D1382913

Jack-Michel Cornil
Philippe Testud

An Introduction to
Maple V

With 105 Figures

 Springer

Jack-Michel Cornil
Philippe Testud
Professeurs en classes préparatoires à Versailles
Lycée Privé Sainte Geneviève
2, rue de l'École des Postes
78029 Versailles Cedex, France
jmcornil@club-internet.fr
ptestud@wanadoo.fr

Translator:
Thierry Van Effelterre
1070 Bruxelles, Belgium
vaneffet@bms.com

Title of the French original edition 1997:
Maple V Release 4 – Introduction raisonnée à l'usage de l'étudiant, de l'ingénieur et du chercheur
ISBN 3-540-63186-0 Springer-Verlag Berlin Heidelberg New York

Library of Congress Cataloging-in-Publication Data
Cornil, Jack-Michel
[Maple V Release 4. English.]
An introduction to Maple V / Jack-Michel Cornil, Philippe Testud;
[translator, Thierry Van Effelterre]. p. cm.
ISBN 3540664424 (softcover: alk. paper)
1. Maple (Computer file) 2. Mathematics – Data processing. I. Testud, Philippe. II. Title.
QA76.95.C68613 2000 510′.285′53042–dc21 00-036581

Mathematics Subject Classification (2000):
00A35, 08-04, 65Y99, 68Q40, 68N15, 51-04

ISBN 3-540-66442-4 Springer-Verlag Berlin Heidelberg New York

Maple and Maple V are registered trademarks of Waterloo Maple, Inc.

Springer-Verlag Berlin Heidelberg New York
a member of BertelsmannSpringer Science+Business Media GmbH
http://www.springer.de
© Springer-Verlag Berlin Heidelberg 2001
Printed in Germany

Typeset in LATEX by the translator and edited by Kurt Mattes, Heidelberg, using a modified Springer LATEX macro-package.
Cover design: Künkel+Lopka, Werbeagentur, Heidelberg
Printed on acid-free paper   SPIN 10647058   46/3142Ko – 5 4 3 2 1 0

Preface

MAPLE is a computer algebra system which, thanks to an extensive library of sophisticated functions, enables both numerical and formal computations to be performed. Until recently, such systems were only available to professional users with access to mainframe computers, but the rapid improvement in the performance of personal computers (speed, memory) now makes them accessible to the majority of users. The latest versions of MAPLE belong to this new generation of systems, allowing a growing audience of users to become familiar with computer algebra.

This work does not set out to describe all the possibilities of MAPLE in an exhaustive manner; there is already a great deal of such documentation, including extensive online help. However, these technical manuals provide a mass of information which is not always of great help to a beginner in computer algebra who is looking for a quick solution to a problem in his own speciality: mathematics, physics, chemistry, etc.

This book has been designed so that a scientist who wishes to use MAPLE can find the information he requires quickly. It is divided into chapters which are largely independent, each one being devoted to a separate subject (graphics, differential equations, integration, polynomials, linear algebra, ...), enabling each user to concentrate on the functions he really needs. In each chapter, deliberately simple examples have been given in order to fully illustrate the syntax used.

The authors have gone to great lengths to give numerous examples of typical incorrect uses of functions in order to help the reader decode and interpret error messages which he may encounter when using MAPLE later on.

How to use this book:

- Chapter 1 is a "guided tour" enabling the reader to catch a glimpse of the different possibilities of MAPLE.

- Chapter 2 presents the basic functions of MAPLE, and it is strongly recommended that Sections 2.1, 2.2 and 2.3 of this chapter be read in order to fully benefit from the rest of the work. In particular, the reader should pay special attention to Section 2.3, which is devoted to evaluation rules, which play a fundamental role in MAPLE.

- The following chapters are to a large extent independent and can be approached directly according to the areas of interest of the user. However, following these guidelines is recommended.

  * Chapter 9 on differential equations is best read after studying Chapter 5 on two-dimensional graphics, and possibly Section 7.2 devoted to derivatives.

  * Chapters 15 to 18, dealing with linear algebra, form a whole which requires a detailed study of Section 15.4, which is devoted to evaluation problems in linear algebra.

  * Chapter 13, on polynomials with irrational coefficients requires a detailed study of Chapter 12.

  * Chapter 22 studies the `subs` et `map` functions which enable the user to work more cleverly with MAPLE, but for a thorough study of this chapter it is necessary to have a good knowledge of Chapter 21, which describes the MAPLE objects.

  * Chapters 23 and 24 introduce some programming notions: loops, branches, and procedures. These tools become indispensable when one wishes to use MAPLE to perform the same series of computations for several different cases. They are presented in an elementary way with simple examples.

It is impossible in a single book to give an exhaustive introduction to all of the MAPLE functions. If the basic functions are described in detail with a precise syntax, the others are presented with the help of sufficiently explicit examples, together with comments enabling their use to be understood. The index, which is very detailed, will help the user to find them.

This book is mainly designed for students, teachers, engineers and researchers who aim to quickly master a software system for formal calculations, which is becoming more and more indispensable for their activity, but also for anyone wishing to solve a problem or test a conjecture for which the calculations appear at first dissuasive.

However, the user should keep in mind that MAPLE is a product in constant development with a few imperfections. He should therefore cast a critical eye on the results obtained and not hesitate to try to check them by different methods.

Table of Contents

1. What MAPLE Can Do for You

In this chapter, we have gathered a few typical examples of MAPLE's use. Except for a few comments, no explanation is provided about the functions used. Further explanation is provided in the following chapters; these sections may be found through the table of contents or index.

1.1 Arithmetic

Ex. 1

```
> 25!;                    MAPLE can compute with integers of any size
```
$$1\,55112\,10043\,33098\,59840\,00000$$

```
> u:=2^(2^7)+1;          Computation of F7: the 7th Fermat number
```
$$u := 340282366920938463463374607431768211457$$

```
> isprime(u);                            to test if F7 is prime
```
$$false$$

```
> ifactor(1234567890987654321);
                              Decomposition into prime factors
```
$$(3)^2\,(7)\,(19)\,(928163)\,(1111211111)$$

1.2 Numerical Computations

Ex. 2

```
> evalf(Pi,25);      approximate value of π with 25 significant
                                                          digits
```
$$3.141592653589793238462643$$

```
> A:=sqrt(5)+sqrt(22+2*sqrt(5));
  B:=sqrt(11+2*sqrt(29))+sqrt(16-2*sqrt(29)
     +2*sqrt(55-10*sqrt(29)));
```

$$A := \sqrt{5} + \sqrt{22 + 2\sqrt{5}}$$

$$B := \sqrt{11 + 2\sqrt{29}} + \sqrt{16 - 2\sqrt{29} + 2\sqrt{55 - 10\sqrt{29}}}$$

Ex. 3

```
> Digits:=25: evalf(A); evalf(B);
```
Evaluation of A and B with 25 significant digits

$$7.381175940895657970987267$$

$$7.381175940895657970987266$$

```
> Digits:=10: evalf(ln(-2));
```
Numerical evaluation of a complex number

$$.6931471806 + 3.141592654I$$

1.3 Polynomials and Rational Functions

Expansion and simplification of polynomials

```
> expand((x^2+x+1)^5);
```
To expand the expression

$$1 + 30\,x^7 + 45\,x^6 + 51\,x^5 + 15\,x^8 + 30\,x^3$$
$$+5\,x + x^{10} + 5\,x^9 + 45\,x^4 + 15x^2$$

Ex. 4

```
> sort(");
```
To sort out the previous expression

$$x^{10} + 5\,x^9 + 15\,x^8 + 30\,x^7 + 45\,x^6 + 51\,x^5 + 45\,x^4$$
$$+30\,x^3 + 15\,x^2 + 5\,x + 1$$

Factorization of polynomials

```
> P:=x^8+x^4+1;
```
$$P := x^8 + x^4 + 1$$

```
> factor(P);
```
factorization over the field of rational numbers

$$(x^2 - x + 1)(x^2 + x + 1)(x^4 - x^2 + 1)$$

Ex. 5

```
> factor(P,sqrt(3));
```
factorization over the subfield generated by $\sqrt{3}$

$$(x^2 - x + 1)(x^2 + x + 1)(x^2 - \sqrt{3}x + 1)(x^2 + \sqrt{3}x + 1)$$

Partial fraction decomposition of rational functions

Ex. 6

```
> f:=1/((x+1)^7-x^7-1);
```

$$f := \frac{1}{(x+1)^7 - x^7 - 1}$$

```
> convert(f,parfrac,x);
```

$$\frac{1}{7}\frac{1}{x} - \frac{1}{7}\frac{1}{x+1} - \frac{1}{7}\frac{1}{x^2+x+1} - \frac{1}{7}\frac{1}{(x^2+x+1)^2}$$

1.4 Trigonometry

Ex. 7

```
> p:=cos(5*x);        Expression of trigonometric expressions of nx
```

$$p := \cos(5x)$$

```
> expand(p);
```

$$16\cos(x)^5 - 20\cos(x)^3 + 5\cos(x)$$

```
> p:=sin(x)^5;        Linearization of trigonometric expressions
```

$$p := \sin(x)^5$$

```
> combine(p,trig);
```

$$\frac{1}{16}\sin(5x) - \frac{5}{16}\sin(3x) + \frac{5}{8}\sin(x)$$

```
> expand(tan(5*x));
```

$$\text{Expression of } \tan(n\,u) \\ \text{in function of } \tan(u)$$

$$\frac{5\tan(x) - 10\tan(x)^3 + 5\tan(x)^5}{1 - 10\tan(x)^2 + 5\tan(x)^4}$$

```
> S:=Sum(cos((2*k+1)*x),k=0..n+1): S=value(S);
```

$$\text{Normalization of some} \\ \text{trigonometric sums}$$

$$\sum_{k=0}^{k=n+1} \cos((2k+1)x) = \frac{\sin(x(n+2))\,\cos(x(n+2))}{\sin(x)}$$

1.5 Differentiation

Computation of derivatives of expressions in a single variable

Ex. 8

```
> p:=arctan(x);
```
$$p := \arctan(x)$$

```
> diff(p,x$5);
```
to compute the fifth derivative

$$384\,\frac{x^4}{(1+x^2)^5} - 288\,\frac{x^2}{(1+x^2)^4} + 24\,\frac{1}{(1+x^2)^3}$$

```
> normal(");
```
$$24\,\frac{5x^4 - 10x^2 + 1}{(1+x^2)^5}$$

Computation of partial derivatives

Ex. 9

```
> p:=ln(x^2+y^2);
```
$$p := \ln(x^2 + y^2)$$

```
> diff(p,x,x,x,y,y);
```
to compute $\partial^5 p/\partial x^3\,\partial y^2$

$$-288\frac{xy^2}{(x^2+y^2)^4} + 48\frac{x}{(x^2+y^2)^3} + 768\frac{x^3y^2}{(x^2+y^2)^5} - 96\frac{x^3}{(x^2+y^2)^4}$$

```
> simplify(");
```
to simplify the previous result

$$-48\frac{x(-10x^2y^2 + 5y^4 + x^4)}{(x^2+y^2)^5}$$

1.6 Truncated Series Expansions

Computation of truncated series expansions

Ex.10

```
> p:=arctanh(sin(x))-sin(arctanh(x));
```
$$p := \operatorname{arctanh}(\sin(x)) - \sin(\operatorname{arctanh}(x))$$

```
> series(p,x,8);
```
$$\frac{1}{90}x^7 + O(x^8)$$

Computation involving generalized series expansions

Ex.11

```
> p:=1/(sin(x)^2)-1/(sinh(x)^2);
```

$$p := \frac{1}{\sin(x)^2} - \frac{1}{\sinh(x)^2}$$

```
> series(p,x,9)
```

$$\frac{2}{3} + \frac{4}{189}x^4 + O(x^6)$$

Computation of asymptotic series expansions

Ex.12

```
> p:=x^2*ln((x+1)/x);
```

$$p := x^2 \ln\left(\frac{x+1}{x}\right)$$

```
> series(p,x=infinity,5);
```

$$x - \frac{1}{2} + \frac{1}{3}\frac{1}{x} - \frac{1}{4}\frac{1}{x^2} + O\left(\frac{1}{x^3}\right)$$

1.7 Differential Equations and Systems

Ex.13

```
> Eq:=4*x*diff(y(x),x,x)+2*diff(y(x),x)+y(x);
```

$$Eq := 4\,x\,\left(\frac{\partial^2}{\partial x^2}y(x)\right) + 2\,\left(\frac{\partial}{\partial x}y(x)\right) + y(x)$$

```
> dsolve(Eq,y(x));
```

$$y(x) = \_C1\,\sin(\sqrt{x}) + \_C2\cos(\sqrt{x})$$

```
> Eq:=5*diff(y(x),x)-y(x)*sin(x)+y(x)^4*sin(2*x);
```

Bernoulli equation

$$Eq := 5\,\left(\frac{\partial}{\partial x}\,y(x)\right) - y(x)\sin(x) + y(x)^4\sin(2x)$$

```
> simplify(dsolve(Eq,y(x)));
```

$$\frac{1}{y(x)^3} = 2\,\cos(x) + \frac{10}{3} + e^{\frac{3}{5}\cos(x)}\,\_C1$$

```
> S:={diff(x(t),t)=x(t)+2*y(t)-z(t),
       diff(y(t),t)=2*x(t)+4*y(t)-2*z(t),
       diff(z(t),t)=-x(t)-2*y(t)+z(t),
       x(0)=1, y(0)=1, z(0)=1};
```

$$S := \quad \left\{ \frac{\partial}{\partial t} x(t) = x(t) + 2\,y(t) - z(t) \,, \right.$$

$$\frac{\partial}{\partial t}\, y(t) = 2\,x(t) + 4\,y(t) - 2\,z(t),$$

Ex.14

$$\frac{\partial}{\partial t}\, z(t) = -x(t) - 2y(t) + z(t),$$

$$\left. x(0) = 1,\; y(0) = 1,\; z(0) = 1 \right\}$$

```
> dsolve(S,{x(t),y(t),z(t)});
```

$$S := \quad \left\{ x(t) = \frac{2}{3} + \frac{1}{3}e^{6t} \,, \right.$$

$$y(t) = \frac{1}{3} + \frac{2}{3}e^{6t},$$

$$\left. z(t) = -\frac{1}{3}e^{6t} + \frac{4}{3} \right\}$$

1.8 Integration

Computation of indefinite and definite integrals

```
> p:=(1-cos(x/3))/(sin(x/2));
```

$$p := \frac{1 - \cos\left(\frac{1}{3}x\right)}{\sin\left(\frac{1}{2}x\right)}$$

```
> int(p,x);
```
                                              Computation of a primitive

$$-3\ln\left(3\tan\left(\frac{1}{12}x\right)^2 - 1\right) + 3\ln\left(\tan\left(\frac{1}{12}x\right)^2 - 3\right)$$

Ex.15

```
> p:=1/(sqrt(1-x*x)+sqrt(1+x*x));
```

$$p := \frac{1}{\sqrt{1 - x^2} + \sqrt{1 + x^2}}$$

```
> int(p,x=-1..1);
```
                                              Computation of an integral

$$-\sqrt{2} - \ln(\sqrt{2} - 1) + \frac{1}{2}\pi$$

Computation of generalized integrals

Ex.16

```
> p:=(arctan(2*t)-arctan(t))/t;
```

$$p := \frac{\arctan(2\,t) - \arctan(t)}{t}$$

```
> Intg:=Int(p,t=0..infinity):
  Intg=value(Intg);
```

$$\int_0^\infty \frac{\arctan(2\,t) - \arctan(t)}{t}\,dt \;=\; \frac{1}{2}\ln(2)\,\pi$$

Computation of integrals depending on a parameter

Ex.17

```
> p:=exp(-t)*cos(x*t)*(t^(-1/2));
```

$$p := \frac{e^{(-t)}\cos(xt)}{\sqrt{t}}$$

```
> int(p,t=0..infinity);
```

$$\frac{(1+x^2)^{1/4}\cos\left(\frac{1}{2}\arctan(x)\right)\sqrt{\pi}}{\sqrt{1+x^2}\cos\left(\frac{1}{2}\arctan(x)\right)^2 + \sqrt{1+x^2}\sin\left(\frac{1}{2}\arctan(x)\right)^2}$$

```
> simplify(");
```

$$\frac{\cos\left(\frac{1}{2}\arctan(x)\right)\sqrt{\pi}}{(1+x^2)^{1/4}}$$

1.9 Plot of Curves

Representation of one or several functions

Ex.18

```
> plot([sin(t), cos(t)],t=-Pi..Pi)
```

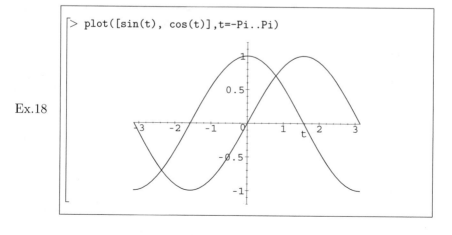

Plot of parametrized curves

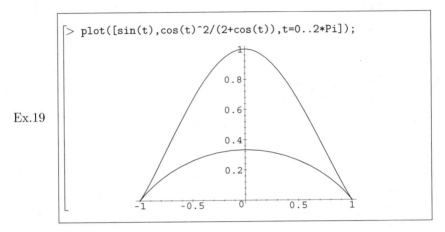

```
> plot([sin(t),cos(t)^2/(2+cos(t)),t=0..2*Pi]);
```

Ex.19

Plot of curves in polar coordinates

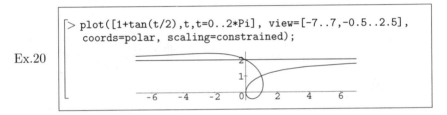

```
> plot([1+tan(t/2),t,t=0..2*Pi], view=[-7..7,-0.5..2.5],
  coords=polar, scaling=constrained);
```

Ex.20

Plot of families of curves

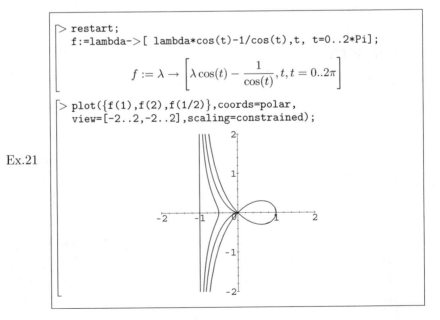

```
> restart;
  f:=lambda->[ lambda*cos(t)-1/cos(t),t, t=0..2*Pi];
```

$$f := \lambda \to \left[\lambda \cos(t) - \frac{1}{\cos(t)}, t, t = 0..2\pi \right]$$

```
> plot({f(1),f(2),f(1/2)},coords=polar,
  view=[-2..2,-2..2],scaling=constrained);
```

Ex.21

1.10 Plot of Surfaces

Plot of a surface given by the equation $z = f(x, y)$

Ex.22

```
> plot3d(x*sin(y)-y*sin(x),x=-3..3,y=-2.5..2.5,
  orientation=[40,67],style=patch);
```

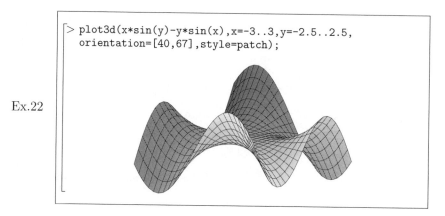

Plot of a parametrized surface patch

Ex.23

```
> plot3d([u*cos(v),u*sin(v),cos(2*v)],u=0..2,
  v=0..2*Pi,grid=[10,60],style=patch);
```

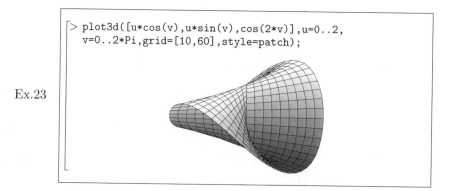

Plot of a surface patch parametrized in cylindrical coordinates

Ex.24

```
> plot3d([r,t,5*sin(r)/sqrt(r)], r=0..2*Pi, t=0..2*Pi,
  coords=cylindrical, scaling=constrained,
  orientation=[44,62],color=black);
```

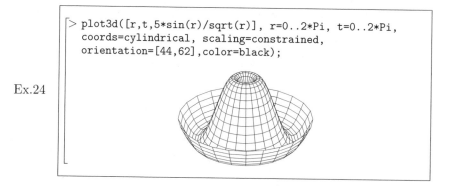

1.11 Linear Algebra

Computation of determinants

Ex.25

```
> with(linalg):                      the linalg library has to be loaded
  Warning, new definition for norm
  Warning, new definition for trace
> M:=matrix(4,4,
      [1,a,a^2,a^4,1,b,b^2,b^4,1,c,c^2,c^4,1,d,d^2,d^4]);
```

$$M := \begin{bmatrix} 1 & a & a^2 & a^4 \\ 1 & b & b^2 & b^4 \\ 1 & c & c^2 & c^4 \\ 1 & d & d^2 & d^4 \end{bmatrix}$$

```
> factor(det(M));              To obtain the determinant
                                        in factorized form
```

$$(-a+b)(-a+c)(c-b)(d-a)(d-b)(d-c)(d+b+a+c)$$

Computation of eigenvalues

Ex.26

```
> M:=matrix(4,4,(i,j)->if i=j then a+b else a fi);
```

$$M := \begin{bmatrix} a+b & a & a & a \\ a & a+b & a & a \\ a & a & a+b & a \\ a & a & a & a+b \end{bmatrix}$$

```
> det(M);
```

$$4b^3a + b^4$$

```
> eigenvals(M);               To obtain the eigenvalues
```

$$b, \ b, \ b, \ b+4a$$

```
> eigenvects(M);              To obtain the eigenvectors
```

$$[b, \ 3, \ \{[-1,0,1,0], [-1,0,0,1], [-1,1,0,0]\}],$$
$$[4a+b, \ 1, \ \{[1,1,1,1]\}]$$

2. Introduction

When a session starts, MAPLE displays a *prompt* (in general the symbol >).
The user can then request that something be executed by entering a MAPLE
assertion – i.e. a mathematical expression, an assignment or other instructions.

2.1 First Steps

2.1.1 Keyboarding an Expression

In order to display the MAPLE evaluation of an expression on the screen,
the user simply types the expression, followed by a *semicolon*, and presses
ENTER.

Ex. 1

> 1+1;   **do not forget to type** ENTER

                              2

> 2^10;

                           1024

> 1+2*3+4;

                             11

When the user types an expression that is syntactically incorrect, MAPLE
returns the message *syntax error, ...*, often indicating the first unexpected
character encountered.

Ex. 2

> 1+2*+4;   **for example, one forgets to type the 3**
Syntax error, '+' unexpected

In the previous example, when the user has forgotten to type the 3, the cursor is positioned between the * and the +. He only has to type 3 and press ENTER. There is no need to position the cursor at the end of the line before typing ENTER.

Warning! Do not forget the semicolon at the end of the line. This punctuation is a separator that indicates the end of the current expression to MAPLE and instructs it to carry out the evaluation. MAPLE returns a warning message if one forgets this *semicolon*.

Ex. 3

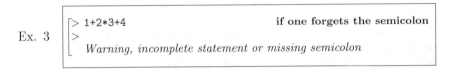

This *semicolon* may then be typed on the line where the cursor stands, although it is better to put it at the end of the appropriate line.

As we notice from the above examples, command areas (containing MAPLE expressions) and text areas (containing comments) may be mixed within the same line.

When the cursor is positioned:

- within a command area, the button Σ is depressed and the context bar related to the commands (Ch. 26) is displayed.
- within a text area, the button T is depressed and the related context bar is displayed (Ch. 26).

By default, the *prompt* that begins a line forms itself a text area when one starts a new line and the cursor stands in the next area, which is a command area: everything one types then is considered as belonging to (executable) MAPLE expressions. To switch into text mode, one only has to click upon the icon T: what one next types is considered as (non executable) text or comments. It suffices to click upon Σ to switch back to command mode.

Warning! Depressing the ENTER key causes the execution of the current line when the cursor stands within a command area. But it causes a line jump into the current area if the cursor stands within a text area.

Throughout this book,

- The executable MAPLE expressions are written with this font.
- **The comments are written with this font.**
- *The error messages are written with this font.*

2.1.2 Operators, Functions and Constants

Basic operators: Besides the basic operators + , - , * , /, MAPLE knows
the following arithmetic operators

Operator	Notation	Example
Factorial	!	7!
Power	** or ^	2.5^3
Quotient of integer division	iquo(.,.)	iquo(17,3)
Remainder of integer division	irem(.,.)	irem(17,3)

Basic functions: MAPLE also knows the following classical basic functions

    exp(x), log(x) or ln(x), log10(x), log[b](x)

    round(x), trunc(x), frac(x), sqrt(x), abs(x)

    sin(x), cos(x), tan(x), cot(x)

    sinh(x), cosh(x), tanh(x), cotanh(x)

    arcsin(x), arccos(x), arctan(x), arccotan(x)

    arcsinh(x), arccosh(x), arctanh(x), arccotanh(x)

Constants: MAPLE also knows the following constants

Identifier	Description
Pi	3.14159........
I	square root of −1
infinity	+ infinity
gamma	Euler constant

Warning! MAPLE distinguishes between upper and lower cases within the names
of constants, as well as within every identifier it uses.

2.1.3 First Computations

MAPLE doesn't give decimal evaluations of quantities such as $10/3$ or $\sqrt{2}$ automatically. The function `evalf` (evaluate using floating-point arithmetic) has to be used in order to obtain such a decimal evaluation.

Ex. 4

```
> 10/3;
                        10/3
> evalf(10/3);
                     3.3333333333
```

The number of significant digits returned by `evalf` is determined by the internal variable `Digits`, whose default value is 10. However, the assignment `Digits:=n` causes all following decimal evaluations to be given with n significant digits.

Ex. 5

```
> Digits:=20;                    Mind the upper case !
                     Digits := 20
> evalf(10/3);
                3.3333333333333333333
> 3+sqrt(2);
                        3 + √2
> evalf(");
                4.4142135623730950488
```

To get an approximate value of the last computed quantity, `evalf` has been used above with " (ditto), which represents the last expression evaluated by MAPLE.

Warning ! The quantity " represents the the last value chronologically that has been computed, not the one that stands on the previous line on the worksheet. These two quantities can be completely different if the user has moved *across* the worksheet.

The function `evalf` can also be used with a second argument, n, which indicates that the first argument should be evaluated with n significant digits.

Ex. 6

```
> ln(2); evalf(",17);
                        ln(2)
                .69314718055994531
```

The function `evalf` is also needed to obtain approximate values of the symbolic constants presented on page 13.

Ex. 7

```
> Digits:=15;
```
$$Digits := 15$$
```
> evalf(Pi);
```
$$3.14159265358979$$
```
> evalf(Pi,50);
```
$$3.1415926535897932384626433832795028841971693993751$$

MAPLE seems to know these constants with unlimited precision. The result of an evaluation depends only on the value of `Digits`. For π, for example, the first evaluation of `evalf(Pi)` loads into memory the procedure `evalf/constant/Pi`, which contains a value with 50 significant digits. If more precision is required, MAPLE accesses a value `_bigPi` that has 10000 decimal digits. Finally, for evaluations with more than 10000 decimal digits, MAPLE uses a hypergeometric series expansion that converges very quickly.

Warning! Since MAPLE distinguishes between upper and lower cases, it distinguishes between `Pi` and `pi`. While `Pi` represents the well-known number, `pi` represents the greek letter, just like `alpha` or `beta`. This explains why one doesn't get the expected evaluation if one types `sin(pi/2)`.

Ex. 8

```
> sin(Pi/2);
```
$$1$$
```
> sin(pi/2);
```
$$\sin\left(\frac{1}{2}\pi\right)$$
```
> sin(Pi/8);
```
value stored within a table (p. 444)
$$\frac{1}{2}\sqrt{2-\sqrt{2}}$$
```
> sin(alpha/2);
```
$$\sin\left(\frac{1}{2}\alpha\right)$$

2.2 Assignment and Evaluation

2.2.1 Identifiers

MAPLE, like many languages, provides the means to work with

- numerical values: real, complex ...
- functions, procedures ...
- sets, lists or arrays ...

Such objects are, as for example in PASCAL, handled through variables that are referenced by names or identifiers. But unlike PASCAL, MAPLE also provides the means to compute symbolically with expressions containing free variables, i.e. variables to which no specific value has been assigned.

For MAPLE, an identifier has to begin with a letter, then possibly followed by letters, digits or symbols. It may not contain more than 499 characters !

**Take care, MAPLE distinguishes
between upper and lower cases for identifiers !**

An identifier may begin with the symbol underscore _ , but one has to keep in mind that MAPLE itself sometimes needs to introduce variables, (integration constants for example) and that, in such a case, the identifiers that are used always begin with an underscore. In order to avoid possible conflicts with such variables, the user is advised against beginning an identifier with an underscore.

2.2.2 Assignment

Assignment is the way identifiers are made to point to values. Given `Ident`, the name of a variable, and an expression `Expr`, MAPLE processes the command `Ident:= Expr` by evaluating the right-hand-side `Expr` and assigning its value to the identifier `Ident`. If the command ends with a semicolon, this assignment is echoed on the screen.

Ex. 9

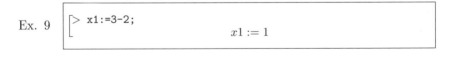

```
> x1:=3-2;
                          x1 := 1
```

Ex.10

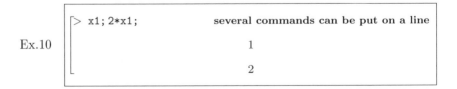

```
> x1; 2*x1;          several commands can be put on a line
                          1
                          2
```

Ex.11

```
> y:=x1+3;
```
$$y := 4$$
```
> y;
```
$$4$$

Some identifiers have a special status for MAPLE, the names of symbolic constants and functions for example. These are protected and an assignment to such an identifier causes an error message.

Ex.12

```
> Pi:=3.14;
```
Error, attempting to assign to 'Pi' which is protected
```
> D:=1;                    D represents the derivation operator
```
Error, attempting to assign to 'D' which is protected
```
> I:=1..2;                          I represents $\sqrt{-1}$
```
Error, Illegal use of an object as a name

2.2.3 Free Variables and Evaluation

If after a restart, which reinitializes the MAPLE session, one assigns to P the quantity x^2+x+1

Ex.13

```
> restart; P:=x^2+x+1;
```
$$P := x^2 + x + 1$$

one can see that MAPLE assigns to P an expression in x. A programming language like PASCAL or C would have evaluated x^2+x+1 using the "random" (i.e. uninitialized) value of the variable x.

If one then assigns x the value 1, or the value 2 and next requests the evaluation of P, one gets the corresponding numerical value of the expression P.

Ex.14

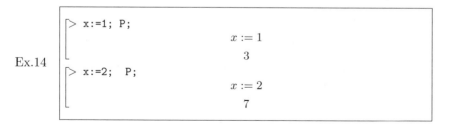

```
> x:=1; P;
```
$$x := 1$$
$$3$$
```
> x:=2;  P;
```
$$x := 2$$
$$7$$

If one then carries out the assignment

Ex.15
```
> Q:=x^3+1;
```
$$Q := 9$$

One can see from the result on the screen that MAPLE assigns Q the value of $x^3 + 1$ for $x = 2$. It isn't an expression in x but a numerical value that is assigned to Q in this case. Let us verify it.

Ex.16
```
> x:=1;
```
$$x := 1$$
```
> Q;
```
$$9$$

In order to return to P as an expression in x, or to construct new expressions in x, one can turn x back into a free variable by assigning its name to itself. The name appears between apostrophes to specify to MAPLE that it isn't a new numerical assignment.

Ex.17
```
> x:='x';
```
To unassign the variable x
$$x := x$$
```
> P;
```
$$x^2 + x + 1$$
```
> Q;
```
$$9$$

From this point on, P is again evaluated as an expression in x, which is once again a free variable, while Q remains equal to 9, since that is the value which it was assigned.

Now that x is free, a polynomial expression in x can be assigned to Q

Ex.18
```
> Q:=x^3+1;
```
$$Q := x^3 + 1$$

For MAPLE, a free (non assigned) variable is a variable to which its own name is assigned. It is therefore a variable pointing to itself.

2.2.4 Full Evaluation Rule

What one observes with the examples of the previous section can be generalized to the evaluation of most expressions used with MAPLE. This can be verified by the following example.

Ex.19

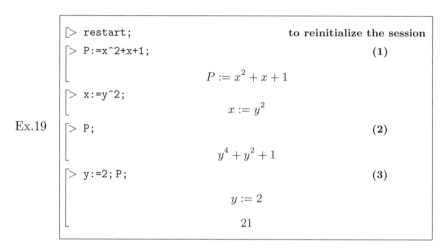

```
[> restart;                          to reinitialize the session
[> P:=x^2+x+1;                                          (1)
```
$$P := x^2 + x + 1$$
```
[> x:=y^2;
```
$$x := y^2$$
```
[> P;                                                   (2)
```
$$y^4 + y^2 + 1$$
```
[> y:=2; P;                                             (3)
```
$$y := 2$$
$$21$$

In this example, we begin **(1)** by defining P as an expression in x. When afterwards the value y^2 is assigned to x, the evaluation **(2)** of P automatically returns the appropriate expression in y. When the value 2 is assigned to y, the evaluation **(3)** of P gives the numerical value 21. This is obtained from P by first replacing x with y^2, and next replacing y with 2.

P points towards the expression x^2+x+1 in each of the three cases.

- In the second case, x points towards y^2 and in the evaluation of P, MAPLE returns is the value of x^2+x+1 for x=y^2.
- In the third case, y points towards 2 and in the evaluation of P, MAPLE returns is the value for y=2 of the value for x=y^2 of x^2+x+1. This little game could be continued ad infinitum.

In brief, MAPLE carries out a full and recursive evaluation of every expression until all possible evaluations have been exhausted.

If one then assigns the value 3 to x, the relation between x and y is broken and the expression P is evaluated by merely replacing x by 3 in x^2+x+1.

Ex.20

```
[> x:=3; P;
```
$$x := 3$$
$$13$$

Now, if the variable x is unassigned by the assignment x:='x', the evaluation of P returns the initial expression in x.

Ex.21

> x:='x':P;   x:='x' is followed by : to avoid a useless echo

$$x^2 + x + 1$$

The full evaluation rule must take care of circular references. In the particular case of an assignment like t:=t+1, for example:

- if t points towards a value a different from t, the consequence of this command is that t will point towards $a + 1$,
- if t points towards itself, i.e. if t is a free variable, such a command gives rise to an infinite loop and to a stack overflow upon evaluating t.

Ex.22

> t:=1; t:=t+1; t;

$$t := 1$$

$$t := 2$$

$$2$$

> t:='t'; t:=t+1;   MAPLE gives only a warning

$$t := t$$

Warning, recursive definition of name

$$t = t + 1$$

> t;   but if one requests the evaluation of t,
Error, too many levels of recursion   one saturates the stack

2.2.5 Use of Apostrophes: Partial Evaluation

We showed before that when x contains a given numerical value, the assignment Q:=x^3+1 assigns Q a numerical value. In order to define Q as an expression in x,

- use the method of "unassigning" the variable x in 2.2.3, or
- a second method using apostrophes.

Ex.23

> x:=1; Q:='x^3+1';

$$x := 1$$

$$Q := x^3 + 1$$

In this example, the apostrophes prevent the full evaluation of the right-hand-side of the last assignment, which causes Q to be assigned an expression in the variable x.

In fact, when MAPLE's evaluator encounters apostrophes, it deletes them and then ceases further evaluation of the expression.

We can verify that if one now assigns a numerical value to x, the evaluation of Q returns the corresponding value of x^3+1.

Ex.24

```
> x:=2: Q;   x:=2 is followed by : in order to avoid a useless echo
```
$$9$$
```
> x:=3: Q;
```
$$28$$

Although x now points towards a numerical value, one can nevertheless display the expression in x pointed to by Q using eval(Q,1), which restricts the evaluation to "the first level".

Ex.25

```
> eval(Q,1);
```
$$x^3 + 1$$

More generally, if n is an integer and Expr is an expression, eval(Expr,n) returns the evaluation of Expr at level n, as one can verify with the following:

Ex.26

```
> restart;                              to reinitialize the session
                                        and thus unassign all the variables
```
```
> P:=x^2+x+1;
```
$$P := x^2 + x + 1$$
```
> x:=y^2;
```
$$x := y^2$$
```
> y:=1;
```
$$y := 1$$
```
> eval(P,1);                            Evaluation at level 1
```
$$x^2 + x + 1$$
```
> eval(P,2);                            Evaluation at level 2
```
$$y^4 + y^2 + 1$$
```
> eval(P,3);                            Evaluation at level 3
```
$$3$$

2.2.6 Evaluation of Function Arguments

When calling a function, MAPLE typically starts by evaluating all its arguments. The following example shows an undesirable consequence of this.

Ex.27

> ```
> restart; i:=2;            simulation of a variable which isn't free
> ```
>
> ```
> sum(i^2,i=1..5);                        to compute $\sum_{i=1}^{5} i^2$
> ```
>
> $$i := 2$$
>
> *Error, (in sum) summation variable previously assigned,*
> *second argument evaluates to, 2 = 1 .. 5*

Contrary to what happens in Mathematics, the i appearing in sum(i^2, i=1..5) isn't a dummy variable: MAPLE evaluates the arguments of the function sum and finds sum(4,2=1..5), which explains the error message.

To solve the previous problem, i can be unassigned before calling sum,

Ex.28

> ```
> i;
> ```
> $$2$$
> ```
> i:='i'; sum(i^2,i=1..5);
> ```
> $$i := 'i'$$
> $$55$$

or apostrophes can be used to prevent the evaluation of the arguments of the function.

Ex.29

> ```
> i:=2; sum('i^2','i'=1..5);
> ```
> $$i := 2$$
> $$55$$

A few functions don't evaluate their arguments or only evaluate them partially. This is true of the function **seq**, for example.

Ex.30

> ```
> restart;                    even with i which isn't free,
> i:=2; seq(i^2,i=1..5);      the function seq allows us to
>                             construct the sequence 1,4,9,16,25
> ```
>
> $$i := 2$$
>
> $$1, 4, 9, 16, 25$$

2.3 Fundamental Operations

MAPLE is designed to keep expressions in the form in which they are initially encountered. It only executes the bare minimum of transformations on its own initiative. This includes:

- setting the rational numbers in irreducible form
- normalizing sums, products, powers of rational numbers
- distributing the product of a numerical value onto a sum of terms
- putting the constant at the beginning of a product of factors
- grouping syntactically identical terms within a sum or a product
- simplifying syntactically identical factors within a quotient
- simplifying remarkable numerical values like $\sin(\pi/3)$
- rewriting expressions that are equivalent to already existing expressions
- simplifying expressions like $\sin(\arcsin(x))$, $(\sqrt{x})^2$, ...

But nothing more!

- It doesn't expand or factor a polynomial on its own initiative.
- It simplifies $\dfrac{(x-y)(x^2 + x\,y + y^2)}{(x-y)}$, but not $\dfrac{x^3 - y^3}{x - y}$.
- It doesn't simplify an expression like $\sin^2(x) + \cos^2(x)$.

Ex.31

```
> restart; ((x-y)*(x^2+x*y+y^2))/(x-y);
```
$$x^2 + x\,y + y^2$$
```
> (x^3-y^3)/(x-y);
```
$$\frac{x^3 - y^3}{x - y}$$
```
> sin(x)^2+cos(x)^2;
```
$$\sin(x)^2 + \cos(x)^2$$

MAPLE thus only carries out the bare minimum of transformations on its own initiative and the user must explicitly request any simplifications required. To do this, MAPLE provides transformation functions such as `expand`, `factor`, `normal`, `simplify`, `convert`, `combine`, ...

2.3.1 The Function expand

The purpose of the function expand is

- to expand the "polynomial expressions",
- to express trigonometric expressions of $n\,x$ into function of x,
- to transform $\exp(x + y)$ into $\exp(x)\,\exp(y)$ and $\ln(x\,y)$ into $\ln(x) + \ln(y)$.

Ex.32

```
> restart; expand((x+1)*(x+2)^2);
```
$$x^3 + 5\,x^2 + 8\,x + 4$$
```
> expand((cos(x)+sin(x))^2);                "Polynomial" expression
```
$$\cos(x)^2 + 2\,\sin(x)\cos(x) + \sin(x)^2$$
```
> expand(ln(x/y^2));
```
$$\ln(x) - 2\ln(y)$$
```
> expand(cos(3*x));
```
$$4\cos(x)^3 - 3\cos(x)$$
```
> expand(tan(3*x));
```
$$\frac{3\,\tan(x) - \tan(x)^3}{1 - 3\,\tan(x)^2}$$

For rational functions, expand only expands the numerator.

Ex.33

```
> expand((x+1)/((x+3)*(x+2)^2));
```
$$\frac{x}{(x + 3)(x + 2)^2} + \frac{1}{(x + 3)(x + 2)^2}$$

If S_Expr is a subexpression of Expr (cf. p. 339), then the evaluation of expand(Expr,S_Expr) expands while keeping the expression S_Expr grouped.

Ex.34

```
> expand((a*(x+1)+y)^2,(x+1));
```
$$a^2\,(x + 1)^2 + 2\,a\,(x + 1)\,y + y^2$$

2.3.2 The Function `factor`

The `factor` function factors "polynomial expressions" in one or several "variables", or quotients of such expressions.

Ex.35

```
> factor(x^8-1);
```
$$(x-1)(x+1)(1+x^2)(1+x^4)$$

```
> factor(x^2-y^2);
```
$$(x-y)(x+y)$$

```
> factor(sin(x)^3-cos(x)^3);          "Polynomial" expression
```
$$\left(\sin(x)-\cos(x)\right)\left(\sin(x)^2+\sin(x)\cos(x)+\cos(x)^2\right)$$

More precisely, `factor` factors a polynomial or rational function over the subfield of the field of complex numbers generated by its coefficients:

Ex.36

```
> f:=(x*x-2); g:=sqrt(2)*f;
```
$$f := x^2 - 2$$
$$g := \sqrt{2}\left(x^2 - 2\right)$$

```
> factor(f) , factor(g);
```
$$x^2 - 2 \quad , \quad \sqrt{2}\left(x - \sqrt{2}\right)\left(x + \sqrt{2}\right)$$

```
> factor((x^2-2*y^2)/(x-sqrt(2)*y));
```
$$x + \sqrt{2}\,y$$

In some cases, one may be surprised to see that MAPLE doesn't carry out factorizations that seem straightforward. For example, the second degree polynomial $x^2 - x\left(e^t + e^{-t}\right) + 1$ obviously has the roots e^t and e^{-t}.

Ex.37

```
> f:=x^2-x*(exp(t)+exp(-t))+1;
```
$$f := x^2 - x\left(e^t + e^{(-t)}\right) + 1$$

```
> factor(f);
```
$$x^2 - x\,e^t + x\,e^{(-t)} + 1$$

On the other hand, if one carries out `expand` before `factor`, one obtains

Ex.38

```
> g:=expand(f);
```

$$g := x^2 - x\,e^t - \frac{x}{e^t} + 1$$

```
> factor(g);
```

$$\frac{\left(x\,e^t - 1\right)\left(x - e^t\right)}{e^t}$$

In the latter case, MAPLE handles g as the rational expression $x^2 - x\,u - \dfrac{x}{u} + 1$, with $u = e^t$. It factors $x^2 - x\,u - \dfrac{x}{u} + 1$ into $\dfrac{(x - u)(u\,x - 1)}{u}$, then replaces u with e^t, providing the expected result.

The factorization of f appears straightforward to a user because he implicitly transforms e^{-t} into $1/e^t$, which then allows him to factor. On the other hand, this transformation has to be explicitly requested from MAPLE; which is precisely what has been done with the function `expand`.

In the computation of Example 6, MAPLE wasn't successful, because it has handled `f` as the polynomial expression $x^2 - x\,(u + v) + 1$ with $u = e^t$ and $v = e^{-t}$. MAPLE was not able to carry out the expected factorization since the polynomial $x^2 - x\,(u + v) + 1$ cannot be factored over the field of rational numbers. The reader can easily verify this by replacing the final 1 with `exp(t)*exp(-t)`.

Just as in the previous example, the factorization of the expression

$$\sin(x)^2 - 2\sin(2x) + 4\cos(x)^2$$

requires a transformation using `expand`.

Ex.39

```
> f:=sin(x)^2-2*sin(2*x)+4*cos(x)^2;
```

$$f := \sin(x)^2 - 2\sin(2x) + 4\cos(x)^2$$

```
> factor(f);
```
                                                            has no effect

$$\sin(x)^2 - 2\sin(2x) + 4\cos(x)^2$$

```
> f:=expand(f);
```

$$f := \sin(x)^2 - 4\sin(x)\cos(x) + 4\cos(x)^2$$

```
> factor(f);
```

$$\left(\sin(x) - 2\cos(x)\right)^2$$

2.3.3 The Function `normal`

The `normal` function normalizes and simplifies "rational expressions" like

$$\frac{x^3 - y^3}{x - y} \quad \text{or} \quad \frac{\sin(x)^3 - \sin(y)^3}{\sin(x) - \sin(y)}.$$

It divides by the "GCD" but doesn't factor.

Ex.40

```
> Fr:=(x^4-y^4)/(x^2-y^2);
```
$$Fr := \frac{x^4 - y^4}{x^2 - y^2}$$
```
> normal(Fr);
```
$$x^2 + y^2$$
```
> Fr:=(sin(x)^3-cos(x)^3)/(sin(x)^2-cos(x)^2);
```
$$\frac{\sin(x)^3 - \cos(x)^3}{\sin(x)^2 - \cos(x)^2}$$
```
> normal(Fr);
```
$$\frac{\sin(x)^2 + \sin(x)\cos(x) + \cos(x)^2}{\sin(x) + \cos(x)}$$

Unlike `factor`, the function `normal` is only able to simplify if the "coefficients" of the numerator and the denominator are rational numbers. The next example demonstrates this.

Ex.41

```
> f:=(x*x-2)/(x-sqrt(2));
```
$$f := \frac{x^2 - 2}{x - \sqrt{2}}$$
```
> normal(f);
```
$$\frac{x^2 - 2}{x - \sqrt{2}}$$
```
> factor(f);
```
$$x + \sqrt{2}$$

2.3.4 The Function convert in Trigonometry

The convert function has many options, summarized in the following table. Some of these allow us to transform trigonometric expressions.

Option	Transformation being carried out
exp	expresses all hyperbolic and circular trigonometric expressions using real or complex exponentials.
ln	expresses inverse functions of the trigonometric functions with the help of logarithms.
expln	combination of the two previous options.
expsincos	expresses hyperbolic expressions with the help of real exponentials and circular expressions with the help of the functions sine and cosine.
sincos	expresses tan and tanh using only sin, cos, sinh, cos and cosh.
tan	expresses circular trigonometric expressions as functions of the tangent of the half arc.
trig	transforms the exponentials into sin, sinh, cos and cosh with the help of Euler formulas.

Examples using convert

Ex.42

```
> restart;
> p:=tan(x)+exp(y)+exp(I*z)+sinh(t)+sin(u);
```
$$p := \tan(x) + e^y + e^{Iz} + \sinh(t) + \sin(u)$$
```
> convert(p,trig);
```
$$\tan(x) + \cosh(y) + \sinh(y) + \cos(z) + I\,\sin(z) + \sinh(t) + \sin(u)$$
```
> convert(p,sincos);
```
$$\frac{\sin(x)}{\cos(x)} + e^y + e^{(Iz)} + \sinh(t) + \sin(u)$$
```
> convert(p,expsincos);
```
$$\frac{\sin(x)}{\cos(x)} + e^y + e^{(Iz)} + \frac{1}{2}e^t - \frac{1}{2}\frac{1}{e^t} + \sin(u)$$

2.3.5 First Approach to the Function `simplify`

The function `simplify` is a multi-purpose command for simplification. It is quite helpful but cannot do everything, particularly in the presence of radicals. The command `simplify` always starts with a call to `normal`.

Use in the Form `simplify(...,symbolic)`

The main transformations carried out by `simplify(...,symbolic)` are summarized in the right column of the table below. These transformations are purely symbolic and for the rows labeled `power`, `radical` and `sqrt`, they are not necessarily valid for all complex values of the variables.

Option	Transformation being carried out
`power`	$\left(a^b\right)^c \quad\rightarrow\quad a^{\,b\,c}$ $\exp\left(5\ln\left(x\right)+1\right) \quad\rightarrow\quad x^5\exp\left(1\right)$ $\ln\left(x\,y\right) \quad\rightarrow\quad \ln\left(x\right)+\ln\left(y\right)$
`radical`	$8^{1/3} \quad\rightarrow\quad 2$ $(x^3+3x^2+3x+1)^{1/3} \quad\rightarrow\quad (x+1)$
`sqrt`	$\sqrt{4} \quad\rightarrow\quad 2$ $\sqrt{x^2+2x+1} \quad\rightarrow\quad (x+1)$
`trig`	$1+\tan(x)^2 \quad\rightarrow\quad 1/\cos(x)^2$ $\sin(x)^2 \quad\rightarrow\quad 1-\cos(x)^2$ $\cos(2x)+\sin(x)^2 \quad\rightarrow\quad \cos(x)^2$ and similarly for the hyperbolic expressions

By default, `simplify(...,symbolic)` carries out all these transformations.

- If one wishes `simplify(...,symbolic)` to carry out only some among the transformations summarized in the table above, one or several of the options listed in the left column of the table may be used. Only the simplifications from the corresponding lines will then be carried out.
- When several simplification options are used, they must be separated by commas, with `symbolic` appearing last.

Example using `simplify(...,symbolic)` without options.

Ex.43

> `f:=(x^a)^b+(u^2+2*u+1)^(1/2)+8^(1/3);`

$$f := (x^a)^b + \sqrt{u^2 + 2\,u + 1} + 8^{1/3}$$

> `g:=simplify(f,symbolic);`

$$g := x^{(a\,b)} + u + 3$$

One can verify that the expressions of `f` and `g` in the previous example are not equal for every value of the variable u.

Ex.44

> `u:=-3: 'f'=f;`

$$f = (x^a)^b + \sqrt{4} + 8^{1/3}$$

> `'g'=g;`

$$g = x^{(a\,b)}$$

Note: The use of apostrophes in the previous example prevents the evaluation of the left-hand-sides of the equalities, providing more informative output.

Examples using `simplify(...,symbolic)` with options:

Ex.45

> `u:='u': simplify(f,sqrt,power,symbolic);`

$$x^{(a\,b)} + u + 1 + 8^{1/3}$$

> `simplify(f,radical,symbolic);`

$$(x^a)^b + u + 3$$

The Function `simplify` Without the Option `symbolic`

When one uses `simplify` as above, the word `symbolic` can be regarded as an option in the same way as `power` or `sqrt`.

When used without the option `symbolic`, the function `simplify` carries out only those of the transformations summarized in the table of the previous page that are valid for all complex values of variables. This deserves explanation, but requires more space and more accurate definitions of the power, exponential, and logarithm functions. It will be the topic of Chapter 5.

Examples using `simplify` without the `symbolic` option.

Ex.46

```
> (1+1/2*cos(2*x))^2+sin(x)^2;
```
$$\left(1 + \frac{1}{2}\cos(2x)\right)^2 + \sin(x)^2$$

```
> simplify(");
```
$$\cos(x)^4 + \frac{5}{4}$$

```
> simplify((x^6)^(1/3)+sqrt(4));
```
$$\left(x^6\right)^{1/3} + 2$$

In the last example, $(x^6)^{1/3}$ is not transformed into x^2 since these quantities are not equal for all complex values of x.

Using Particular Simplification Rules

The rules `simplify` uses to transform expressions can turn out to be unsuitable in some cases. For example, with trigonometric expressions the function `simplify` systematically replaces $\sin(x)^2$ with $1 - \cos(x)^2$ as indicated in the table page 29.

Ex.47

```
> u:=sin(x)^2-sin(x)^2*cos(x)^2;
```
$$\sin(x)^2 - \cos(x)^2\sin(x)^2$$

```
> simplify(u);
```
$$\cos(x)^4 - 2\cos(x)^2 + 1$$

To obtain $\sin(x)^4$, which looks simpler than the expression returned in the previous example, one may use `simplify` while imposing simplification rules other than the ones defined in MAPLE's kernel.

In order to transform $\sin(x)^2 - \cos(x)^2\sin(x)^2$ to $\sin(x)^4$, the relation `cos(x)^2=1-sin(x)^2` must be imposed as a simplification rule. This relation is given between square brackets as the second argument to `simplify`.

Ex.48

```
> simplify(u,[cos(x)^2=1-sin(x)^2]);
```
$$\sin(x)^4$$

One may give several `simplify` simplification relations in a comma-separated list within brackets. One nice application of this is the expression of symmetric functions in terms of the elementary symmetric functions.

Ex.49

```
> restart; f:=sum(a^i*b^(4-i),i=0..4);
```

$$f := b^4 + a\,b^3 + a^2\,b^2 + a^3\,b + a^4$$

```
> simplify(f,[a+b=s,a*b=p]);
```

$$s^4 - 3\,p\,s^2 + p^2$$

Although each simplification relation is written as an equation, the order in which individual members are written is important: the quantities one wishes to appear in the result must be put on the right side. The previous example can be compared with the next formulation :

Ex.50

```
> simplify(f,[s=a+b,p=a*b]);
```

$$b^4 + a\,b^3 + a^2\,b^2 + a^3\,b + a^4$$

Finally, note that the simplification relations have to be polynomial expressions (possibly in a broad sense as shown in the example `cos(x)^2=1-sin(x)^2`), and thus without denominator. In the next example, the use of `simplify` with the relation `a/b=t` gives an error message.

Ex.51

```
> restart; f:=(a^3+3*a*b^2)/(3*a^2*b+b^3);
```

$$f := \frac{a^3 + 3\,a\,b^2}{3\,a^2\,b + b^3}$$

```
> simplify(f,[a/b=t]);
Error, (in simplify/siderels) side relations must
be polynomials in (name or function) variables
```

However, the expected simplification can be obtained by evaluating the quantity `simplify(simplify(f,[a=b*t]))` or, more simply, by setting `a:=b*t`.

Ex.52

```
> a:=b*t: simplify(f);
```

$$\frac{t\,\left(t^2 + 3\right)}{3\,t^2 + 1}$$

2.3.6 Simplification of Radicals: `radnormal` and `rationalize`

Using `simplify` with expressions containing radicals is unadvisable, because it is often unsuccessful. It is better to use `radnormal` or `rationalize`.

The Function `radnormal`

The function `radnormal` can be used to simplify the nested radicals. This function doesn't belong to the standard library and must therefore be loaded before its first use with the command `readlib(radnormal)`.

Ex.53

```
> x:=(1+sqrt(2))^3;
```
$$x := \left(1 + \sqrt{2}\right)^3$$

```
> y:=expand(x)^(1/3);
```
$$y := \left(5\sqrt{2} + 7\right)^{1/3}$$

```
> simplify(y);
```
$$\left(5\sqrt{2} + 7\right)^{1/3}$$

```
> readlib(radnormal): radnormal(y);
```
$$1 + \sqrt{2}$$

The Function `rationalize`

While `radnormal` handles nested radicals very well, it is better to use `rationalize` to rationalize denominators. Again, this function doesn't belong to the standard library and must therefore be loaded before its first use with the command `readlib(rationalize)`.

Ex.54

```
> readlib(rationalize):
  u:=2^(3/4); x:=(1+u)/(1-u);
```
$$u := 2^{3/4}$$
$$x := \frac{1 + 2^{3/4}}{1 - 2^{3/4}}$$

```
> rationalize(x);
```
$$-\frac{1}{7}\left(1 + 2^{3/4}\right)\left(1 + 2^{3/4} + 2\sqrt{2} + 4\,2^{1/4}\right)$$

2.3.7 The Functions `collect` and `sort`

The Function `collect`

The `collect` function provides a way to group together terms that have the same power within a "polynomial expression". If `var` is a free variable or an object of type `function`, i.e. a non-evaluated expression of the form `f(x)`, and `Expr` is a polynomial expression in `var`, `collect(Expr,var)` returns the expression obtained from `Expr` by grouping together terms that have the same power in `var`.

Example using `collect` with polynomials in one unknown

Ex.55

```
> restart;                          To reinitialize the session
  f:=(x-a)*(x-b)*(x-c);
```
$$f := (x - a)(x - b)(x - c)$$
```
> f:=expand(f);
```
$$f := x^3 - x^2 c - x^2 b + x b c - a x^2 + a x c + a b x - a b c$$
```
> collect(f,x);
```
$$f := x^3 + (-a - b - c) x^2 + (ac + ab + bc) x - abc$$

Example using collect with an object of type `function`.

Ex.56

```
> Expr:=expand(sin(3*x)+cos(3*x));
```
$$Expr := 4\sin(x)\cos(x)^2 - \sin(x) + 4\cos(x)^3 - 3\cos(x)$$
```
> collect(Expr,sin(x));          sin(x) is of type function
```
$$\left(4\cos(x)^2 - 1\right)\sin(x) + 4\cos(x)^3 - 3\cos(x)$$

Functions like `factor`, `normal` or `simplify` may be given as a third argument to `collect`, indicating that they are applied individually to the coefficients of the collected expression.

Applied to the expression of the previous example, `collect(Expr,sin(x), factor)` produces a grouped expression in which the coefficents appear in factored form.

Ex.57

```
> collect(Expr,sin(x),factor);
```
$$(2\cos(x) - 1)(2\cos(x) + 1)\sin(x) + \cos(x)\left(4\cos(x)^2 - 3\right)$$

Note: The function `collect` begins by calling `expand`, so `collect` can be used on a polynomial that isn't in expanded form.

Ex.58

```
[> f:=(x-a)*(x-b)*(x-c);
```
$$f := (x - a)(x - b)(x - c)$$
```
[> collect(f,x);
```
$$f := x^3 + (-a - b - c)\,x^2 + (a\,c + a\,b + b\,c)\,x - a\,b\,c$$

If `Expr` is a polynomial expression in several "unknowns", and if `var_1`, `var_2`, ...`var_p` are unknowns or objects of type `function`, then evaluating `collect(Expr,[var_1,var_2,...var_p])` returns the expression obtained by grouping together the terms in `Expr` that have the same power in `var_1`, the terms in each of those coefficients being themselves grouped together according to the powers of `var_2` and so forth recursively until `var_p`.

Ex.59

```
[> f:=expand((x-a)*(x-b)*(x-c));
```
$$f := x^3 - x^2\,c - x^2\,b + x\,b\,c - a\,x^2 + a\,x\,c + a\,b\,x - a\,b\,c$$
```
[> collect(f,[a,b]);
```
$$\left((x - c)\,b - x^2 + x\,c\right)a + \left(-x^2 + x\,c\right)b + x^3 - x^2\,c$$
```
[> collect(f,[b,a]);
```
$$\left((x - c)a - x^2 + x\,c\right)b + \left(-x^2 + x\,c\right)a + x^3 - x^2\,c$$

Adding `distributed` as a third parameter results in grouping together of terms of the same degree with respect to the "unknowns" in the list.

Ex.60

```
[> collect(f,[a,b],distributed);
```
$$x^3 - x^2\,c + (x - c)\,a\,b + \left(-x^2 + x\,c\right)a + \left(-x^2 + x\,c\right)b$$

The Function `sort`

The `sort` function arranges a polynomial expression in descending order. If `var` is an unknown or an object of type `function` and if `Expr` is an expanded polynomial expression in `var` (possibly obtained with the help of `expand`) then `sort(Expr,var)` returns the expression obtained from `Expr` by arranging the powers of `var` in descending order.

Ex.61

```
> expand((x^2+x+1)^5);
```

$$1 + 15\,x^2 + 45\,x^4 + 30\,x^3 + 45\,x^6 + 51\,x^5$$
$$+15\,x^8 + 5\,x + 30\,x^7 + x^{10} + 5\,x^9$$

```
> sort(");
```

$$x^{10} + 5\,x^9 + 15\,x^8 + 30\,x^7 + 45\,x^6 + 51\,x^5$$
$$+45\,x^4 + 30\,x^3 + 15\,x^2 + 5\,x + 1$$

```
> u:=expand((x^2+sin(y)+z)^3);
```

$$u := x^6 + 3\sin(y)\,x^4 + 3\,x^4\,z + 3\sin(y)^2\,x^2 + 6\sin(y)\,x^2\,z$$
$$+3\,x^2\,z^2 + \sin(y)^3 + 3\sin(y)^2\,z + 3\sin(y)\,z^2 + z^3$$

```
> sort(u,sin(y));
```

$$\sin(y)^3 + 3\,x^2\sin(y)^2 + 3\,z\sin(y)^2 + 6\,z\,x^2\sin(y)$$
$$+3\,x^4\sin(y) + 3\,z^2\sin(y) + 3\,z^2\,x^2 + 3\,z\,x^4 + x^6 + z^3$$

To sort by exponent using several variables, one provides these variables as a set (between braces) or a list (between square brackets). The expression is arranged, in descending order, as a function of the total degree with respect to this set of variables. When the variables are given as a list, each subset of terms of like total degree is itself recursively arranged in descending order with respect to this list.

Ex.62

```
> sort(u,[x,z]);
```

$$x^6 + 3\,z\,x^4 + 3\sin(y)\,x^4 + 3\,x^2\,z^2 + 6\sin(y)\,x^2\,z + z^3$$
$$+3\sin(y)^2\,x^2 + 3\sin(y)\,z^2 + 3\sin(y)^2\,z + \sin(y)^3$$

```
> sort(u,[z,x]);
```

$$x^6 + 3\,z\,x^4 + 3\,x^2\,z^2 + 3\sin(y)\,x^4 + z^3 + 6\sin(y)\,x^2\,z$$
$$+3\sin(y)\,z^2 + 3\sin(y)^2\,x^2 + 3\sin(y)^2\,z + \sin(y)^3$$

Warning! The function `sort` is "destructive". The rearrangement is carried out on the contents of the variable passed to `sort` (which is thus modified). Since MAPLE only keeps one copy of each expression it uses during a session.

Ex.63

```
> u;
```

$$x^6 + 3\,z\,x^4 + 3\,x^2z^2 + 3\sin(y)\,x^4 + z^3 + 6\sin(y)\,x^2\,z$$
$$+3\sin(y)\,z^2 + 3\sin(y)^2\,x^2 + 3\sin(y)^2\,z + \sin(y)^3$$

2.4 First Approach to Functions

2.4.1 Functions of One Variable

MAPLE allows the user to create his own functions via a syntax which is very similar to that used in Mathematics.

In the following example, a function, defined with the help of -> (arrow operator), is assigned to the identifier My_Funct. My_Funct can then be used like any other function name in MAPLE.

Ex.64

```
> My_Funct:=x -> x^2+x+1;
```
$$My\_Funct := x \to x^2 + x + 1$$

```
> My_Funct(2);
```
$$7$$

```
> My_Funct(sqrt(2));
```
$$3 + \sqrt{2}$$

```
> My_Funct(t);
```
$$t^2 + t + 1$$

Functions may be defined with if-statements, although MAPLE doesn't echo such definitions in the same nice mathematical syntax. This will be explained in Chapter 24. However, functions like this are used in the same way.

The function x -> x^(1/3) returns a non-real value when its argument is negative (p. 43). However, we can use the if-statement to construct a function that returns the real cubic root of any real number, even a negative one.

Ex.65

```
> Rac_Cub:=x -> if x>0 then x^(1/3) else -(-x)^(1/3) fi:
```
$$Rac\_Cub := proc(x) \ options \ operator, \ arrow;$$
$$if \ 0<x \ then \ x^{\wedge}(1/3) \ else \ -(-x)^{\wedge}(1/3) \ fi \ end$$

```
> Rac_Cub(-2);
```
$$-2^{1/3}$$

```
> evalc((-2)^(1/3));          to see the real and imaginary parts
```
$$\frac{1}{2} \, 2^{1/3} + \frac{1}{2} \, I \, 2^{1/3} \sqrt{3}$$

2.4.2 Functions of Several Variables

Functions of several variables can be defined in the same way, however, one should not forget to put the family of identifiers that appear on the left-hand side of the operator `->` in parentheses.

Ex.66

```
> f_1:=(x,y) -> (x^3-y^3)/(x-y);
```
$$f\_1 := (x,y) \to \frac{x^3 - y^3}{x - y}$$

```
> f_1(1,a);
```
$$\frac{1 - a^3}{1 - a}$$

As with functions of one variable, functions of several variables may be defined using if-statements. In this case MAPLE echos a procedure definition, but the function can be used in the same way. As given above, the function f_1 isn't defined if $x = y$; a more complete definition of it can be given as:

Ex.67

```
> f_1(a,a);
  Error, (in f_1) division by zero
> f_2:=(x,y) -> if x <> y then (x^3-y^3)/(x-y)
          else 3*x^2 fi:
```
$f\_2 := proc(x,y)$ *options operator, arrow;*
$\quad$ *if x<>y then (x^3-y^3)/(x-y) else 3*x^2 fi end*

```
> f_2(1,a);
```
$$\frac{1 - a^3}{1 - a}$$

```
> f_2(a,a);
```
$$3\,a^2$$

Warning! Forgetting the parentheses around the list of variables doesn't produce an error message but gives a result which is completely different from what is expected.

Ex.68

```
> f:=x,y -> (x^3-y^3)/(x-y); f(1,a);
```
$$f := x, y \to \frac{x^3 - y^3}{x - y}$$

$$x(1, a) \,,\ \frac{x^3 - 1}{x - 1}$$

2.4.3 The Difference Between Functions and Expressions

As in Mathematics, one has to distinguish between a function and an expression in MAPLE. In the next example, f is a function while P is an expression.

Ex.69

```
> f:=x -> x^2+x+1;
```
$$f := x \rightarrow x^2 + x + 1$$
```
> x:='x': P:=x^2+x+1;
```
$$P := x^2 + x + 1$$

One difference between functions and expressions lies in the kind of variable used at the time of their definition: it isn't necessary to use free variables in order to define a function, while the definition of an expression requires a free variable or the use of apostrophes.

Ex.70

```
> x:=1;
```
$$x := 1$$
```
> f:=x -> x^2+x+1;
```
$$f := x \rightarrow x^2 + x + 1$$
```
> P:=x^2+x+1;
```
$$P := 3$$
```
> P:='x^2+x+1';
```
$$P := x^2 + x + 1$$

If f is a function, one only has to request the evaluation of f(a) to obtain the value of f when its argument is equal to a.

Ex.71

```
> f(2);
```
$$7$$

If P is an expression that depends on a free variable x, its value for x=a can be obtained

- either by assigning a to x and requesting the evaluation of P (be aware that x is no longer free),
- or by using subs(x=a,P), which returns the result obtained by replacing x with a in the expression P (x remains a free variable in this case).

```
▷ x:='x' : P:=x^2+x+1 :
▷ P;                          the evaluation of P returns an expression
```
$$x^2 + x + 1$$
```
▷ x:=1: P;                    the evaluation of P returns a number
```
Ex.72
$$3$$
```
▷ x:='x' : subs(x=2,P);
```
$$7$$
```
▷ P;                          x is free, hence the evaluation of P
                                      returns an expression in x
```
$$x^2 + x + 1$$

In order to use the function subs, x has to be a free variable. Suppose, for example, x has been assigned the value 5. Since MAPLE fully evaluates all the arguments of the function subs, the expression subs(x=2,P) is transformed into subs(5=2,P), which is not, of course, what one expects.

2.4.4 Links Between Expressions and Functions

If P is an expression in the free variable x, the evaluation of unapply(P,x) returns the function that maps x onto P.

```
▷ restart:                                              restart
                                         reinitializes the variables
▷ Q:=a*x*x+1;
```
$$Q := a\,x^2 + 1$$
Ex.73
```
▷ g:=unapply(Q,x);
```
$$g := x \rightarrow a\,x^2 + 1$$

Similarly, if P is an expression in the free variables x and y, the evaluation of unapply(P,x,y) returns the function that maps (x,y) onto P.

```
▷ R:=x^2+x*y+y^2;
```
$$R := x^2 + xy + y^2$$
Ex.74
```
▷ h:=unapply(R,x,y);
```
$$h := (x,y) \rightarrow x^2 + xy + y^2$$

Conversely, if f is a function in one variable and if g is a function in two variables, then f(x) and g(x,y) are expressions with which one can compute just as with any expression that has been typed in or returned as the result of a computation.

2.5 Simplification of Power Functions

This section, which is a bit more theoretical than previous sections, is devoted to a precise definition of the function exp, the function ln and the exponentiation operator, $(x, y) \mapsto x\hat{\,}y = x^y$. We shall also study in the behavior of simplify on expressions using these types of functions. It can be skipped in the first reading, but will provide the necessary details when the need arises.

2.5.1 The Functions exp, ln and the Exponentiation Operator

In this part, we assume the following functions of one real variable t to be known

$$\left\{ \begin{array}{ccc} \mathbb{R} & \to & \mathbb{R} \\ t & \mapsto & e^t \end{array} \right. \quad \left\{ \begin{array}{ccc} \mathbb{R}_+^* & \to & \mathbb{R} \\ t & \mapsto & \ln t \end{array} \right. \quad \left\{ \begin{array}{ccc} \mathbb{R} & \to & \mathbb{C} \\ t & \mapsto & \exp(I\,t) = \cos t + I\,\sin t \end{array} \right.$$

Definition of the functions exp and ln

For every complex number z one sets:

$$\exp(z) = e^{\operatorname{Re}(z)} e^{i\operatorname{Im}(z)} = e^{\operatorname{Re}(z)}(\cos(\operatorname{Im}(z)) + i\,\sin(\operatorname{Im}(z)))$$

and, likewise, for every $z \neq 0$, one sets

$$\ln(z) = \ln(\,|z|\,) + i\,\text{argument}(z)$$

where argument(z) denotes the unique real number t in $]-\pi, \pi]$ such that $z = |z|\, e^{i\,t}$.

According to this definition, the function exp is periodic with period $2\pi i$. Hence, it isn't *injective* as it is when restricted to the real domain, and solving the equation $z = \exp(u)$ for $z \neq 0$ gives

$$u = \ln(\,|z|\,) + i\,(\text{argument}(z) + 2k\pi) \quad \text{with } k \in \mathbb{Z}$$

which is equal to

$$u = \ln(z) + 2\,I\,k\,\pi \quad \text{with } k \in \mathbb{Z}.$$

Ex.75

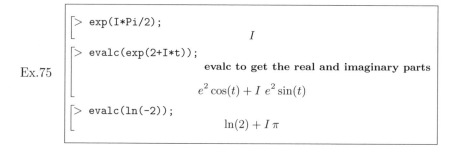

```
[> exp(I*Pi/2);
                                    I

[> evalc(exp(2+I*t));
                          evalc to get the real and imaginary parts
                          e² cos(t) + I e² sin(t)

[> evalc(ln(-2));
                          ln(2) + I π
```

With these definitions for the functions `exp` and `ln`, one has for all complex numbers z, z_1, z_2:

$$\exp(\ln(z)) = z$$

$$\ln(\exp(z)) = z \Leftrightarrow \mathrm{Im}(z) \in \left]-\pi, \pi\right]$$

$$\exp(z_1 + z_2) = \exp(z_1)\,\exp(z_2)$$

$$\ln(z_1\,z_2) = \ln(z_1) + \ln(z_2) \Leftrightarrow \mathrm{argument}(z_1) + \mathrm{argument}(z_2) \in \left]-\pi, \pi\right]$$

$$\forall n \in \mathbb{Z} \quad \exp(n\,z) = \exp(z)^n$$

$$\forall n \in \mathbb{Z} \quad \ln(z^n) = n\,\ln(z) \Leftrightarrow n\,\mathrm{argument}(z) \in \left]-\pi, \pi\right]$$

The Exponentiation Operator

While the definition of the exponentiation operator $(x, y) \longmapsto x^y$ and its use are well-known when y is a positive or negative integer, they may not be obvious when y takes fractional, real or complex values. MAPLE allows expressions of the form x^y in which x and y are allowed any complex value.

In order to define x^y, MAPLE works in the complex domain and sets

$$x^y = \exp(y\,\ln(x)) = \exp\left[y\left(\ln|x| + i\,\mathrm{argument}(x)\right)\right] \qquad (*)$$

When y is an integer, $(*)$ is another way to write the formula for a complex number written in trigonometric form raised at an integer power, since

$$x^y = \exp\left[y\left(\ln|x| + i\,\mathrm{argument}(x)\right)\right] = |x|^y \exp(i\,y\,\mathrm{argument}(x)).$$

When x is a positive real number and y is any real number, the argument of x is equal to zero and $(*)$ can be written

$$x^y = \exp\left[y \cdot \ln|x|\right] = e^{y\,\ln x}.$$

Hence, the relation $(*)$ is a generalization of the more classical definitions of x^y.

With this definition of the exponential, one has for all complex numbers z, z_1, z_2, a, b:

$$z^a\,z^b = z^{a+b}$$

$$(z^a)^b = z^{a\,b} \Leftrightarrow b\,a\,\ln(z)) = b\,\ln(e^{a\,\ln(z)}) \quad [2\,i\,\pi]$$

$$z_1^a\,z_2^a = (z_1\,z_2)^a \Leftrightarrow a\,\ln(z_1\,z_2) = a\,\ln(z_1) + a\,\ln(z_2) \quad [2\,i\,\pi]$$

In particular, the equalities on the right-hand sides of the two equivalences are true when a is an integer, which yields well-known identities.

Square Roots, Cubed Roots and the Function surd

Taking the formula $(*)$ from page 42 with $y = 1/2$ and any z, one has:

$$z^{1/2} = \exp\left[\frac{1}{2} \cdot (\ln|z| + i\operatorname{argument}(z))\right] = \sqrt{|z|}\,\exp\left(\frac{1}{2} i\operatorname{argument}(z)\right)$$

It can then be verified that $z^{1/2}$ is a square root of z, i.e. a number whose square is equal to z. It is in fact the root of z whose argument belongs to the range $]-\pi/2, \pi/2]$.

With this definition of $\sqrt{z} = z^{1/2} =$ sqrt(z), one can verify that

$$\left(z^{1/2}\right)^2 = z$$
$$\left(z^2\right)^{1/2} = z \Leftrightarrow \operatorname{argument}(z) \in \left]-\tfrac{\pi}{2}, \tfrac{\pi}{2}\right]$$

In particular, $\sqrt{-1} =$ sqrt(-1) $= \exp\left(i\frac{\pi}{2}\right) =$ I, which indeed corresponds to MAPLE's definition of I.

Since one obviously has $-1 = \sqrt{-1}\sqrt{-1} \neq \sqrt{1} = 1$, one can see that the relation

$$\sqrt{u}\sqrt{v} = \sqrt{uv}$$

isn't true for all complex numbers u and v.

Taking the formula $(*)$ from page 42 with $x = -1$ and $y = 1/3$, one has

$$(-1)\hat{\ }(1/3) = \exp\left(\frac{1}{3}\left(\ln(1) + i\pi\right)\right) = \exp\left(i\,\frac{\pi}{3}\right) = \frac{1}{2} + i\,\frac{\sqrt{3}}{2}$$

In contrast, one usually considers the cubed root of -1 to be -1 when working over the real domain.

Since the operator $\hat{\ }$ returns a non-real value of the cubed root of a negative number, MAPLE provides the function surd, which gives a real result.

- If x is a real number and n is an odd integer, then surd(x,n) returns the real n^{th} root of x.
- More generally, if x is a complex number and n is an integer, surd(x,n) returns the nth root of x whose argument is closest to the argument of x.

Ex.76

```
> surd(-1,3);
                              -1
> evalc(surd(-1,8));
```
$$-\frac{1}{2}\sqrt{2+\sqrt{2}} + \frac{1}{2}I\sqrt{2-\sqrt{2}}$$

2.5.2 The Function `simplify`

Having given clear definitions of the functions `exp`, `ln` and the exponentiation operator, we come back to the behavior of the function `simplify`. Since the transformations corresponding to the three first lines `power`, `radical` and `sqrt` of the table page 29 are not valid for all complex value of the arguments, the function `simplify` only executes these transformations in two cases:

- when `simplify` is used with the option `symbolic` (p. 29)
- when they are valid for all values of the domain one works in via `assume` (p. 46)

Study of an Example: `simplify((a^b)^c)`

With the option `symbolic`, the function `simplify` returns a^{bc}, while without the option, it returns the argument unchanged since, as one can verify, the two quantities are not equal for all values of the variables a, b and c.

Ex.77

```
[> restart; u:=(a^b)^c:        the symbol : suppresses the echo
[> u1:=simplify(u,symbolic);
```
$$u1 := a^{(bc)}$$
```
[> u2:=simplify(u);
```
$$u2 := (a^b)^c$$
```
[> a:=-1: b:=3: c:=1/3: u1; evalc(u2);
```
$$-1$$
$$\frac{1}{2} + \frac{1}{2}I\sqrt{3}$$

The transformation is carried out even without the option symbolic when b and c are integers, since it is valid for every value of a in that case. On the other hand, when b is fractional, the transformation is carried out only when c is an integer, since this is the only case for which the two quantities are always equal.

Ex.78

```
[> a:='a': b:=3: c:=4: simplify(u), u1;
```
$$a^{12} , a^{12}$$
```
[> b:=5/2: c:=2: simplify(u), u1;
```
$$a^5 , a^5$$
```
[> a:=-1: b:=5/2: c:=2: simplify(u), u1;
```
$$-1 , -1$$

Using the Function `assume`

When one knows that some variables belong to specific domains, one can specify it to MAPLE with the help of the function `assume`. So,

- `assume(a,real)` specifies that a is a real number.
- `assume(b>0)` specifies that b is a positive real number.

Many other hypotheses may be specified using the function `assume`. A detailed list of these can be obtained by typing `?assume`.

If, with the help of `assume`, one specifies to MAPLE that a is positive and that b and c are real numbers, the function `simplify` can transform $(a^b)^c$ into a^{bc}, since the two quantities are equal under these hypotheses.

Ex.79

> `a:='a':b:='b':c:='c':`   the variables have to be unassigned before using assume

> `assume(b,real);assume(c,real);assume(a>0);`

> `u1:=simplify(u);`   u contains (a^b)^c

$$u1 := a \sim^{(b\sim\, c\sim)}$$

Note: By default, a variable for which a hypothesis has been set using `assume` is displayed on the screen followed by the symbol $\sim$. This symbol acts as a reminder for the user. The option **Assumed Variables** in the **Options** menu can be used to replace this symbol $\sim$ with the phrase *with assumptions on a*, or even to suppress all annotations.

Hypotheses that have been set concerning a given variable can be retrieved with the help of the function `about`.

Ex.80

> `about(a);`

Originally a, renamed a $\sim$:
is assumed to be: RealRange(Open(0),infinity)

Warning! If a constraint has been set for the variable a using `assume`, one cannot make an assignment like `a~:=b`. If the variable a occurs within an expression `Expr` and if one wishes to compute the value of `Expr` for a=b, then one has to use `subs(a=b,Expr)`.

If one wishes the value of `u1` for a=1 in example 79, the function `subs` must be used instead of assignment, since one cannot make an assignment on an assumed variable.

Ex.81
```
> subs(a=1,u1);
```
$$1$$

Not only does the assignment `a:=1` not work, it also locks any subsequent usage of `subs`:

Ex.82
```
> a:=1; u1;
```
$$a := 1$$
$$a \sim^{(b\sim\, c\sim)}$$
```
> a:='a': subs(a=1,u1);
```
$$a \sim^{(b\sim c\sim)}$$

Using the Option `assume` within `simplify`

A hypothesis can be set upon all the variables occuring within an expression to which one applies `simplify` by adding an argument of the form `assume=<prop>` when calling `simplify`. For example, `assume=positive` indicates that all the variables occuring within the expression can only take positive real values.

Ex.83
```
> a:='a': b:='b': c:='c':            These assignments
                                     clear previous hypotheses.
> simplify(u);           Thus no transformations are performed.
```
$$(a^b)^c$$
```
> simplify(u,assume=positive);         With assume=positive,
                                the transformation is again performed.
```
$$a^{(b\,c)}$$

Note: Any hypotheses given with `simplify` are only used during the simplification stage and don't affect the variables occuring in the expression to be simplified. Thus, they won't appear followed by the symbol $\sim$ afterward. We can verify this for the variables of the previous example with the help of the function `about`.

Ex.84
```
> about(a);
  a:
  nothing known about this object
```

The Function `sqrt` and the Function `csgn`

With the definition of $z^{1/2} = $ `sqrt(z)` $= \exp(\ln(z)/2)$, one can verify that

- $\left(z^{1/2}\right)^2$ is always equal to z.
- $\left(z^2\right)^{1/2}$ is equal to z only if the argument of z belongs to $]-\pi/2, \pi/2]$.

MAPLE carries out the simplification $\left(z^{1/2}\right)^2 \rightarrow z$ automatically.

On the other hand, the quantity $\left(z^2\right)^{1/2}$ isn't simplified automatically and `simplify((z^2)^(1/2))` returns $csgn(z)\,z$ where the function `csgn` is defined by

$$\text{csgn(z)} = \begin{cases} 1 & \text{if } \mathrm{Re}(z) > 0 \text{ or } (\mathrm{Re}(z) = 0 \text{ and } \mathrm{Im}(z) > 0) \\ -1 & \text{if } \mathrm{Re}(z) < 0 \text{ or } (\mathrm{Re}(z) = 0 \text{ and } \mathrm{Im}(z) < 0) \\ 0 & \text{if } z = 0 \end{cases}$$

Ex.85

```
> restart; u:=x^2+2*x+1; v:=u^(1/2);
```
$$u := x^2 + 2\,x + 1$$
$$v := \sqrt{x^2 + 2\,x + 1}$$
```
> simplify(v);
```
$$csgn(x + 1)\,(x + 1)$$
```
> simplify(v, symbolic);
```
$$x + 1$$

2.5.3 The Function `combine`

The main transformations carried out by `combine` are summarized in the right column of the following table

Option	Transformation being carried out
trig	linearization of the trigonometric expressions (circular or hyperbolic)
exp	$e^x * e^y \rightarrow e^{x+y} \qquad (e^x)^a \rightarrow e^{x*a}$ $e^{x+n*\ln(y)} \rightarrow e^x * y^n$
ln	$\ln(x) + \ln(y) \rightarrow \ln(x * y)$ $a * \ln(x) \rightarrow \ln(x^a)$
power	$z^x * z^y \rightarrow z^{x+y} \qquad (z^x)^a \rightarrow z^{x*a}$ $\sqrt{-a} \rightarrow i\sqrt{a}$

Regarding transformations in rows `exp`, `ln` and `power`, the function `combine`, like the function `simplify`, executes only those transformations that are valid for all complex values of the variables.

If one wishes `combine` to carry out only some subset of the transformations from the previous table, it may be passed a second argument comprised of options from the first column in the table. If more than one option is used, the set must be enclosed in braces. Without any option, `combine` carries out all transformations appearing in the table.

Ex.86

```
> combine(sin(a)*cos(b));
```
$$\tfrac{1}{2}\sin(a+b) - \tfrac{1}{2}\sin(-a+b)$$
```
> combine(x^a*x^b+exp(x)*exp(y),exp);
```
$$x^a\,x^b + e^{(x+y)}$$
```
> combine(x^a*x^b+exp(x)*exp(y)+sin(x)^4,power);
```
$$x^{(a+b)} + e^{(x+y)} + \sin(x)^4$$
```
> combine(x^a*x^b+exp(x)^5+sin(x)^4,{trig,exp});
```
$$x^a\,x^b + e^{(5\,x)} + \tfrac{3}{8} + \tfrac{1}{8}\cos(4x) - \tfrac{1}{2}\cos(2x)$$

With `symbolic` as a third argument, the function `combine` carries out all transformations from the previous table, even those that aren't valid for some complex values of the variables. An empty set `{ }` has to be used as a second argument if one doesn't wish to give any transformation options.

Ex.87

```
> combine(ln(x)+ln(y)+sin(x)^4);
```
$$\ln(x) + \ln(y) + \frac{3}{8} + \frac{1}{8}\cos(4x) - \frac{1}{2}\cos(2x)$$
```
> combine(ln(x)+ln(y)+sin(x)^4,ln);
```
$$\ln(x) + \ln(y) + \sin(x)^4$$
```
> combine(ln(x)+ln(y)+sin(x)^4,ln,symbolic);
```
$$\ln(x\,y) + \sin(x)^4$$
```
> combine(ln(x)+ln(y)+sin(x)^4,symbolic);
   Error, (in combine) unable to combine with respect to, symbolic
> combine(ln(x)+ln(y)+sin(x)^4,{ },symbolic);
```
$$\ln(x\,y) + \tfrac{3}{8} + \tfrac{1}{8}\cos(4x) - \tfrac{1}{2}\cos(2x)$$

3. Arithmetic

3.1 Divisibility

3.1.1 Quotient and Remainder

The functions `iquo` (integer quotient) and `irem` (integer remainder) are used to compute the quotient and the remainder respectively of integer division. If a and b are two integers

- `iquo(a,b)` returns the quotient of the integer division of a by b,
- `irem(a,b)` returns the remainder of the integer division of a by b.

Ex. 1

```
> restart; iquo(24,7);                          restart to
                                          reinitialize the session

                          3
> irem(12,7);

                          5
```

An optional third parameter can be given to the function `iquo` (or `irem`) that will be set to the remainder (or the quotient) of the integer division after evaluation.

Ex. 2

```
> iquo(24,9,r);r;
                          2

                          6
```

However, if one gives the same command with two more integers, MAPLE returns an error message that isn't easy for a beginner to understand.

Ex. 3

```
> iquo(12,7,r);
   Error, wrong number (or type) of parameters in function iquo;
```

Indeed, when MAPLE encounters `iquo(12,7,r)`, it starts by evaluating all arguments, which gives `iquo(12,7,6)`. It is now easier to understand the content of the error message, since the function `iquo` is programmed in such a way that it doesn't accept a numerical value as a third argument.

There are two ways to use this function `iquo` with a third argument `r`

- either one unassigns `r` before calling `iquo`, using the assignment `r:='r'`,
- or one puts the identifier `r` in apostrophes.

Ex. 4

```
> r:='r': iquo(24,9,r) : r ;
                            6
> iquo(12,7,'r') : r ;
                            5
```

The apostrophes around `r` prevent MAPLE from carrying out a full evaluation of that argument and restrict its evaluation to the first level: hence it is the name `r` which is passed on to the procedure and not the value towards which `r` is pointing. Using apostrophes everywhere may seem to be a good method, but the user has to take care of the fact that he may modify links that exist between variables without noticing it.

3.1.2 G.c.d. and Euclid's Algorithm

The Functions `igcd` and `ilcm`

The functions `igcd` (integer greatest common divisor) and `ilcm` (integer least common multiple) are use to compute the gcd and the lcm, respectively.

Given k integers `a1`, `a2`,..., `ak`

- `igcd(a1,a2,...,ak)` returns the gcd of the integers `a1`, `a2`, ...,`ak`
- `ilcm(a1,a2,...,ak)` returns the lcm of the integers `a1`, `a2`, ...,`ak`

Ex. 5

```
> igcd(12,16);
                            4
> ilcm(12,16);
                            48
> ilcm(12,16,15);
                            240
```

Extended Euclidean Algorithm: The Function `igcdex`

Given two integers a and b and two free variables u and v, `igcdex(a,b,u,v)` returns the gcd of a and b, and assigns to the variables u and v values u0 and v0 such that: u0 a+v0 b= `pgcd(a,b)`.

Ex. 6

```
> u:='u': v:='v' : d:=igcdex(12,7,u,v);
                        d := 1
> u ; v;
                          3
                         −5
> 12*u+7*v-d;                              To verify
                          0
```

Warning! On calling the function `igcdex`, the identifiers u and v have to represent unassigned variables or be in apostrophes, otherwise MAPLE returns an error message (p. 50).

Ex. 7

```
> d:=igcdex(27,12,u,v);
    Error, (in igcdex) Illegal use of a formal parameter
```

Once again, this is a consequence of the way MAPLE evaluates a function call, namely by first evaluating all its arguments.

In the previous example, u and v are first replaced respectively with 3 and −5, which causes MAPLE to evaluate `igcdex(12,7,3,-5)` and leads to the error message *Error, (in igcdex) Illegal use of a formal parameter*, since the function `igcdex` receives a numerical value instead of a variable name as its third argument.

A shown on page 50, one can either unassign the variables or use apostrophes in such a case.

Ex. 8

```
> u:='u' : v:='v' : igcdex(27,12,u,v) : u, v;
                        1, −2
> igcdex(27,12,'u','v'): u, v;
                        1, −2
```

3.1.3 Decomposition into Prime Factors

Given a natural number n,

- nextprime(n)   returns the smallest prime number strictly bigger than n.
- prevprime(n)   returns the greatest prime number strictly smaller than n.
- ithprime(n)   returns the nth prime number.
- isprime(n)   returns true if n is prime and false otherwise.
- ifactor(n)   returns the decomposition of n into prime factors

Ex. 9

```
> isprime(561);
                        false
> ithprime(17);
                          59
> prevprime(1001) , nextprime(1001);
                        997 , 1009
> ifactor(561) ; ifactor(2727);

                      (3)(11)(17)

                      (3)³(101)
```

Note: The function isprime is a probabilistic primality test that returns a boolean value

- If it returns false, the number is certainly composite
- If it returns true, it is very likely that the number is prime.

3.1.4 Congruences

By default, the operator mod computes positive remainders.

Given three natural numbers a, b and n such that n and b are relatively prime,

- a mod n   returns the unique integer in $[0, n[$ congruent to a modulo n.
- (1/b) mod n   returns the unique integer c in $[0, n[$ such that $bc \equiv 1\,[n]$
- (a/b) mod n   returns the unique integer d in $[0, n[$ such that $bd \equiv a\,[n]$

Ex.10

```
> 14 mod 4; 1/2 mod 17;
                        2
                        9
```

> 1/2 mod 14 ;   **2 and 14 are not relatively prime**
  Error, the modular inverse does not exist

Ex.11

> 4/3 mod 14;
                                  6

If one makes the assignment 'mod':= mods, the operator mod computes symmetric remainders. If a, b and n are natural numbers such that n and b are relatively prime, and J is the range -trunc((n-1)/2)..trunc(n/2), i.e. the set of integers lying between -(n-1)/2 and n/2,

- a mod n   returns the unique integer in J congruent to a modulo n
- (1/b) mod n   returns the unique integer c in J such that b c ≡ 1 [n]
- (a/b) mod n   returns the unique integer d in J such that b d ≡ a [n]

Warning ! In the assignment 'mod':=mods, one must not forget to put mod between backwards apostrophes (ALTGR-7 on a standard P.C. keyboard), so that MAPLE carries out an assignment and not an evaluation of the operator mod.

> 'mod':=mods;
                          $mod := mods$

Ex.12

> 1/2 mod 17;
                          -8

Entering 'mod':=modp switches back to the first definition of mod, which returns the positive remainder.

To compute remainders of big powers modulo a given integer, it is better to use the operator &^, which doesn't evaluate its arguments and forces MAPLE to cleverly compute powers with the help of congruences, instead of beginning by computing powers in the set of integers. It is interesting to compare the computation times of the two following formulations:

> 'mod':=modp: 7&^12345 mod 17;
                          10

Ex.13

> 7^12345 mod 17;
                          10

3.2 Diophantian Equations

3.2.1 Chinese Remainder Theorem

The function chrem (chinese remainder) is used to solve a system of multiple congruences. Given k integers r1, r2, ... rk and k integers n1, n2, ... nk that are pairwise relatively prime, chrem([r1,r2,...,rk],[n1,n2,...nk]) returns an integer x such that

$$\forall i \in [1, k], \text{ x} \equiv \text{r i mod n i}.$$

When the environment variable mod contains modp, chrem returns the positive remainder modulo n1 n2...nk. When mod contains mods, it returns the symmetric remainder (p. 53).

Ex.14

```
> chrem([9,6,4],[3,5,7]);
                                81
> 'mod':=mods : chrem([9,6,4],[3,5,7]);
                               -24
```

When the ni's are not relatively prime, MAPLE returns one of the following messages:

Ex.15

```
> chrem([9,6,4],[3,5,15]);
  Error, (in chrem) division by zero
> chrem([9,6,4],[5,15,3]);
  Error, (in chrem) the modular inverse does not exist
```

3.2.2 Solution of Equations Modulo n

The function msolve can be used to solve equations modulo n. Calling this function requires two arguments: first is the equation (or the system of equations) to be solved, and the second the module defining the congruence.

Example of equation solving

Ex.16

```
> restart; Sol:=msolve(x^4=1,33);
```
$$Sol := \{x = 23\}, \{x = 10\}, \{x = 32\}, \{x = 1\}$$

When an equation has no solution, `msolve` doesn't return anything

Ex.17

```
> Sol:=msolve(x^2=-1,33);
```
$$Sol :=$$

When an equation holds for every value of x, `msolve` returns $\{x = x\}$.

Ex.18

```
> msolve(x^561=x,561);
```
$$\{x = x\}$$

When `msolve` is used to solve a system of equations, the equations have to appear in braces.

Ex.19

```
> msolve({2*x+3*y=3,4*x+y=5},13);
```
$$\{y = 8, x = 9\}$$

3.2.3 Classical Equations

To solve an equation over the integers, one calls `isolve` with the equation to be solved as its only argument. The function `isolve` is able primarily to solve the classical equations of degree two, like the *Pell-Fermat* equation or the *Pythagorean* equation.

Ex.20

```
> isolve(x*x-y*y=9);
```
$$\{x = 5, y = -4\}, \{x = -5, y = -4\}, \{y = 0, x = 3\},$$
$$\{y = 0, x = -3\}, \{x = -5, y = 4\}, \{x = 5, y = 4\}$$

Ex.21

```
> isolve(x^2-11*y^2=1);
```
$$\left\{x = -\frac{1}{2}\%2 - \frac{1}{2}\%1, y = \frac{1}{22}\sqrt{11}\,(\%2 - \%1)\right\},$$
$$\left\{x = -\frac{1}{2}\%2 - \frac{1}{2}\%1, y = -\frac{1}{22}\sqrt{11}\,(\%2 - \%1)\right\},$$
$$\left\{x = \frac{1}{2}\%2 + \frac{1}{2}\%1, y = -\frac{1}{22}\sqrt{11}\,(\%2 - \%1)\right\}$$
$$\%1 \quad : \quad = \left(10 - 3\sqrt{11}\right)^{-N1}$$
$$\%2 \quad : \quad = \left(10 + 3\sqrt{11}\right)^{-N1}$$

In the last example, MAPLE uses the parameter _N1. The name of this variable begins with _ (underline character), like all variables introduced by MAPLE.

Moreover, MAPLE uses the *labels* %1 and %2 in place of the quantities $\left(10 - 3\sqrt{11}\right)^{-N\,1}$ and $\left(10 + 3\sqrt{11}\right)^{-N\,1}$, which occur frequently in the result, to give a more compact solution.

The user is not allowed to introduce such labels but he may use them once they introduced by MAPLE. In order to compute the value of $\left(10 - 3\sqrt{11}\right)^{-N\,1}$ $+\left(10 + 3\sqrt{11}\right)^{-N\,1}$ when _N1 = 10 in the previous example, one only has to write

Ex.22

```
> expand(subs(_N1=10,%1+%2));
                        9986232009998
```

MAPLE may be prevented from introducing *labels* by executing the command interface(labelling=false). As an example, the reader may try

Ex.23

```
> restart; interface(labelling=false);
  isolve(x^2-11*y^2=1);
```

4. Real Numbers, Complex Numbers

4.1 The Real Numbers

4.1.1 Display of Real Numbers

The Type `integer`

An integer value is automatically set in integer form and always displayed in base 10. Output may possibly span several lines on the screen. An integer value has the type `integer`.

Ex. 1

```
> a:=2^10+1;
```
$$a := 1025$$
```
> whattype(a);
```
whattype returns the
type of an expression

$$integer$$

The Type `fraction`

A fractional value which is not an integer is automatically set as a quotient of two relatively prime integers, with a strictly positive denominator, and displayed as such on the screen. It is of type `fraction`.

Ex. 2

```
> a:=15*(-5^(-2))+3;
```
$$a := \frac{12}{5}$$
```
> whattype(a);
```
$$fraction$$

The Type `float`

A value which is expressed from rational numbers, using the the four operations and at least one occurrence of a decimal point is automatically simplified and stored as two numbers: an integer, the mantissa, and a power of 10, the exponent. Such an element is of type `float`.

A value of type float is usually displayed on the screen in the classical decimal form, like 123456.789, or with a scientific writing, like .602 10^{24}. The user may type decimal numbers in either of these two forms, but should take care not to forget the symbol * between the mantissa and the power of 10.

Ex. 3

> `123456.789 , 1234567.89 , 123.456789*10^(-15);`

$$123456.789,\ .123456789\ 10^{7},\ .123456789\ 10^{-12}$$

> `a:=10.; whattype(a);`   **with a decimal point,**
     a is of type float

$$a := 10.$$

$$float$$

> `b:=10; whattype(b);`   **without a decimal point,**
     b is of type integer

$$b := 10$$

$$integer$$

If a and b are two integers, `Float` (a,b) denotes the decimal number $a \times 10^{b}$. MAPLE also uses this function instead of the decimal notation to write the number $a \times 10^{b}$ when the b is too big or too small in absolute value.

Ex. 4

> `Float(6023,20);`

$$.6023\ 10^{24}$$

> `10000.^10000;`

$$Float(1000000000,\ 39991)$$

The Other Real numbers

For MAPLE, the real numbers of type `integer` and `fraction` are combined in the type `rational`. Likewise, the real numbers of type `rational` and `float` are combined in the type `numeric`. These two types aren't basic types returned by `whattype`, but can nevertheless be tested using the function `type`.

Numbers like `ln(2)`, `sin(1)`, `Pi+1`, `sqrt(2)` are displayed on the screen using their literal classical expressions; they aren't of type `numeric`. MAPLE groups all the real numerical values, together within the type `realcons` including those which aren't of type `numeric`. This type `realcons` (Ch. 21) isn't a basic type returned by `whattype`, but can nevertheless be tested with the help of `type`.

4.1.2 Approximate Decimal Value of Real Numbers

The Function `evalf`

In general, MAPLE doesn't carry out any decimal evaluation of real numbers. The function `evalf` can be used to obtain an approximate decimal value of a real number.

- If `a` contains a real numerical value, `evalf(a)` returns an approximate value of `a` written in decimal form, with a number of significant digits equal to the value of the global variable `Digits`.
- If `n` contains an integer value, `evalf(a,n)` returns an approximate value of `a` with `n` significant digits.

In either case, the expression that is returned is of type `float`.

Ex. 5

```
> a:=22/7; b:=Pi; c:=sqrt(2);
```
$$a := \frac{22}{7} \quad b := \pi \quad c := \sqrt{2}$$
```
> evalf(a);
```
the default value of **Digits** is **10**
$$3.142857143$$
```
> Digits:=18: evalf(b);
```
or **evalf(b,18)** directly
$$3.14159265358979324$$
```
> evalf(c), evalf(c,3);
```
$$1.41421356237309505, \ 1.41$$

The expression returned by `evalf` can either be written in elementary decimal form as above, or using scientific notation (with a mantissa between 0.1 and 1), or using the function `Float`.

Ex. 6

```
> restart; evalf(Pi*(6400)^2); evalf(1/");
```
$$.1286796351 \ 10^9$$
$$.7771237455 \ 10^{-8}$$
```
> evalf(2.^(2^(20)));
```
$$Float(6741140125, 315643)$$

Expressions Containing an Element of Type `float`

Every mathematical expression constructed from the operators +, -, *, ^ and / from terms of type `numeric`, is automatically evaluated in decimal form if any term is of type `float`.

Ex. 7

```
> a:=1+2/3; b:=1.0+2/3;
```

$$a := \frac{5}{3}$$

$$b := 1.666666667$$

Likewise, every function of MAPLE's kernel – except functions with integer values – which is called with an argument of type `float` returns a result that is automatically evaluated in decimal form.

Ex. 8

```
> a:=sin(1);
```

$$a := \sin(1)$$

```
> b:=sin(1.0);
```

$$b := .8414709848$$

Approximate Value of a List or a Set of Real Numbers

`evalf` can be directly applied to a list (or a set) of real numbers: it returns then the list (or the set) of approximate values of these real numbers.

Ex. 9

```
> s:=2*Pi, sqrt(2)+1, gamma;
```
construction of a sequence

$$s := 2\pi, \ \sqrt{2}+1, \ \gamma$$

```
> Ens:={s};
```
One constructs a set with { }.
The order of the elements of a set may vary from one session to another.

$$Ens := \left\{ \gamma, 2\pi, \sqrt{2}+1 \right\}$$

```
> Lst=[s];
```
One constructs a list with [].
Its elements appear always in the same order.

$$Lst := \left[2\pi, \sqrt{2}+1, \gamma \right]$$

```
> Digits:=4: evalf(Ens); evalf(Lst);
```

$$\{6.284, 2.414, .5772\}$$

$$[6.284, \ 2.414, \ .5772]$$

The Function evalhf

If a contains a real numerical value, evalhf(a) (*hardware floating point*) returns, an approximate decimal value using about 15 significant digits (depending upon the architecture of the machine used), regardless of the value of the variable Digits. Since the function evalhf uses the hardware structure of the machine, its execution time is very much faster than the one of the function evalf.

Ex.10

```
> Digits:=3; evalf(Pi); evalhf(Pi);
```

$$Digits := 3$$

$$3.14$$

$$3.141592653589793$$

Continued Fraction Series Expansions of a Real Number

The function convert with the option confrac returns the continued fraction series expansion of a real number.

If a is an expression of type **numeric**, the evaluation of convert(a,confrac) returns the list of first terms of the continued fraction series expansion of a. The number of terms that are computed depends on the content of the variable Digits. The last term is often wrong.

A variable that is free or set between apostrophes may be given as an optional third argument to convert. After evaluation, this variable contains the list of successive quotients corresponding to the list convert returns.

Ex.11

```
> Digits:=4; a:=sqrt(2);
  convert(evalf(a),confrac,'t');
```

$$Digits := 4$$

$$a := \sqrt{2}$$

$$[1, 2, 2, 2, 2, 5]$$

```
> t;
```

$$\left[1, \frac{3}{2}, \frac{7}{5}, \frac{17}{12}, \frac{41}{29}, \frac{222}{157}\right]$$

```
> evalf(t);
```
The function evalf can be used with a list

$$1, 1.500, 1.400, 1.417, 1.414, 1.414$$

4.2 The Complex Numbers

4.2.1 The Different Types of Complex Numbers

A complex numerical value, obtained from the real numbers of type numeric and the number I = sqrt(-1) using the operations +, -, *, ^ and /, is automatically evaluated in the form a+Ib, where a and b are real numbers of type numeric.

Ex.12

```
> restart; (1+2*I)^3;
```
$$-11 - 2I$$
```
> (1/2+I/3)^3;
```
$$-\frac{1}{24} + \frac{23}{108}I$$
```
> (0.5+I/3)^3;
```
$$-0.4166666663 + .2129629629I$$

A complex numerical value that uses a real number which is of type realcons but not of type numeric is not automatically set in the form a+I b.

Ex.13

```
> (1+sqrt(2)*I)^3;
```
$$\left(1 + \sqrt{2}I\right)^3$$

MAPLE has no specific basic type for storing all complex values. However, the function type can be used to ascertain the type of the coefficients a and b of a complex number of the form a+Ib (p. 348).

Ex.14

```
> z:=(1+I*sqrt(2))^3: z1:=expand(z);
```
$$z1 := -5 + I\sqrt{2}$$
```
> whattype(z), whattype(z1);
```
$$\wedge, +$$
```
> type(z,complex(realcons)),
  type(z1,complex(realcons));
```
$$false, \ true$$

As can be seen in the previous example, a complex numerical value z is of type complex(realcons) if z is written in the form a+Ib, where a and b are two real numbers of type realcons. This data type is not returned by whattype but can be determined with the help of type.

4.2.2 Algebraic Form of the Complex Numbers

The Function evalc

The function evalc can be used to set a complex number in algebraic form. If z contains a complex numerical value, evalc(z) returns the complex number z in the form a+Ib, with a and b real numbers.

Ex.15

```
> u:=(sqrt(2)+I)*(1+I); evalc(u);
```

$$u := (1 + I)(\sqrt{2} + I)$$

$$\sqrt{2} - 1 + I(1 + \sqrt{2})$$

```
> v:=(sqrt(2)+I)/(1+sqrt(2)*I); evalc(v);
```

$$v := \frac{\sqrt{2} + I}{1 + I\sqrt{2}}$$

$$\frac{2}{3}\sqrt{2} - \frac{1}{3}I$$

Note: Every numerical value of type complex(numeric) is automatically written in algebraic form without using the function evalc.

Ex.16

```
> z:=(1+I)/(1-2*I);
```

$$z := -\frac{1}{5} + \frac{3}{5}I$$

Like evalf, the function evalc can also be applied directly to a list or a set of complex numerical values.

Ex.17

```
> s:=(sqrt(2)+I)/(sqrt(2)-I), (1+sqrt(2)*I)*(1-I);
```

construction of a sequence

$$s := \frac{\sqrt{2} + I}{\sqrt{2} - I}, \ (1 - I)(1 + I\sqrt{2})$$

```
> evalc({s});
```

Using evalc with a set

$$\left\{ 1 + \sqrt{2} + I(\sqrt{2} - 1), \frac{1}{3} + \frac{2}{3}I\sqrt{2} \right\}$$

```
> evalc([s]);
```

Using evalc with a list

$$\left[\frac{1}{3} + \frac{2}{3}I\sqrt{2}, 1 + \sqrt{2} + I(\sqrt{2} - 1) \right]$$

The Functions `Re` and `Im`

If `z` contains a complex numerical value, then `Re(z)` and `Im(z)` return the real part and the imaginary part respectively of the complex number `z`.

Ex.18

```
> z:=(1+I)*(1+I*sqrt(2));
```
$$z := (1 + I)\left(1 + I\sqrt{2}\right)$$

```
> a:=Re(z);
```
$$a := 1 - \sqrt{2}$$

```
> b:=Im(z);
```
$$b := 1 + \sqrt{2}$$

Sometimes, `Re(z)` or `Im(z)` returns a non evaluated form using $R(z)$ or $I(z)$. The function `evalc` can be used in such cases to force the evaluation of the result.

Ex.19

```
> z:=(1+I)/(1-sqrt(2)*I);
```
$$z := \frac{1 + I}{1 - I\sqrt{2}}$$

```
> a:=Re(z); b:=Im(z);
```
$$a \;:\; = R\left(\frac{1 + I}{1 - I\sqrt{2}}\right)$$
$$b \;:\; = I\left(\frac{1 + I}{1 - I\sqrt{2}}\right)$$

```
> evalc(a), evalc(b);
```
$$\frac{1}{3} - \frac{1}{3}\sqrt{2}\,,\ \frac{1}{3} + \frac{1}{3}\sqrt{2}$$

Complex Conjugate of a Complex Number

If `z` contains a complex value, `conjugate(z)` returns the conjugate of `z`.

Ex.20

```
> z1:=1+2*I; z2:=(1+I)/(1-sqrt(2)*I);
```
$$z1 := 1 + 2I$$
$$z2 := \frac{1 + I}{1 - I\sqrt{2}}$$

```
> conjugate(z1), conjugate(z2);
```
$$1 - 2I\,,\ \frac{1 - I}{1 + I\sqrt{2}}$$

4.2.3 Trigonometric Form of the Complex Numbers

The Function abs

If z contains a complex value, abs(z) returns the absolute value of the complex number z.

Ex.21

```
> z:=2+3*I; abs(z);
```
$$z := 2 + 3I$$
$$\sqrt{13}$$

The Function argument

If z contains a complex numerical value different from zero, argument(z) returns the unique real number t belonging to $[-\pi, \pi]$ such that

$$z = |z| \, e^{I\,t}.$$

Given the complex number 0, the function argument returns the value 0.

Ex.22

```
> argument(1+I);
```
$$\frac{1}{4}\pi$$

```
> argument(-3-2*I);
```
$$\arctan\left(\frac{2}{3}\right) - \pi$$

```
> argument(0);
```
argument(0)=0 for MAPLE !
$$0$$

4.2.4 Computing with Expressions with Complex Coefficients

The function evalc can be used to set any complex expression in algebraic form. In general, if z is a complex expression, evalc(z) returns an expression of the form a+I*b, where a and b are expressions with real coefficients in the free variables occuring in z.

In fact, the function evalc carries out its computation assuming that all the free variables occuring in z only take real values.

Ex.23

```
> restart; z:=(a+I)^3;
```
$$z := (a + I)^3$$
```
> evalc(z);
```
$$a^3 - 3\,a + I\,(3\,a^2 - 1)$$
```
> z:=(a+I)^2;
```
$$z := (a + I)^2$$
```
> evalc(z);
```

**with a single term in I,
the other terms aren't grouped together**

$$a^2 + 2\,I\,a - 1$$

If **f** is a function from MAPLE's kernel, `evalc` can also decompose expressions like `f(x+Iy)`.

Ex.24

```
> z:=sin(x+I*y): evalc(z);
```
$$\sin(x)\cosh(y) + I\,\cos(x)\sinh(y)$$

The functions `Re` and `Im` are always ineffective for complex expressions containing free variables. To compute the real or the imaginary part of an expression **z** containing unassigned variables, in addition to `Re` and `Im` use `evalc` (which assumes all variables take real values).

Ex.25

```
> z:=sin(x+I*y);
```
$$\sin(x + I\,y)$$
```
> Re(z);
```
$$R\left(\sin(x + I\,y)\right)$$
```
> evalc(Re(z)); evalc(Im(z));
```
$$\sin(x)\cosh(y)$$
$$\cos(x)\sinh(y)$$

Likewise, `evalc` must be used with the function `conjugate` (or `abs`) to obtain the complex conjugate (or the absolute value) of a complex expression **z** containing free variables.

Ex.26

```
> z:=sin(x+I*y): evalc(conjugate(z));
```

$$\sin(x)\cosh(y) - I\cos(x)\sinh(y)$$

```
> z:=a+I;
```

$$z := a + I$$

```
> abs(z);
```

used alone, abs
returns a non evaluated form

$$|a + I|$$

```
> evalc(abs(z));
```

with evalc the variable a
is assumed to be a real value

$$\sqrt{a^2 + 1}$$

4.2.5 Approximate Decimal Value of the Complex Numbers

As with real numbers, the function `evalf` can be used to obtain the approximate decimal value of a complex numerical value. If `z` contains a complex numerical value, `evalf(z)` returns the complex number a+I b, the numbers a and b being the approximate decimal values of the real and imaginary parts of `z` respectively.

Ex.27

```
> evalf(1+sqrt(2)*I+ln(2));
```

$$1.693147181 + 1.414213562\,I$$

5. Two-Dimensional Graphics

5.1 Curves Defined by an Equation $y = f(x)$

This section explains how to use MAPLE to plot curves defined by an equation $y = f(x)$. Such a curve may be defined either by an expression or by a function.

5.1.1 Graphic Representation of an Expression

Given an expression p depending on a single free variable x, and two numerical values a and b such that a<b, the evaluation of plot(p,x=a..b) plots the graphic representation of p for x ranging from a to b.

Ex. 1

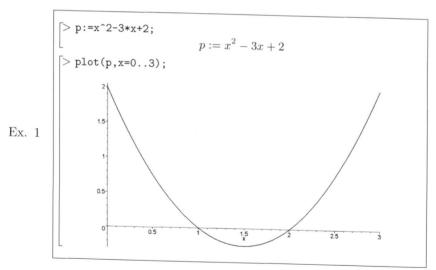

By default the plot is included within the worksheet, and its size can be modified with the help of the mouse. However, if the option **Plot Display Window** is selected in the **Options** menu before executing the plot command, the plot is displayed in its own separate window. This option is very useful if one wishes to print only the plot, without the rest of the worksheet.

As can be seen in the previous example, `plot` automatically adjusts the scale of the ordinates in such a way that the graph uses the whole window. This doesn't necessarily give an interesting picture of the curve. Therefore, the range of the images can be specified as a third argument.

If p is an expression depending on a single free variable x, and a, b, c, d are values such that a<b and c<d , the evaluation of `plot(p,x=a..b,y=c..d)` or of `plot(p,x=a..b,c..d)` plots the graphic representation of p for x ranging from a to b while restricting the values of y to the range $[c, d]$.

Any other name can be used in place of y, since it is only used to label the vertical axis.

Example with a third parameter `c..d`

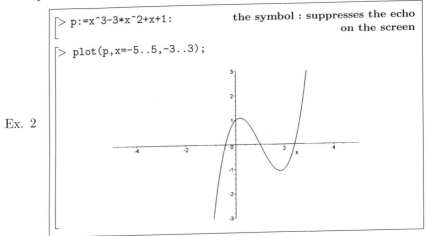

Ex. 2

Example with a third parameter `y=c..d`

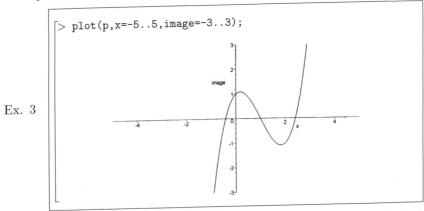

Ex. 3

Warning ! When `plot(p,x=a..b)` is evaluated, MAPLE begins by evaluating the two arguments of the function `plot`, which produces an error if x isn't a free variable. This explains the error message one obtains when evaluating `plot(2,1=0..5)`.

Ex. 4
```
> x:=1: plot(x+1,x=0..5);
  Error, (in plot) invalid arguments
```

Warning!

- If the identifier x is missing in the second argument, MAPLE returns a message indicating that the graph is empty, without specifying why.
- The same happens if p depends on a free variable other than the one appearing in the second argument of plot.

Ex. 5
```
> x:='x': plot(p,0..5);          doesn't return any graph
  Plotting error, empty plot

> y:='y': q:=x+y:        example of an expression depending on
  plot(q,x=0..5);              a free variable other than x
  Plotting error, empty plot
```

Warning! If a is bigger than b, MAPLE doesn't give any error message but returns an empty graph.

Ex. 6
```
> x:='x': plot(p,x=5..0);
                  returns an empty graph without error message
```

5.1.2 Graphic Representation of a Function

Given two numerical values a and b such that a<b and a function f in a single variable, one may use either plot(f(x),x=a..b) or plot(f,a..b) to graphically represent the curve $y = f(x)$ for x ranging from a to b.

- The first syntax plot(f(x),x=a..b) corresponds to the one studied in Section 5.1.1 since f(x) is an expression in x.
- In the second syntax plot(f,a..b), one has to take care **not to put the variable identifier for the domain**.

In the previous syntaxes, the identifier f may denote either a function belonging to MAPLE's kernel or a user-defined function or procedure.

Whether one uses the first or the second syntax, the scale of the vertical axis can always be specified, and the vertical axis can be given a name, by giving a third parameter y=c..d or c..d.

To plot, for example, the function $x \to \frac{5\,\sin(x)}{x}$ continuously extended at 0, one may write

Ex. 7

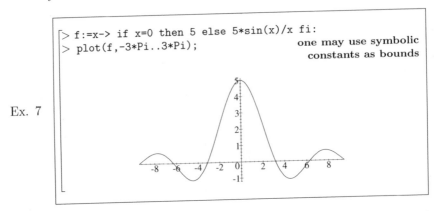

For a function which is unbounded over the given range, one has to restrict the ordinates with a third argument c..d or y=c..d. Otherwise, the graph will be unreadable.

Ex. 8

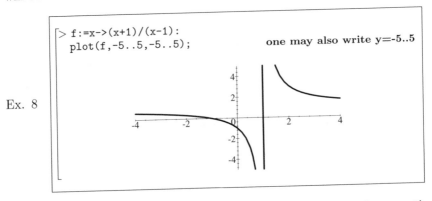

It may be surprising to get the vertical asymptote $x = 1$ when only requesting a plot of the curve. In fact, MAPLE plots the segment linking the last point whose x-coordinate is smaller than 1 to the first point whose x-coordinate is bigger than 1. Since the x-coordinates of these points are close to 1, they are outside the limits of the screen on both sides of x=1. Since their ordinates have opposite signs and are very big, this segment is vertical and looks like an asymptote (p. 81 to suppress the asymptote).

5.1.3 Simultaneous Plot of Several Curves

Given two real numbers a and b such that a<b,

- if p1, p2,..., pk are k expressions depending on the single free variable x, the evaluation of plot([p1,p2,...,pk],x=a..b) plots p1, p2,..., pk for x ranging from a to b all in the same picture.
- if f1, f2, ..., fk are k functions or procedures in a single variable, the evaluation of plot([f1,f2,...,fk],a..b) plots f1, f2,..., fk all in the same picture.

In each of these cases, the scale of the vertical axis can be specified by using a third argument y=c..d or c..d .

MAPLE automatically plots the different curves with different colors on the screen.

Ex. 9

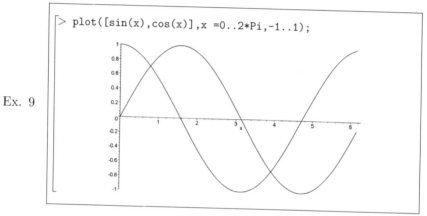

```
> plot([sin(x),cos(x)],x =0..2*Pi,-1..1);
```

To get the same plot, one may also write

Ex.10
```
> plot([sin,cos],0..2*Pi,-1..1);
```

Warning! The variable x has to appear in the two arguments of plot when the curves are defined by expressions, but it must not appear in any of them when the curve is defined by funtions.

5.1.4 Plot of a Family of Curves

One often needs to plot a family of curves depending on a real parameter t for $x \in [a, b]$. In order to do this, one can

- either use an application f that maps the variable t onto the expression f(t) that depends on x and t.
- or use an expression p that depends on t and x.

First Method

If one for example wishes to study the family of curves defined by $y = t\,e^x + x^2$, one may write

Ex.11

```
> f:=t->t*exp(x)+x^2;
```
$$f := t \to t\,e^x + x^2$$

With such a formulation, `f(1)` is an expression that depends on the single variable x and a sample of the family of curves can be obtained by typing

```
> plot([f(-1),f(1),f(2)],x=-3..3,y=-5..5);
```

Ex.12

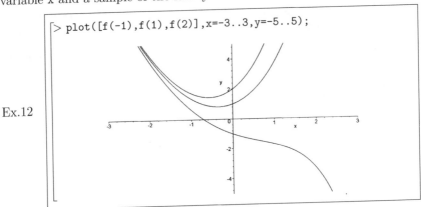

The function `seq` can be used to obtain a set of curves of the family with values of the parameter `t` that are evenly spaced out. This function `seq` will be studied p. 350 but, for the moment, it suffices to know that the evaluation of `seq(f(t),t=-1..3)` returns the sequence `f(-1),f(0),f(1),f(2),f(3)`.

```
> seq(f(t),t=-1..3);
```
$$-e^x + x^2,\ x^2,\ e^x + x^2,\ 2e^x + x^2,\ 3e^x + x^2$$
```
> Lst:=["];              "represents the last computed quantity
```
$$Lst := [-e^x + x^2,\ e^x + x^2,\ 2e^x + x^2,\ 3e^x + x^2,\ x^2]$$
```
> plot(Lst,x=-3..3,y=-5..5);
```

Ex.13

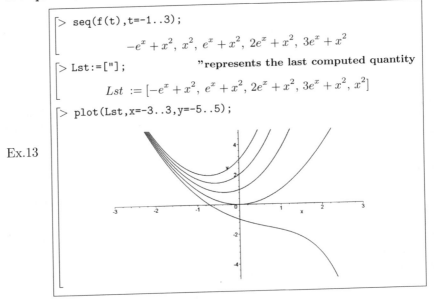

Note: In the previous example, one could also have directly typed plot([seq(f(t),t=-1..3)], x=-3..3,y=-5..5) which avoids the use of the intermediary variable Lst.

The function seq can also be used even if the values of the parameter aren't evenly spaced out. Indeed, if L is a list of values [t1,t2,...,tr], the evaluation of seq(f(t),t=L) returns the sequence p(t1),p(t2),...,p(tr).

With this syntax, Example 13 can be written

Ex.14
> plot([seq(f(t),t=[-1,1,2])],x=-3..3,y=-5..5);

Second Method

If one has an expression p depending on t and x, which is frequently the case in a worksheet, one may use

- plot([seq(p,t=t0..t1)],x=a..b), which produces parameter values that are evenly spaced in steps of 1.
- t := k*h: plot([seq(p,k=k0..k1)],x=a..b), which produces values of the parameter that are evenly spaced in steps of h.
- plot([seq(p,t=L)],x=a..b), where L is a list of parameter values.

With this syntax, the example 13 can be written

Ex.15

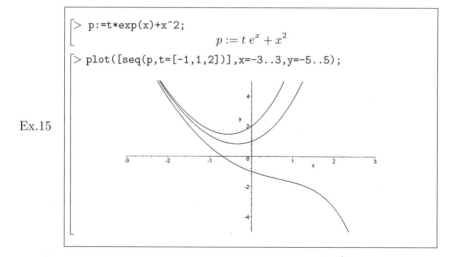

> p:=t*exp(x)+x^2;
$$p := t\,e^x + x^2$$
> plot([seq(p,t=[-1,1,2])],x=-3..3,y=-5..5);

5.2 The Environment of plot

By default, plots are rendered in the worksheet. However, if the option **Plot Display→Window** has been selected in the **Options** menu before executing plot, the plot appears in its own window. Several options, most of which described below, can be used to modify aspects of this picture; they are directly available when the drawing is plotted within an external window. If the plot is included within the worksheet, you must click on the plot to access them.

5.2.1 The plot Menu in Windows

In graphic mode, there is a menu bar, a tool bar and a context bar at the top of the window and a status line at the bottom of the window.

The Menu Bar

In graphics mode, options on the menu bar are

File   to print the drawing displayed within an external graphics window (**Print**), to set up printer parameters (**Printer set-up**) and to close the graphics window (**Close**).

Edit   to copy the drawing displayed within the graphics window to the clipboard, where it can be pasted into any Windows compatible application.

View   to enable or to suppress the display of the tool bar (**Tool bar**), the status line (**Status line**) or the context bar (**Context bar**).

Style   to choose among two plot styles: plot by points (**Points**) and a continuous plot that interpolates between consecutive points (**Line**).

to choose (**Symbol**) the symbol used to represent points, choices are: **Cross**, **Diamond**, **Point**, **Circle** ...

to choose (**Line Style**) the line style used to represent the curves, choices are: continuous (**Solid**), dashes (**Dash**), points (**Point**).

to choose the line width, choices are: **Thin**, **Medium**, **Thick** or the current width (**Default**).

Axes   to choose the position of the axes.

Boxed the axes form a rectangle around the graph.

Framed the two axes are drawn at the border of the graph.

Normal the two axes pass through the origin when it appears in the drawing. When the origin of one of the axes doesn't belong to the portion of the plane being represented, the other axis is shifted towards the border of the graph.

None no axis is plotted.

Projection to choose a frame which is orthonormal (**Constrained**) or not (**Unconstrained**).

The Tool Bar and the Context Bar

Icons on the tool bar and the context bar can be used to directly activate some options of the previous menu. Each icon is fairly suggestive and a message summarizing its use is displayed in the status line when left mouse button is pressed while the cursor is above the icon. Moving off the icon before letting up the mouse button stops the corresponding option from being activated.

- The two icons on the left can be used to select the **Line** or **Point** plot option.
- There are icons for the axes styles **Boxed**, **Framed**, **Normal** and **None**.
- On the right, the icon $\boxed{1:1}$ toggles between the **Constrained** and **Unconstrained** modes.

5.2.2 The Options of `plot`

When calling `plot`, options can be used to specify a representation style or to refine the plot. Several options can be given, separated with commas.

**These options must follow the two or three
mandatory arguments already discussed.**
(function(s) or expression(s), range in x, range in y).

Presentation Options Corresponding to Menu Options

Some `plot` options previously discussed as menu options can be passed directly to `plot`. These are:

style   used in the form `style=POINT` or `style=LINE` according to the plot style one wishes.

linestyle   used in the form `linestyle=n`. According to the values of n, the plots are rendered as a continuous line (n=1), dashes (n=2), points (n=3), point-dashes (n=4) ...

thickness   used in the form `thickness=n` where n is 1, 2 or 3 according to the thickness one wishes for the line.

axes   used in the form `axes=BOXED`, `axes=FRAMED`, `axes=NORMAL` or `axes=NONE` according to the type of axes one wishes.

scaling   `scaling=CONSTRAINED` or `scaling=UNCONSTRAINED` can be used to choose a representation with orthonormal axes or a representation making the best use of the whole window.

Presentation Options Not Available as Menu Options

There are other options that cannot be obtained through menus:

xtickmarks the option `xtickmarks=n`, where n is an integer, can be used to display approximately n values on the x axis.

ytickmarks likewise, `ytickmarks=n`, where n is an integer, can be used to display approximately n values on the y axis.

title   `title='Title of the graph'` can be used to display a title at the top of the window. Backwards apostrophes must be used to delimit the title (ALTGR-7 key on a standard P.C. keyboard).

color   `color=c`, where c is the name of a color (cf. the on-line help by typing `?color`), is used to choose the color in which the plot is rendered. For example, `color=black` ensures that all the curves are black, which is useful for black and white printers.

Example using a single option

Ex.16   `[> plot(sin(x),x=-5..5,-3..3,scaling=constrained);`

Multiple options must be separated by commas.

Ex.17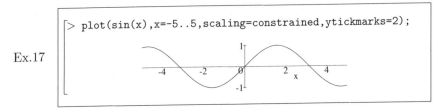

`[> plot(sin(x),x=-5..5,scaling=constrained,ytickmarks=2);`

Warning ! When an option is used, it must follow the three first parameters which are the expression(s) or function(s) and the ranges in x and in y, otherwise MAPLE returns an error message which isn't very informative.

Ex.18   `[> plot(sin(x) ,x = -5..5 ,scaling=constrained,-3..3);`
        Error, (in plot) invalid arguments

When plotting several curves simultaneously, one may choose a style for each curve by using lists for the options `style`, `linestyle`, `thickness`, `color`. For example, the representation of the function sin with a continuous black line and the representation of cos with red dashes in the same drawing can be obtained by writing

Ex.19

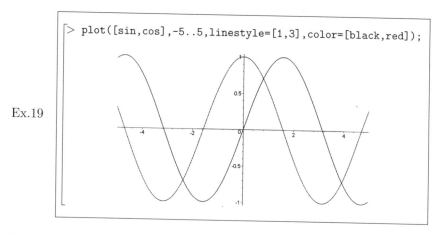

Note: The contents of a variable can be inserted within the `title` option by using the *period*, which is MAPLE's concatenation operator. If the value is an integer, it has to be stored within a variable beforehand with the help of `convert(...,string)`.

Ex.20

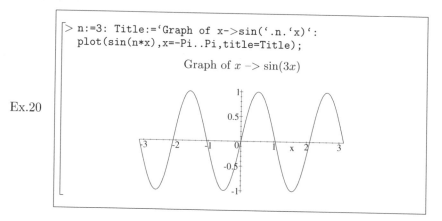

Options for Improving Quality of Plots

If the plot of a curve is not accurate enough, the options `numpoints` and `resolution` increase the number of points that are computed and refine the drawing.

The option numpoints (by default numpoints=49) defines the minimal number of points MAPLE computes to plot the curve. MAPLE's technique uses a variable number of points; more points are computed above ranges in which the function varies very more. The number of points that are added in this way is limited by the value of the option resolution which corresponds to the horizontal resolution of the graphic display being used (by default resolution=200).

It is better to use a big value of resolution than a big value of numpoints when the function has only one or two singularities. It avoids computing too many points in regions where the function behaves nicely.

Ex.21

```
> plot(x*sin(1/x),x=0..0.5,-0.5..0.5,resolution=2000);
                 this resolution may seem excessive for the screen
                     but it produces a nice curve on the printer
```

Warning! These last options require time and memory. They should therefore be used in moderation according to the limitations of the system and the time one has to plot the curve.

The Option discont

If plot is used to plot the graphic representation of an expression that has a discontinuity, the drawing which is returned may contain an extraneous vertical segment.

Ex.22

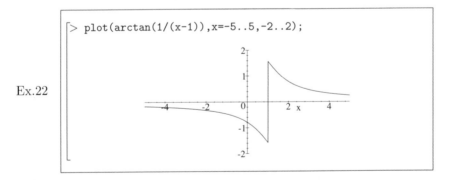

```
> plot(arctan(1/(x-1)),x=-5..5,-2..2);
```

The option discont=true forces plot to test for discontinuities of the expression to be represented. The curve is then plotted only in the ranges where the given expression is continuous, avoiding vertical segments like the one appearing in the previous plot.

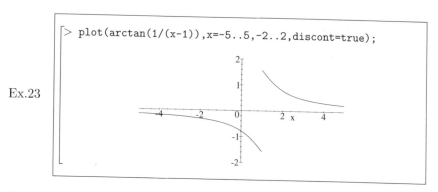

Ex.23

This option `discont` could have been used on p. 72, to suppress the asymptote obtained when plotting the graph of $(x+1)/(x-1)$, provided that one uses `plot` with an expression.

Ex.24

```
[> plot((x+1)/(x-1),x=-5..5,-5..5,discont=true);
```

Warning! The option `discont` can only be used for the graphic representation of an expression, not for a function.

Lifetime of Options

Options specified when calling `plot` are active for that call only. When the user wishes to work with given options during a whole session without retyping them every time he calls `plot`, he may use the function `setoptions` of the `plots` library.

This function can be used with one or several arguments separated by commas. An option that has been chosen with `setoptions` can always be locally modified during a call to the function `plot`.

For example, all plots can be executed in an orthonormal frame without drawing the axes by writing

Ex.25

```
[> with(plots,setoptions):        to load the function setoptions
   setoptions(scaling=constrained,axes=none);
```

5.3 Parametrized Curves in Cartesian Coordinates

5.3.1 Plot of a Parametrized Curve

Given two numerical values u0 and u1 such that u0<u1,

- If p and q are two expressions in the single free variable u, then the evaluation of plot([p,q,u=u0..u1]) plots the curve whose parametric representation is x=p, y=q for u ranging from u0 to u1.
- If f and g are two functions in a single variable, then plot([f,g,u0..u1]) or plot([f(u),g(u),u=u0..u1]) plots the curve whose parametric representation is x=f(u), y = g(u) for u ranging from u0 to u1.

Warning ! The parameter u has either to appear in the three elements of the list (when the two first parameters are expressions) or to appear nowhere (when the two first parameters are functions).

For such a plot, MAPLE automatically adapts the scale in an optimal way, but ranges for x and y that force MAPLE to restrict the drawing can still be specified.

- plot([p,q,u=u0..u1],x=a..b) restricts the plot of the curve to points whose domain lies between a and b, and uses x to label the horizontal axis.
- plot([p,q,u=u0..u1],x=a..b,y=c..d) restricts the plot to the window [a,b]×[c,d] and uses x and y to label the axes.
- plot([p,q,u=u0..u1],a..b,c..d) or plot([p,q,u=u0..u1],view=[a..b,c..d]) restricts the plot to the window $[a,b] \times [c,d]$ without labeling the axes.

Such a definition of a window, which is necessary when the curve has infinite branches (otherwise the graph is unreadable), and can also to zoom in on a specific portion of a curve.

Example with the coordinates written as expressions

Ex.26

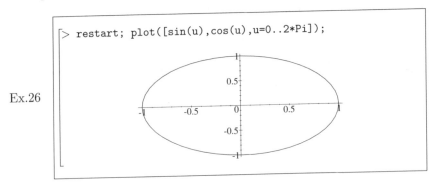

The same example can be written with functions as

Ex.27
```
[> plot([ sin,cos,0..2*Pi ]);
```

The options seen previously on p. 77 can also be used in plotting parametrized curves. In particular here, it is essential to add the option `scaling=constrained` in order to obtain a true circle.

Ex.28
```
[> plot([sin,cos,0..2*Pi ] ,scaling=constrained);
```

Example of a curve that has infinite branches for which the scaling is essential

Ex.29
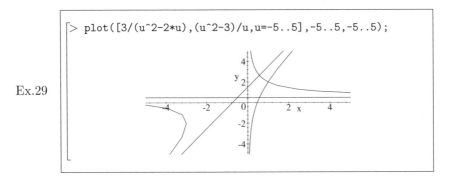
```
[> plot([3/(u^2-2*u),(u^2-3)/u,u=-5..5],-5..5,-5..5);
```

5.3.2 Simultaneous Plot of Several Parametrized Curves

Let a1, b1, a2, b2 be four real numbers such that a1<b1 and a2<b2 and p1, p2, q1, q2 be four expressions depending on u, then the evaluation of plot([[p1,q1,u=a1..b1] , [p2,q2,u=a2..b2]}) plots the parametrized curve x=p1, y=q1 for u ranging from a1 to b1 and the parametrized curve x=p2, y=q2 for u ranging from a2 to b2 in the same picture.

- The scale of the horizontal axis can be specified and the horizontal axis can be labeled, by writing plot([[p1,q1,u=a1..b1] , [p2,q2,u=a2..b2]], x=a..b).
- The scales of the two axes can be specified and the two axes can be labeled, by writing plot([[p1,q1,u=a1..b1] , [p2,q2,u=a2..b2]],x=a..b, y=c..d).
- The scales of the two axes can also be specified without labeling the axes, by writing plot([[p1,q1,u=a1..b1] , [p2,q2,u=a2..b2]],a..b,c..d) or plot([[p1,q1,u=a1..b1] , [p2,q2,u=a2..b2]],view=[a..b,c..d]).

The syntax described above can easily be generalized to two or more curves.

MAPLE automatically plots the different curves in different colors. If one wishes to print out the drawing, one can use the option `color=black` in order to plot all curves in black. One can also define specific plot styles for each curve by using lists of options.

Ex.30

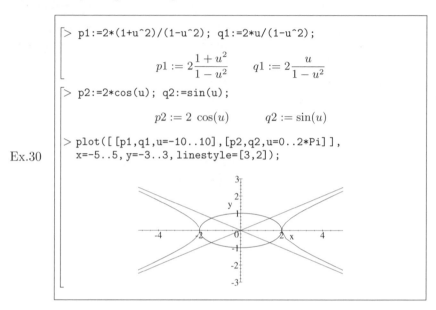

```
> p1:=2*(1+u^2)/(1-u^2); q1:=2*u/(1-u^2);
```

$$p1 := 2\frac{1+u^2}{1-u^2} \qquad q1 := 2\frac{u}{1-u^2}$$

```
> p2:=2*cos(u); q2:=sin(u);
```

$$p2 := 2\,\cos(u) \qquad q2 := \sin(u)$$

```
> plot([[p1,q1,u=-10..10],[p2,q2,u=0..2*Pi]],
   x=-5..5, y=-3..3, linestyle=[3,2]);
```

5.3.3 Plot of a Family of Parametrized Curves

To plot the family of curves Γ_t parametrized by $x = f_t(u)$, $y = g_t(u)$ for u ranging from $u_0(t)$ to $u_1(t)$, one may use

- an application G that maps t onto the list `[p(t),q(t),u=a(t)..b(t)]` where `p(t)`, `q(t)`, `a(t)` and `b(t)` are respectively the expressions of $f_t(u)$, $g_t(u)$, $u_0(t)$ and $u_1(t)$,
- a list of the form `[p,q,u=a..b]` where `p`, `q`, `a` and `b` are respectively the expressions of $f_t(u)$, $g_t(u)$, $u_0(t)$ and $u_1(t)$.

First Method

To plot a family of hypocycloïds, for example, one can define:

Ex.31

```
> G:=t->[cos(u/t)+cos(u)/t,sin(u/t)-sin(u)/t,u=0..2*Pi*t];
```

$$G := t \rightarrow \left[\cos\left(\frac{u}{t}\right) + \frac{\cos(u)}{t}, \sin\left(\frac{u}{t}\right) - \frac{\sin(u)}{t}, u = 0..2\pi\,t\right]$$

To then obtain the curves corresponding to the values 3, 4, 5 and 6 of the parameter t, one only has to write

Ex.32

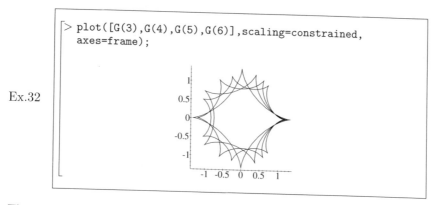

```
> plot([G(3),G(4),G(5),G(6)],scaling=constrained,
  axes=frame);
```

The function seq can be used to obtain a larger sample with values of t that are evenly spaced out.

Ex.33

```
> Lst_G:=[seq(G(2*t),t=1..5)]:     the symbol : suppresses the
                                   echo, which isn't very informative
> plot( Lst_G,scaling=constrained,axes=frame);
```

The function seq can also be used, though with a different syntax, even if the values of t aren't evenly spaced out.

Ex.34

```
> Lst_t:=[2,3,5,10,20]:
> Lst_G:=[seq(G(t),t=Lst_t)]:
```

Second Method

When a family of curves is given by p, q, a and b which are respectively the expressions of $f_t(u)$, $g_t(u)$, $u_0(t)$ and $u_1(t)$, one may use

- `plot([seq([p,q,u=a..b],t=t0..t1)])` which provides values of the parameter that are evenly spaced out in steps of 1.
- `t:=k*h: plot([seq([p,q,u=a..b],k=k0..k1)])` which provides values of the parameter that are evenly spaced out in steps of h.
- `plot([seq([p,q,u=a..b],t=L)])` where L is the list of values of the parameter.

Example of plot of a family of cycloïdal curves

Ex.35

```
> p:=cos(u)+t*cos(2*u); q:=sin(u)-t*sin(2*u);
```

$$p \quad : \quad = \cos(u) + t \, \cos(2\,u)$$
$$q \quad : \quad = \sin(u) - t \, \sin(2\,u)$$

```
> Lst_t:={0,0.3,0.5,0.7}:
  Lst_G:=[seq([p,q,u=0..2*Pi],t=Lst_t)]:
  plot(Lst_G,scaling=constrained);
```

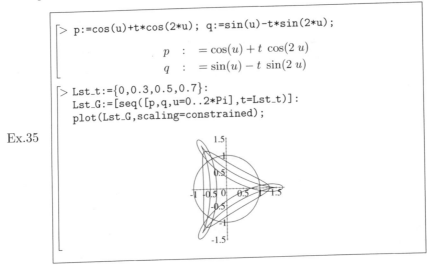

5.4 Curves in Polar Coordinates

5.4.1 Plot of a Curve in Polar Coordinates

Given two real numbers u0 and u1 such that u0<u1,

- if p is an expression in the single free variable u, then the evaluation of plot(p,u=u0..u1,coords=polar) plots the curve defined by the polar equation $r = p$.
- if p and q are two expressions in the single free variable u, then the evaluation of plot([p,q,u=u0..u1],coords=polar) plots the curve which is parametrically represented in polar coordinates by $r = p$ and $\theta = q$ for u ranging from u0 to u1.

Example of a curve defined by the polar equation $r = f(\theta)$

Ex.36

```
> plot([1+cos(theta),theta,theta=0..2*Pi],coords=polar,
  scaling=constrained);
```

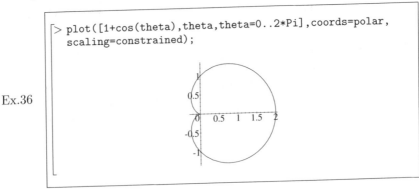

Example of a curve for which r and θ are defined in terms of u :

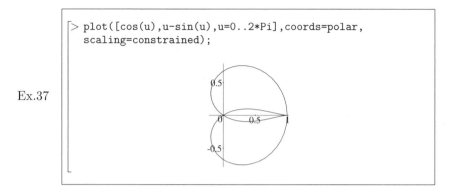

Ex.37

Warning! The option `coords=polar` doesn't force MAPLE to use an orthonormal frame. This is reason why `scaling=constrained` was used in the previous examples.

MAPLE adjusts the scale automatically just like it does for plots of parametrized curves. However, the use of `view=[a..b,c..d]` as a second parameter restricts the plot to the window $[a, b] \times [c, d]$. Such a scale specification is needed when the curve has infinite branches, otherwise one obtains an unreadable picture.

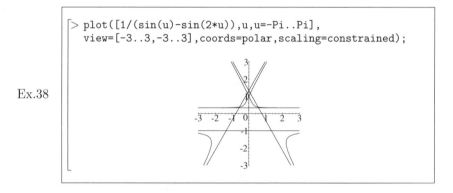

Ex.38

The asymptotes in the previous picture don't belong to the curve and again illustrate the phenomenon mentioned on page 81. For a parametrized curve, they cannot be suppressed with the option `discont=true`.

5.4.2 Plot of a Family of Curves in Polar Coordinates

Let a1, b1, a2, b2 be four real numbers such that a1<b1 and a2<b2 and p1, p2, q1, q2 be four expressions in u.

- plot([[p1,q1,u=a1..b1], [p2,q2,u=a2..b2]],coords=polar) can be used to plot the curves defined in polar coordinates by $r = p1$, $\theta = q1$ for $u \in [a1, b1]$ and by $r = p2$, $\theta = q2$ for $u \in [a2, b2]$ in a single picture.
- The scales of the two axes can be specified with plot([[p1,q1,u=a1..b1], [p2,q2,u=a2..b2]], view=[a..b,c..d], coords=polar).

Example of plot of a family of Pascal snails.

Ex.39

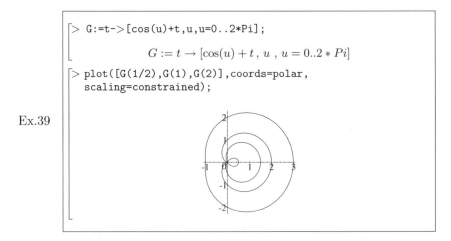

One may also write

Ex.40

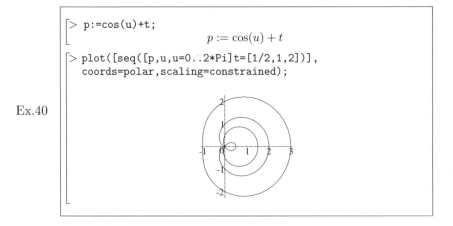

5.5 Curves Defined Implicitly

The function `implicitplot`, which plots curves that are defined implicitly, doesn't belong to the standard library and must therefore be loaded with

Ex.41
```
[> with (plots,implicitplot):
```

5.5.1 Plot of a Curve Defined Implicitly

Given four real numbers a, b, c, d such that a<b and c<d and an expression p in the two free variables x and y, the evaluation of `implicitplot(p,x=a..b, y=c..d)` plots the curve defined by the equation p=0 for $(x,y) \in [a,b] \times [c,d]$. The expression p may be replaced by the equation p=0 and, more generally, by the equation p=q.

Ex.42
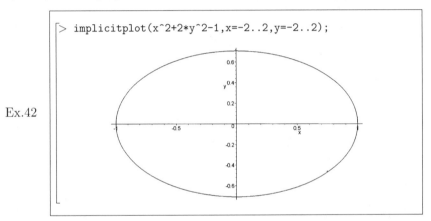
```
[> implicitplot(x^2+2*y^2-1,x=-2..2,y=-2..2);
```

The implicit equation of the curve to be plotted can also be given by a function. Given four real numbers a, b, c, d such that a<b and c<d and a function f in two variables, the evaluation of `implicitplot(f,a..b,c..d)` plots the curve defined by the equation $f(x,y) = 0$ for $(x,y) \in [a,b] \times [c,d]$. One could have written the previous example

Ex.43
```
[> f:=(x,y)->x^2+2*y^2-1;
```
$$f := (x,y) \rightarrow x^2 + 2y^2 - 1$$
```
[> implicitplot (f,-2..2,-2..2);
```

Warning! As has already been seen, one should take care not to mix syntaxes. In the previous example, `implicitplot(f, x=-2..2, y=-2..2)` wouldn't give any error message but would return an empty graph.

The ranges `x=a..b` and `y=c..d` passed to the function `implicitplot` are mainly used to determine the points of the curve. MAPLE starts by deter-

mining all the points of the curve that lie within the rectangle $[a, b] \times [c, d]$,
next it adapts the scale in order to obtain a "full page" plot. For the ellipse in the previous example, the window has been restricted to the square
$[-1, +1] \times [-1, +1]$.

5.5.2 Plot of a Family of Implicit Curves

Given four real numbers a, b, c, d such that a<b, c<d and expressions p1,
p2,..., pk in the free variables x and y, the evaluation of

$$\texttt{implicitplot([p1,p2,...,pk], x=a..b, y=c..d)}$$

simultaneously plots the curves defined by the equations p1=0, p2=0,..., pk=0
for $(x, y) \in [a, b] \times [c, d]$.

Warning ! To plot a family of curves, one must to apply the function `implicitplot`
to a set of expressions, not a list: it is a holdover from the syntax used by `plot`
until after *release 3* included.

Ex.44

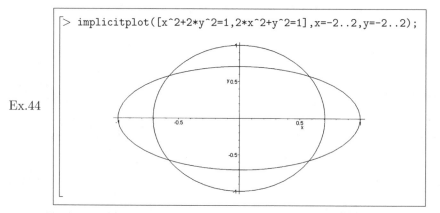

Example of a plot of a family of curves which are defined implicitly

Ex.45

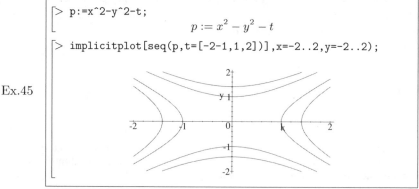

5.5.3 Precision of the Plot of Implicit Curves

As one can see in the next example, the function `implicitplot` without options doesn't always provide as precise a plot as those encountered in the previous section.

Ex.46

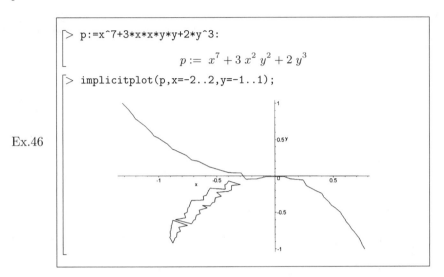

The plot can be made more precise by zooming in on a part of the curve and using the option `grid`, which refines the grid that analyzes sign changes of the function. The option `grid=[m,n]` (by default m=n=25) defines a grid that has m points horizontally and n points vertically.

Ex.47

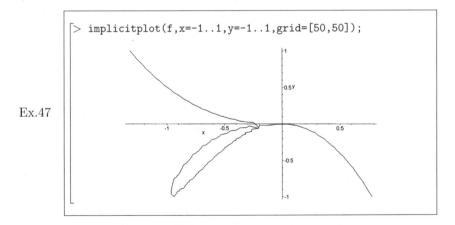

Warning ! Big values of m or of n may slow down and even cause a memory overflow. It is therefore better to use a parametric representation of a curve whenever possible.

5.6 Polygonal Plots

To plot a polygonal line, one calls the function `plot` with a list of points (between square brackets) as first argument. Each point is itself represented by a list of two coordinates.

Given the points $M_1(x1, y1)$, $M_2(x2, y2)$, ..., $M_k(xk, yk)$, the evaluation of `plot([[x1,y1],[x2,y2],...,[xk,yk]])` plots the polygonal line linking these points.

Ex.48

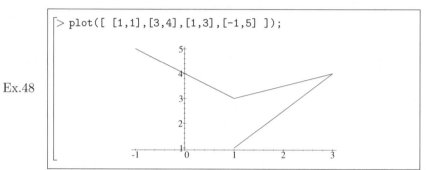

To plot a regular pentagon inscribed within a circle of unit radius, one can write

Ex.49

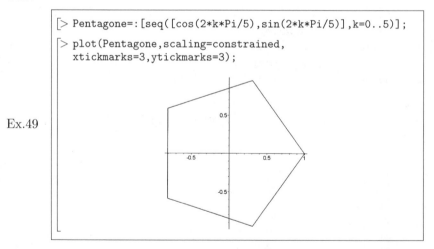

5.7 Mixing Drawings

One may wish to simultaneously plot in the same window graphs of different types: parametric curve, curve given by an implicit equation, etc....

The function `plot` alone can't deal with this kind of problem. The graphs have to be stored in variables that can then be displayed with the help of the function `display` from the `plots` library.

5.7.1 How Does `plot` Work

The function `plot` returns a MAPLE object, like any function of the `plots` library. It is an object like any other, just a bit more complex than the ones encountered up till now. Such an object is of type `PLOT`.

When MAPLE evaluates an expression that has the form `plot(....)`, it starts by computing the list of points sed in the plot, next

- if the expression `plot(....)` appears alone, MAPLE plots the corresponding drawing in a graphics window.
- if the expression `plot(....)` is assigned to a variable, MAPLE carries out this assignment without plotting the drawing. The echo of this assignment is displayed on the screen if the corresponding line ends with a semicolon.

As can be seen in the following example, an object of type `PLOT` contains the list of the points to be plotted and of the instructions for customizing the picture.

Ex.50

```
> Gr:=plot(sin(x),x=0..2*Pi,scaling=constrained);
```

$Gr := PLOT(CURVES([[0,0],[12522,12489],$
$\quad .../...$
$\quad .../...$
$\quad .../...$
$\quad [6.28318,.8204110\,10^{-9}]],COLOR(RGB,1.0,0.0),$
$\quad SCALING(CONSTRAINED),AXESLABELS(x,),$
$\quad VIEW(0.6.28318,DEFAULT))$

Note: Assigning a plot structure to a variable produces an echo containing a large number of coordinates. As before the echo may be suppressed with the use of the colon (:) instead of the semicolon (;) to terminate the line.

To display the drawing stored in the variable `Gr`, one can either evaluate `Gr` or type `print(Gr)`. On the other hand, `lprint(Gr)` displays the contents of the variable `Gr` without plotting the drawing.

5.7.2 The Function `display`

If `Gr_1,Gr_2,...,Gr_k` contain objects of type `PLOT`, the evaluation of `display([Gr_1,Gr_2,...,Gr_k])` plots the corresponding drawings simultaneously. Some options of the function `plot` may be used with `display`.

To simultaneously plot a pentagon and the circle round it, one can write

Ex.51

```
[> with(plots):
[> Pentagon :=
   [seq([cos(2*k*Pi/5),sin(2*k*Pi/5)],k=0..5)]:
   Gr_1:=plot([1,u,u=0..2*Pi],coords=polar):
   Gr_2:=plot(Pentagon):
   display([Gr_1,Gr_2],scaling=constrained);
```

This function **display** can also be used to add text to a plot, using information transformed into graphic objects via the function **textplot**, which also belongs to the **plots** library

Ex.52

```
[> Txt_1:=textplot([0,-1.2,'Circle around the pentagon']):
   display([Gr_1,Gr_2,Txt_1],scaling=constrained);
```

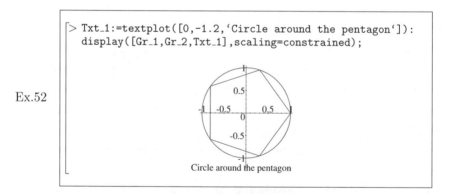

Circle around the pentagon

5.8 Animation

A family of curves can be represented dynamically using either the function **animate** or the function **display** with the option **insequence=true**.

The Function `animate`

The function **animate** doesn't belong to the standard library and must therefore be loaded with

Ex.53
```
> with(plots):
```

The evolution of the family of curves defined by the equation $y = t\,e^x + x^2$ when t runs over the interval $[-1, 2]$ can be displayed by writing

Ex.54

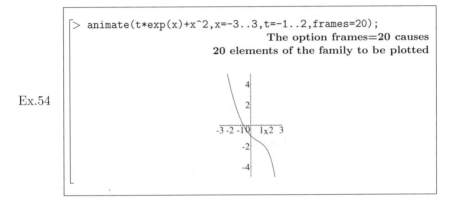

```
> animate(t*exp(x)+x^2,x=-3..3,t=-1..2,frames=20);
```
**The option frames=20 causes
20 elements of the family to be plotted**

MAPLE draws the first curve of the family. By clicking on this drawing, or by default if the option **Plot Display→Window** of the **Options** menu is selected, a context bar is displayed with an icon for starting the animation.

In the previous example, the first 8 curves are

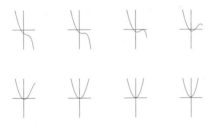

To display the family of Pascal snails, one may use **animate** with a parametrized curve and the option `coords=polar`.

Ex.55
```
> animate([cos(u+t),u,u=0..2*Pi],t=0..2,
   coords=polar,frames=30);
```

The Function display

animate cannot be used to carry out an animation with values of the parameter that aren't regularly distributed. In this case, one has to use display with the option insequence=true after constructing a list of drawings to be displayed.

To display the evolution of the family of curves defined by the equation $y = t e^x + x^2$ when t only takes the values -1, -0.5, -0.2, -0.1, 0 and 1, one can write

Ex.56

```
> Lst_Val:=[-1,-0.5,-0.2,-0.1,0,1]:
  Lst_Gr:=[seq(plot(t*exp(x)+x^2,x=-3..3),t=Lst_Val)];
> plots[display](Lst_Gr,insequence=true);
```

Note: Animations with curves that are defined implicitly can only be carried out using display with insequence=true.

Animation with a Fixed Background

For an animation against a fixed background, use the function display on a list of two elements, the first a graph and the second obtained with the function animate.

For example, a planet and its orbit can be dynamically represented by writing

Ex.57

```
> a:=5: b:=2: r:=0.2:
  Orbit:=plot([a*cos(t),b*sin(t),t=0..2*Pi]):
> Planet:=animate([a*cos(t)+r*cos(u),b*sin(t)+r*sin(u),
  u=0..2*Pi], t=0..2*Pi,frames=50):
> display([Orbit,Planet],scaling=constrained);
```

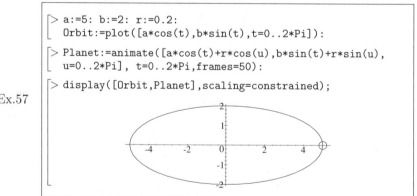

5.9 Using Logarithmic Scales

To represent functions while using logarithmic or semi-logarithmic scales, one must use the functions `loglogplot` or `logplot` from the `plots` library.

- `logplot(p,x=a..b)` provides a graphic representation of the variations of p as a function of `ln(x)`.
- `loglogplot(f,x=a..b)` provides a graphic representation of the variations of `ln(f)` as a function of `ln(x)`.

In electricity, for example, one frequently uses transfer functions that characterize the response of a circuit to a given input. Such a function is expressed as: $H = 1/(1 - x^2 + I * a * x)$ where a is a constant depending on the circuit. It is common practice to plot $\ln(|H|)$ as a function of $\ln(x)$; this can be done for the value $a = 1/2$ in the following way:

Ex.58

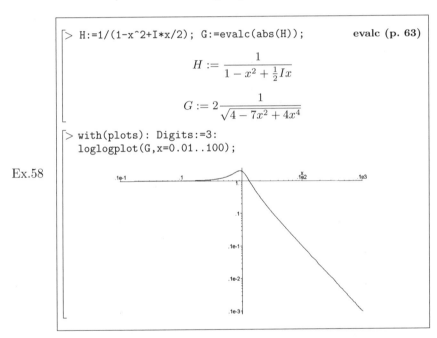

6. Equations and Inequations

6.1 Symbolic Solution: `solve`

6.1.1 Univariate Polynomial Equations

The function `solve` determines all the solutions of a polynomial equation in one unknown. If `p` is a polynomial expression in the free variable `x`, the evaluation of `solve(p,x)` returns all solutions in `x` of the equation p=0. One may simply write `solve(p)` if `p` contains no variable other than `x`.

If `p` contains at least one element of type `float`, all the numerical values occuring in the expression of `p`'s roots are computed as floating point numbers and expressed with `n` digits, where `n` is given by the system variable `Digits`.

Polynomials of Degree at Most 3

For a polynomial `p` of degree at most 3, `solve(p,x)` returns the family of roots written as a sequence (cf. p. 349). The index operator `[ ]` (p. 353) can be used access each root in this sequence.

Ex. 1

```
> Sol:=solve(x^3-3*x^2*sqrt(2)+4*sqrt(2)-4);
```
$$Sol := 1 + \sqrt{2} + \sqrt{3}\ ,\ 1 + \sqrt{2} - \sqrt{3}\ ,\ -2 + \sqrt{2}$$

```
> Sol[1];
```
$$1 + \sqrt{2} + \sqrt{3}$$

```
> evalf({Sol},4);                    evalf can be applied to a set
```
$$\{4.146\ ,\ .682\ ,\ -.586\}$$

```
> Digits:=4: p:=x^3-3*x^2*sqrt(2)+4*sqrt(2)-4.0: solve(p);
                The decimal point leads to a floating point computation
```
$$.6821\ ,\ 4.146\ ,\ -.5858$$

In some cases, the function `solve` returns a result that uses *labels,* which are abbreviations of frequently occurring subexpressions. Such labels are made up of the symbol % followed by a positive integer. The user isn't allowed to introduce labels on his own initiative but he may use them once MAPLE has introduced them (cf. p. 56).

Ex. 2

```
> solve(x^3+5*x^2+6*x-2);
```

$$\tfrac{1}{3}\%2 + \tfrac{7}{3}\%1 - \tfrac{5}{3}, -\tfrac{1}{6}\%2 - \tfrac{7}{6}\%1 - \tfrac{5}{3} + \tfrac{1}{2}I\sqrt{3}\left(\tfrac{1}{3}\%2 - \tfrac{7}{3}\%1\right),$$
$$-\tfrac{1}{6}\%2 - \tfrac{7}{6}\%1 - \tfrac{5}{3} - \tfrac{1}{2}I\sqrt{3}\left(\tfrac{1}{3}\%2 - \tfrac{7}{3}\%1\right)$$

$$\%1 := \frac{1}{\left(37 + 3\sqrt{114}\right)^{1/3}} \quad \%2 := \left(37 + 3\sqrt{114}\right)^{1/3}$$

```
> u:=%2;
```

$$u := \left(37 + 3\sqrt{114}\right)^{1/3}$$

Warning! When the equation contains several free variables, it is imperative to specify as a second argument of solve the variable with respect to which one wishes to solve, otherwise the answer returned isn't what's expected.

Ex. 3

```
> Sol:= solve(1/3*x^2+3*x+a+1);
```

$$Sol := \{x = x, a = -\tfrac{1}{3}x^2 - 3x - 1\}$$

```
> Sol:= solve(1/3*x^2+3*x+a+1,x);
```

$$Sol := -\tfrac{9}{2} + \tfrac{1}{2}\sqrt{69 - 12a}, -\tfrac{9}{2} - \tfrac{1}{2}\sqrt{69 - 12a}$$

Note: One may use the abbreviated form `solve(p)` when the expression p doesn't contain any variable other than x, but it is better to use the complete form `solve(p,x)` which, among other things, allows MAPLE to detect the error when x isn't a free variable, as shown in the following example.

Ex. 4

```
> x:=1;
```

$$x := 1$$

```
> s1:=solve(x^2+x+1,x);
```
Error, (in solve) a constant is invalid as a variable, 1

```
> s2:=solve(x^2+x+1);
```
no error message in this case, in fact solve solves the equation 3=0 !

$$s2 :=$$

Note: If `p` is a polynomial expression in `x` that depends on other parameters, all elements of type `float` are converted into fractions when `solve(p,x)` is evaluated.

Ex. 5

```
> restart; solve(33/100*x^2+3*x+a+1,x);
```
$$-\frac{50}{11} + \frac{10}{33}\sqrt{192 - 33\,a}\,,\ -\frac{50}{11} - \frac{10}{33}\sqrt{192 - 33\,a}$$

```
> solve(0.33*x^2+3*x+a+1,x);
```
$$-\frac{50}{11} + \frac{10}{33}\sqrt{192 - 33\,a}\,,\ -\frac{50}{11} - \frac{10}{33}\sqrt{192 - 33\,a}$$

Another example of solution of an equation of degree 2 with several simplifications of the returned results

Ex. 6

```
> s:=solve(x^2-2*x*sin(a)+1,x);
```
$$s := \sin(a) + \sqrt{\sin(a)^2 - 1},\, \sin(a) - \sqrt{\sin(a)^2 - 1}$$

```
> s1:=simplify({s},symbolic);
```
$$s1 := \{\sin(a) + I\cos(a),\, \sin(a) - I\cos(a)\}$$

```
> normal(convert(s1,exp));
```
$$\left\{ -I\,e^{(Ia)}\,,\ \frac{I}{e^{(Ia)}} \right\}$$

The use of the option `symbolic` is correct in the previous example since the function `simplify` is applied to the set of expressions that are obtained, a set that contains the values $+i\sqrt{\cos(a)^2}$ and $-i\sqrt{\cos(a)^2}$ in a symmetric way.

Note: The operator `{ }` can be used to transform the result of `solve`, which is a sequence, into a set. This transformation is essential, otherwise the function `simplify` receives the expression `sin(a)+I*cos(a)` followed by the options `sin(a)-I*cos(a)` and `symbolic`, which it isn't able to handle.

Ex. 7

```
> simplify(s,symbolic);
```
Error, (in simplify) invalid simplification command

Polynomials of Degree 5 or Greater

The roots of a polynomial of degree greater than or equal to 5 cannot, in general, be expressed with radicals. However, when it can be done, MAPLE returns the sequence of roots written with the help of radicals, as for polynomials of degree lower than 3.

Ex. 8

```
> solve(x^8+x^4+1);
```

$$\frac{1}{2} - \frac{1}{2}I\sqrt{3}, \; \frac{1}{2} + \frac{1}{2}I\sqrt{3}, \; -\frac{1}{2} + \frac{1}{2}I\sqrt{3},$$

$$-\frac{1}{2} - \frac{1}{2}I\sqrt{3}, \frac{1}{2}\sqrt{2 - 2I\sqrt{3}}, \; -\frac{1}{2}\sqrt{2 - 2I\sqrt{3}},$$

$$\frac{1}{2}\sqrt{2 + 2I\sqrt{3}}, \; -\frac{1}{2}\sqrt{2 + 2I\sqrt{3}}$$

In other specific cases, the function `solve` may return a result using trigonometric functions.

Ex. 9

```
> solve(x^7=1);                              the equation can be
                                             written in the form p=q
```

$$1, \; \cos\left(\frac{2}{7}\pi\right) + I \; \sin\left(\frac{2}{7}\pi\right), \; -\cos\left(\frac{3}{7}\pi\right) + I \; \sin\left(\frac{3}{7}\pi\right),$$

$$-\cos\left(\frac{1}{7}\pi\right) + I \; \sin\left(\frac{1}{7}\pi\right), \; -\cos\left(\frac{1}{7}\pi\right) - I \; \sin\left(\frac{1}{7}\pi\right),$$

$$-\cos\left(\frac{3}{7}\pi\right) - I \; \sin\left(\frac{3}{7}\pi\right), \; \cos\left(\frac{2}{7}\pi\right) - I \; \sin\left(\frac{2}{7}\pi\right)$$

If the function `solve` can use neither radicals nor trigonometric expressions, it returns a result in implicit form that uses the function `RootOf`: if p is a polynomial in the variable x, the expression `RootOf(p,x)` represents a generic root of the polynomial p. The function `RootOf` can be used with any polynomial p, but MAPLE introduces `RootOf`'s for irreducible polynomials only.

Ex.10

```
> solve(x^7-2*x+1);
```

$$1, RootOf(\_Z^6 + \_Z^5 + \_Z^4 + \_Z^3 + \_Z^2 + \_Z - 1)$$

```
> solve(x^8-x^6+2*x^4+1);
```

$$RootOf(\_Z^4 + \_Z^3 + 1),$$
$$RootOf(\_Z^4 - \_Z^3 + 1)$$

```
> solve(x^5+3*x-1);
```

$$RootOf(\_Z^5 + 3\_Z - 1)$$

Note: The use of the function `RootOf`, particularly in the last example, may appear to be mere subterfuge, but we shall see in Chapter 13 that it is fundamental to computation in algebraic extensions of $\mathbb{Q}$.

Polynomials of Degree 4

Although the roots of polynomials of degree 4 can always be expressed with radicals, their expression is in general too complicated to be useful. Thus, MAPLE, by default, does not generally express the solutions of an equation of degree 4 with radicals; it uses `RootOf` as for polynomials of higher degree.

For the next example, MAPLE uses the function `RootOf` by default, but it can be forced to use radicals by modifying the system variable `_EnvExplicit` (`false` by default).

Ex.11

```
> solve(x^4+x^3+1,x);
```
$$RootOf(\_Z^4 + \_Z^3 + 1)$$
```
> _EnvExplicit:=true: solve(x^4+x^3+1,x);
```
Result not written to avoid wasting a page

In some specific cases, like bisquare polynomials, MAPLE returns an expression using radicals regardless of the value of the variable `_EnvExplicit`.

Ex.12

```
> restart;                                    to give its default value
                                              back to _EnvExplicit
> Sol:=solve(x^4+x^2+1);
```
$$Sol := \frac{1}{2} + \frac{1}{2}I\sqrt{3},\ \frac{1}{2} - \frac{1}{2}I\sqrt{3},\ -\frac{1}{2} + \frac{1}{2}I\sqrt{3},\ -\frac{1}{2} - \frac{1}{2}I\sqrt{3}$$

6.1.2 Other Equations in One Variable

The function `solve` also returns a result when it is applied to non-polynomial expressions. However, the results are purely symbolic and use the inverses of classical functions.

Ex.13

```
> solve(2*sin(3*x)+1,x);
```
$$-\frac{\pi}{18}$$
In fact, MAPLE returns -1/3 arcsin(1/2)

In order to obtain all solutions of the previous equation, one may force the value of the global variable _EnvAllSolutions to be **true**.

Ex.14

```
> _EnvAllSolutions:=true;
```
$$\_EnvAllSolutions := true;$$
```
> solve(2*sin(3*x)+1,x);
```
$$-1/18\,\pi + 4/9\,\pi\,\_B1 \sim\ +2/3\,\pi\,\_Z1 \sim$$

As can be seen in the previous example, MAPLE introduces variables whose names begins with the character _

- the variables beginning with _Z have integer values.
- the variables beginning with _B have their values in $\{0,1\}$.

The results returned by **solve** may use less classical functions like Lambert's function, which is the inverse of $x \mapsto x \exp(x)$.

Ex.15

```
> restart; solve(ln(x)=x/4);
```
$$-4\,LambertW\left(-\frac{1}{4}\right), -4\,LambertW\left(-1,-\frac{1}{4}\right)$$

When the function **solve** isn't able to determine the result explicitly,

- it may return an implicit expression using the function **RootOf**. When the equation depends on a parameter, this answer may be used with the function **series** to obtain a truncated series expansion of the root.
- it may also return an empty sequence, although the equation may well have solutions. In such a case, the system variable _SolutionsMayBeLost is set to **true**.

Ex.16

```
> p:=tan(x)+x+a: s:=solve(p,x);
```
$$s := RootOf(tan(\_Z) + \_Z + a)$$
```
> series(s,a);
```
series to obtain a truncated
series expansion of the root
$$-\frac{1}{2}a + \frac{1}{48}a^3 - \frac{1}{1920}a^5 + O\left(a^6\right)$$
```
> s:=solve(cos(x)-x^2+1);
```
$$s :=$$
```
> _SolutionsMayBeLost;
```
$$true$$

It is in fact naive to use `solve` to try to solve any non algebraic equation. For most practical problems, it is more useful to obtain an approximation of solutions rather than their exact expressions, which can be done with the function `fsolve`.

6.1.3 Systems of Equations

The function `solve` can also to be used to solve systems of algebraic equations symbolically. It takes the set (hence between braces) of equations to solve as its first argument, and the set (hence between braces) of variables with respect to which one wishes to solve the system as its second argument.

The result returned by the function `solve` is a set or a sequence of sets, each made up of equations defining a parametrization of a family of solutions.

Ex.17

```
> restart; Sol:=solve({x+y=3,x*y=2},{y,x});
```
$$Sol := \{ x = 1, y = 2 \}, \{ x = 2, y = 1 \}$$

Because of the form of the result returned by `solve`, the function `subs` (p. 373) must be used to retrieve values of solutions.

Ex.18

```
> Sol[1];
```
The index operator [ ] gives the means to extract an element of Sol
$$\{ x = 1, y = 2 \}$$

```
> subs(Sol[1],x);
```
returns the value of x, while keeping x free
$$1$$

```
> subs(Sol[2],[x,y]);
```
returns the list made up of the values of x and y
$$[1, 2]$$

For systems with infinitely many solutions, MAPLE returns a parametric representation of a set of solutions expressed in terms of some unknowns.

Ex.19

```
> Eq:={x+2*y+3*z=0,2*x+3*y+4*z=1,3*x+4*y+5*z=2};
```
$$Eq := \{ x + 2y + 3z = 0, 2x + 3y + 4z = 1, 3x + 4y + 5z = 2 \}$$

```
> solve(Eq,{x,y,z});
```
$$\{ y = -2z - 1, \quad x = z + 2, \quad z = z \}$$

For inconsistent systems, MAPLE neither returns nor displays anything. In fact, it returns the value NULL but, since there is no assignment, no echo is displayed on the screen.

Ex.20

```
> Eq:={x+2*y+3*z=0,2*x+3*y+4*z=1,3*x+4*y+5*z=0};
```
$$Eq := \{x + 2\,y + 3\,z = 0,\ 2\,x + 3\,y + 4\,z = 1,\ 3\,x + 4\,y + 5\,z = 0\}$$
```
> s:=solve(Eq,{x,y,z});
```
$$s :=$$

The function solve is effective for symmetric systems for which, in general, it returns the whole set of solutions.

Ex.21

```
> S:={x+y+z=6,x^2+y^2+z^2=14,x*y*z=6};
```
$$S := \left\{ x\,y\,z = 6,\ x^2 + y^2 + z^2 = 14,\ x + y + z = 6 \right\}$$
```
> solve(S,{x,y,z});
```
$$\{x = 3, y = 1, z = 2\}, \{y = 1, z = 3, x = 2\},$$
$$\{z = 1, x = 3, y = 2\}, \{z = 3, y = 2, x = 1\},$$
$$\{y = 3, z = 1, x = 2\}, \{y = 3, z = 2, x = 1\}$$

solve is also able to solve linear systems that depend on parameters.

Ex.22

```
> eqn:={cos(a)*x+sin(a)*y=u,sin(a)*x-cos(a)*y=v};
```
$$eqn := \{\cos(a)\,x + \sin(a)\,y = u,\ \sin(a)\,x - \cos(a)\,y = v\}$$
```
> Sol:=solve(eqn,{x,y});
```
$$Sol := \{x = \cos(a)\,u + \sin(a)\,v,\ y = -\cos(a)\,v + \sin(a)\,u\}$$

Warning! One must keep in mind that the function solve solve works in the symbolic mode. In the next example:

- The determinant of the system is $a^2 - 1$, which is a non-zero expression. Thus the system has one and only one solution.

- In computations one can simplify by $a - 1$, which is non-zero, and leave $a + 1$ as the denominator, which is again a non-zero expression.

A user that wants to consider a as a real or complex parameter must deal with the cases $a = 1$ and $a = -1$ separately.

```
> Eq:={a*x+y=1,x+a*y=1};
```

$$Eq := \{\, a\,x + y = 1\,,\ x + a\,y = 1\,\}$$

```
> solve(Eq,{x,y});
```

$$\left\{\, y = \frac{1}{a+1}\,,\quad x = \frac{1}{a+1}\,\right\}$$

Ex.23

```
> solve(subs(a=1,Eq),{x,y});
```

$$\{\, x = -y + 1\,,\ y = y\,\}$$

```
> Sol:=solve(subs(a=-1,Eq),{x,y});
```

$$Sol\ :=$$

**the system is impossible, solve returns
an empty sequence without echo**

6.1.4 Inequations

The function `solve` can also solve some simple inequalities in one variable.
The result is most often expressed with the help of the function `RealRange`,
and can thus be used in a call to `assume`.

Ex.24

```
> solve(x^2-1<=0, x);
```

$$RealRange(-1, 1)$$

```
> assume(x,");about(x);
```

Originally x, renamed x˜: is assumed to be: RealRange(-1,1)

Ex.25

```
> S:=solve(x^3-3*x^2+x+2>0);
```

$$S\ :\ = RealRange\left(Open\left(\frac{1}{2} - \frac{1}{2}\sqrt{5}\right), Open\left(\frac{1}{2} + \frac{1}{2}\sqrt{5}\right)\right),$$
$$RealRange\left(Open(2), \infty\right)$$

```
> assume(x,S[1]);about(x);
```

Originally x, renamed x˜: is assumed to be:
RealRange(Open(1/2-1/2*5^(1/2)),Open(1/2+1/2*5^(1/2)))

The function `solve` cannot deal with systems of inequalities. On the other
hand, systems of inequalities in two variables can be solved graphically with
the help of the function `inequal` of the `plots` library.

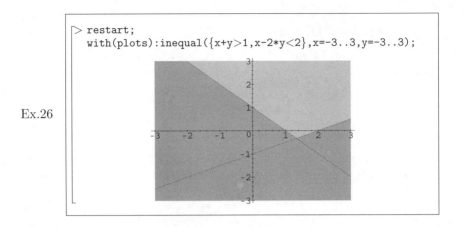

Ex.26

6.2 Approximate Solution of Equations: fsolve

The function fsolve can be used to solve equations numerically, as well as systems of equations involving as many unknowns as equations. Take note, however, that fsolve returns at most one real root of an equation or system of equations, except for polynomials, for which fsolve returns all real roots.

6.2.1 Algebraic Equations in One Variable

If p is a polynomial expression in x whose coefficients are all real numbers (of type realcons cf. p. 59), the evaluation of fsolve(p,x) or of fsolve(p) returns a sequence containing all the real roots of p.

Ex.27

```
> restart; p:=x^4-3*x^2+x+1;        restart, to reinitialize Digits
```
$$p := x^4 - 3x^2 + x + 1$$
```
> fsolve(p);
```
$$-1.801937736 , \ -.4450418679 , \ 1. , \ 1.246979604$$

One may specify a range for solutions as an option of fsolve. If a and b are two real numbers, the evaluation of fsolve(p,x,x=a..b) or of fsolve(p,x=a..b) returns the sequence of roots of p contained within the interval $[a, b]$.

Ex.28

```
> fsolve(p,x=-1..0);
```
$$-.4450418679$$

To obtain all the roots, including non real roots, of a polynomial p, one must use the option complex and request the evaluation of fsolve(p,x,complex).

Ex.29

```
> p:=x^4-3*x^2+x+sqrt(2);
```
$$p := x^4 - 3x^2 + x + \sqrt{2}$$
```
> Digits:=4;fsolve(p);
```
$$Digits := 4$$
$$-1.764 \, , \, -.5632$$
```
> fsolve(p,x,complex);          The x is mandatory in this case
```
$$-1.764 \, , \, -.5632 \, , \, 1.164 - .2627 \, I \, , \, 1.164 + .2627 \, I$$

The option `maxsols` can be used to obtain a given number of roots. The evaluation of `fsolve(p,x,maxsols=n)` returns at most n real solutions of the equation p=0. This option can be combined with the option `complex`. For example, `fsolve(p,x,complex,maxsols=n)` returns at most n complex solutions of the equation p=0.

Ex.30

```
> restart; p:=x^4-3*x^2+x+1;
```
$$p := x^4 - 3x^2 + x + 1$$
```
> fsolve(p,x,maxsols=3);
```
$$-1.801937736 \, , \, -.4450418679 \, , \, 1.$$

6.2.2 Other Equations in One Variable

If p is a non polynomial expression depending on the free variable x and on no other free variable, `fsolve(p,x)` or `fsolve(p)` returns at most one root of p=0.

Ex.31

```
> p:= x^3-x+2-exp(x): fsolve(p);
```
$$1.806570269$$

Only one solution was returned in the previous example, although a graphic study clearly shows that there are several.

Ex.32

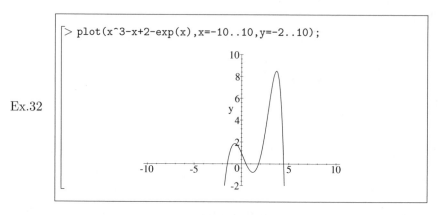

```
> plot(x^3-x+2-exp(x),x=-10..10,y=-2..10);
```

As for algebraic equations, a range for the solution can be specified as an option. If a and b are two real numbers, `fsolve(p,x,x=a..b)` or `fsolve(p,x=a..b)` returns at most one root of p in the interval [a, b]. To obtain the negative solution from the previous example, one can write

Ex.33

```
> fsolve(p,x=-2..0);
```
$$-1.481974815$$

When the function `fsolve` doesn't find a solution to a non polynomial equation, it returns an unevaluated form and not an empty sequence as for algebraic equations.

Ex.34

```
> p:=(x^2+1)*exp(x);
```
$$(x^2 + 1)\exp(x)$$
```
> fsolve(p,x);
```
$$fsolve\left((x^2 + 1)\exp(x),\ x\right)$$

6.2.3 Systems of Equations

The function `fsolve` solves systems of equations numerically. It is given a set (hence between braces) of equations to solve as a first argument, and a set (hence between braces) of variables with respect to which one wishes to solve the system as a second argument. The function `fsolve` returns a set of equations defining one solution of the given system.

Warning! The number of equations must be equal to the number of unknowns.

Ex.35

```
[> fsolve({y^2-x,y-x^2+4*x-2},{x,y});
```
$$\{\, x = 4.\,,\ y = 2.\,\}$$

A graphic study that can be carried out with the help of the function `plot` to show that there exist other solutions:

Ex.36

```
[> plot({sqrt(x),-sqrt(x),x^2-4*x+2},x=-1..5,y=-2.5..2.5);
```

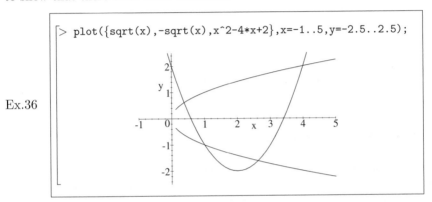

As for equations, one may specify a domain for the solution as a third parameter to `fsolve`, written

- `{x=a..b}` to solve within the strip $a \leq x \leq b$
- `{y=c..d}` to solve within the strip $c \leq y \leq d$
- `{x=a..b,y=c..d}` to solve within the rectangle $a \leq x \leq b, c \leq y \leq d$

To find the solution of the previous system whose ordinate lies between 0 and 1, one can write

Ex.37

```
[> fsolve({y^2-x, y-x^2+4*x-2},{x,y},{y=0..1});
```
$$\{\, x = .3819660113\,,\ y = .6180339888\,\}$$

An attempt to determine the solution whose ordinate is strictly less than -1 fails. However, this proves nothing, as is shown the next example, in which both a range for `x` and a range for `y` are specified.

Ex.38

```
[> fsolve({y^2-x,y-x^2+4*x-2},{x,y},{y=-2..-1.4});
[> fsolve({y^2-x,y-x^2+4*x-2},{x,y},{y=-2..-1.4,x=2..3});
```
$$\{\, x = 2.618033989\,,\ y = -1.6180339989\,\}$$

Finally we consider a few typical errors encountered using the function `fsolve`.

If there are fewer equations than unknowns:

Ex.39

> ```
> >restart;fsolve({a*x+1=0,a*y+1=0},{x,y,a});
> ```
> *Error, (in fsolve/gensys)case not implemented, # of equations<> # of variables*

If not all unknowns of the equation are used:

Ex.40

> ```
> > fsolve({a*x+1=0,a*y+1=0},{x,y});
> ```
> *Error, (in fsolve) should use exactly all the indeterminates*

6.3 Solution of Recurrences: `rsolve`

The function `rsolve` can be used to study certain series expansions defined by recurrence relations: linear recurrences, homographic recurrences and a few other particular cases.

6.3.1 Linear Recurrences

Given two free variables, `u` and `n`, and four expressions, `a`, `b`, `u0` and `u1`, not depending on `n`,

- `rsolve(u(n)-a*u(n-1)-b*u(n-2),u)` returns, in terms of $u(0), u(1)$ and n, a formula for the nth term in the series expansion defined by the recurrence relation $u_n - a\,u_{n-1} - b\,u_{n-2} = 0$.
- `rsolve({u(n)-a*u(n-1)-b*u(n-2),u(0)=u0,u(1)=u1},u)` returns, in terms of $u0, u1$ and n, a formula for the nth term in the series expansion defined by the recurrence relation $u_n - a\,u_{n-1} - b\,u_{n-2} = 0$ and the initial conditions $u_0 = u0$ and $u_1 = u1$.

The function `rsolve` solves linear recurrences of any order. The syntax is the same as that used above for order 2.

For a relation of order p, the "initial" conditions may be given with the help of any p consecutive terms; these conditions can be abbreviated as follows

- If `c` is independent of `n`, the initial condition `u(a..b)=c` is equivalent to `u(a)=c, u(a+1)=c,...u(b)=c`.
- If `f(m)` is an expression of `m` which is independent of `n`, the initial condition `u(m=a..b)=f(m)` is equivalent to `u(a)=f(a),u(a+1)=f(a+1),...` and `u(b)=f(b)`.

Ex.41

```
> rsolve(u(n)=-3*u(n-1)-2*u(n-2),u);
```

$$\left(2u\left(0\right)+u\left(1\right)\right)\left(-1\right)^{n}+\left(-u\left(0\right)-u\left(1\right)\right)\left(-2\right)^{n}$$

```
>
rsolve({u(n)=6*u(n-1)-11*u(n-2)+6*u(n-3),u(m=0..2)=m},u);
```

$$-\frac{3}{2}-\frac{1}{2}\,3^{n}+2\,2^{n}$$

In the previous syntaxes, the u that occurs as the second argument to `rsolve` can be replaced with u(k). The function `rsolve` then returns a formula for the kth term.

Example of the computation and simplification of a term in the Fibonacci sequence.

Ex.42

```
> u_n:=rsolve({u(n)=u(n-1)+u(n-2),u(0..1)=1},u);
```

$$u\_n:=\frac{2}{5}\frac{\sqrt{5}\left(2\frac{1}{-1+\sqrt{5}}\right)^{n}}{-1+\sqrt{5}}+\frac{2}{5}\frac{\sqrt{5}\left(-2\frac{1}{1+\sqrt{5}}\right)^{n}}{1+\sqrt{5}}$$

```
> x:=subs(n=10,u_n);              to obtain the expression of u(10)
```

$$x:=\frac{2048}{5}\frac{\sqrt{5}}{(-1+\sqrt{5})^{11}}+\frac{2048}{5}\frac{\sqrt{5}}{(1+\sqrt{5})^{11}}$$

```
> rationalize(x);                              cf. p. 33
```

$$89$$

The function `rsolve` can be used with the option 'genfunc' (x): it then returns the generating function of the series expansion, i.e. a function whose coefficients of the series expansion at 0 are the values of the terms of the series expansion.

Ex.43

```
> x:='x':
  rsolve({F(n)=F(n-1)+F(n-2),F(1..2)=1},F,'genfunc'(x));
```

$$-\frac{x}{-1+x+x^{2}}$$

```
> series(",x);
```

$$x+x^{2}+2\,x^{3}+3\,x^{4}+5\,x^{5}+O(x^{6})$$

The function `rsolve` can also deal with a set of series expansions defined by coupled recurrence relations. The syntax can be easily deduced from the following example.

Ex.44

```
> rsolve({u(n)=3*u(n-1)+2*v(n-1),v(n)=u(n-1)+2*v(n-1)},
  {u,v});
```

$$\left\{ u(n) = \tfrac{2}{3} \, 4^n \, u(0) + \tfrac{2}{3} \, 4^n \, v(0) + \tfrac{1}{3} \, u(0) - \tfrac{2}{3} \, v(0) \right.$$

$$\left. v(n) = \tfrac{1}{3} \, 4^n \, u(0) + \tfrac{1}{3} \, 4^n \, v(0) - \tfrac{1}{3} \, u(0) + \tfrac{2}{3} \, v(0) \right\}$$

The function `rsolve` isn't restricted to linear recurrence relations; it can also deal with affine recurrence relations, as the following example shows:

Ex.45

```
> rsolve({f(n)=-3*f(n-1)-2*f(n-2)+n,f(1..2)=1},f);
```

$$-\frac{7}{4} \, (-1)^n + \frac{5}{9} \, (-2)^n + \frac{1}{6} \, n + \frac{7}{36}$$

6.3.2 Homographic Recurrences

The function `rsolve` also solves homographic recurrences , provided they are written without denominator.

Given two free variables u and n, an integer r and five expressions a, b, c, d, e that don't depend on n,

- `rsolve( u(n+1)*(c*u(n)+d)=a*u(n)+b,u)` returns, in terms of $u(0)$ and n, the expression of the general term u_n in the series expansion defined by the relation $u_{n+1} = \dfrac{a \, u_n + b}{c \, u_n + d}$.
- `rsolve({u(n+1)*(c*u(n)+d)=a*u(n)+b,u(r)=e},u)` returns, in terms of n, the expression of the general term u_n in the series expansion defined by the relation $u_{n+1} = \dfrac{a \, u_n + b}{c \, u_n + d}$ and the initial condition $u_r = e$.

Ex.46

```
> restart; u_n:=rsolve(u(n)*(5*u(n-1)+4)=1,u);
```

$$u\_n := -\frac{5 \, (-1)^n \, u(0) - (-1)^n + 5^n \, u(0) + 5^n}{5 \, (-1)^n \, u(0) - (-1)^n - 5 \, 5^n \, u(0) - 5 \, 5^n}$$

As usual, MAPLE returns a symbolic expression that doesn't take particular cases into account: the expression of `u_n` above is undefined for a particular value of $u(0)$, which can be determined with the help of the function `solve`. The function `seq` can be used to obtain the first "back" values of $u(0)$.

Ex.47

```
> solve(denom(u_n),u(0));
```

$$-\frac{-(-1)^n - 5\,5^n}{5\,(-1)^n - 5\,5^n}$$

```
> seq(",n=1..5);
```
to see the first 5 values

$$-\frac{4}{5},\ -\frac{21}{20},\ -\frac{104}{105},\ -\frac{521}{520},\ -\frac{2604}{2605}$$

6.3.3 Other Recurrence Relations

The function rsolve can also solve a few other recurrence relations, like for example:

Ex.48

```
> restart;rsolve({y(n)=n*y(n-1),y(0)=1},y);
```

$$\Gamma(n+1)$$

or relations often encountered in analyzing the complexity of algorithms

Ex.49

```
> rsolve(f(n)=3*f(n/2)+5*n,f(n));
```

$$f(1)\,n^{\left(\frac{\ln(3)}{\ln(2)}\right)} + n^{\left(\frac{\ln(3)}{\ln(2)}\right)}\left(-15\left(\frac{2}{3}\right)^{\left(\frac{\ln(n)}{\ln(2)}+1\right)} + 10\right)$$

7. Limits and Derivatives

7.1 Limits

7.1.1 Limit of Expressions

The function `limit` computes limits of expressions in a single real variable. If `p` is an expression depending on the free variable `x`

- `limit(p,x=a)`   returns the limit of `p` as `x` tends towards `a`
- `limit(p,x=a,right)`   returns the limit of `p` as `x` tends towards a^+
- `limit(p,x=a,left)`   returns the limit of `p` as `x` tends towards a^-
- `limit(p,x=infinity)`   returns the limit of `p` as `x` tends towards $+\infty$
- `limit(p,x=-infinity)`   returns the limit of `p` as `x` tends towards $-\infty$
- `limit(p,x=infinity,real)` returns the limit of `p` as $|x|$ tends towards $+\infty$

Examples of limits at `a`:

Ex. 1

```
> p:=(x^2-1)*ln((1+x)/(1-x));
```
$$p := \left(x^2 - 1\right) \ln \left(\frac{1+x}{1-x}\right)$$

```
> limit(p,x=1);
```
$$0$$

```
> limit(p/x,x=0);
```
$$-2$$

```
> limit(ln(tan(x))/(tan(x)-1),x=Pi/4);
```
$$1$$

Examples of limits from the right and from the left at a:

Ex. 2

```
> limit(exp(1/x),x=0,right);
```
$$\infty$$
```
> limit(exp(1/x),x=0,left);
```
$$0$$

Examples of limits at infinity:

Ex. 3

```
> limit(exp(x)/x,x=infinity);
  limit(exp(x)/x,x=-infinity);
```
$$\infty$$
$$0$$
```
> p:=(x^2+1)/(x^2-1);
```
$$p := \frac{x^2 + 1}{x^2 - 1}$$
```
> limit(p,x=infinity,real);
```
$$1$$

Warning! In evaluating `limit(p,x=a)`, MAPLE begins by evaluating the two arguments, `p` and `x=a` and it returns an error message, which isn't very easy to understand, if the variable `x` isn't free.

Ex. 4

```
> x:=y+1: limit(p,x=1);
  Error, (in limit) invalid arguments
```

When MAPLE realizes that the limit doesn't exist, `limit` returns `undefined`.

Ex. 5

```
> x:='x': limit(exp(1/x),x=0);
```
$$undefined$$

In some cases, `limit` returns an interval. It means that the expression takes on values in this interval in the neighbourhood of the limit point. However, this does not mean that every value belonging to this interval is reached.

$$\begin{array}{l}
\text{> limit(sin(1/x),x=0);}\\
\qquad\qquad\qquad -1..1\\
\text{> limit(sin(x)+cos(x),x=infinity);}\\
\qquad\qquad\qquad\qquad\qquad |\sin x + \cos x| \le \sqrt{2}\\
\qquad\qquad\qquad -2..2
\end{array}$$

Ex. 6

MAPLE returns an unevaluated form when it doesn't succeed in determining a limit; it is just printed out in a nice format.

Ex. 7

$$\begin{array}{l}
\text{> limit(abs(sin(x)),x=infinity);}\\
\qquad\qquad\qquad \lim_{x \to \infty} \; |\sin(x)|
\end{array}$$

7.1.2 Limit of Expressions Depending on Parameters

One can compute limits of expressions depending on parameters, i.e. of free variables other than that for which one computes the limit.

Ex. 8

$$\begin{array}{l}
\text{> p:=(1+t/n)\textasciicircum n;}\\
\qquad\qquad p := \left(1 + \dfrac{t}{n}\right)^n\\
\text{> limit(p,n=infinity);}\\
\qquad\qquad e^t
\end{array}$$

The computation, however, is symbolic: MAPLE doesn't deal with special cases, and it is up to the user to handle them separately.

Ex. 9

$$\begin{array}{l}
\text{> a:='a': p:=(x*ln(x)\textasciicircum2-a*ln(a)\textasciicircum2)/((x-a)*(x-1));}\\
\qquad\qquad p := \dfrac{x \ln(x)^2 - a \ln(a)^2}{(x-a)\,(x-1)}\\
\text{> limit(p, x=a);}\\
\qquad\qquad \dfrac{2 \ln(a) + \ln(a)^2}{a - 1}\\
\text{> limit(subs(a=1,p),x=1);} \qquad\qquad \textbf{To compute}\\
\qquad\qquad\qquad\qquad\qquad\qquad\qquad \textbf{the limit for a=1}\\
\qquad\qquad 1
\end{array}$$

In the following example, MAPLE returns an unevaluated form because the limit is equal to 0, 1 or $+\infty$, depending on whether the parameter t is negative, zero or strictly positive.

Ex.10

```
> Lim:=limit(exp(t*x),x=+infinity);
```
$$Lim := \lim_{x \to \infty} e^{(t\,x)}$$

The limit can then be computed for some specific values of the parameter t by using the function subs.

Ex.11

```
> subs(t=1,Lim);
```
$$\lim_{x \to \infty} e^x$$

```
> eval(subs(t=1,Lim));
```
eval is essential because subs doesn't provoke any evaluation

$$\infty$$

```
> eval(subs(t=-1,Lim));
```
$$0$$

Hypotheses concerning the parameter t can also be introduced with the help of the function assume (p. 45), which allows MAPLE to determine the limit. To study the cases t>0 and t<0, one has only to write:

Ex.12

```
> assume(t>0);
```
assume doesn't cause any echo

```
> Lim;
```
$$\infty$$

```
> assume(t<0);
```
Another use of assume cancels any previous hypothesis about t

```
> Lim;
```
$$0$$

In the following example, MAPLE returns ∞ as the limit since, symbolically, abs(t-1) is different from zero and positive.

Ex.13

```
> restart; limit(exp(abs(t-1)*x),x=infinity);
```
$$\infty$$

On the other hand, since release 3 onward, the function limit doesn't assume that parameters are real numbers. The following limit in which the expression t^2 is not necessarily positive cannot be computed.

Ex.14

```
> limit(exp(t^2*x),x=infinity);
```
$$\lim_{x \to \infty} e^{(t^2 x)}$$

One may use **assume** again to indicate to MAPLE that the parameter **t** is in the real domain.

Ex.15

```
> assume(t,real); limit(exp(t^2*x),x=infinity);
```
$$\infty$$

7.1.3 Limit of Functions

In order to compute the limit of a function **f** at a point, one must study the limit of its associated expression **f(x)** :

Ex.16

```
> f:=x->((ln(x+1)/ln(x))^x-1)*ln(x);
```
$$f := x \to \left(\left(\frac{\ln(x+1)}{\ln(x)} \right)^x - 1 \right) \ln(x)$$

```
> limit(f(x),x=infinity);
```
$$1$$

Unlike to the function **plot** (p. 71), **limit** cannot be used with a function if one leaves out the variable in the second argument.

Ex.17

```
> limit(f,0);
   Error, (in limit) invalid arguments
```

The function **limit** also computes limits of expressions in several variables. If **p** is an expression depending on the free variables **x** and **y**, the evaluation of **limit(p,{x=a,y=b})** returns the limit of **p** as the point **(x,y)** tends towards **(a,b)**.

Ex.18

```
> limit((x*x-y*y)/(x-y),{x=0,y=0});
```
$$0$$

As can be seen in the next example, the function `limit` often returns an unevaluated expression.

Ex.19

```
> limit(x*y/sqrt(x^2+y^2),{x=0,y=0});
```

$$limit\left(\frac{xy}{\sqrt{x^2+y^2}}, \{x=0, y=0\}\right)$$

7.2 Derivatives

7.2.1 Derivatives of Expressions in a Single Variable

The function `diff` performs differentiation.

First Derivative of an Expression

If `p` is an expression depending on the free variable `x`, `diff(p,x)` returns the derivative of `p` with respect to `x`.

Ex.20

```
> p:=(x^2+1)*arctan(x);
```

$$p := (x^2 + 1)\arctan x$$

```
> diff(p,x);
```

$$2x\arctan x + 1$$

Warning! When evaluating `diff(p,x)`, MAPLE begins by evaluating the two arguments `p` and `x`, and MAPLE returns an error message which isn't very easy to understand if the variable `x` isn't free.

Ex.21

```
> x:=y+1: diff(arctan(x),x);
   Error, wrong number (or type) of parameters in function diff
```

If the expression to be derived includes terms of type `function` (p. 341) of the form `f(x)`, where `f` is free, the function `diff` uses classical formulas to differentiate and gives its result written with the help of expressions like $\frac{\partial f}{\partial x}$.

Ex.22

```
> restart; diff(arctan(f(x)),x);
```

$$\frac{\frac{\partial}{\partial x}f(x)}{1 + f(x)^2}$$

Higher Order Derivatives of an Expression

Given a natural number n and an expression p depending on the free variable x, diff(p,x,...,x) or diff(p,x$n) returns the nth derivative of p with respect to x.

Ex.23

```
> diff(arctan(x),x,x,x);
```

$$-8\frac{x^2}{(1+x^2)^3} - 2\frac{1}{(1+x^2)^2}$$

```
> diff(arctan(x),x$4);
```

$$-48\frac{x^3}{(1+x^2)^4} + 24\frac{x}{(1+x^2)^3}$$

```
> normal(");
```
                                                    to normalize the expression

$$-24\frac{x(x^2-1)}{(1+x^2)^4}$$

When n doesn't contain a **numeric** value, diff(p,x$n) returns unevaluated.

Ex.24

```
> n:='n': diff(arctan(x),x$n);
```

$$\text{diff}(\arctan(x),\, x \, \$ \, n)$$

7.2.2 Partial Derivatives of Expressions in Several Variables

Given an expression expr and free variables x1,x2,...,xn (not necessarily distinct) diff(p,x1,x2,...,xn) returns $\dfrac{\partial^n p}{\partial x_1 \partial x_2 \ldots \partial x_n}$.

Ex.25

```
> p := ln(sqrt(x^2+y^2)):
> r:=diff(p,x,x); s:=diff(p,x,y); t:=diff(p,y,y);
```

$$r := -2\frac{x^2}{(x^2+y^2)^2} + \frac{1}{x^2+y^2}$$

$$s := -2\frac{x\,y}{(x^2+y^2)^2}$$

$$t := -2\frac{y^2}{(x^2+y^2)^2} + \frac{1}{x^2+y^2}$$

Ex.26

```
> normal(s*s-r*t);
```

$$\frac{1}{(x^2+y^2)^2}$$

7.2.3 Derivatives of Functions in One Variable

First Derivative of a Function

Whereas `diff` differentiates expressions and returns expressions, the function D differentiates a function, whether it is a MAPLE function or a user-defined function, and returns a function.

Warning! Make sure to use an upper case D, as MAPLE is case-sensitive.

If `f` is a function of a single variable, then `D(f)` returns the function which is the derivative of `f`.

Ex.27

```
> f:=x->arctan(x)/(1+x^2); f_1:=D(f);
```

$$f := x \to \frac{\arctan(x)}{1+x^2}$$

$$f\_1 := x \to \frac{1}{(1+x^2)^2} - 2\frac{\arctan(x)\,x}{(1+x^2)^2}$$

Normalization of the function `f_1` from the previous example must be done using the expression `f_1(x)`, because `normal` can only be applied to expressions. The function `unapply` (p. 40) can be used to recover the derivative, if necessary.

Ex.28

```
> normal(f_1);
```

$$f\_1$$

```
> normal(f_1(x));
```

$$\frac{1 - 2\arctan(x)\,x}{(1+x^2)^2}$$

```
> f_1:=unapply(",x);  transforms the expression into a function
```

$$f\_1 := x \to \frac{1 - 2\arctan(x)\,x}{(1+x^2)^2}$$

If `diff` is used to differentiate an expression with respect to a variable on which the expression does not depend, MAPLE returns zero of course; this is in particular the case if one tries to differentiate a free variable with respect to another variable. On the other hand, D can be applied to a free variable; it then returns a partially evaluated form.

```
[> restart; diff(f,x); D(f);
```

$$0$$

$$D(f)$$

```
[> D(g@f);
```
Computation of the derivative of a composition of functions in one variable

$$D(g)@f \; D(f)$$

Ex.29

Higher Order Derivatives of a Function

Given an integer n and a function in one variable f, (D@@n)(f) returns a function which is the n-th derivative of f.

Warning! The @@ is the exponentiation operator for functions and D@@n represents the nth power of D. The parentheses around D@@n are necessary for MAPLE to interpret the formula correctly.

```
[> f:=x->(1+x^2)^(-1):
[> f_3:=(D@@3)(f);
```

$$f\_3 := x \rightarrow -48\frac{x^3}{(1+x^2)^4} + 24\frac{x}{(1+x^2)^3}$$

Ex.30

7.2.4 Partial Derivatives of Functions in Several Variables

If f is a function in p variables and i1,i2,...,ir is a family of r integral values in the interval [1,p], D[i1,i2,...,ir](f) returns the function $(x_1, x_2, \ldots, x_p) \rightarrow \dfrac{\partial^r f}{\partial x_{i1} \partial x_{i2} \ldots \partial x_{ir}}(x_1, x_2, \ldots, x_p)$. As for partial derivatives of expressions, MAPLE may permute differentials with respect to different variables.

Example displaying the computation and simplification of a partial derivative of a function of 2 variables.

```
[> f:=(x,y)->arctan(y/x);
```

$$f := (x,y) \rightarrow \arctan\left(\frac{y}{x}\right)$$

```
[> f_1:=D[2](f);
```
derivative with respect to the second variable

$$f\_1 := (x,y) \rightarrow \frac{1}{x\left(1 + \dfrac{y^2}{x^2}\right)}$$

Ex.31

Ex.32

```
> normal("(x,y));          one needs an expression to apply normal
```

$$\frac{x}{x^2 + y^2}$$

```
> f_1:=unapply(",x,y);          unapply to recover the function
```

$$f\_1 := (x, y) \to \frac{x}{x^2 + y^2}$$

Example displaying the computation and simplification of a mixed partial derivative:

Ex.33

```
> f_2:=D[1,2](f);                                computation of \frac{\partial^2 f}{\partial x \partial y}
```

$$f\_2 := (x, y) \to -\frac{1}{x^2\left(1 + \dfrac{y^2}{x^2}\right)} + 2\frac{y^2}{x^4\left(1 + \dfrac{y^2}{x^2}\right)^2}$$

```
> normal("(x,y));                    simplification of \frac{\partial^2 f}{\partial x \partial y}(x, y)
```

$$-\frac{x^2 - y^2}{(x^2 + y^2)^2}$$

```
> f_3:=unapply(normal(D[1,1,2](f)(x,y)),x,y);
                        computation and simplification of \frac{\partial^3 f}{\partial x^2 \partial y}
```

$$f\_3 := (x, y) \to 2\frac{x(x^2 - 3y^2)}{(x^2 + y^2)^3}$$

Used to differentiate an expression of type function (p. 341) like f(x), f(x,y) or, more generally, f(u,v) in which f is a free variable and u, v are expressions depending on x and y, diff returns a form using partial derivatives of f. In performing such a computation, diff assumes the function f to be "fair", i.e. it assumes that partial derivatives with respect to all variables occurring in the computation may be permutated.

Ex.34

```
> restart; diff(f(x,y),x,y,x);
```

$$\frac{\partial^3}{\partial x^2 \partial y} f(x, y)$$

```
> diff(f(x^2+y^2),x,y);
```

$$4 D^{(2)}(f)(x^2 + y^2) y x$$

8. Truncated Series Expansions

8.1 The Function series

8.1.1 Obtaining Truncated Series Expansions

The function series computes truncated series expansions of expressions depending on a single free variable.

Truncated Series Expansion About a

If p is an expression depending on the free variable x, and a is an expression which is independent of x and n and is a non-zero integer, the evaluation of series(p,x=a,n) returns a truncated series expansion of p in the neighbourhood of a whose order depends on n. series(p,x=a) is equivalent to series(p,x=a,n), where n is equal to the global variable Order, whose default value is 6.

In the returned result, the supplementary term is written in the form $O\left((x-a)^m\right)$ where O represents Landau's notation, which corresponds to a series expansion truncated at order $m-1$.

Since all computations of intermediary truncated series expansions are carried out to an order at most equal to n-1, one has n=m in nice cases.

Ex. 1
```
> series(1/(1+x),x=1,4);
```
$$\frac{1}{2} - \frac{1}{4}(x-1) + \frac{1}{8}(x-1)^2 - \frac{1}{16}(x-1)^3 + O\left((x-1)^4\right)$$

However, it sometimes happens that m>n without extra work.

Ex. 2
```
> series(1/(1-x^4),x,5);
```
$$1 + x^4 + O\left(x^8\right)$$

It may be that m<n if a power of (x-a) is a factor of denominator.

Ex. 3

> `series((sin(x)-x)/x^3,x=0,7);`   **Here, one has m=n-3**

$$-\frac{1}{6} + \frac{1}{120}x^2 + O(x^4)$$

The next sequence of computations may nevertheless be surprising.

Ex. 4

> `restart; series((log(1+x)-x+x^2/2)/x^2,x=0,5);`

Here, m=n-2

$$\frac{1}{3}x - \frac{1}{4}x^2 + O\left(x^3\right)$$

> `series((log(1+x)-x+x^2/2)/x^2,x=0,10);`

$$\frac{1}{3}x - \frac{1}{4}x^2 + \frac{1}{5}x^3 - \frac{1}{6}x^4 + \frac{1}{7}x^5 - \frac{1}{8}x^6 + \frac{1}{9}x^7 + O\left(x^8\right)$$

> `series((log(1+x)-x+x^2/2)/x^2,x=0,5);`   **but here, m=n**

$$\frac{1}{3}x - \frac{1}{4}x^2 + \frac{1}{5}x^3 - \frac{1}{6}x^4 + O\left(x^5\right)$$

The function **series** keeps track of the series expansions it computes within a **remember** table (p. 444). In the previous example, the function **series**, when called the third time, has found a result within this table that allows it to return, without any computation, a truncated series expansion for which m=n.

One may replace x=0 with x to obtain a series expansion about 0, but for an expansion about a one cannot replace x=a with x-a.

Ex. 5

> `series(sin(x),x,8);`   **=0 can be omitted by default**

$$x - \frac{1}{6}x^3 + \frac{1}{120}x^5 - \frac{1}{5040}x^7 + O\left(x^8\right)$$

To obtain the truncated series expansion of a function f, one must apply **series** to the expression f(x). When f is a free variable, the evaluation of **series(f(x),x=a,n)** returns Taylor's formula up to order n-1 in a symbolic form.

Ex. 6

> `f:='f': series(f(x),x,4);`

$$f(0) + D(f)(0)x + \frac{1}{2}\left(D^{(2)}\right)(f)(0)x^2 + \frac{1}{6}\left(D^{(3)}\right)(f)(0)x^3 + O\left(x^4\right)$$

Truncated Series Expansion at Infinity

The function `series` can also be used to compute truncated series expansions at infinity. Simply replace x=a with x=infinity (resp. x=-infinity) in the previous syntax to obtain a series expansion at $+\infty$ (resp. at $-\infty$).

Ex. 7

```
> series(1/(1+x),x=infinity);
```
$$\frac{1}{x} - \frac{1}{x^2} + \frac{1}{x^3} - \frac{1}{x^4} + \frac{1}{x^5} + O\left(\frac{1}{x^6}\right)$$

8.1.2 Generalized Series Expansions

The function `series` not only computes truncated series expansions but also generalized series expansions that may be Laurent series (positive and negative integer powers) or Puiseux series (fractional exponents).

Ex. 8

```
> series(cot(x),x,6);
```
Laurent series
$$x^{-1} - \frac{1}{3}x - \frac{1}{45}x^3 - \frac{2}{945}x^5 + O\left(x^6\right)$$
```
> series(sqrt(x*(1+x)),x,4);
```
Puiseux series
$$\sqrt{x} + \frac{1}{2}x^{3/2} - \frac{1}{8}x^{5/2} + \frac{1}{16}x^{7/2} - \frac{5}{128}x^{9/2} + O\left(x^{11/2}\right)$$

The evaluation of `series(p,x=a,n)` may sometimes return a series expansion whose coefficients contain expressions in the variable x that cannot be expanded in the neighbourhood of the point a.

Ex. 9

```
> p:=sin(x)/(1+x);
```
$$\frac{\sin(x)}{1+x}$$
```
> series(p,x=infinity,6);
```
$$\frac{\sin(x)}{x} - \frac{\sin(x)}{x^2} + \frac{\sin(x)}{x^3} - \frac{\sin(x)}{x^4} + \frac{\sin(x)}{x^5} + O\left(\frac{1}{x^6}\right)$$

When MAPLE keeps expressions in x as coefficients of a generalized series expansion in x, these coefficients need to satisfy in the neighborhood of a a relation like $k_1 |x - a|^r < |\texttt{coeff[i]}| < k_2 |x - a|^r$, where `coeff[i]` denotes the coefficient of x^i and k_1, k_2 and r denote positive constants.

Another example of series expansion whose coefficients are expressions in **x**:

Ex.10

```
> p:=x^x;
```
$$p := x^x$$
```
> series(p,x,4);
```
$$1 + \ln(x)\, x + \frac{1}{2} \ln(x)^2\, x^2 + \frac{1}{6} \ln(x)^3\, x^3 + O\left(x^4\right)$$

The function **series** can be used to obtain more general series expansions like Stirling's formula, which is computed with the help of the Gamma function.

Ex.11

```
> series(n!,n=infinity,3);
```
$$\frac{\dfrac{\sqrt{2\pi}}{\sqrt{\dfrac{1}{n}}} + \dfrac{\sqrt{2\pi}}{12}\sqrt{\dfrac{1}{n}} + \dfrac{\sqrt{2\pi}}{288}\left(\dfrac{1}{n}\right)^{3/2} + O\left(\left(\dfrac{1}{n}\right)^{5/2}\right)}{\left(\dfrac{1}{n}\right)^n e^n}$$

8.1.3 Regular Part of a Series Expansion

Since the regular part of a truncated series expansion of a function is a good approximation of this function, one sometimes wants to compute values for it, or even to represent it graphically. In order to carry out such operations, one then must extract the regular part of the series expansion returned by the function **series**, i.e. suppress the O term.

If **u** contains a truncated series expansion, **convert(u,polynom)** returns the polynomial part of **u**.

Ex.12

```
> p:=sin(x):u:=series(p,x,6);
```
$$u := x - \frac{1}{6} x^3 + \frac{1}{120} x^5 + O\left(x^6\right)$$
```
> subs(x=2,u);                    Impossible substitution
Error, invalid substitution in series
```
```
> u1:=convert(u,polynom);
```
$$u1 := x - \frac{1}{6} x^3 + \frac{1}{120} x^5$$

The quality of the approximation of the function sin by the polynomial u1 can be assessed by representing the two curves on the same graph.

Ex.13

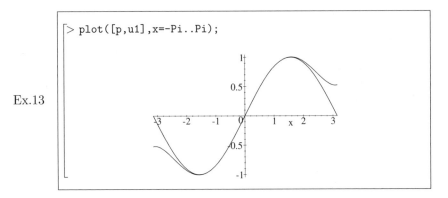

```
> plot([p,u1],x=-Pi..Pi);
```

When u contains a Laurent series or a Puiseux series, one may still use convert(u,polynom), though the result returned isn't a polynomial.

8.1.4 Obtaining an Equivalent

The function series can also to be used to obtain an equivalent.

If p is an expression depending on the free variable x, the evaluation of series(leadterm(p),x=a) or of series(leadterm(p),x=a,n) provides an equivalent of p in the neighbourhood of a, i.e. only the leading term of the series expansion of p in the neighbourhood of a.

It is better to use a big value of n or the variable Order in order to be sure to obtain the expected answer: no computation time will be needlessly wasted since only the leading term is computed. On the other hand, MAPLE returns an error message if n is not big enough.

Ex.14

```
> f:=x->tan(sin(x))-sin(tan(x));
```
$$f := x \rightarrow \tan(\sin(x)) - \sin(\tan(x))$$
```
> series(leadterm(f(x)),x,5);
```
Error, (in series/leadterm) unable to compute leading term
```
> series(leadterm(f(x)),x,20);
```
$$\frac{1}{30}x^7$$

8.1.5 Limits of the Function series

One should pay attention to the fact that series can only compute a truncated series expansion about a provided that the function can be series expanded (in a quite general sense) in the neighbourhood of a.

The function $x \rightarrow \exp(-1/x^2)$, for example, is infinitely differentiable for $x \neq 0$ and all its derivatives tend towards 0 as x tends towards 0, which can be verified with MAPLE in a few specific cases. This function can thus be infinitely differentiated about 0 and all its derivatives vanish there. By Taylor's formula, it thus has a truncated series expansion about 0 that vanishes at every order, which MAPLE isn't able to discover.

Ex.15

```
> p:=exp(-1/x^2);
```
$$p := e^{\left(-\frac{1}{x^2}\right)}$$

```
> n:=4: limit(diff(p,x$n),x=0);
```
try also
other values of n

$$0$$

```
> series(p,x=0);
  Error, (in series/exp) unable to compute series
```

When the series expansion exists on the right side and on the left side of a point a but hasn't the same analytical expression on both sides, the function series either doesn't return anything or returns a series expansion which is only valid on the right side.

Ex.16

```
> restart; p:=x^2/(1+abs(x));
```
$$p := \frac{x^2}{1 + |x|}$$

```
> series(p,x);
  Error, (in series/abs) no series at 0
```

Ex.17

```
> p:=arccos(sin(x)/x): u:=series(p,x);
```
$$u := \frac{1}{3}\sqrt{3}\,x - \frac{1}{270}\sqrt{3}\,x^3 + O\left(x^4\right)$$

```
> limit((p-u)/x^3,x=0,right);
```
It is the series expansion
on the right side,

$$0$$

```
> limit((p-u)/x^3,x=0,left);
```
but not on the left side

$$-\infty$$

8.2 Operations on Truncated Series Expansions

Although MAPLE automatically computes the truncated series expansions of most expressions, it may be useful to perform some computations on the truncated series expansions.

8.2.1 Sums, Quotients, Products of Truncated Series Expansions

The operators `*`, `/` or `^` may be used to express the products, quotients and powers of truncated series expansions, but since the "real" truncated series expansions have a specific type in MAPLE, the type `series` (p 364), the functions `expand` or `simplify` don't have the expected effect: one must use the function `series` every time.

Ex.18

```
> restart; u:=series(sinh(x),x); v:=series(cos(x),x);
```

$$u := x + \frac{x^3}{6} + \frac{1}{120}x^5 + O\left(x^6\right)$$

$$v := 1 - \frac{1}{2}x^2 + \frac{1}{24}x^4 + O\left(x^6\right)$$

```
> expand(u*v);
```

$$\left(x + \frac{x^3}{6} + \frac{1}{120}x^5 + O\left(x^6\right)\right)\left(1 - \frac{1}{2}x^2 + \frac{1}{24}x^4 + O\left(x^6\right)\right)$$

```
> series(u*v,x);
```

$$x - \frac{1}{3}x^3 - \frac{1}{30}x^5 + O\left(x^6\right)$$

```
> series(u/v,x);
```

$$x + \frac{2}{3}x^3 + \frac{3}{10}x^5 + O(x^6)$$

As the following example shows, MAPLE will not answer to unreasonable questions. It is useless to ask, using the previous expansions, for a power expansion of `sinh(x)*cos(x)` to the order 11.

Ex.19

```
> series(u*v,x,12);
```

$$x - \frac{1}{3}x^3 - \frac{1}{30}x^5 + O\left(x^6\right)$$

8.2.2 Compositions and Inverses of Truncated Series Expansions

Compositions of Truncated Series Expansions

The compositions of truncated series expansions can also be directly obtained with the function `series`.

Ex.20

```
> restart; u:=series(sin(x),x,5);
```

$$u := x - \frac{x^3}{6} + O\left(x^5\right)$$

```
> v:=series(tan(u),x,5);
```

$$v := x + \frac{x^3}{6} + O\left(x^5\right)$$

Truncated Series Expansion of a Reciprocal "Function"

If f is a bijective function that has a truncated series expansion about a whose coefficient of $(x - a)$ doesn't vanish, then f^{-1} has a truncated series expansion up to the same order in the neighbourhood of $b = f(a)$. If `u` contains `series(f(x),x=a,n)` where `n` is an integer less than or equal to `Order`, and if `y` is a free variable, `solve(u=y,x)` returns the truncated series expansion of f^{-1} about $b = f(a)$ up to order `n-1`.

Let us find the series expansion of `arctan` in this way.

Ex.21

```
> u:=series(tan(x),x); solve(u=y,x);          T.S.E. about 0
```

$$u := x + \frac{1}{3}x^3 + \frac{2}{15}x^5 + O\left(x^6\right)$$

$$y - \frac{1}{3}y^3 + \frac{1}{5}y^5 + O\left(y^6\right)$$

```
> solve(series(tan(x),x=Pi/4,3)=y,x);          T.S.E. about 1
```

$$\frac{1}{4}\pi + \frac{1}{2}(y - 1) - \frac{1}{4}(y - 1)^2 + O\left((y - 1)^3\right)$$

Note: When `n` is strictly bigger than `Order`, the order of the series expansion returned by `solve` is `Order-1` which is equal to 5 by default. Thus, one must modify `Order` to obtain a truncated series expansion up to a higher order.

Ex.22

```
> Order:=8; solve(series(tan(x),x)=y,x);
```

$$y - \frac{1}{3}y^3 + \frac{1}{5}y^5 - \frac{1}{7}y^7 + O\left(y^8\right)$$

When the coefficient of $(x - a)$ in the truncated series expansion of f about a vanishes, `solve(u=y,x)` returns the sequence containing the Puiseux series of the various branches of the "reciprocal function" of f.

Ex.23

```
> u:=series(cos(x),x,6);
```

$$u := 1 - \frac{1}{2}x^2 + \frac{1}{24}x^4 + O\left(x^6\right)$$

```
> solve(u=y,x);
```

$$I\sqrt{2}\sqrt{y-1} - \frac{1}{12}I\sqrt{2}\,(y-1)^{3/2} + O\left((y-1)^{5/2}\right),$$

$$-I\sqrt{2}\sqrt{y-1} + \frac{1}{12}I\sqrt{2}\,(y-1)^{3/2} + O\left((y-1)^{5/2}\right)$$

One can see that MAPLE introduces the complex number I in the previous computation, because it uses the increment (y-1) instead of (1-y). To obtain the expression of the series expansions with real coefficients corresponding to y<1 in the previous example, one may replace y with 1-h when calling the function `solve`. Then MAPLE carries out a series expansion with respect to powers of h, i.e. of 1-y.

Ex.24

```
> solve(u=1-h,x);
```

$$\sqrt{2}\sqrt{h} + \frac{1}{12}\sqrt{2}\,h^{3/2} + O\left(h^{5/2}\right),$$

$$-\sqrt{2}\sqrt{h} - \frac{1}{12}\sqrt{2}\,h^{3/2} + O\left(h^{5/2}\right)$$

```
> subs(h=1-y,["]);                    [] essential so that subs
                                      sees only two arguments
```

$$\left[\sqrt{2}\sqrt{1-y} + \frac{1}{12}\,\sqrt{2}\,(1-y)^{3/2} + O((1-y)^{5/2}),\right.$$

$$\left.-\sqrt{2}\sqrt{1-y} - \frac{1}{12}\,\sqrt{2}\,(1-y)^{3/2} + O((1-y)^{5/2})\right]$$

8.2.3 Integration of a Truncated Series Expansion

The function `int` can be used to integrate truncated series expansions, asymptotic series expansions or Puiseux series. If u contains the truncated series expansion up to order n of f about a, then `int(u,x)` returns the series expansion up to order n+1 about a of the primitive of f that vanishes at a.

Ex.25

```
> u:=series(1/(x^2+x+1),x=1,3);
```

$$\frac{1}{3} - \frac{1}{3}(x-1) + \frac{2}{9}(x-1)^2 + O\left((x-1)^3\right)$$

```
> int(u,x);
```

$$\frac{1}{3}(x-1) - \frac{1}{6}(x-1)^2 + \frac{2}{27}(x-1)^3 + O\left((x-1)^4\right)$$

Example displaying the integration of a Laurent series, in which MAPLE integrates the truncated series expansion symbolically without introducing an integration constant.

Ex.26

```
> u:=series(cos(x)/x,x,4);
```

$$u := x^{-1} - \frac{1}{2}x + O\left(x^3\right)$$

```
> int(u,x);
```

$$\ln(x) - \frac{1}{4}x^2 + O\left(x^4\right)$$

8.3 Series Expansion of an Implicit Function

In this section, we study the truncated series expansions of "implicit functions". For MAPLE, it most often concerns expressions defined with the help of RootOf.

Evaluation of RootOf(p,y,b)

If b contains a real or complex numerical value, and p contains an expression in the free variable y, RootOf(p,y,b) represents the root of the equation p=0 which is "closest" to b. The result returned by MAPLE uses the function RootOf unless p is a polynomial of degree one in y.

Ex.27

```
> restart; P:=x^3-3*x+1: s:=RootOf(P,x,2);
```

$$s := RootOf(\_Z^3 - 3\_Z + 1, 2)$$

One may simply use the function evalf to obtain a numerical approximation of such a quantity.

Ex.28

```
> evalf(s);
```

$$1.532088886$$

Truncated Series Expansion of an Implicit Function

The functions `series` and `RootOf` can be combined to compute truncated series expansions of implicit functions.

Given a real or complex numerical value b, a numerical value a which isn't of type `float`, and an expression p=f(x,y) in the free variables x and y that doesn't contain elements of type `float`, `series(RootOf(p,y,b),x=a)` returns a truncated series expansion of the expression g(x) defined implicitly by f(x,g(x))=0 and g(a) "near" b. It is a series expansion in (x-a) whose coefficients are expressed with the help of quantities that are symbolically equal to `RootOf(subs(x=a,p),y,b)`.

Using `series(RootOf(p,y,b),x=a)` we can make a local study of a branch of a curve defined by an equation f(x,y)=0. We explain the method with an example.

We consider the expression p=f(x,y)=x^3+y^3-3*x*y-2 and represent its associated curve as well as the line defined by the equation x=1 with the help of `plots[implicitplot]`: this syntax allows us to use the function `implicitplot` of the `plots` library without loading it permanently in memory.

Ex.29

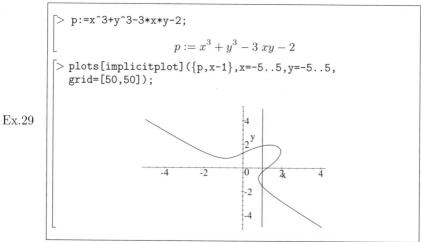

```
> p:=x^3+y^3-3*x*y-2;
```
$$p := x^3 + y^3 - 3\,xy - 2$$
```
> plots[implicitplot]({p,x-1},x=-5..5,y=-5..5,
  grid=[50,50]);
```

One can see from the picture that, in the neighbourhood of $x = 1$, this curve defines three implicit functions of x, which correspond to the three roots of the equation $f(1,y) = 0$. These three roots can be computed with the function `fsolve`.

Ex.30

```
> Digits:=4: fsolve(subs(x=1,p));
```
$$-1.532,\ -0.3473,\ 1.879$$

Denoting by s1, s2 and s3 the truncated series expansions up to order 2 of the corresponding implicit functions, we have

Ex.31

```
> Order:=3: s1:=series(RootOf(p,y,-1.5),x=1);
```

$$s1 \quad : \quad = \%1 + \left(-\%1^2 + \%1 + 2\right)(x - 1)$$
$$+ \left(-\%1 + \%1^2 - 2\right)(x - 1)^2 + O(x - 1)^3$$
$$\%1 \quad : \quad = RootOf(-1 + \_Z^3 - 3\_Z, -1.5)$$

The previous result reads more easily using `alias(b1=%1)`, equivalent to `alias(b1=RootOf(-1+_Z^3-3*_Z,-1.5))`, which forces MAPLE to write its results in terms of b1.

Ex.32

```
> alias(b1=%1);                          MAPLE returns
                                         the list of existing aliases
```

$$I, b1$$

```
> s1;
```

$$b1 + \left(-b1^2 + b1 + 2\right)(x - 1)$$
$$+ \left(-b1 + b1^2 - 2\right)(x - 1)^2 + O\left((x - 1)^3\right)$$

The same can be done for the two other branches, starting by defining the aliases b2 and b3 with the help of `RootOf(subs(x=a,p),y,b)`:

Ex.33

```
> alias(b2=RootOf(subs(x=1,p),y,-0.3));
```

$$I, b1, b2$$

```
> s2:=series(RootOf(p,y,-0.3),x=1);
```

$$s2 \quad : \quad = b2 + \left(-b2^2 + b2 + 2\right)(x - 1)$$
$$+ \left(-b2 + b2^2 - 2\right)(x - 1)^2 + O\left((x - 1)^3\right)$$

```
> alias(b3=RootOf(subs(x=1,p),y,1.8)):
> s3:=series(RootOf(p,y,1.8),x=1);
```

$$s3 \quad : \quad = b3 + \left(-b3^2 + b3 + 2\right)(x - 1)$$
$$+ \left(-b3 + b3^2 - 2\right)(x - 1)^2 + O\left((x - 1)^3\right)$$

These truncated series expansions are in fact purely symbolic and their coefficients depend only on b through $RootOf(\_Z^3 - 3\_Z - 1, b)$. To grasp the differences between these three expressions and benefit from what has been done so far, one must compute the numerical evaluations of the coefficients of these truncated series expansions using the function `evalf`.

Ex.34

```
> evalf(s1); evalf(s2); evalf(s3);
```

$$-1.532 - 1.879(x - 1.) + 1.879(x - 1.)^2 + O((x - 1.)^3)$$
$$-.3473 + 1.532(x - 1.) - 1.532(x - 1.)^2 + O((x - 1.)^3)$$
$$1.879 + .348(x - 1.) - .348(x - 1.)^2 + O((x - 1.)^3)$$

If a is a numerical value of type `float`, or if `p=f(x,y)` is an expression containing an element of type `float`, then `evalf` is useless since `series(RootOf(p,y,b),x=a)` directly returns a truncated series expansion whose coefficients are of type `float`.

Ex.35

```
> evalf(series(RootOf(p,y,-1.5),x=1.1));
```

$$-1.705 - 1.612(x - 1.100) + .9520(x - 1.100)^2 + O((x - 1.100)^3)$$

9. Differential Equations

The MAPLE function `dsolve` solves differential equations or systems of differential equations with or without initial conditions (or boundary conditions). It can be used to obtain an exact solution, a truncated series expansion of a solution, or a procedure that compute approximate numerical values of a solution.

The function `DEplot` of the `plots` library graphically represents a family of integral curves of a differential equation or a system of differential equations corresponding to various given initial conditions, without explicitly solving the equation or the system.

9.1 Methods for Solving Exactly

The function `dsolve` requires at least two arguments:

- The first is a set containing the equations and, if required, the initial conditions.
- The second is a set containing the names of the unknown functions (in the form y(x) for a function y whose variable is x).

These sets are delimited by braces, as is often the case with MAPLE. These braces are however not mandatory for sets containing a single element.

9.1.1 Differential Equations of Order 1

In a differential equation of order 1, the unknown function has to be written y(x), its derivative may be written `diff(y(x),x)` or `D(y)(x)`, but **it absolutely has to be written with the operator D if one uses an initial condition involving the derivative**.

The braces around the equation are not required when one wishes to solve a differential equation without initial conditions. Nor are the braces required around the name of the unknown function.

Equations of Order 1 Without Initial Conditions

It is better to first store the differential equation to be solved in a variable. One can then check it with the help of the echo returned by MAPLE.

Ex. 1

```
> Eq_1:=2*diff(y(x),x)+y(x)=cos(x);
```
$$Eq\_1 := 2 \left(\frac{\partial}{\partial x} y(x) \right) + y(x) = \cos(x)$$

When one has to deal with several differential equations during the same session, time can be saved by using subsidiary variables like y0 and y1 in which one stores the quantities y(x) and diff(y(x),x) at the beginning of the session.

Ex. 2

```
> y0:=y(x); y1:=diff(y0,x);
```
$$y0 := y(x)$$
$$y1 := \frac{\partial}{\partial x} y(x)$$

Every differential equation can then be written in an easy way.

Ex. 3

```
> Eq_1:=2*y1+y0=cos(x);
```
$$Eq\_1 := 2 \left(\frac{\partial}{\partial x} y(x) \right) + y(x) = \cos(x)$$
```
> dsolve(Eq_1,y(x));
```
$$y(x) = \frac{1}{5} \cos(x) + \frac{2}{5} \sin(x) + \_C1\, e^{-\frac{1}{2} x}$$

The solution of such a differential equation requires an integration constant for which MAPLE uses an identifier starting with an underscore. The user should therefore avoid introducing identifiers starting with underscores.

Warning! The y(x) specifying "function" to be solved for is required. The following error message is returned if one puts y instead:

Ex. 4

```
> dsolve(Eq_1,y);
```
Error, (in dsolve) dsolve/inputck1 expects its 2nd argument,
vars, to be of type {list, set, function}, but received y

Notice that in the previous example `dsolve` hasn't returned the expression of a solution of the differential equation but only the equation of an integral curve in the form $y(x) = \langle expr\_of\_x \rangle$. The expression of the solution isn't stored in `y(x)` after the evaluation of `dsolve`. One can, however, obtain this expression by using the function `subs`.

Ex. 5

```
> Sol := dsolve(Eq_1, y0):
> Expr := subs(Sol, y(x));
```

$$Expr := \frac{1}{5}\cos(x) + \frac{2}{5}\sin(x) + \_C1\, e^{-\frac{1}{2}x}$$

In some cases, the function `dsolve` returns an implicit equation for the integral curves. However, the function `dsolve` used with the option `explicit` returns an explicit equation for the integral curves whenever possible, or possibly a sequence of such equations.

Ex. 6

```
> Eq_2:=y(x)*diff(y(x),x)+x-1;
```

$$Eq\_2 := y(x)\left(\frac{\partial}{\partial x}y(x)\right) + x - 1$$

```
> dsolve(Eq_2,y(x));
```

$$\frac{1}{2}y(x)^2 + \frac{1}{2}x^2 - x = \_C1$$

```
> dsolve(Eq_2,y(x),explicit);
```

$$y(x) = \sqrt{-x^2 + 2x + 2\_C1},\ y(x) = -\sqrt{-x^2 + 2x + 2\_C1}$$

The function `dsolve` may also return an empty sequence (without any echo). This doesn't mean that the equation has no solution, only that the function `dsolve` isn't able to find one.

Ex. 7

```
> Eq_3:=2*y(x)^2*diff(y(x),x)-y(x)+x;
```

$$Eq\_3 := 2\,y(x)^2\left(\frac{\partial}{\partial x}y(x)\right) - y(x) + x$$

```
> s:=dsolve(Eq_3,y(x));
```

$$s :=$$

Equations of Order 1 with Initial Conditions

To deal with a differential equation with initial conditions, `dsolve` must be called with a set made up of the equation and the initial condition as first argument. This initial condition is an additional equation the solution must satisfy, hence **this condition is written with = and not :=** .

Ex. 8

```
> Sol:=dsolve({Eq_1,y(0)=0},y(x));
```
with the previous value of Eq_1

$$Sol := y(x) = \frac{1}{5}\cos(x) + \frac{2}{5}\sin(x) - \frac{1}{5}e^{-\frac{1}{2}x}$$

The use of an assignment for the initial condition would give

Ex. 9

```
> dsolve({Eq_1,y(0):=0},y(x));
```
Syntax error, ':=' unexpected

9.1.2 Differential Equations of Higher Order

Equations of Order 2

The function `dsolve` can also be used to solve differential equations of order 2. In such an equation, the second derivative of `y(x)` is written `diff(y(x),x,x)` or `(D@@2)(y)(x)`, but **the initial conditions concerning the derivatives must be written** with the operator D.

Entering differential equations is once again facilitated by using the subsidiary variables y0, y1 and y2 as in the following example.

Ex.10

```
> y0:=y(x); y1:=diff(y0,x); y2:=diff(y1,x);
```

$$y0 := y(x) \quad y1 := \frac{\partial}{\partial x}y(x) \quad y2 := \frac{\partial^2}{\partial x^2}y(x)$$

The general case of the classical equation $y'' + a\,y = 0$ with the initial conditions $y(0) = 1$ and $y'(0) = 1$ can then be solved by writing

Ex.11

```
> dsolve({y2+a*y0=0,y(0)=1,D(y)(0)=1},y0);
```
the initial condition has to be written with D

$$y(x) = \frac{1}{2}\frac{(1+\sqrt{-a})\,e^{(\sqrt{-a}x)}}{\sqrt{-a}} + \frac{1}{2}\frac{(\sqrt{-a}-1)\,e^{(-\sqrt{-a}x)}}{\sqrt{-a}}$$

In the general case, the formula one obtains isn't very appealing. The result is closer to what is expected if a is set equal to b^2.

Ex.12

```
> a:=b*b: dsolve({y2+a*y0=0,y(0)=1,D(y)(0)=1},y0);
```

$$y(x) = \frac{\sin(bx)}{b} + \cos(bx)$$

Likewise, if a is set equal to $-b^2$, one obtains

Ex.13

```
> a:=-b*b: dsolve({y2+a*y0=0,y(0)=1,D(y)(0)=1},y0);
```

$$y(x) = \frac{1}{2}\frac{(b+1)\,e^{(bx)}}{b} + \frac{1}{2}\frac{(b-1)\,e^{(-bx)}}{b}$$

```
> simplify(convert(", trig));
```

$$y(x) = \frac{b\,\cosh(bx) + \sinh(bx)}{b}$$

Another way to obtain a result for the previous equation which reads more easily is to specify the domain the parameter a belongs to. This can be done with the function **assume**, which can be used to indicate to MAPLE that some variables satisfy given "conditions". The easiest conditions being that a number is an integer, is a real number, is positive, is negative, etc.

For example, one can indicate that **a** is assumed to be strictly positive by writing

Ex.14

```
> a:='a': assume(a>0);
```

And MAPLE takes into account the fact that a is positive to express the solution returned by **dsolve** in function of trigonometric expressions of $\sqrt{a}$.

Ex.15

```
> Sol:=dsolve({y2+a*y0=0,y(0)=1,D(y)(0)=1},y0);
```

$$Sol := y(x) = \cos\left(\sqrt{a}\sim x\right) + \frac{\sin\left(\sqrt{a}\sim x\right)}{\sqrt{a}\sim}$$

One should however keep in mind for later computations that $a \sim$ is a variable different from a for MAPLE. If, for example, one wishes to assign a numerical value to a afterwards and deduce from it the new expression of the solution, then one has to use **subs** instead of an ordinary assignment.

Hence, to replace **a** with 1 in the solution one obtains, one has to type

Ex.16

```
> Sol1:=subs(a=1,Sol);
```

$$Sol1 := y(x) = \cos(x) + \sin(x)$$

If one tries make an assignment instead of using **subs**, one obtains

Ex.17

```
> a:=1;
```

$$a := 1$$

```
> Sol;
```

$$y(x) = \cos\left(\sqrt{a}\sim x\right) + \frac{\sin\left(\sqrt{a}\sim x\right)}{\sqrt{a}\sim}$$

which isn't the expected result. It is however too late to use subs, since subs(a=1,Sol) is then evaluated to subs(1=1,Sol).

Equation of Order Greater Than Two

MAPLE can also solve differential equations of higher order as, for example, the following equation, which is written with the operator D for a change.

Ex.18

```
> Eq:=(D@@3)(y)(x)-y(x);
```
$$Eq := D^{(3)}(y)(x) - y(x)$$

```
> dsolve(Eq,y(x));
```
$$y(x) = \_C1\, e^x + \_C2\, e^{(-\frac{1}{2}x)} \sin\left(\frac{\sqrt{3}}{2}x\right) + \_C3\, e^{(-\frac{1}{2}x)} \cos\left(\frac{\sqrt{3}}{2}x\right)$$

For such a differential equation, **the initial conditions concerning the derivatives must be written with the operator D.**

Ex.19

```
> dsolve({Eq,y(0)=1,D(y)(0)=0,(D@@2)(y)(0)=0},y(x));
```
$$y(x) = \frac{1}{3}e^x + \frac{2}{3}e^{(-\frac{1}{2})x} \cos\left(\frac{1}{2}\sqrt{3}x\right)$$

Warning ! Be careful to make proper use of parentheses in writing (D@@2)(y)(0)=0.

9.1.3 Classical Equations

MAPLE can solve most equations encountered in the literature: homogeneous equations, Riccati equations, Bessel equations, etc. It usually uses one of the many functions belonging to its mathematical library (Chapter 25).

The following example concerns a Riccati equation MAPLE solves with the help of the function erf defined by: $erf(x) = \frac{2}{\sqrt{\pi}} \int_0^x e^{-t^2} dt$.

Ex.20

```
> Eq:=diff(y(x),x)=x^2-y(x)^2+1;
```
$$Eq := \frac{\partial}{\partial x}y(x) = x^2 - y(x)^2 + 1$$

```
> dsolve(Eq,y(x));
```
$$y(x) = x + \frac{e^{-x^2}}{\_c1 + \frac{1}{2}\sqrt{\pi}\,erf(x)}$$

Another example, in which MAPLE uses Bessel functions to express the solution.

Ex.21

```
> Eq:=x^2*diff(y(x),x,x)+x*diff(y(x),x)+x^2*y(x);
```

$$Eq := x^2 \left(\frac{\partial^2}{\partial x^2} y(x) \right) + x \left(\frac{\partial}{\partial x} y(x) \right) + x^2 y(x)$$

```
> dsolve(Eq,y(x));
```

$$y(x) = \_C1\, BesselJ(0, x) + \_C2\, BesselY(0, x)$$

9.1.4 Systems of Differential Equations

Writing and Solving a System of Equations

To solve a differential system, `dsolve` is called with two arguments:

- The first is the set, between braces, of equations of the system and possibly of initial conditions.
- The second is the set of unknown functions.

If one wishes to impose initial conditions on the solutions of a differential system, one has to write them within the set of equations using = instead of :=.

Example for a system of two differential equations, without initial condition

Ex.22

```
> Eq:={diff(x(t),t)=-y(t),diff(y(t),t)=x(t)};
```

$$Eq := \left\{ \frac{\partial}{\partial t} x(t) = -y(t), \quad \frac{\partial}{\partial t} y(t) = x(t) \right\}$$

```
> dsolve(Eq,{x(t),y(t)});
```

$$\{ y(t) = \sin(t)\, \_C1 + \cos(t)\, \_C2,$$
$$x(t) = \cos(t)\, \_C1 - \sin(t)\, \_C2 \}$$

MAPLE returns a set of equations and introduces the constants it needs using identifiers beginning, as usual, with an underscore.

The same system, but with initial conditions

Ex.23

```
>Eq:={diff(x(t),t)=-y(t),diff(y(t),t)=x(t),x(0)=1,y(0)=0};
```

$$Eq := \left\{ \frac{\partial}{\partial t} x(t) = -y(t), \frac{\partial}{\partial t} y(t) = x(t), x(0) = 1, y(0) = 0 \right\}$$

```
> Sol:=dsolve(Eq,{x(t),y(t)});
```

$$Sol := \{ y(t) = \sin(t), x(t) = \cos(t) \}$$

To solve a system, one must provide as many unknown functions as equations, otherwise one gets an error message, which isn't very helpful when there are initial conditions.

Ex.24

```
> dsolve(Eq,x(t));
    Error, (in dsolve) invalid initial condition
```

Graphic Representation

To graphically represent the solution of a differential system, one has to extract the expression for the solutions from the result returned by dsolve. The syntax dsolve uses for its result makes it easy to use the function subs.

If one wishes to plot $x(t)$ and $y(t)$ from the previous example as functions of t, one simply has to write

Ex.25

```
> x_y:=subs(Sol,[x(t),y(t)]);
```
$$x\_y := [\cos(t) \ , \ \sin(t)]$$
```
> plot(x_y,t=0..2*Pi,-2..2);
```

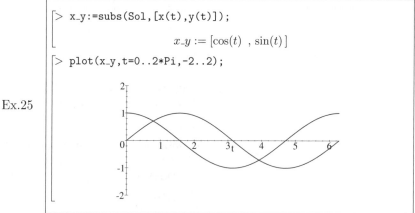

If, for the same system, one wishes to plot the parametrized curve associated with a solution (phase difference in electricity, trajectory in mechanics), one simply has to write

Ex.26

```
> Par_Curve:=subs(Sol,[x(t),y(t),t=0..2*Pi]);
```
$$Par\_Curve := [\cos(t), \sin(t), t = 0..2\pi]$$
```
> plot (Par_Curve,-2..2,-2..2);
```

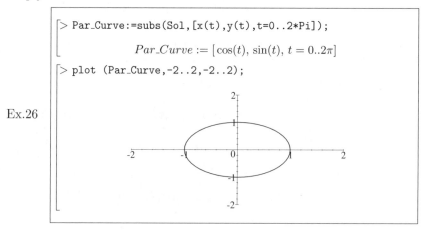

9.2 Methods for Approximate Solutions

9.2.1 Numerical Solution of an Equation of Order 1

The function `dsolve` returns an empty sequence when it isn't able to find a symbolic expression for the solution of a differential equation. This occurs, for example, when trying to determine the equation of the tractrix containing a given point.

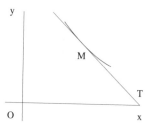

A tractrix is a curve whose tangent at a point M intersects Ox at a point T such that the length MT is equal to a given constant a. Finding the equation of the tractrix corresponding to $a = 2$ and containing the point $(3, 1.5)$ comes down to a differential problem written

Ex.27

```
> restart:
  Eq:={y(3)=1.5,diff(y(x),x)=-y(x)/sqrt(4-y(x)^2)};
```

$$Eq := \left\{ y(3) = 1.5, \ \frac{\partial}{\partial x} y(x) = -\frac{y(x)}{\sqrt{4 - y(x)^2}} \right\}$$

```
> Sol:=dsolve(Eq,y(x));
```
dsolve returns the expression NULL without echo on the screen

$$Sol :=$$

The Option `numeric`

For a differential equation without parameter and with enough initial conditions that its solution does not depend on any integration constants (Cauchy problem), the use of `dsolve` with the option `numeric` returns a procedure for producing numerical values of the solution.

For the tractrix, one can write

Ex.28

```
> Sol:=dsolve(Eq,y(x),numeric);
```

$$Sol := proc(rkf45\_x)...end$$

The function `dsolve` returns a procedure with one parameter that returns a list $[x = a, y(x) = val\_of\_y(a)]$ when applied to a value a of the variable x. The structure of this result makes it easy to use the function `subs` to extract the value of $y(a)$.

With the procedure of the previous example, one has

Ex.29

```
> Sol(4);
              [ x = 4 , y(x) = .814430348531400 ]
> subs(Sol(4),y(x));
                      .814430348531400
```

To plot the solution curve of the differential equation, one can write

Ex.30

```
> f:=t->subs(Sol(t),y(x));
              f := t → subs(Sol(t), y(x));
> plot(f,3..10,y=0..1.5);
```

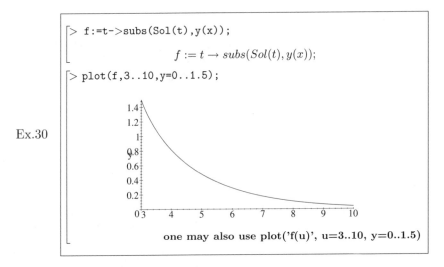

one may also use plot('f(u)', u=3..10, y=0..1.5)

Note: If one uses `f(u)` instead of `f` with `plot`, the apostrophes around `f(u)` are necessary since the function `plot` evaluates all its arguments when called. In particular `f(u)` would be evaluated as `Sol(u)`, which MAPLE isn't able to carry out since `u` doesn't contain any numerical value. Without apostrophes the same error message is returned as for the direct evaluation of `Sol(u)`.

Ex.31

```
> Sol(u);
  Error, (in Sol) cannot evaluate boolean
```

No problems arise with the syntax `plot(f,3..10,y=0..1.5)`, since a function is never fully evaluated.

Warning ! Be cautions the names of the variables used in the definition of `f`:

- The second argument of the function `subs` absolutely has to be `y(x)`, i.e. the name of the unknown function given `dsolve`.
- the parameter of the function `f` has to be different from `x`, since the evaluation of `f(a)` gives `subs(Sol(a),y(a))` instead of `subs(Sol(a),y(x))` if the same variable is used.

The function `odeplot` of the `plots` library can also be directly used to plot the solution curve of the previous differential equation.

Ex.32

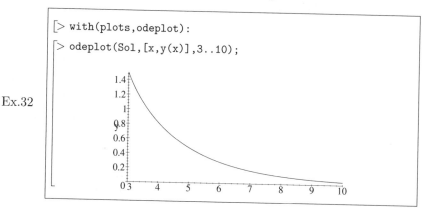

```
[> with(plots,odeplot):
[> odeplot(Sol,[x,y(x)],3..10);
```

9.2.2 Numerical Solution of an Equation of Higher Order

The option `numeric` can also be used to solve a differential equation of order greater than 1. For a second order equation, the function `dsolve` returns a procedure with one parameter which returns a list $[x = a, y(x) = val\_of\_y(a), \frac{\partial}{\partial x}y(x) = val\_of\_y'(a)]$ when it is applied to a value a of the variable x. The structure of this result makes it easy to use the function `subs` to extract $y(a)$ and $y'(a)$.

The process is similar for equations of higher order.

Simple Pendulum

For a non damped pendulum, one may write

Ex.33

```
[> Eq:=diff(y(x),x,x)=-sin(y(x)):
   Sol:=dsolve({Eq,y(0)=0,D(y)(0)=0.5},y(x),numeric);
```
$$Sol := proc(rkf45\_x)...end$$
```
[> Sol(1);                        To check the structure of the result
```
$$\left[x = 1,\ y(x) = .4215341926928455,\ \frac{\partial}{\partial x}y(x) = .2737235288022365\right]$$

To plot the solution, one may write

Ex.34

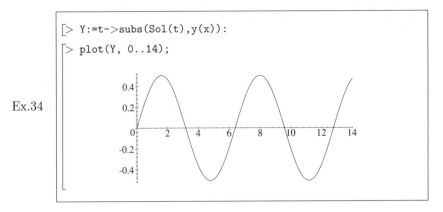

```
[> Y:=t->subs(Sol(t),y(x)):
[> plot(Y, 0..14);
```

The graph shows that the period of this pendulum lies between 6 and 7, which helps us use the function **fsolve** to compute the period numerically.

Ex.35

```
[> fsolve('Y(t)',t=6..7);                    Apostrophes mandatory
                                              like in example 30.

                        6.384968902
```

van der Pol's Oscillator

In the case of a van der Pol's oscillator, one obtains

Ex.36

```
[> Eq:=diff(y(x),x,x)=(1-y(x)^2)*diff(y(x),x)-y(x);
```

$$Eq := \frac{\partial^2}{\partial x^2} y(x) = \left(1 - y(x)^2\right) \frac{\partial}{\partial x} y(x) - y(x)$$

```
[> Sol:=dsolve({Eq,y(0)=0,D(y)(0)=0.1},y(x),numeric);
```

$$Sol := proc(rkf45\_x)...end$$

To represent the phase portrait, for example, we can use the function **odeplot** as follows:

Ex.37

```
[> with(plots,odeplot);
```

$$[\,odeplot\,]$$

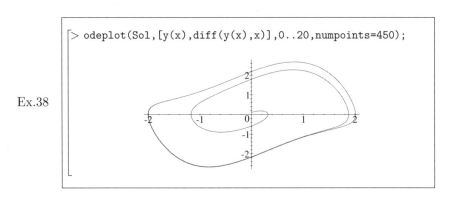

```
> odeplot(Sol,[y(x),diff(y(x),x)],0..20,numpoints=450);
```

Ex.38

Gravitation Equation with Perturbation

Studying the motions of some planets using polar coordinates requires solving
the following type of differential equation:

Ex.39

```
> u:=1/r(theta): Eq:=diff(u,theta,theta)=-u+1+u^2/100;
```

$$Eq := 2\frac{\left(\frac{\partial}{\partial t}\, r(\theta)\right)^2}{r(\theta)^3} - \frac{\frac{\partial^2}{\partial t^2}\, r(\theta)}{r(\theta)^2} = -\frac{1}{r(\theta)} + 1 + \frac{1}{100}\frac{1}{r(\theta)^2}$$

in which the term $\frac{1}{100\, r(\theta)^2}$ corresponds to a small perturbation with respect
to the classical equation of Newtonian mechanics. The function dsolve isn't
able to solve this differential equation with initial conditions. To plot the
corresponding trajectory, one may solve this differential equation with the
option numeric, and use the function plot with the option coords=polar.

```
> Sol:=dsolve({Eq,r(0)=10,D(r)(0)=0},r(theta),numeric);
```

$$Sol := proc(rkf45\_x)...end$$

```
> R:=u->subs(Sol(u),r(theta)):
  plot(R,0..6*Pi,coords=polar,numpoints=350);
```

Ex.40

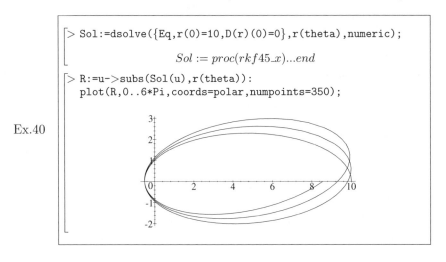

The previous picture shows us the influence of the perturbation of the differential equation on the trajectory. It behaves here as a slightly turning ellipse.

Note: Although `odeplot` doesn't allow the option `coords=polar`, it can nevertheless be used to obtain the previous drawing by typing

Ex.41
```
> odeplot(Sol,[r(theta)*cos(theta),r(theta)*sin(theta)],
    0..6*Pi,numpoints=350);
```

Note: The values returned by procedures obtained from the evaluation of `dsolve(...,numeric)` are computed with the help of the function `evalhf` (p. 61) and thus contain about fifteen significant digits. The precision of these values may be modified by changing the value of `Digits` **before calling the function** `dsolve`. The computation time quickly increases as `Digits` is increased.

9.2.3 Computing a Truncated Series Expansion of the Solution

The function `dsolve`, used with the option `series`, can be used to obtain a truncated series expansion of the solution of a differential equation.

- When the option `series` is used on an equation with initial conditions, the truncated series expansion is computed in the neighbourhood of the point where the initial conditions are given.
- Without initial conditions, the truncated series expansion is computed in the neighbourhood of 0 and expressed as a function of `y(0)`, `D(y)(0)`,...

In both cases, the order of this truncated series expansion is specified by the variable `Order` (mind the upper case) and cannot be locally defined in `dsolve`.

In the case of the simple pendulum, with initial conditions $y(0) = 0$ and $y'(0) = v$, one obtains

Ex.42
```
> Eq:=diff(y(x),x,x)=-sin(y(x));
```
$$Eq := \frac{\partial^2}{\partial x^2} y(x) = -\sin(y(x))$$
```
> dsolve({Eq, y(0)=0,D(y)(0)=v},y(x),series);
```
$$y(x) = v - \frac{1}{6} v x^3 + \left(\frac{1}{120} v + \frac{1}{120} v^3\right) x^5 + O(x^6)$$

And one can verify that this last truncated series expansion, up to the term $\frac{1}{120} v^3 x^5$, is equal to the truncated series expansion of $v \sin x$, which is the solution of the approximate equation $y'' = -y$ that is classically used for the oscillator.

9.3 Methods to Solve Graphically

For a differential equation (or a first order differential system) without parameters and with enough initial conditions for its solution not to depend on any integration constants (Cauchy problem), the function DEplot can be used to quickly obtain a set of integral curves.

Since the function DEplot doesn't belong to the standard library, it must first be loaded using with(DEtools,DEplot) or with(DEtools).

9.3.1 Differential Equation of Order 1

Calling DEplot to plot integral curves of an equation $y' = f(x, y)$ requires four parameters which are, in order:

- the equation, written diff(y(x),x)=f(x,y(x)) or D(y)(x)=f(x,y(x)),
- the function one seeks, in the form y(x),
- the range of the variable, in the form x=a..b or a..b,
- a set of initial conditions: each condition a list of the form [y(a)=y0]. The curves corresponding to these initial conditions will be plotted. Note that it is necessary to write {[y(a)=y0]} to obtain a single curve.

Example of a plot of a few curves of the equation $y'(x) = y(x)$.

Ex.43

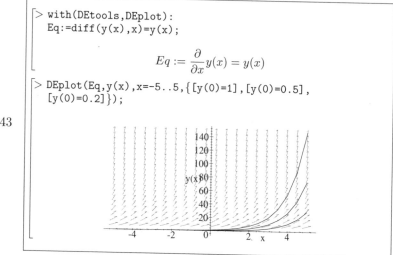

```
> with(DEtools,DEplot):
  Eq:=diff(y(x),x)=y(x);
```

$$Eq := \frac{\partial}{\partial x} y(x) = y(x)$$

```
> DEplot(Eq,y(x),x=-5..5,{[y(0)=1],[y(0)=0.5],
  [y(0)=0.2]});
```

9.3.2 The Options of DEplot for a Differential Equation

The previous example shows that the plots one obtains from the four required parameters are often too inaccurate. This inaccuracy is due either to a bad scale in y or to an overly large step used for the approximate solution; moreover, these plots contain a representation of the vector field of the differential equation which is often useless.

The following options may be used to control the plots returned by DEplot

stepsize=h   which specifies the step h used to increment the variable when solutions are evaluated numerically. The default value is (b-a)/20, what is often too coarse.

y=c..d   which specifies the scale of the vertical axis and restricts the plot to values of y in the interval $[c, d]$. If this option isn't present, MAPLE adapts the scale to plot the integral curves for x ranging from a to b. Note that y is mandatory here.

scene=[y,x]   which inverts the coordinates, i.e. to carry out an orthogonal symmetry of axes y=x first bisecting line. This is useful when one for example needs to solve an equation by expressing x in function of y.

arrows=NONE   which suppresses the plot of the vector field.

grid=[n,m]   which modifies the step of the grid used to plot the vector field. MAPLE uses a 20×20 grid by default.

linecolor=black which plots in black for printer output.

Example displaying the use of some options with the equation $y'(x) = y(x)$

Ex.44

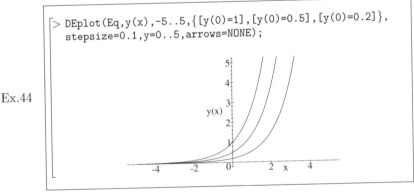

```
> DEplot(Eq,y(x),-5..5,{[y(0)=1],[y(0)=0.5],[y(0)=0.2]},
    stepsize=0.1,y=0..5,arrows=NONE);
```

One only obtains the vector field of the differential equation if no initial conditions are given. On the other hand, one must use the option y=c..d in this case, in order to specify the scale of the vertical axis.

Ex.45

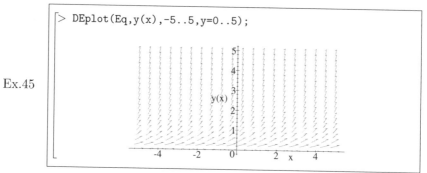

9.3.3 Differential Equation of Order n

Calling DEplot to plot integral curves of a differential equation of the form $y^{(n)} = f(x, y, y', \ldots, y^{(n-1)})$ requires four parameters which are, in order

- the equation, written
  `diff(y(x),x$n)=f(x,y(x),...diff(y(x),x$(n-1)))`,
- the function one seeks, in the form y(x),
- the range of the variable, written x=a..b or a..b,
- a set of initial conditions: each initial condition being a list of the form [y(a)=y0,D(y)(a)=y1,...]. The curves corresponding to these initial conditions will be plotted. Mind that one must put the initial condition between braces even if one wishes to plot a single curve.

Optional parameters are the same as in the previous case except those concerning the plot of the vector field, which is meaningless for an equation of order $n > 1$.

Example displaying the plot of a few curves of the pendulum equation $y = -\sin(y)$

Ex.46

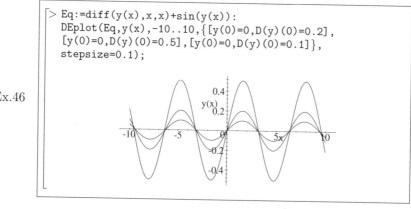

9.3.4 Necessity of the Option stepsize

In the case of a van der Pol oscillator, the plot one gets using DEplot without the option stepsize is far from accurate.

Ex.47

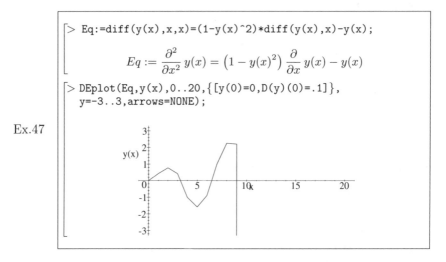

```
> Eq:=diff(y(x),x,x)=(1-y(x)^2)*diff(y(x),x)-y(x);
```

$$Eq := \frac{\partial^2}{\partial x^2} y(x) = \left(1 - y(x)^2\right) \frac{\partial}{\partial x} y(x) - y(x)$$

```
> DEplot(Eq,y(x),0..20,{[y(0)=0,D(y)(0)=.1]},
  y=-3..3,arrows=NONE);
```

On the other hand, with stepsize=0.1 a quite satisfactory plot is obtained.

Ex.48

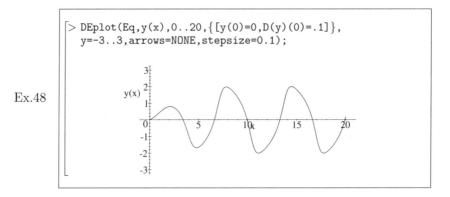

```
> DEplot(Eq,y(x),0..20,{[y(0)=0,D(y)(0)=.1]},
  y=-3..3,arrows=NONE,stepsize=0.1);
```

9.3.5 Differential System of Order 1

The function DEplot provides planar graphic representations of solutions of differential systems like

$$(S_1) \begin{cases} x' = f(t, x, y) \\ y' = g(t, x, y) \end{cases} \qquad (S_2) \begin{cases} x' = f(t, x, y, z) \\ y' = g(t, x, y, z) \\ z' = h(t, x, y, z) \end{cases}$$

In this context `DEplot` requires five parameters which are, in order

- the system of equations, written as a set.
- a set describing the unknown functions, of the form
  * $\{x(t),y(t)\}$ for (S_1).
  * $\{x(t),y(t),z(t)\}$ for (S_2).
- the range of the variable t, of the form `t=a..b` or `a..b`.
- a set of initial conditions, each condition a list of the form
  * $\{x(a)=x0,y(a)=y0\}$ for (S_1).
  * $\{x(a)=x0,y(a)=y0,z(a)=z0\}$ for (S_2).

Warning! One must to put the initial conditions between braces even if plotting a single curve.

- a relation `scene=...` specifying the curve to be plotted
  * In the case of the system (S_1), the relation `scene=` $[x,y]$ yields the curve $t \mapsto (x(t),y(t))$ while `scene=` $[t,x]$ gives the curve $t \mapsto (t,x(t))$
  * In the case of the system (S_2), the relation `scene=` $[x,z]$ yields the curve $t \mapsto (x(t),z(t))$ while `scene=` $[t,x]$ gives the curve $t \mapsto (t,x(t))$.

The function `DEplot` applied to a differential system uses most of the options described on page 156.

Ex.49

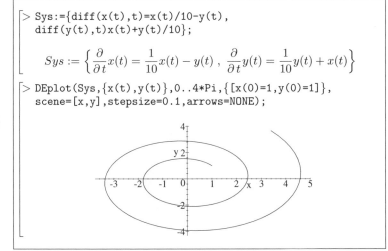

```
> Sys:={diff(x(t),t)=x(t)/10-y(t),
  diff(y(t),t)x(t)+y(t)/10};
```

$$Sys := \left\{\frac{\partial}{\partial t}x(t) = \frac{1}{10}x(t) - y(t) , \ \frac{\partial}{\partial t}y(t) = \frac{1}{10}y(t) + x(t)\right\}$$

```
> DEplot(Sys,{x(t),y(t)},0..4*Pi,{[x(0)=1,y(0)=1]},
  scene=[x,y],stepsize=0.1,arrows=NONE);
```

To obtain a 3D representation of solutions of one of the previous systems, the function `DEplot3D` must be used, which also belongs to the `DEtools` library and has the same syntax as `DEplot`. For the previous example, the curve $t \mapsto (t,y(t),z(t))$ can be plotted by

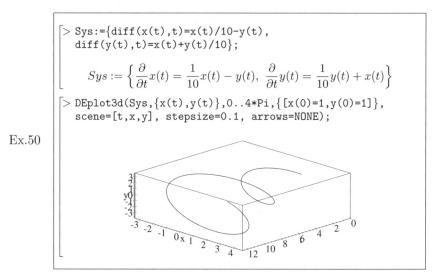

```
> Sys:={diff(x(t),t)=x(t)/10-y(t),
   diff(y(t),t)=x(t)+y(t)/10};
```

$$Sys := \left\{ \frac{\partial}{\partial t} x(t) = \frac{1}{10} x(t) - y(t), \; \frac{\partial}{\partial t} y(t) = \frac{1}{10} y(t) + x(t) \right\}$$

```
> DEplot3d(Sys,{x(t),y(t)},0..4*Pi,{[x(0)=1,y(0)=1]},
   scene=[t,x,y], stepsize=0.1, arrows=NONE);
```

Ex.50

Likewise, the Lorenz attractor is obtained with

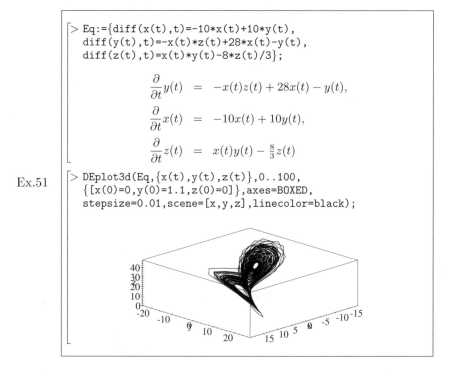

```
> Eq:={diff(x(t),t)=-10*x(t)+10*y(t),
   diff(y(t),t)=-x(t)*z(t)+28*x(t)-y(t),
   diff(z(t),t)=x(t)*y(t)-8*z(t)/3};
```

$$\frac{\partial}{\partial t} y(t) = -x(t)z(t) + 28x(t) - y(t),$$

$$\frac{\partial}{\partial t} x(t) = -10x(t) + 10y(t),$$

$$\frac{\partial}{\partial t} z(t) = x(t)y(t) - \tfrac{8}{3}z(t)$$

```
> DEplot3d(Eq,{x(t),y(t),z(t)},0..100,
   {[x(0)=0,y(0)=1.1,z(0)=0]},axes=BOXED,
   stepsize=0.01,scene=[x,y,z],linecolor=black);
```

Ex.51

9.3.6 Study of an Example

To finish this chapter, let us try to plot a few integral curves of the differential equation: $y'(x) = \frac{1}{y(x) - x^2}$ with DEplot.

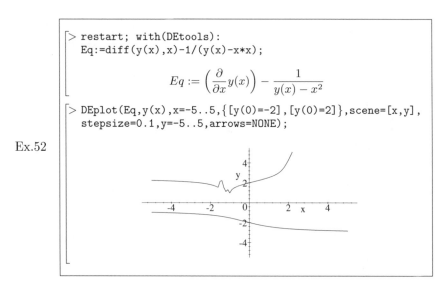

```
> restart; with(DEtools):
  Eq:=diff(y(x),x)-1/(y(x)-x*x);
```

$$Eq := \left(\frac{\partial}{\partial x}y(x)\right) - \frac{1}{y(x) - x^2}$$

```
> DEplot(Eq,y(x),x=-5..5,{[y(0)=-2],[y(0)=2]},scene=[x,y],
  stepsize=0.1,y=-5..5,arrows=NONE);
```

Ex.52

Since the upper graph of the previous plot seems to exhibit a singular behavior between -2 and 0, one might try using a finer step. However, this tends to make things even worse, as can be verified with `stepsize=0.03`.

The problem is due to the fact that the derivative of y tends towards infinity in the neighbourhood of the points of the parabola $y - x^2 = 0$, which doesn't allow the numerical method to proceed correctly. One can verify this by plotting this parabola on the same drawing as the previous solutions, with the help of the function `display` (p. 93). One then must first store the previous drawing in a variable G_1 and the drawing of the parabola in the variable P_xy.

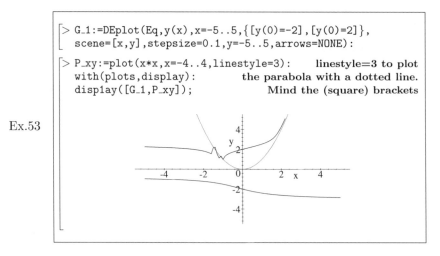

```
> G_1:=DEplot(Eq,y(x),x=-5..5,{[y(0)=-2],[y(0)=2]},
  scene=[x,y],stepsize=0.1,y=-5..5,arrows=NONE):
> P_xy:=plot(x*x,x=-4..4,linestyle=3):      linestyle=3 to plot
  with(plots,display):                      the parabola with a dotted line.
  display([G_1,P_xy]);                       Mind the (square) brackets
```

Ex.53

To obtain an accurate plot of the integral curves of the previous equation, one should look for solutions of the form $y \mapsto x(y)$, and thus solve the differential equation $x' \Pi(y) = y - x(y)^2$.

Ex.54

```
> Eq_inv:=diff(x(y),y)=y-x(y)^2;
```

$$Eq\_inv := \left(\frac{\partial}{\partial y} x(y) \right) = y - x(y)^2$$

Then `scene=[x,y]` yields a plot of a solution of the initial problem.

Ex.55

```
> G_2:=DEplot(Eq_inv,x(y),-5..5,{[x(-2)=0],[x(2)=0]},
    scene=[x,y],x=-4..4,stepsize=0.1,arrows=NONE):
> display([G_2,P_xy]);
```

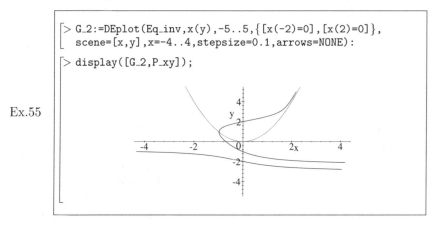

A few integral curves of the given equation can then be plotted.

Ex.56

```
> G_3:=DEplot(Eq_inv,x(y),-5..5,
    {[x(-2)=0],[x(2)=0],[x(3)=0],[x(4)=0]},
    x=-4..4,stepsize=0.1,scene=[x,y],arrows=NONE):
> display([G_3,P_xy]);
```

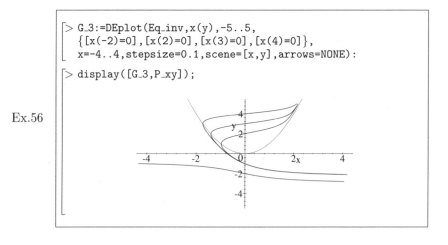

10. Integration and Summation

10.1 Integration

The function `int` gives the means to compute integrals or primitives.

10.1.1 Exact Computation of Definite and Indefinite Integrals

- If `p` is an expression in the free variable `x`,
  * `int(p,x=a..b)` returns an expression of $\int_a^b p\,dx$.
  * `int(p,x)` returns the anti-derivative of `p` with respect to `x`, without integration constants.
- If `f` is a function in one variable, one uses `int(f(x),x=a..b)` or `int(f(x),x)`.

Ex. 1

```
> restart; int(sin(x)^2,x=0..Pi/2);
```
$$\frac{1}{4}\pi$$
```
> p:=(2*x^2+x+3)*exp(x);
```
$$p := (2x^2 + x + 3)\,e^x$$
```
> int(p,x);
```
$$2\,e^x\,x^2 - 3\,e^x\,x + 6\,e^x$$

MAPLE doesn't use integration constants when it computes indefinite integrals.

Warning! If the integration variable `x` isn't free when `int` is called, MAPLE returns an error message which isn't very helpful for a beginner: *Error, (in int) wrong number (or type) of arguments*

Warning ! The identifier I represents `sqrt(-1)` for MAPLE and may therefore not be used to store an integral.

Ex. 2

```
> I:=int(sin(x),x=0..Pi/4);
  Error, Illegal use of an object as a name
```

MAPLE isn't limited to the "elementary functions" in expressing the integrals, it can also use Legendre functions, Bessel functions or any the many functions belonging to its library (see Chapter 25).

Ex. 3

```
> f:=1/sqrt((1-x^2)*(x^2+5));
```

$$f := \frac{1}{\sqrt{(1-x^2)\,(5+x^2)}}$$

```
> int(f,x=1/2..1);
```

$$\frac{1}{6}\,\sqrt{6}\,EllipticF\left(\frac{1}{2}\,\sqrt{3},\frac{1}{6}\,\sqrt{6}\right)$$

When an expression involves the Heaviside function or the "Dirac function", MAPLE computes its integral as a distribution.

Ex. 4

```
> int(exp(x)*Heaviside(x),x=-5..5);
```

$$e^5 - 1$$

```
> int(exp(x)*Dirac(x),x=-2..2);
```

$$1$$

MAPLE returns an unevaluated expression when it isn't able to return an explicit form of an integral; it is just written in a nicer way in Windows.

Ex. 5

```
> p:=1/sqrt(2*cos(x)^3+3*sin(x)^2);
```

$$p := \frac{1}{\sqrt{2\cos(x)^3 + 3\sin(x)^2}}$$

```
> Int_p:=int(p,x=0..Pi/2);
```

$$Int\_p := \int_0^{\pi/2} \frac{1}{\sqrt{2\cos(x)^3 + 3\sin(x)^2}}\,dx$$

10.1.2 Generalized Integrals

The function `int` computes generalized integrals over bounded or unbounded intervals.

Example of integral over a bounded interval

Ex. 6

```
> f:=1/sqrt((1-x)*(x+1));
```

$$f := \frac{1}{\sqrt{(1-x)(1+x)}}$$

```
> int(f,x=-1..1);
```

$$\pi$$

In the following example, MAPLE returns an expression using the B function; `convert(...,GAMMA)` yields an expression that uses the Γ function.

Ex. 7

```
> int(sin(x)/x,x=0..infinity);
```

$$\pi/2$$

```
> f:=1/(x^(1/3)*(1-x)^(1/3));
```

$$f := \frac{1}{x^{1/3}(1-x)^{1/3}}$$

```
> int(f,x=0..1);
```

$$B\left(\frac{2}{3}, \frac{2}{3}\right)$$

```
> convert(",GAMMA);
```

$$\frac{3}{2} \frac{\Gamma\left(\frac{2}{3}\right)^3 \sqrt{3}}{\pi}$$

As for definite integrals, the function `int` sometimes returns a result in an unevaluated form. As the two following examples show, the fact that MAPLE returns such a result doesn't say anything about the convergence of the integral.

Ex. 8

```
> int(sin(x)^2/(1+x^(3/2)),x=0..infinity);
```
convergent integral

$$\int_0^\infty \frac{\sin(x)^2}{1+x^{3/2}}\, dx$$

```
> int(sin(x)^2/(1+x^(1/2)),x=0..infinity);
```
divergent integral

$$\int_0^\infty \frac{\sin(x)^2}{1+\sqrt{x}}\, dx$$

When the integral diverges towards $+\infty$ (resp. towards $-\infty$), MAPLE returns $+\infty$ (resp. $-\infty$) or the integral in an unevaluated form. MAPLE returns the value $\mathtt{undefined}$ when it realizes that the integral diverges without tending towards $\pm\infty$.

Ex. 9

```
> int(1/x,x=0..1);
```
$$\infty$$

```
> int(abs(sin(x)/x),x=0..infinity);
```
$$\int_0^\infty \left| \frac{\sin(x)}{x} \right| dx$$

```
> int(x*sin(x),x=0..infinity);
```
$$undefined$$

10.1.3 Inert Form Int

One may request MAPLE to return an integral in an unevaluated form using $\mathtt{Int}$ (mind the upper case) instead of $\mathtt{int}$. The "function" $\mathtt{Int}$ is the inert form of $\mathtt{int}$: it isn't really a MAPLE function, but only a keyword that is recognized

- by the display program which returns a nice integral,
- by a few functions belonging to MAPLE's kernel, like the function $\mathtt{value}$ which transforms it into $\mathtt{int}$ and tries to compute the integral.

$\mathtt{Int}$ and $\mathtt{value}$ can be used together, as in the next examples, to express the equality between the initial integral and the result returned by MAPLE.

Ex.10

```
> Intg:=Int(sin(x)^2,x=0..Pi/2);
```
$$Intg := \int_0^{\pi/2} \sin(x)^2 \, dx$$

```
> Intg=value(Intg);
```
$$\int_0^{\pi/2} \sin(x)^2 \, dx = \frac{\pi}{4}$$

```
> Int(1/(x^(2/3)*(1-x)^(1/3)),x=0..1): "=value(");
```
$$\int_0^1 \frac{1}{x^{2/3}(1-x)^{1/3}} \, dx = \frac{2}{3}\pi\sqrt{3}$$

Int can also be used to write an integral one doesn't wish to compute immediately, but either one wishes to evaluate numerically (see below) or upon which one later wishes to carry out transformations: differentiation, integration by parts (p. 168), etc.

One may apply simplify, convert, ... to an integral which is in an unevaluated form, which amounts to applying the corresponding function to all elements appearing within the integral: both to the bounds and to the function to integrate.

Ex.11

```
> Intg:=Int(1/sqrt(2*cos(x)^2+3*sin(x)^2),x=0..Pi/2);
```

$$Intg := \int_0^{\pi/2} \frac{1}{\sqrt{2\cos(x)^2 + 3\sin(x)^2}}\, dx$$

```
> simplify(Intg);
```

$$\int_0^{\pi/2} \frac{1}{\sqrt{-\cos(x)^2 + 3}}\, dx$$

10.1.4 Numerical Evaluation of Integrals

The function evalf can be used to obtain the numerical evaluation of an integral which is in unevaluated form. All computations are carried out with n digits, where n is either the content of the environmental variable Digits or the optional second argument of evalf, when specified.

Ex.12

```
> p:=1/sqrt(2*cos(x)^3+3*sin(x)^2): int(p,x=0..Pi/2);
```

$$\int_0^{\pi/2} \frac{1}{\sqrt{2\cos(x)^3 + 3\sin(x)^2}}\, dx$$

```
> evalf(");
```

$$1.033315425$$

For a generalized convergent integral that has been returned in unevaluated form by MAPLE, a numerical evaluation can also be obtained using evalf.

Ex.13

```
> int(sin(x)^2/(1+x^(3/2)),x=0..infinity);
```

$$\int_0^\infty \frac{\sin(x)^2}{1 + x^{3/2}}\, dx$$

```
> evalf(",5);
```

$$1.1179$$

When `evalf` is applied to a divergent integral, MAPLE may return an error message simply pointing out that the function to be integrated has a pole in the interval *(Error, (in evalf/int) integrand has a pole in the interval)*, but it may also lead to a system crash, in which case the user will have to reinitialize the system.

It is faster to use the inert form `Int` for the numerical evaluation of a given integral (generalized or not). It defines an integral without requesting MAPLE to compute an exact expression of it. This saves the time to try, perhaps unsuccessfully, to compute a closed form.

Ex.14

```
> p:=1/sqrt(2*cos(x)^3+3*sin(x)^2): Intgr:=Int(p,x=0..Pi/2);
```

$$Intgr := \int_0^{\pi/2} \frac{1}{\sqrt{2\cos(x)^3 + 3\sin(x)^2}} dx$$

```
> evalf(Intgr);
```
$$1.033315425$$

```
> Digits:=20: evalf(Intgr);
```
$$1.0333154249774588724$$

10.2 Operations on Unevaluated Integrals

10.2.1 Integration by Parts

Although MAPLE can compute many integrals without any external help, one must sometimes compute substitutions of variables or integration by parts on unevaluated integrals. The functions for carrying out such transformations don't exist within MAPLE's kernel, but belong to an external library called `student`. To use them, they must first be loaded with the function `with`.

Ex.15

```
> restart; with(student):
```
Using : avoids the echo of the list of functions MAPLE loads

In the following example, the graph of the function $f : x \mapsto x \arctan\left(\sqrt{\frac{1-x}{1+x}}\right)$ seems to be incompatible with the result returned by `int(f(x),x=0..1)`; using `evalf` and the inert form `Int` together confirms our doubts.

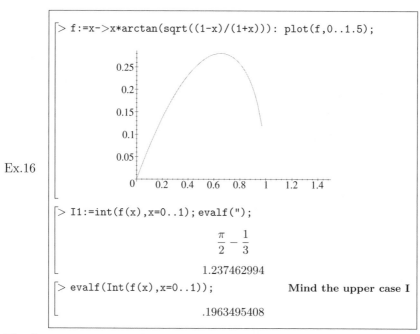

Ex.16

```
> I1:=int(f(x),x=0..1); evalf(");
```

$$\frac{\pi}{2} - \frac{1}{3}$$

$$1.237462994$$

```
> evalf(Int(f(x),x=0..1));                    Mind the upper case I
```

$$.1963495408$$

The function `intparts` from the `student` library may be used to compute the previous integral by parts, as one usually does by hand. If `Intgr` is an unevaluated integral of an expression `u*v`, then `intparts(Intgr,u)` carries out an integration by parts by deriving `u` and by integrating `v`. Even if the initial integral is defined with the help of `int`, the integral appearing in the result returned by `intparts` is an inert form that uses `Int`, hence the function `value` is needed in order to complete the evaluation of the integral.

```
> p:=arctan(sqrt((1-x)/(1+x))):
  I2:=intparts(Int(f(x),x=0..1),p);
```

$$I2 := -\int_0^1 \frac{1}{4} \frac{\left(-\frac{1}{1+x} - \frac{1-x}{(1+x)^2}\right) x^2}{\sqrt{\frac{1-x}{1+x}} \left(1 + \frac{1-x}{1+x}\right)} \, dx$$

```
> assume(x,RealRange(0,1));                    To specify x ∈ [0,1]
```

Ex.17
```
> I3:=combine(simplify(I2),radical);
```

$$I3 := \frac{1}{4} \int_0^1 \frac{x \sim^2 \sqrt{1 - x \sim^2}}{1 - x \sim^2} \, dx$$

```
> value(I3); evalf(");
```

$$\frac{\pi}{16}$$

$$.1963495409$$

Hence it is the last result of example 16 that is correct

10.2.2 Variable Substitution in an Integral

Variable Substitution of the Type $x = f(u)$

Let `Intgr` be an unevaluated integral in the form `Int(p,x=a..b)` or `Int(p,x)`. To make the variable substitution `x=f(u)`, one uses the function `changevar` with three arguments:

- the formula `x=f(u)` that defines the old integration variable as a function of the new one,
- the integral,
- the new integration variable.

It is thus written `changevar(x=f(u),Intgr,u)`.

Ex.18

```
> restart;with(student):
  Intgr:=Int(x^2/sqrt(1-x^2),x=0..1);
```

$$Intgr := \int_0^1 \frac{x^2}{\sqrt{1-x^2}}\, dx$$

```
> changevar(x=sin(u),Intgr,u);
```

$$\int_0^{\pi/2} \frac{\sin^2(u)\cos(u)}{\sqrt{1-\sin(u)^2}}\, du$$

To simplify the previous integral, use `simplify` with the option `symbolic` to indicate to MAPLE that the simplification $\cos(x) = \sqrt{\cos(x)^2}$ is allowed.

Ex.19

```
> simplify(",symbolic);
```

$$\int_0^{\frac{1}{2}\pi} 1 - \cos(u)^2\, du$$

```
> value(");
```

$$\frac{\pi}{4}$$

Variable Substitution of Type $g(x) = f(u)$

Let `Intgr` be an unevaluated integral of the form `Int(p,x=a..b)` or `Int(p,x)`. It isn't necessary to write `x` as a function of `u` to carry out a variable substitution upon `Intgr`, it is sufficient to give a relation of the type `g(x)=f(u)` as the first argument and to write `changevar(g(x)=f(u),Intgr,u)`.

Ex.20

```
> g:=sqrt((1-x)/(1+x));
```

$$g := \sqrt{\frac{1-x}{1+x}}.$$

```
> Intgr1:=Int(x*arctan(sqrt((1-x)/(1+x))),x);
```

$$Intgr1 := \int x \arctan\left(\sqrt{\frac{1-x}{1+x}}\right) dx$$

```
> Intgr2:=value(changevar(g=t,Intgr1,t));
```

$$Intgr2 \quad : \quad = 2\,\frac{\arctan(t)}{(1+t^2)^2} - 2\,\frac{\arctan(t)}{1+t^2} - \frac{1}{2}\,\frac{t}{(1+t^2)^2}$$
$$+ \frac{1}{4}\,\frac{t}{1+t^2} + \frac{1}{4}\,\arctan(t)$$

```
> F:=simplify(subs(t=g,Intgr2));
```
                                   To come back to the initial variable

$$-\frac{1}{4}\,\arctan\left(\sqrt{-\frac{-1+x}{1+x}}\right) + \frac{1}{2}\,\arctan\left(\sqrt{-\frac{-1+x}{1+x}}\right)\,x^2$$
$$-\frac{1}{8}\,\sqrt{-\frac{-1+x}{1+x}}\,x - \frac{1}{8}\,\sqrt{-\frac{-1+x}{1+x}}\,x^2$$

```
> eval(subs(x=1,F)-subs(x=0,F));
```
                                   To confirm the result of example 17

$$\frac{\pi}{16}$$

10.2.3 Differentiation Under the Integral Sign

The function `diff` can be used to apply the formula of "differentiation under the summation symbol" to an unevaluated integral. If p is an expression depending on t and x and if a and b are expressions that don't depend on x,

- `diff(int(p,x=a..b),t)` returns the value of `int(diff(p,t),x=a..b)`.
- `diff(Int(p,x=a..b),t)` returns the value of `Int(diff(p,t),x=a..b)`.

The function value must be used to evaluate this last quantity.

Differentiation under the integral sign is often used to compute the definite integral of a function that doesn't have a closed form anti-derivative.

This method can be used to compute, for $x > 0$, the quantity $\int_0^{\pi/2} \ln(x^2 \cos(t)^2 + \sin(t)^2)\, dt$ for which MAPLE returns a result that isn't very useful. To do this, one defines the integral using Int in order to carry out differentiation under the summation symbol afterwards.

Ex.21

```
> restart: F:=Int(ln(x^2*cos(t)^2+sin(t)^2),t=0..Pi/2);
```

$$F := \int_0^{\frac{1}{2}\pi} \ln\left(x^2 \cos(t)^2 + \sin(t)^2\right) \, dt$$

```
> F1:=diff(F,x);
```

$$F1 := \int_0^{\frac{1}{2}\pi} 2\, \frac{x \cos(t)^2}{x^2 \cos(t)^2 + \sin(t)^2} \, dt$$

`F1` cannot be computed with the help of `value` in Release 4. On the other hand, the classical variable substitution `u=tan(t)` can be used to compute the integral in such a case, which can be written

Ex.22

```
> with(student): F1:=changevar(tan(t)=u,F1,u);
```

$$F1 := \int_0^\infty 2\, \frac{x}{(1+u^2)^2 \left(\frac{x^2}{1+u^2} + \frac{u^2}{1+u^2}\right)} \, du$$

```
> F1:=value(F1);
```

$$F1 := -\frac{\pi\left(csgn\left(\overline{x}\right) - x\right)}{(x^2 - 1)}$$

The expression of the previous result reminds us that MAPLE assumes that all variables may take complex values. In our example, x represents a strictly positive real number, which we tell MAPLE with the help of `assume`.

Ex.23

```
> assume(x>0); F1:=simplify(F1);
```

$$F1 := \frac{\pi}{1 + x \sim}$$

Since it is obvious that F equals zero for x=1, F can be determined by integrating F1 between 1 and x.

Ex.24

```
> F=Int(subs(x=t,F1),t=1..x);
```

$$\int_0^{\pi/2} \ln\left(x \sim^2 \cos(t)^2 + \sin(t)^2\right) \, dt = \int_1^{x\sim} \frac{\pi}{t+1} \, dt$$

```
> F=value(rhs("));
```

$$\int_0^{\pi/2} \ln\left(x \sim^2 \cos(t)^2 + \sin(t)^2\right) \, dt = \ln(x \sim +1)\,\pi - \ln(2)\,\pi$$

The function `rhs` in the previous line allows us to apply `value` to the right hand side of the equality `F=Int(subs(x=t,F1),t=1..x)` only.

10.2.4 Truncated Series Expansion of an Indefinite Integral

One can obtain a truncated series expansion of an unevaluated indefinite integral by calling the function `series`. The truncated series expansion can then only be computed in the neighbourhood of 0. Any request for a truncated series expansion about another point will lead to an error message.

Ex.25

```
> restart; intgr:=int(exp(-x^3),x);
```
$$intgr := \int e^{-x^3}\, dx$$

```
> series(intgr,x=0,6);
```
$$x - \frac{1}{4}x^4 + O(x^7)$$

```
> series(intgr,x=1,6);
```
Error, (in series/int) invalid arguments

To obtain a truncated series expansion of an unevaluated indefinite integral about a point other than 0, express it as a definite integral function of its upper bound, and then use `series`.

Ex.26

```
> intgr:=int(exp(-x^3),x=0..t);
```
$$intgr := \int_0^t e^{-x^3}\, dx$$

```
> series(intgr,t=1,3);
```
$$\int_0^1 e^{-x^3}\, dx + e^{-1}(t-1) - \frac{3}{2}e^{-1}(t-1)^2 + O\left((t-1)^3\right)$$

The function `series` can be used to obtain a generalized series expansion of an unevaluated indefinite integral of a function f which is unbounded in the neighbourhood of 0, provided that the function f has an asymptotic series expansion about zero with only integer powers.

Ex.27

```
> intgr:=int(sin(1+t^3)/t,t); series(intgr,t);
```
$$intgr := \int \frac{\sin(1+t^3)}{t}\, dt$$

$$\sin(1)\ln(t) + \frac{1}{3}\cos(1)\, t^3 + O\left(t^6\right)$$

On the other hand, MAPLE returns an error message when the function f has a series expansion with fractional exponents.

Ex.28

```
> intgr:=int(exp(-sqrt(x^3)),x);
```

$$intgr := \int e^{-\sqrt{x^3}}\, dx$$

```
> series(intgr,x);
  Error, (in series/int) unable to compute series
```

In such a case, the result can be obtained by reversing the sequence of calls of the functions int and series.

Ex.29

```
> int(series(exp(-sqrt(x^3)),x),x);
```

$$x - \frac{2}{5}\, x^{5/2} + \frac{1}{8}\, x^4 - \frac{1}{33}\, x^{11/2} + O\left(x^7\right)$$

10.3 Discrete Summation

The function sum is the discrete analogue of int, it defines a finite sum or an indefinite sum of a quantity f(k) depending on a variable k.

10.3.1 Indefinite Sums

If f(k) is an expression in the free variable k, sum(f(k),k) returns an indefinite sum of f(k) i.e. an expression g(k) that satisfies g(k+1)-g(k)=f(k).

For polynomial expressions, MAPLE uses a method based on Bernoulli polynomials, and Moenck's method is used for rational functions.

Ex.30

```
> sum(k^3,k);
```

$$\frac{1}{4}\, k^4 - \frac{1}{2}\, k^3 + \frac{1}{4}\, k^2$$

```
> factor(");
```

$$\frac{1}{4}\, k^2 \left(k - 1\right)^2$$

MAPLE can also compute indefinite sums of some expressions involving factorials, as in the following example

Ex.31

```
> sum(k*k!,k);
```

$$k!$$

One way encounters less common functions, like Ψ, the *digamma* function, which is the logarithmic derivative of the Γ function (see Chapter 25).

Ex.32

```
> sum(1/k,k);
```
$$\Psi(k)$$

One should finally note that MAPLE can also give exact expressions for geometric sums as well as the classical sums of trigonometric functions.

Ex.33

```
> sum(cos((2*k+1)*a),k);
```
$$\frac{\sin(a\,k)\,\cos(a\,k)}{\sin(a)}$$

However, MAPLE doesn't seem to know how to compute analogous sums of hyperbolic sines or of hyperbolic cosines. One must convert them to exponential form, and then force the evaluation of the new quantity with the help of `eval`.

Ex.34

```
> sum(sinh((2*k+1)*a),k);
```
$$\sum_k \sinh((2k+1)\,a)$$

```
> S:=eval(convert(",exp));
```
$$S := \frac{1}{2}\,\frac{e^a\left(\left(e^{ak}\right)^4+1\right)}{\left(\left(e^a\right)^2-1\right)\left(e^{ak}\right)^2}$$

```
> S:=simplify(simplify(convert(S,trig)),
  {cosh(a)^2=sinh(a)^2+1});
```
$$\frac{1}{2}\,\frac{-1+2\,\cosh(a\,k)^2}{\sinh(a)}$$

If the summation variable isn't free when `sum` is called, MAPLE will indicate it

Ex.35

```
> k:=1; '.........': sum(k^3,k);
```
Error, (in sum) summation variable previously assigned, second argument evaluates to, 1

A common way to compute the previous sum without losing the contents of k is to use apostrophes in order to prevent MAPLE from fully evaluating the arguments passed to sum.

Ex.36

```
> sum('k^3','k');
```
$$\frac{1}{4} k^4 - \frac{1}{2} k^3 + \frac{1}{4} k^2$$

10.3.2 Finite Sums

Given two integers m and n and an expression f(k) in the free variable k, the expression sum(f(k),k=n..m) represents

- if $n \leq m$ $f(n) + f(n+1) + \ldots f(m-1) + f(m)$,
- if $n > m$ $- (f(m+1) + f(m+2) + \ldots f(n-2) + f(n-1))$.

In both cases, it is thus g(m+1)-g(n), where g(k) is an expression in k such that g(k+1)-g(k)=f(k), i.e. such that g(k)=sum(f(k),k).

Warning! One shouldn't believe that inverting the summation bounds corresponds to a simple change in the order of computation.

The sum sum(f(k),k=n..m) is computed arithmetically when abs(m-n) is a numerical value less than 1000, otherwise MAPLE uses the corresponding indefinite discrete sum, if it knows it.

Ex.37

```
> k:='k'; sum(1/k,k=1..30);
```
$$\frac{9304682830147}{2329089562800}$$

```
> sum(1/k,k=1..n);
```
$$\Psi(n+1) + \gamma$$

```
> sum(1/k,k=1..1000);
```
$$\Psi(1001) + \gamma$$

It may be that the expression resulting from sum(1/k,k=1..1000) is inconvenient if one needs the exact fractional expression, for example to handle an arithmetic problem. One may obtain such an expression by first constructing the list of numbers to sum using seq, and then converting it into an expression of type sum with convert. MAPLE's automatic simplifier does the rest.

```
[> S:=[seq(1/k,k=1..1000)]:  : to prevent the echo of the result
[> convert(S,'+');
```

Ex.38

$$53362913282294785045591045624042980409652472280384260097101349248456268889497101757506097901985035691409088731550468098378442172117885009464302344326566022502100278425632852081405544941210442142672770294774712708917963967779610453224692426664688888281582071984897105110796873249319155529301750893156451997608573447301418328401172441228064907430770373668317005580029365923508858936023528585280816075957473783665541317550813152251 / 712886527466509305316638415571427292066835886188589304045200199115432408758111149947644415191387158691171781701957525651298026406762100925146587100430513107268626814320019660997486274593718834370501543445252373974529896314567498212823695623282379401106880926231770886197954079124775455804932647573782992335275179673524804246363805113703433121478174685087845348567802188807537324992199567205693202909939089168748767269795093160352000$$

```
[> isprime(numer(")");
```
$$false$$

11. Three-Dimensional Graphics

11.1 Surfaces Defined by an Equation $z = f(x, y)$

In this part, we study surfaces defined by an equation $z = f(x, y)$. In MAPLE, such a surface can be defined either by an expression depending on the variables x and y or by a function in two variables.

11.1.1 Plot of a Surface Defined by an Expression

If p is an expression in the free variables x and y, and if a, b, c and d are four numerical values such that a<b and c<d, then plot3d(p,x=a..b,y=c..d) plots the surface S defined by

$$S = \{(x, y, p) \mid a \leq x \leq b \text{ and } c \leq y \leq d\}$$

Since the function plot3d doesn't plot any axes by default, using axes=frame or axes=boxed as an option, which displays the axes, is recommended. This way plots are produced are more easily understood.

Ex. 1

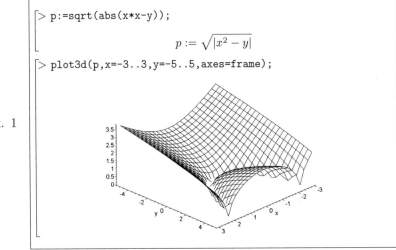

By default, the plot is included in the worksheet and its size can be adjusted with the help of the mouse. However, if the option **Plot Display→Window** in the **Options** menu has been selected before the execution of `plot`, the plot is displayed alone in another window, where it can be printed without the other computations.

As the previous example shows, MAPLE automatically adjusts the scale of z in order to represent all the points of the surface S, the plot is then displayed "full page". To restrict the range of z to [z1,z2], either to zoom in on a subset of the surface or because the suface "goes to infinity", use the option `view=z1..z2`.

Example of zooming in on a subset of the previous surface.

Ex. 2

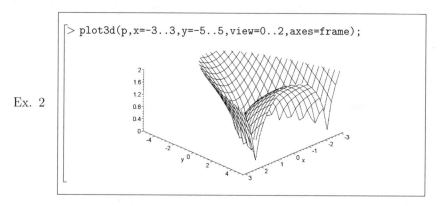

Example in which the use of `view` is essential since the surface is defined by an expression that has an infinite limit at a point in the domain.

Ex. 3

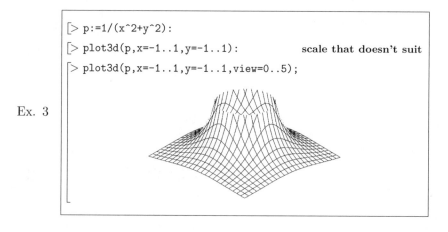

Warning! If either of the variables x or y isn't free when MAPLE evaluates plot3d(p,x=a..b,y=c..d), it returns the following error message:

Ex. 4

```
> x:=t^2+1: plot3d(p,x=-1..1,y=-1..1);
  Error, (in plot3d/expression) bad range arguments,
  t^2+1=-1..1, y=-1..1
```

Warning!

- If one forgets the identifiers x and y appearing as second and third parameters, MAPLE returns a message saying that the plot is empty without further explanation.
- If only one of the identifier x and y is forgotten, MAPLE returns an error message saying that the arguments are not suitable.

Ex. 5

```
> plot3d(1/(x^2+y^2),-1..1,-1..1);
  Plotting error, empty plot
> plot3d(1/(x^2+y^2),x=-1..1,-1..1);
  Error, (in plot3d/expression) bad range arguments,
  x=-1..1,-1..1
```

11.1.2 Plot of a Surface Defined by a Function

If f is a function in two variables (or a procedure) and if a, b, c and d are four real numbers such that a<b and b<d, then plot3d(f(x,y),x=a..b,y=c..d) or plot3d(f,a..b,c..d) plots the surface defined by $z = f(x, y)$, for x ranging from a to b and y ranging from c to d. The range of z can be restricted to the interval $[z1, z2]$ by using the option view=z1..z2.

Ex. 6

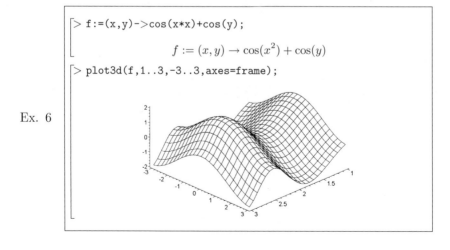

```
> f:=(x,y)->cos(x*x)+cos(y);
```
$$f := (x, y) \rightarrow \cos(x^2) + \cos(y)$$
```
> plot3d(f,1..3,-3..3,axes=frame);
```

11.1.3 Simultaneous Plot of Several Surfaces

If p and q are two expressions in the free variables x and y, and if a, b, c and d are numerical values such that a<b and b<d, then the evaluation of plot3d({p,q},x=a..b,y=c..d) plots the surfaces S_1 and S_2 defined by

$$S_1 = \{(x,y,p) \mid a \leq x \leq b \text{ and } c \leq y \leq d\}$$
$$S_2 = \{(x,y,q) \mid a \leq x \leq b \text{ and } c \leq y \leq d\}$$

Warning! Do not forget the braces around p and q, and do not replace them with square brackets, which have a totally different meaning as explained in Section 11.3, p. 189.

Example showing the simultaneous plot of a cone and of the classical Plücker's conoid.

Ex. 7

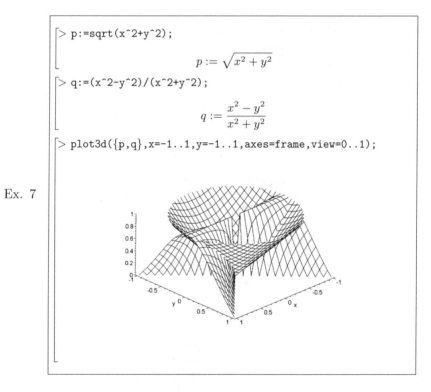

11.2 The Environment of `plot3d`

By default, a plot is included in the worksheet. However, if the option **Plot Display**→**Window** of the **Options** menu has been selected before the execution of `plot`, the plot is displayed alone in an external window. Several options which can be accessed through menus, most of them described below, can be used to modify the appearance of the plot; they can be directly accessed when the plot is displayed in an external window. If the drawing is included in the worksheet, one must click onto the plot to access them.

11.2.1 The Menu of `plot3d` in Windows

In graphic mode, there is a menu bar, a tool bar and a context bar that contain, among other things, the button $\boxed{R}$, which replots the surface after any style modification.

The Menu Bar

In graphic mode, the most useful options of the menu bar are:

File   same functions as in Section 5.2, p. 75.

Edit   to copy the plot into the clipboard (*copy*) in order to transfer it to another Windows compatible application.

View   to validate or suppress the display of the tool bar (*Toolbar*) or of the status bar (*Statusbar*).

Style   to choose among the following plot styles:

Patch colored surface and grid obtained by joining the computed points.

Patch w/o grid colored surface, without grid.

Patch and contour colored surface, plot of the level curves in z.

Hidden line grid obtained by joining the computed points, hidden lines not plotted.

Contour plot of the level lines in z.

Wireframe grid obtained by joining the computed points, hidden lines included.

Point plot of the computed points only.

Style   to choose the **Symbol** being used when the surface is plotted with points, which can be: **Cross, Diamond, Point, Circle**, ...

to choose the **Line Style** being used to represent the curves, which can be: continuous (**Solid**), dashes (**Dash**), ...

to choose the **Grid Style**, either quadrilaterals (**Grid Half**) or quadrilaterals with a diagonal (**Grid Full**).

to choose the **line width**, which can be **thin, medium, thick** or the **default** width.

Color   to choose, in **Patch** style, the distribution mode of the colors

XYZ colors varying in function of **X, Y** and **Z**.

XY colors varying in function of **X** and **Y**.

Z colors varying in function of **Z** alone.

Z(Hue) as the previous one, but with stronger variations.

Z(Greyscale) grey tinted surface with shades varying in function of **Z**.

NoColoring white surface.

to choose a lighting of the surface or not and to specify its origin, it can be **No Lighting, light scheme1, light scheme2**, ...

Axes   to choose the kind and the position of the axes.

Boxed axes forming a parallelepiped around the surface.

Framed axes plotted at the edges of the reference parallelepiped.

Normal axes through, in general, the origin.

None no axes plotted.

Projection   to choose the type of perspective used: **No Perspective, Near Perspective, Medium Perspective** or **Far Perspective**.

to choose among an orthonormal frame (**Constrained**) or a plot using the window best (**Unconstrained**).

The Tool Bar and the Context Bar

The icons of the tool bar and the context bar allow one, by clicking upon them with the mouse's left button, to directly activate some options of the previous menu. Every icon is suggestive enough and a message describing its use can be displayed in the status bar by clicking upon the mouse's left button while the cursor stands above this icon. The choice will only be activated if the mouse's button let up inside the icon.

Orientation of the Reference Parallelepiped

When one clicks on the plot window with the mouse, the plotted surface disappears and is replaced by a "parallelepiped" whose sides are parallel to the axes while the values of θ and φ, which determine the angle from which the surface is viewed, are displayed on the left side of the context bar.

The orientation of the reference parallelepiped can then be manually modified, which means modifying the position of the observer, by sliding the mouse's pointer while the mouse's left button is depressed. During this process, the values of θ and φ, which determine the position of the observer, are continuously displayed in the context bar. Once an orientation has been chosen, one has only to depress the $\boxed{\text{ENTER}}$ key or to click upon the icon $\boxed{\text{R}}$ to obtain the new plot.

Note: The values of θ and φ can also be directly modified either by entering numerical values (in degrees) or by using the variation arrows.

11.2.2 The Options of `plot3d`

Some options can be added when calling `plot3d` which can be used to specify a presentation style or to refine the plot. Several options may be used, separated with commas. As for the function `plot`, these options have to be put after the three first parameters, which are the expression or the function and the intervals in x and in y.

Presentation Options Corresponding to Some Menu Options

Some options of `plot3d` can be used to directly obtain some options of the previous menu.

style   used in the form `style=hidden`, `style=contour`, `style=patch`, `style=patchnogrid`, `style=patchcontour`, `style=wireframe` or
`style=point`, according to the plot style one wishes. The default style is `hidden`.

thickness   used in the form `thickness=n` where n equals 0, 1, 2 or 3, according to the line width one wishes.

axes   used in the form `axes=boxed`, `axes=framed`, `axes=normal`, or `axes=none` according to the kind of axes one wishes.

scaling   `scaling=constrained` or `scaling=unconstrained` which chooses between a representation with orthonormal axes and a representation that uses the window best.

shading   used in the form `shading=s`, where s is equal to `xyz`, `xy`, `z`, `zhue`, `zgreyscale`, `none`, according to the distribution of shades one wishes.

Comparison between the different plot styles for the surface of Example 6, p. 181

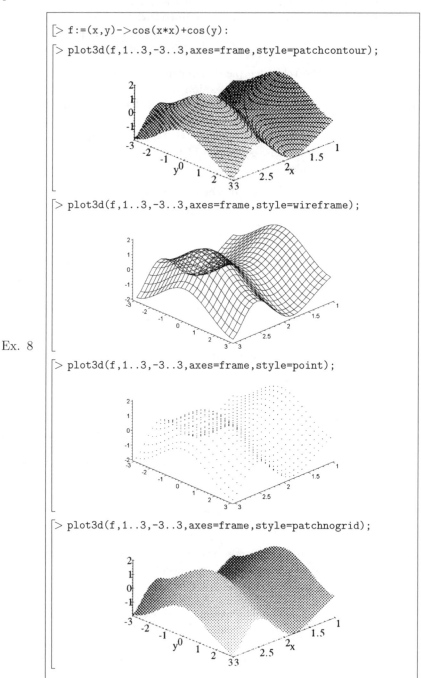

Ex. 8

Presentation Options Not Corresponding to a Menu Option

tickmarks   tickmarks=[l,m,n] is used to display about l values on the x axis, m values on the Oy axis and n values on the Oz axis.

orientation   orientation=[m,n] is used to choose the values in degrees of *theta* (longitude) and of *phi* (latitude) which determine the angle from which the surface is viewed. By default we have *theta* = *phi* = 45°.

view   view=z1..z2 is used to restrict the values of z to $[z1, z2]$. view=[x1..x2,y1..y2,z1..z2] is used to restrict the values of the three coordinates.

labels   labels=[x,y,z] is used to label the axes.

title   title='surface name' is used to display a title.

Examples of plots of the same surface viewed from different view points.

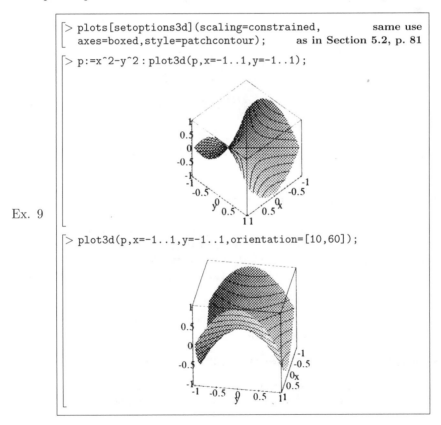

Ex. 9

The previous surface viewed from other angles

Ex.10

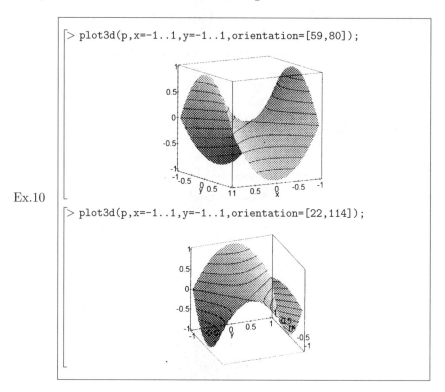

```
> plot3d(p,x=-1..1,y=-1..1,orientation=[59,80]);
```

```
> plot3d(p,x=-1..1,y=-1..1,orientation=[22,114]);
```

The Options numpoints and grid

When evaluating plot3d(p,x=a..b,y=c..d), MAPLE computes p for a set of values (x, y) forming a grid of points in the rectangle $[a, b] \times [c, d]$ whose abscissas and ordinates are regularly spaced. By default, this grid is square and contains $25^2 = 625$ points. The two following options can be used to refine this grid.

grid   with grid=[m,n], the grid contains m points along the axis of abscissas and n points along the axis of ordinates.

numpoints   with numpoints=n, MAPLE uses a grid of about $\sqrt{n} \times \sqrt{n}$.

Warning ! Even more than for the function plot, these options should be managed according to the capabilities of the system and the time at one's disposal.

11.3 Surface Patches Parametrized in Cartesian Coordinates

This section concerns parametrized surface patches, i.e. surfaces comprised of points whose coordinates, (x, y, z), depend on two parameters. Such a parametric representation can be defined either by expressions depending on two variables or by functions or procedures of two variables.

Given four numerical values, a, b, c, d, such that a<b and c<d

- If p, q and r are expressions in the two free variables u and v, then plot3d([p,q,r],u=a..b,v=c..d) plots the surface S which is defined parametrically by

$$S = \{(p, q, r) \mid a \leq u \leq b \text{ and } c \leq v \leq d\}$$

- If f, g and h are functions (or procedures) of two variables, then the evaluation of plot3d([f(u,v),g(u,v),h(u,v)],u=a..b,v=c..d) or of plot3d([f,g,h],a..b,c..d) plots the surface S which is defined parametrically by

$$S = \{(f(u, v), g(u, v), h(u, v)) \mid a \leq u \leq b \text{ and } c \leq v \leq d\}$$

The plot of parametrized surface patches uses the environment of plot3d described in part II, for the menu as well as for options.

Example of parametrized surface patch whose coordinates are given in the form of expressions:

Ex.11

```
> p:=u*cos(v)-u*sin(v)+u;q:=u*cos(v)+u*sin(v)-u;
  r:=u*sin(v)+u;
```

$$p := u \cos(v) - u \sin(v) + u$$

$$q := u \cos(v) + u \sin(v) - u$$

$$r := u \sin(v) + u$$

```
> plot3d([p,q,r], u=0..2*Pi, v=0..2*Pi,axes=framed,
  style=hidden);
```

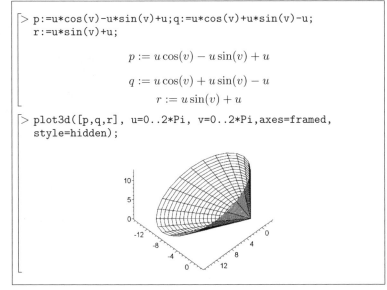

Example of parametrized surface patch whose coordinates are given in the form of functions:

Ex.12

```
> f:=(u,v)->2*u*cos(v); g:=(u,v)->2*u*sin(v);
  h:=(u,v)->2*cos(2*v);
```

$$f := (u, v) \rightarrow 2\, u \cos(v)$$

$$g := (u, v) \rightarrow 2\, u \sin(v)$$

$$h := (u, v) \rightarrow 2\, \cos(2v)$$

```
> plot3d([f,g,h],0..1,0..2*Pi,
  grid=[35,35],scaling=constrained);
```

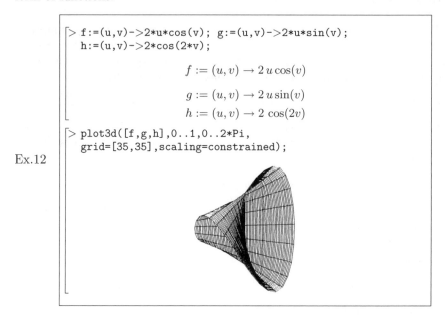

11.4 Surfaces Patches Parametrized
in Cylindrical Coordinates

The function plot3d with the option coords=cylindrical can be used to represent a surface which is defined in cylindrical coordinates.

- Given an expression p depending on the two free variables theta and z, and the numerical values a, b, c, d such that a<b and c<d, the evaluation of plot3d(p,theta=a..b,z=c..d,coords=cylindrical) plots the surface which is defined in cylindrical coordinates by $r = p$ for θ ranging from a to b and z ranging from c to d, i.e. the surface which is defined parametrically by

$$S = \{(p\cos\theta, p\sin\theta, z) \mid a \le \theta \le b,\ c \le z \le d\}.$$

- Given expressions p, alpha, q depending on the free variables u and v, and the numerical values a, b, c, d such that a<b and c<d, plot3d([p,alpha,q], u=a..b,v=c..d,coords=cylindrical) plots the surface which is defined in cylindrical coordinates by $r = p$, $\theta = \alpha$ and $z = q$, for u ranging from a to b and v ranging from c to d, i.e. the surface which is defined parametrically by

$$S = \{(p\cos\alpha,\, p\sin\alpha,\, q) \mid a \le u \le b,\ c \le v \le d\}.$$

Warning! The option `coords=cylindrical` doesn't force the function `plot3d` to use an orthonormal frame. One must to specify `scaling=constrained` to obtain the plot with orthonormal axes.

Ex.13

```
> restart; p:=z+cos(theta);
```

$$p := z + \cos(\theta)$$

```
> plot3d(p,theta=0..2*Pi,z=0.1..0.9,coords=cylindrical,
  grid=[35,35],scaling=constrained,orientation=[44,72]);
```

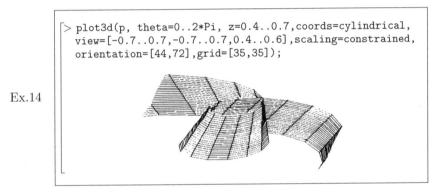

Plot of a part of the previous surface by using the option `view`:

Ex.14

```
> plot3d(p, theta=0..2*Pi, z=0.4..0.7,coords=cylindrical,
  view=[-0.7..0.7,-0.7..0.7,0.4..0.6],scaling=constrained,
  orientation=[44,72],grid=[35,35]);
```

And to finish up, the classical Möbius strip:

Ex.15

```
> r:=2-v*sin(Pi/4+theta/2): z:=v*cos(theta/2):
> plot3d([r,theta,z],theta=0..2*Pi,v=-1..1,
  coords=cylindrical,orientation=[120,67],
  grid=[150,5],scaling=constrained);
```

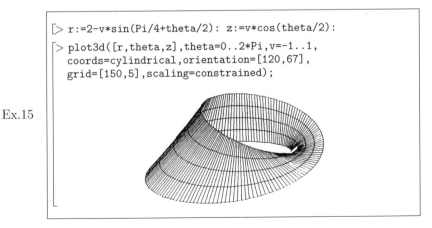

11.5 Surface Patches Parametrized in Spherical Coordinates

The function `plot3d` with the option `coords=spherical` can be used to represent a surface which is defined in spherical coordinates.

- Given an expression p depending on two free variables `theta` and `phi` and numerical values a, b, c and d such that a<b and c<d, the evaluation of `plot3d(p,theta=a..b,phi=c..d,coords=spherical)` plots the surface which is defined in spherical coordinates by $r = p$ for θ ranging from a to b and φ ranging from c to d, i.e. the surface which is defined parametrically by

$$S = \{(p \cos\theta \sin\varphi, p \sin\theta \sin\varphi, p \cos\varphi) \mid a \leq \theta \leq b \text{ and } c \leq \varphi \leq d\}.$$

- Given expressions p, `alpha` and `beta` depending on the free variables u and v and numerical values a, b, c and d such that a<b and c<d, `plot3d([p,alpha,beta],u=a..b,v=c..d,coords=spherical)` plots the surface which is defined in spherical coordinates by $r = p$, $\theta = \alpha$ and $\varphi = \beta$, for u ranging from a to b and v ranging from c to d, i.e. the surface which is defined parametrically by

$$S = \{(p \cos\alpha \sin\beta, p \sin\alpha \sin\beta, p \cos\beta) \mid a \leq u \leq b \text{ and } c \leq v \leq d\}.$$

Warning ! The option `coords=spherical` doesn't force the function `plot3d` to use an orthonormal frame. One must specify `scaling=constrained` to obtain the plot with orthonormal axes.

```
> plot3d(cos(theta)*cos(phi),theta=0..2*Pi,phi=0..Pi,
  grid=[50,50],coords=spherical,orientation=[54,67],
  style=patchcontour,view=[-0.3..0.3,-0.5..0.5,-0.3..0.3],
  scaling=constrained);
```

Ex.16

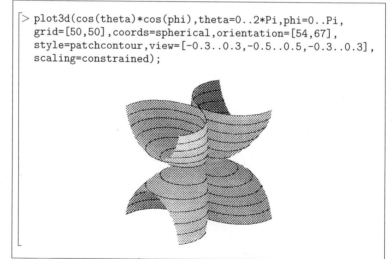

11.6 Parametrized Space Curves

The function `spacecurve` is used to represent a parametrized space curve. It doesn't belong to the standard library and has therefore to be loaded with

Ex.17
```
> with(plots,spacecurve):          To load only the spacecurve
function
                                   of the plots library
```

11.6.1 Plot of a Parametrized Curve

Given two numerical values `a` and `b` such that `a<b`,

- if `p`, `q` and `r` are expressions in a free variable `u` then the evaluation of `spacecurve([p,q,r,u=a..b])` plots the curve which is defined parametrically by $x = p$, $y = q$ and $z = r$ for u ranging from a to b.
- if `f`, `g` and `h` are functions in one variable, `spacecurve([f,g,h,a..b])` or `spacecurve([f(u),g(u),h(u),u=a..b])` plots the curve which is defined parametrically by $x = f(u)$, $y = g(u)$ and $z = h(u)$ for u ranging from a to b.

The option `numpoints` can be used to increase the number of points MAPLE uses to plot the curve (by default `numpoints=50`). Except for the option `grid`, all options already described for the function `plot3d` can be used with `spacecurve`.

Ex.18
```
> with(plots,spacecurve):     To load the spacecurve function
> p:=(t^2+3)*sin(15*t): q:=(t^2+3)*cos(15*t): r:=t:
  spacecurve([p,q,r,t=-3..3],numpoints=800,
  orientation=[51,70]);
```

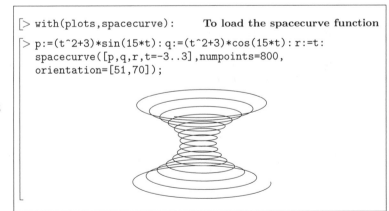

11.6.2 Simultaneous Plot of Several Parametrized Curves

Given real numbers a1, b1, a2 and b2 such that a1<b1 and a2<b2 and expressions p1, p2, q1, q2, r1 and r2 in the free variable u, the evaluation of spacecurve({[p1,q1,r1,u=a1..b1],[p2,q2,r2,u=a2..b2]}) plots the curve defined by $x = p1$, $y = q1$ and $z = r1$ for u ranging from $a1$ to $b1$ as well as the curve defined by $x = p2$, $y = q2$ and $z = r2$ for u ranging from $a2$ to $b2$.

This syntax can be generalized to any number of curves. Three curves are used in the following example.

Ex.19

```
> f:=sin(40*t^(4/3)):
  g:=(3+cos(40*t^(4/3)))*cos(t):
  h:=(3+cos(40*t^(4/3)))*sin(t):

> spacecurve({[f,g,h,t=0..Pi],
  [sin(t),3+cos(t),0,t=0..2*Pi],
  [sin(t),-3+cos(t),0,t=0..2*Pi]},scaling=constrained,
  orientation=[32,69],numpoints=800,shading=none);
```

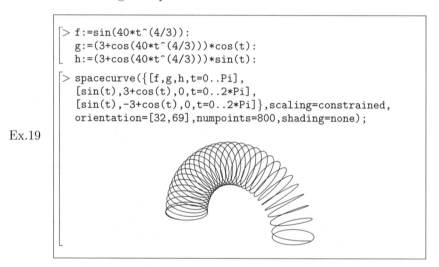

11.7 Surfaces Defined Implicitly

The function implicitplot3d plots a surface which is defined implicitly. It doesn't belong to the standard library and must therefore be loaded with

Ex.20

```
> restart; with(plots,implicitplot3d):
```

If x1, x2, y1, y2, z1 and z2 are six real numbers such that x1<x2, y1<y2, z1<z2 and if p is an expression in the three free variables x, y and z, then implicitplot3d(p,x=x1..x2,y=y1..y2,z=z1..z2) plots the part of the surface defined by the equation $p = 0$ that is contained in $[x1, x2] \times [y1, y2] \times [z1, z2]$.

The equation p=0 and more generally the equation p=q can be used as first argument of implicitplot3d. All options already described for the function plot3d (p. 185) can be used for the function implicitplot3d.

```
> implicitplot3d(x^2+y^2-z^2-1,x=-2..2,y=-2..2,z=-2..2,
  style=patchcontour,shading=zhue);
```

Ex.21

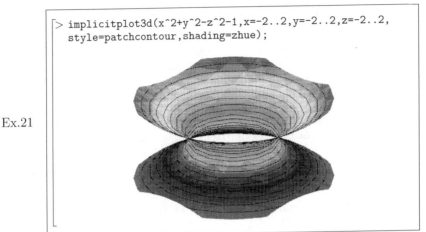

The implicit equation of the surface to be plotted can also be given by a function. Given six real numbers x1, x2, y1, y2, z1, z2 such that x1<x2, y1<y2, z1<z2 and a function f in three variables, the evaluation of implicitplot3d(f,x1..x2,y1..y2,z1..z2) plots the part of the surface defined by the equation $f(x, y, z) = 0$ that is contained in the volume $[x1, x2] \times [y1, y2] \times [z1, z2]$.

The previous example could have been written

Ex.22

```
> f:=(x,y,z)->x^2+y^2-z^2-1;
> implicitplot3d(f,-2..2,-2..2,-2..2, style=patchcontour,
  shading=zhue);
```

As for implicit plane curves, grid can be used to improve the quality of plots of implicitly defined surfaces. The option grid=[m,n,p] defines a grid that has m points along Ox, n points along Oy and p points along Oz (grid=[10,10,10] by default). As for the 2D case, this option should be used with moderation!

```
> implicitplot3d(x^7+3*x^2*y^3+3*y^2*z^2+z^3,
  x=-0.5..0.5,y=-0.5..0.5,z=-0.5..0.5,grid=[20,20,20],
  orientation=[-72,49],style=patchcontour,shading=zhue);
```

Ex.23

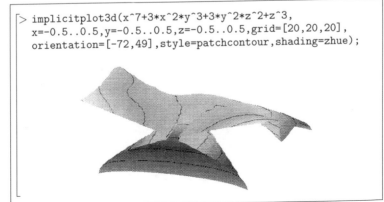

11.8 Mixing Plots from Different Origins

As for the 2D case, the function display can be used to represent surfaces or curves created in different ways in the same picture: parametrized surface patches, surfaces defined implicitly ... The function display doesn't belong to the standard library and must therefore be loaded before its first use.

Before using the function display one must, as in the planar case, start by storing the different objects (surfaces, curves) in variables. The function display can then be called with the list of variables to be plotted as its first argument. The function display can be used with the options described on p. 185.

To use display with a sphere and a torus, we start by storing these surfaces into the variables S and T:

Ex.24

```
> f:=sin(u): g:=(3+cos(u))*cos(v)-3: h:=(3+cos(u))*sin(v):
> S:=plot3d(1.75,u=0..2*Pi,v=0..Pi,grid=[15,20],
  coords=spherical,scaling=constrained):
> T:=plot3d([f,g,h],u=0..2*Pi,v=0..2*Pi,grid=[15,25],
  scaling=constrained):
```

To verify the contents of S and T, we write:

Ex.25

```
> T; S;
```
The evaluation of T and S returns the plots

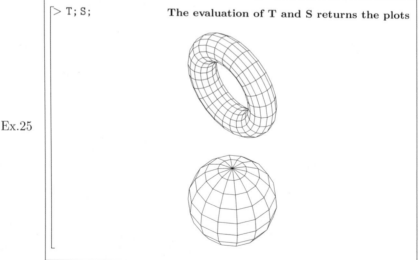

With the option `style=hidden`, the function `display` returns the union of
the surfaces without hidden parts

Ex.26

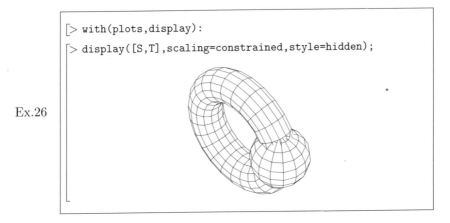

We see the union of the two structures with the style `wireframe`

Ex.27

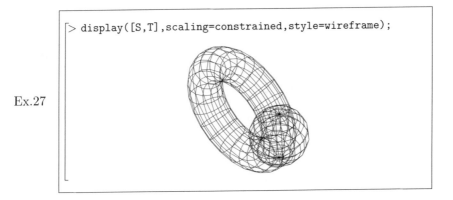

12. Polynomials with Rational Coefficients

12.1 Writing Polynomials

Polynomials in one or several variables have a specific type in MAPLE, the type `polynom`. However, introducing such objects doesn't require any specific declaration. The user simply enters the polynomials with the help of the usual arithmetic operators `+`, `-`, `*` and `^`.

12.1.1 Reminders: `collect`, `sort`, `expand`

The usual arithmetic operators can be applied to the polynomials: sum, difference, product and raising to an integer power. The results one obtains can be expanded using the function `expand`, terms with the same power can be grouped together using the function `collect` and the polynomial's terms can be sorted by decreasing powers of a given variable using the function `sort` (for more details about these functions see p. 23).

Ex. 1

```
> f:=2*x+1; g:=x^2+x+1; h:=x^2+1;
```
$$f := 2x + 1$$
$$g := x^2 + x + 1$$
$$h := x^2 + 1$$

```
> k:=f*g+h^2;
```
$$k := (2x + 1)(x^2 + x + 1) + (x^2 + 1)^2$$

```
> k:=expand(k);
```
$$k := 2x^3 + 5x^2 + 3x + 2 + x^4$$

```
> sort(k,x);
```
$$x^4 + 2x^3 + 5x^2 + 3x + 2$$

For a polynomial in several variables, **expand** groups identical monomials but
collect must be used to group together terms of the same power in a given
indeterminate.

Ex. 2

```
> f:=(x+y)^2+y*x^2+y*x;
```
$$f := (x + y)^2 + y x^2 + y x$$
```
> g:=expand(f);
```
$$g := x^2 + 3 y x + y^2 + y x^2$$
```
> collect(g,x);
```
$$(1 + y) x^2 + 3 y x + y^2$$

However, MAPLE starts by expanding the expression when the function
collect is called. It is therefore redundant to call **expand** beforehand.

Ex. 3

```
> collect(f,x); collect(f,y);
```
$$(1 + y) x^2 + 3 y x + y^2$$
$$y^2 + (3 x + x^2) y + x^2$$

One must call **collect** with **factor** as a third argument to obtain the coefficients of the polynomial in factorized form. The reader may refer to page 34
where the other options of the function **collect** are also described.

Ex. 4

```
> collect(f,y,factor);
```
$$y^2 + x (x + 3) y + x^2$$

Even for a polynomial in a single variable, the name of this variable must be
given as the second argument of **collect**.

Ex. 5

```
> f:=x^2+(x+1)^2;
```
$$f := x^2 + (x + 1)^2$$
```
> collect(f);
```
Error, (in collect) collect uses a 2nd argument, x, which is missing

When the polynomial has several variables, terms of the same power with
respect to a subset of the variables can be grouped together by using the
function **collect** with the list (between square brackets) of these variables
as second parameter. This grouping is carried out recursively according to
the powers of the variables of this list.

Ex. 6

```
> f:=(x*y+1)^2+(y+1)^2*x;
```
$$f := (x\,y + 1)^2 + (1 + y)^2\,x$$
```
> collect(f,x); collect(f,y);
```
$$x^2\,y^2 + \left(2\,y + (1 + y)^2\right)x + 1$$
$$\left(x^2 + x\right)y^2 + 4\,x\,y + 1 + x$$
```
> collect(f,[x,y]);
```
$$x^2\,y^2 + (y^2 + 4\,y + 1)\,x + 1$$

12.1.2 Indeterminates of a Polynomial

If f is a polynomial, indets(f) returns the set of indeterminates in f.

Ex. 7

```
> f:=x*y+z;
```
$$f := x\,y + z$$
```
> indets(f);
```
$$\{\,x\,,\,y\,,\,z\,\}$$

This function operates on any expression, polynomial or otherwise, to determine the set of terms from which the expression is built up.

Ex. 8

```
> f:=exp(x*x)+x^(1/2);
```
$$f := e^{\left(x^2\right)} + \sqrt{x}$$
```
> indets(f);
```
$$\left\{\,x\,,\,\sqrt{x}\,,\,e^{\left(x^2\right)}\,\right\}$$
```
> g:=x^2-exp(a)^2; indets(g);
```
$$g := x^2 - (e^a)^2$$
$$\{\,x\,,\,e^a\,,\,a\,\}$$
```
> h:=x^2-exp(2*a); indets(h);
```
$$h := x^2 - e^{2a}$$
$$\left\{\,x\,,\,e^{(2a)}\,,\,a\,\right\}$$

12.1.3 Value of a Polynomial at a Point

The easiest way to compute the value of a polynomial expression at a point is to use the function `subs` (Chapter 22, p. 373). The evaluation of `subs(x=a,f)` returns the expression obtained by replacing the variable x by the value a in the polynomial f.

Ex. 9

```
> f:=(x+1)^4-x*(x+1)^3+x;
```
$$f := (x+1)^4 - x\,(x+1)^3 + x$$
```
> subs(x=2,f);
```
$$29$$

The previous computation can also be carried out by assigning the value 2 to the variable x. The evaluation of f then returns the expected value.

Ex.10

```
> x:=2;
```
$$x := 2$$
```
> f;
```
$$29$$

In order to recover the initial expression of f after such an assignment, one can either unassign x with the command `x:='x'` or use `eval(f,1)` (p. 21), which restricts evaluation to the first level.

Ex.11

```
> eval(f,1);
```
$$(x+1)^4 - x\,(x+1)^3 + x$$
```
> x:='x':f;
```
$$(x+1)^4 - x\,(x+1)^3 + x$$

12.2 Coefficients of a Polynomial

12.2.1 Degree and Low Degree

The functions `degree` and `ldegree` compute the degree and the low degree of a polynomial. The evaluations of `degree(f,x)` and `ldegree(f,x)` return the degree and the low degree of the polynomial f with respect to the variable x. The x isn't mandatory if f is a polynomial in a single variable. For MAPLE, the degree and the low degree of the zero polynomial are equal to 0.

Ex.12

```
> restart; f:=2*x^4+x^5-3*x^2;
```
$$2\,x^4 + x^5 - 3\,x^2$$
```
> degree(f), ldegree(f);
```
$$5\,,\,2$$

Although MAPLE doesn't return any error message, the result may be surprising if one uses these functions **degree** and **ldegree** with a polynomial which isn't written as a sum of monomials of different degree. For such polynomials, the user must call **collect** before these functions.

Ex.13

```
> f:=(x+1)^4-x*(x+1)^3+x; n:=degree(f,x);
```
$$f := (x + 1)^4 - x\,(x + 1)^3 + x$$
$$n := 4$$
```
> f:=collect(f,x); n:=degree(f,x);
```
$$f := x^3 + 3\,x^2 + 4\,x + 1$$
$$n := 3$$

When **f** is a polynomial in several variables, **degree(f)** returns the total degree of the polynomial **f** with respect to the complete set of its variables. The degree with respect to a subset of the variables can also be obtained by specifying this subset of variables (between braces) as second argument.

Ex.14

```
> f:=a*b*x^2+b^3*x+c;
```
$$f := a\,b\,x^2 + b^3\,x + c$$
```
> degree(f), degree(f,{a,b});
```
$$4\,,\,3$$

Warning ! The functions **degree** and **ldegree** don't produce the expected results when some exponents are not evaluated to integer values.

Ex.15

```
> n:='n': f:=(x^n)^2+x^n+1; degree(f);
```
$$f := (x^n)^2 + x^n + 1$$
$$2$$

In the previous example, the function **degree** sees in fact a polynomial expression of degree two in x^n and returns its degree with respect to x^n.

The function `degree` can also be used in a wider scope than just polynomials: when an expression `f` is a polynomial function of a subexpression `g`, the evaluation of `degree(f,g)` returns the degree of the expression `f` with respect to `g`.

Ex.16

> f:=x^2*sin(x)^2+x; degree(f,sin(x));

$$f := x^2 \, \sin(x)^2 + x$$

$$2$$

12.2.2 Obtaining the Coefficients

Three functions are available for retrieving coefficients of a polynomial `f`

- `coeff(f,x,k)` returns the coefficient of the term in x^k
- `lcoeff(f,x)` (leading coefficient) returns the coefficient of the term of highest degree.
- `tcoeff(f,x)` (trailing coefficient) returns the coefficient of the term of lowest degree.

In each case the polynomial `f` must be in the form of a sum of terms whose degrees are all different from each other.

Ex.17

> f:=2*x^4+x^5-3*x^2;

$$f := 2\,x^4 + x^5 - 3\,x^2$$

> coeff(f,x,4); lcoeff(f,x); tcoeff(f,x);

$$2$$

$$1$$

$$-3$$

The functions `lcoeff` and `tcoeff` can also be used with a third parameter which is either unassigned or between apostrophes. The evaluation of `lcoeff(f,x,'t')` returns the coefficient of the term of highest degree d and assigns the value x^d to the variable t.

Ex.18

> f:=2*x^4+3*x^5-3*x^2;

$$f := 2\,x^4 + 3\,x^5 - 3\,x^2$$

> lcoeff(f,x,'t'); t;

$$3$$

$$x^5$$

Warning! One must apply `collect` before using one of the previous functions if the polynomial isn't in the form of a sum of monomials of distinct degree.

Ex.19

```
> f:=(x+1)^4-x*(x+1)^3+x; g:=expand(f);
```
$$f := (x+1)^4 - x(x+1)^3 + x$$
$$g := x^3 + 3x^2 + 4x + 1$$

Ex.20

```
> coeff(f,x,3);
```
$$4$$
```
> lcoeff(f,x);
```
$$0$$

12.3 Divisibility

12.3.1 The Function `divide`

If `f` and `g` are two polynomials in one or several variables, with rational coefficients, `divide(f,g)` returns the value `true` if `f` is divisible by `g`, and `false` otherwise.

Ex.21

```
> f:=(x-1)^4+x^5; g:=x^2-x+1;
```
$$f := (x-1)^4 + x^5$$
$$g := x^2 - x + 1$$
```
> divide(f,g);
```
$$true$$

Example of divisibility with polynomials in several variables:

Ex.22

```
> f:=x^3-y^3; g:=x-y;
```
$$f := x^3 - y^3$$
$$g := x - y$$
```
> divide(f,g);
```
$$true$$

The function `divide` can also be used with a third parameter that must be either an unassigned variable or a variable between apostrophes. When `divide(f,g,'q')` evaluates to `true`, the variable `q` contains the quotient of the division of `f` by `g`.

Ex.23

```
> divide(f,g,'q'); q;
```
$$true$$
$$x^2 + x\,y + y^2$$

The function `divide` should absolutely not be used outside the domain of polynomials with rational coefficients.

When the coefficients aren't rational, as in the following example, MAPLE may return an error message warning the user, but it may also return `true` or `false`: the result can moreover vary between different calls.

Ex.24

```
> restart;
  divide(x^4-2*cos(2*a)*x^2+1,x^2-2*cos(a)*x+1);
```
$$true$$
```
> restart;
  divide(x^4-2*cos(2*a)*x^2+1,x^2-2*cos(a)*x+1);
  Error, invalid arguments to divide
```

In the case of the next example, one should keep in mind that MAPLE doesn't regard `f` and `g` as polynomials in `x`, even if the reader strongly assumes `n` to be an integer, and even if he declares it with the function `assume`. One can verify this with the help of the function `indets`.

Ex.25

```
> assume(n,integer);
  f:=x^(3*n)-1; g:=x^(2*n)+x^n+1;
```
$$f \; : \; = x^{(3n\sim)} - 1$$
$$g \; : \; = x^{(2n\sim)} + x^{n\sim} + 1$$
```
> divide(f,g);
  Error, invalid arguments to divide
```
```
> indets(f); indets(g);
```
$$\{x, n \quad \sim \quad , x^{n\sim}, x^{(2n\sim)}\}$$
$$\{x, n \quad \sim \quad , x^{(3n\sim)}\}$$

12.3.2 Euclidean Division

The functions `quo` and `rem` (*remainder*) compute the quotient and the remainder respectively of a Euclidean division. If `f` and `g` are two polynomials in the variable `x` whose coefficients may depend on other variables.

- `quo(f,g,x)` returns the quotient of the Euclidean division, with respect to the variable `x`, of the polynomial `f` by the polynomial `g`.
- `rem(f,g,x)` returns the remainder of the Euclidean division, with respect to the variable `x`, of the polynomial `f` by the polynomial `g`.

Warning ! The `x` is necessary even when the expressions `f` and `g` depend on a single indeterminate.

Ex.26

```
> f:=x^4+4*x^3-3*x+7;
```
$$f := x^4 + 4x^3 - 3x + 7$$
```
> g:=3*x^2-5*x+9;
```
$$g := 3x^2 - 5x + 9$$
```
> q:=quo(f,g,x);
```
$$q := \frac{1}{3}x^2 + \frac{17}{9}x + \frac{58}{27}$$
```
> r:=rem(f,g,x);
```
$$r := -\frac{250}{27}x - \frac{37}{3}$$
```
> q:=quo(f,g);
    Error, (in quo) wrong number (or type) of arguments
```

The function `quo` (resp. `rem`) can be used with a fourth optional parameter which is either an unassigned variable or a variable between apostrophes. This variable will contain the remainder (resp. the quotient) of the Euclidean division after the evaluation.

Ex.27

```
> q:=quo(f,g,x,'r');r;
```
$$q := \frac{1}{3}x^2 + \frac{17}{9}x + \frac{58}{27}$$
$$-\frac{250}{27}x - \frac{37}{3}$$

The evaluation of `rem(f,g,x)` can be used to test the divisibility of `f` by `g` with respect to `x` even if the coefficients aren't polynomials, which differentiates it from the function `divide` described before.

Ex.28

```
> f:=x^4*sin(a)-x*sin(4*a)+sin(3*a);
  g:=x*x-2*x*cos(a)+1;
```

$$f := x^4 \sin(a) - x \sin(4a) + \sin(3a)$$

$$g := x^2 - 2x \cos(a) + 1$$

```
> r:=rem(f,g,x,'q');
```

$$\sin(3a) + \sin(a) - 4\sin(a)\cos(a)^2$$
$$+ \left(-\sin(4a) - 4\sin(a)\cos(a) + 8\sin(a)\cos(a)^3\right)x$$

```
> combine(r,trig);                    To simplify the result
```

$$0$$

```
> divide(f,g);          Result that may vary between sessions
  Error, invalid arguments to divide
```

12.3.3 Resultant and Discriminant

If f and g are two polynomials in the variable x, resultant(f,g,x) returns the resultant of the polynomials with respect to x. This resultant is a polynomial expression in the coefficients of f and g and its being zero is a necessary and sufficient condition for the two polynomials in the variable x to have a common root.

Ex.29

```
> restart; f:=x^3+p*x+q; g:=y*x+y-1;
```

$$f := x^3 + p x + q$$

$$g := y x + y - 1$$

```
> collect(resultant(f,g,x),y);
```

$$(-q + p + 1) y^3 + (-p - 3) y^2 + 3y - 1$$

If f is a polynomial in the variable x, discrim(f,x) returns the discriminant of f with respect to x, i.e. the resultant of f and f up to the sign. This discriminant is a polynomial expression in the coefficients of f and its being equal to zero is a necessary and sufficient condition for f to have a multiple root.

Ex.30

```
> discrim(f,x); resultant(f,diff(f,x),x);
```

$$-4p^3 - 27q^2$$

$$4p^3 + 27q^2$$

12.4 Computation of the g.c.d. and the l.c.m.

12.4.1 The Functions gcd and lcm

The functions gcd (*greatest common divisor*) and lcm (*least common multiple*) return respectively a g.c.d. and a l.c.m. of two polynomials in one or several variables. If f and g are polynomials with rational coefficients,

- gcd(f,g) returns a g.c.d. of f and g.
- lcm(f,g) returns a l.c.m. of f and g.

Example with one variable:

Ex.31

```
> f:=1/2*x^3-1/2;g:=x^2-1;
```
$$f := \frac{1}{2}x^3 - \frac{1}{2}$$
$$g := x^2 - 1$$
```
> gcd(f,g);lcm(f,g);
```
$$x - 1$$
$$\frac{1}{2}x^4 + \frac{1}{2}x^3 - \frac{1}{2}x - \frac{1}{2}$$

Example with several variables:

Ex.32

```
> f:=x^4*y-y*z^4; g:=x^3-z^3;
```
$$f := x^4 y - y z^4$$
$$g := x^3 - z^3$$
```
> gcd(f,g);
```
$$x - z$$

The function gcd can be used with two optional parameters which are either unassigned variables or variables between apostrophes. After the evaluation, these variables will contain respectively the quotient of f by gcd(f,g) and the quotient of g by gcd(f,g).

Ex.33

```
> f:=1/2*x^3-1/2:
  g:=x^2-1: gcd(f,g,f1,g1):
  f1; g1;
```
$$\frac{1}{2}x^2 + \frac{1}{2}x + \frac{1}{2}$$
$$x + 1$$

The function `gcd` can only compute the g.c.d. of polynomials with rational coefficients. MAPLE returns a clear error message when the coefficients of one of the polynomials are not all rational.

Ex.34

> `f:=sqrt(2)*x^3-sqrt(2); g:=x^2-1;`

$$f := \sqrt{2}x^3 - \sqrt{2}$$

$$g := x^2 - 1$$

> `gcd(f,g);`

Error, (in gcd) arguments must be polynomials over the rationals

> `f:=x^2-sin(a)^2; g:=x-sin(a);`

$$f := x^2 - \sin(a)^2$$

$$g := -\sin(a) + x$$

> `gcd(f,g);`

Error, (in gcd) arguments must be polynomials over the rationals

12.4.2 Content and Primitive Part

If `f` is a polynomial in one or several variables with integer coefficients, the content of `f` with respect to `x` is the greatest common divisor of the coefficients of the polynomial `f`, considered as a polynomial in `x`.

• `content(f,x)` returns the content of `f` with respect to `x`.
• `primpart(f,x)` returns the quotient of `f` by `content(f,x)`.

Example with one variable:

Ex.35

> `f:=6*x^2+2*x+2;`
$$f := 6x^2 + 2x + 2$$

> `content(f);`   **x is optional for a**
  `primpart(f);`   **polynomial in one variable**

$$2$$

$$3x^2 + x + 1$$

Example with several variables:

Ex.36

```
> p:=(a^2-1)*(a+2)^2*x+a*(a+1);
```
$$p := (a^2 - 1)(a + 2)^2 x + a(a + 1)$$
```
> content(p,x);
```
$$a + 1$$

When f is a polynomial in x whose coefficients are rational functions, the content of f is the quotient content(m*f,x)/m where m is the l.c.m. of the denominators of the coefficients of f.

- content(f,x) returns the content of f with respect to x.
- primpart(f,x) returns the polynomial f/content(f,x).

Ex.37

```
> p:=1/a*x+1/(a+1);
```
$$p := \frac{x}{a} + \frac{1}{a + 1}$$
```
> content(p,x); primpart(p,x);
```
$$\frac{1}{a(a + 1)}$$
$$x\,a + x + a$$

Using content and primpart we compute the g.c.d. of two polynomials in one indeterminate whose coefficients are rational functions, which cannot be done by calling gcd directly.

Ex.38

```
> f:=1/a*x^2-a; g:=1/a*x^3-a^2;
```
$$f := \frac{x^2}{a} - a$$
$$g := \frac{x^3}{a} - a^2$$
```
> gcd(f,g);
  Error, (in gcd) arguments must be polynomials over the rationals
> gcd(primpart(f,x),primpart(g,x));
```
$$x - a$$

12.4.3 Extended Euclid's Algorithm: The Function gcdex

Given two non-constant polynomials with rational coefficients f and g, and two free variables u and v, gcdex(f,g,x,u,v) returns the g.c.d. of f and g with respect to the variable x and assigns to the variables u and v polynomials u0 and v0 such that u0*f+v0*g=gcd(f,g), the degree of the polynomial u0 (resp. v0) being strictly smaller than the degree of g (resp. f). The parameters u and v are optional.

Ex.39

```
> f:=(x-1)^4; g:=(x+1)^4; gcdex(f,g,x,u,v);
```

$$f := (x-1)^4$$

$$g := (x+1)^4$$

$$1$$

```
> u; v;
```

$$\frac{29}{32}\,x + \frac{1}{2} + \frac{5}{32}\,x^3 + \frac{5}{8}\,x^2$$

$$\frac{1}{2} - \frac{29}{32}\,x + \frac{5}{8}\,x^2 - \frac{5}{32}\,x^3$$

With polynomials in x whose coefficients are rational functions, the evaluation of gcdex(f,g,x) indeed returns the g.c.d. with respect to x of the polynomials f and g. However, gcdex cannot be used with polynomials with arbitrary coefficients although MAPLE doesn't return an error message.

Ex.40

```
> f:=1/a*x^2-a; g:=1/a*x^3-a^2;
```

$$f := \frac{x^2}{a} - a$$

$$g := \frac{x^3}{a} - a^2$$

```
> gcdex(f,g,x);
```

$$-a + x$$

```
> f:=x^4-2*x^2*cos(2*a)+1; g:=x^2-2*x*cos(a)+1;
```

$$f := x^4 - 2\,x^2\,\cos(2\,a) + 1$$

$$g := x^2 - 2\,x\,\cos(a) + 1$$

```
> gcdex(f,g,x);
```
                                                    gcdex returns 1

$$1$$

```
> combine(rem(f,g,x),trig);
```
                                                    and yet g divides f !

$$0$$

12.5 Factorization

In this section, we only study the factorization of a polynomial with rational coefficients into a product of polynomials with rational coefficients. Indeed, the factorization of a polynomial over $\mathbb{Q}$ reduces to the factorization of a polynomial over $\mathbb{Z}$ and can thus be handled with modular methods (using congruences), while the factorization over $\mathbb{R}$ or over $\mathbb{C}$ requires algorithms of a different kind. The study of this last type of factorization will be tackled in the next chapter.

12.5.1 Decomposition into Irreducible Factors

The function `factor` factors a polynomial with rational coefficients. If `f` is a polynomial with rational coefficients, in one or several variables, `factor(f)` returns the factorization of `f` into a product of irreducible polynomials in the field of rational numbers.

Ex.41

```
> f:=(x+1)^7-x^7-1;
```
$$f := (x+1)^7 - x^7 - 1$$
```
> factor(f);
```
$$7\,x\,(x+1)(x^2+x+1)^2$$
```
> f:=x^4+y^2*x^2+y^4;
```
$$f := x^4 + y^2\,x^2 + y^4$$
```
> factor(f);
```
$$(x^2 - x\,y + y^2)\,(x^2 + x\,y + y^2)$$

The polynomials returned by the function `factor` are irreducible in the field of rational numbers, but are not necessarily irreducible in the field of real numbers: one can thus obtain polynomials in one indeterminate of degree 3 with such a factorization, as in the following example.

Ex.42

```
> factor(x^6-4);
```
$$(x^3 - 2)(x^3 + 2)$$

In the following example, the function `factor` returns a factorization into a product of irreducible polynomials with respect to the indeterminates x and a, despite the name of the second variable which classically represents a parameter.

Ex.43

```
> f:=x^4-4*x^2*a^2+2*x^2+1;
```
$$f := x^4 - 4a^2 x^2 + 2x^2 + 1$$

```
> factor(f);
```
$$(x^2 + 2ax + 1)(x^2 - 2ax + 1)$$

The polynomials one obtains are of course not irreducible as polynomials in x, for any value of the "parameter" a, as one can verify for a=1.

Ex.44

```
> subs(a=1,f);
```
$$x^4 - 2x^2 + 1$$

```
> factor(");
```
$$(x - 1)^2 (x + 1)^2$$

12.5.2 Square-Free Factorization

Used with the option sqrfree, the function convert carries out a *square-free* factorization. If f is a polynomial with rational coefficients, in one or several variables, convert(f,sqrfree) returns the expression of the polynomial f in the form $f = \lambda f_1 f_2^2 f_3^3 ... f_k^k$ where λ is a constant and $f_1, f_2, f_3, ..., f_k$ are relatively prime polynomials without multiple roots. In fact, f_r is the unit polynomial whose roots are the complex roots of order r of f. Some among the polynomials f_r may be equal to 1 and don't appear in the result in this case.

This square-free factorization which mainly relies on a g.c.d. computation is often used in computer algebra, in particular in some integration algorithms.

Ex.45

```
> f:=x^10+x^9-x^8-x^7-x^6-x^5+x^4+x^3;
```
$$f := x^{10} + x^9 - x^8 - x^7 - x^6 - x^5 + x^4 + x^3$$

```
> convert(f,sqrfree);
```
$$(x^2 + 1)(x - 1)^2 (x^2 + x)^3$$

12.5.3 Irreducibility Test

The function `irreduc` tests the irreducibility of a polynomial over the field of rational numbers. If `f` is a polynomial with rational coefficients, in one or several variables, `irreduc(f)` returns `true` if `f` is irreducible in the field of rational numbers and `false` otherwise.

Ex.46

```
> f:=x^4+x^3+x^2+x+1;
```
$$f := x^4 + x^3 + x^2 + x + 1$$

```
> irreduc(f);
```
$$true$$

```
> f:=x^4+y^2*x^2+y^4;
```
$$f := x^4 + y^2 x^2 + y^4$$

```
> irreduc(f);
```
$$false$$

```
> factor(f);
```
$$(x^2 - x\,y + y^2)(x^2 + x\,y + y^2)$$

For a polynomial like the one of the following example, the function `irreduc` tests the irreducibility of the polynomial with respect to the indeterminates `x` and `a`, which doesn't mean that the polynomial is irreducible, as a polynomial in `x`, for any value of the "parameter" `a`.

Ex.47

```
> f:=x^4+a*x^2+1;
```
$$f := x^4 + a\,x^2 + 1$$

```
> irreduc(f);
```
$$true$$

```
> subs(a=1,f); irreduc(");
```
$$x^4 + x^2 + 1$$
$$false$$

```
> factor(");
```
"" represents the next to last computed value
$$\left(x^2 + x + 1\right)\left(x^2 - x + 1\right)$$

13. Polynomials with Irrational Coefficients

13.1 Algebraic Extensions of $\mathbb{Q}$

In the previous chapter, the study of the functions `divide`, `factor`, etc. was restricted to polynomials with rational coefficients. In this chapter, we generalize their use to polynomials whose coefficients may be algebraic, i.e. roots of a polynomial equation with integer coefficients.

Factorization of Polynomials with Algebraic Coefficients

If `f` is a polynomial in one or several variables, with algebraic coefficients, `factor(f)` returns the factorization of `f` into a product of irreducible polynomials over the field generated by the coefficients of the polynomial `f`.

Ex. 1

```
> f:=x^2-2;
```
$$f := x^2 - 2$$

```
> g:=(x^2-2)*(x-sqrt(2));
```
$$g := \left(x^2 - 2\right)\left(x - \sqrt{2}\right)$$

```
> factor(f);
```
$$x^2 - 2$$

```
> factor(g);
```
$$\left(x + \sqrt{2}\right)\left(x - \sqrt{2}\right)^2$$

Since `f` has rational coefficients, it is factorized over the field of rationals where it is irreducible, But since $\sqrt{2}$ appears in the coefficients of `g`, it is factorized into a product of first degree polynomials whose coefficients are expressed as functions of $\sqrt{2}$.

Another example of factorization over the field generated by the coefficients:

Ex. 2

```
> f:=x^2-(sqrt(2)+sqrt(3))*x+sqrt(6);
```
$$f := x^2 - \left(\sqrt{2} + \sqrt{3}\right)x + \sqrt{6}$$
```
> factor(f);
```
$$\left(x - \sqrt{2}\right)\left(x - \sqrt{3}\right)$$

13.1.1 Irreducibility Test

Following the example of the function `factor`, the function `irreduc` tests if a polynomial is irreducible over the field generated by its coefficients.

Ex. 3

```
> f:=sqrt(2)*x^4-2*sqrt(2); g:=x^4-2;
```
$$f := \sqrt{2}\,x^4 - 2\sqrt{2}$$
$$g := x^4 - 2$$
```
> irreduc(f); irreduc(g);
```
$$false$$
$$true$$

13.1.2 Roots of a Polynomial

The function `roots` constructs a list of the roots of a polynomial belonging to the field generated by its coefficients.

If `f` is a polynomial in one indeterminate with algebraic coefficients, `roots(f)` returns the list $[[x_1, \alpha_1], [x_2, \alpha_2], \ldots, [x_k, \alpha_k]]$ where $x_1, x_2, \ldots, x_k$ are the roots of `f` belonging to the field generated by the coefficients of `f` and where $\alpha_1, \alpha_2, \ldots, \alpha_k$ are the multiplicities of these roots.

Ex. 4

```
> f:=x^7-2*x^5-x^4+x^3+2*x*x-1;
```
$$f := x^7 - 2x^5 - x^4 + x^3 + 2x^2 - 1$$
```
> roots(f);
```
$$[[-1, 2], [1, 3]]$$

The function `solve` returns the sequence of all the roots of a polynomial, even those not belonging to the field generated by its coefficients. In this sequence, a multiple root appears a number of times equal to its multiplicity. The function `solve` will be studied in detail in Chapter 6.

Ex. 5

```
> solve(f);
```
$$-\frac{1}{2} + \frac{1}{2} I \sqrt{3}, \ -\frac{1}{2} - \frac{1}{2} I \sqrt{3}, \ -1, \ -1, \ 1, \ 1, \ 1$$

The function `solve` returns an answer using the function `RootOf` when it isn't able to express some root of the polynomial with radicals.

Ex. 6

```
> f:=x^6-2*x+1;
```
$$f := x^6 - 2\,x + 1$$
```
> solve(f);
```
$$1, \ RootOf(\_Z^5 + \_Z^4 + \_Z^3 + \_Z^2 + \_Z - 1)$$

The previous result means that the set of roots of `f` is made up of 1 and of the set of roots of the polynomial $Z^5 + Z^4 + Z^3 + Z^2 + Z - 1$ which is itself irreducible over $\mathbb{Q}$.

The remainder of this section is devoted to the study of the function `RootOf`.

13.1.3 The Function `RootOf`

In the algebraic framework, the function `RootOf` can be used with two different meanings that should be clearly distinguished. It represents

- either the set of roots of a polynomial.
- or an algebraic number or, better, an algebraic extension.

There is another use of `RootOf` in representing an implicit function, which is studied on page 136.

Using `RootOf` to Describe the Roots of a Polynomial

We saw in Example 6 how the function `solve` uses `RootOf` in order to describe the set of roots of a polynomial.

Likewise, a `RootOf` used with the functions `sum` and `product` allows the user to express and to compute a symmetric expression in the roots of a polynomial.

To compute the sum of `1/(x+1)` as x takes all values in the set of roots of
the polynomial `x^3+x+1`, one writes:

Ex. 7

```
> f:=x^3+x+1;
                        f := x^3 + x + 1
> sum(1/(x+1),x=RootOf(f));
                        4
```

For a polynomial in x whose coefficients depend on one or several parameters,
one has to specify the name of the indeterminate as second argument to
the function RootOf in order to allow MAPLE to distinguish it from the
parameters.

Ex. 8

```
> f:=x^3+p*x+q;
                        f := x^3 + px + q
> product(1/(u+1),u=RootOf(f,x));
                             1
                        ───────────
                         -q + p + 1
> product(1/(u+1),u=RootOf(f));   If one forgets the x ... Error
  Error, (in RootOf) expression independent of, _Z
```

Using RootOf to Represent an Algebraic Number

Even when the roots of a polynomial can be expressed, doing so explicitly
often doesn't help to simplify rational expressions in these roots and to deduce
some of their properties. With its second type of use, RootOf describes an
algebraic number (root of a polynomial) or rather an algebraic extension.

If f is an irreducible polynomial in the variable x, the quantity RootOf(f,x)
represents a root of this polynomial. The assignment a:=RootOf(f,x) corresponds to the sentence: "let a be a root of f".

For example, one can prove that if $k \in \mathbb{R}$, the polynomial $f(x) = x^3 - 3x$
$-k(1 - 3x^2)$ has three real roots by reasoning as follows.

- One computes $f'(x) = 3x^2 - 3 + 6kx$. This polynomial f' has two real
  roots whose product is -1 : let a be the negative root and b be the positive
  one.

- By denoting one of the roots of f' as u, thanks to the relation $u^2 = 1 - 2\,k\,u$, one may write

$$
\begin{aligned}
f(u) &= u\,(1 - 2\,k\,u) - 3\,u - k\,(1 - 3\,u^2)\\
&= k\,u^2 - 2\,u - k\\
&= -2\,(1 + k^2)\,u
\end{aligned}
$$

- By this last result, one can see that $f(u)$ and u have opposite signs. Thus $f(a) > 0$ and $f(b) < 0$. Since the coefficient of x^3 in f is positive, studying the variations of f, one concludes that the polynomial f has three real roots.

The computation of the previous example doesn't use an explicit expression of the roots of f, only the algebraic relation they satisfy. MAPLE proceeds in the same way when requested to compute with an expression containing RootOf's.

As an example, let us give the MAPLE worksheet corresponding to the previous computation.

Ex. 9

```
> restart; f:=x^3-3*x-k*(1-3*x^2);
```
$$f := x^3 - 3\,x - k\,(1 - 3\,x^2)$$
```
> f1:=diff(f,x):                          computation of f'
> u:=RootOf(f1,x):                         let u be a root of f' ...
> extrem:=subs(x=u,f);                     Expression of f(u)
```
$$
\begin{aligned}
extrem := &\; RootOf\left(\_Z^2 - 1 + 2k\_Z\right)^3\\
&- 3\,RootOf\left(\_Z^2 - 1 + 2k\_Z\right)\\
&- k\left(1 - 3\,RootOf\left(\_Z^2 - 1 + 2k\_Z\right)^2\right)
\end{aligned}
$$
```
> simplify(extrem);
```
$$-2\left(1 + k^2\right)RootOf\left(\_Z^2 - 1 + 2k\_Z\right)$$

It can be seen from the previous example that, unlike with radicals, MAPLE does not automatically simplify an expression containing RootOf's. Simplification must be explicitly requested with the function simplify.

Results involving RootOf's can read more easily with the help of the function alias. The advantage of alias(a=RootOf(f)) over a:=RootOf(f) is that MAPLE will next use a instead of RootOf(f) to return its results, which makes for a more pleasant presentation.

Ex.10

```
> alias(alpha=RootOf(f1,x));                MAPLE displays then
                                     the list of all the existing alias
```

$$I, \alpha$$

```
> extrem:=subs(x=u,f);                      Expression of f(u)
```

$$extrem := \alpha^3 - 3\,\alpha - k\,(1 - 3\,\alpha^2)$$

```
> simplify(extrem);
```

$$-2\,\left(1 + k^2\right)\alpha$$

Another example of computation upon `RootOf`'s:

Ex.11

```
> restart; alias(a=RootOf(x^4+x+1));
```

$$I, a$$

```
> simplify(1/(a^2+1));
```

$$\frac{3}{5} + \frac{1}{5}\,a^3 - \frac{1}{5}\,a - \frac{2}{5}\,a^2$$

Note: The usual syntax of the function `RootOf` is `RootOf(f,x)`, but `RootOf(f)` suffices if `f` is a polynomial in a single indeterminate with numerical coefficients. MAPLE returns an error message if the coefficients of the polynomial contain parameters and one forgets to specify the name of the indeterminate.

Ex.12

```
> restart; f:=x^5+a*x+1: RootOf(f);
   Error, (in RootOf) expression independent of, _Z
```

The text of this error message, not very clear at first sight, reflects the fact that MAPLE systematically replaces `RootOf(f(x),x)` by `RootOf(f(_Z))`, as one can verify with the following example:

Ex.13

```
> restart; u:=RootOf(x^4+a*x+1,x);
```

$$u := RootOf(\_Z^4 + a\,\_Z + 1)$$

13.1.4 Numerical Values of Expressions Containing `RootOf`'s

If `f` is a polynomial with numerical coefficients, `evalf(RootOf(f))` returns an approximate decimal value of one of the roots of `f`.

Ex.14

```
> a:=RootOf(x^4+x+1);
```
$$a := RootOf(\_Z^4 + \_Z + 1)$$
```
> evalf(a);
```
$$-.7271360845 - .4300142883\, I$$

The Function `allvalues`

If P is a polynomial in the single variable x with numerical coefficients, and if f is an expression containing `RootOf(P,x)`, then `allvalues(f)` returns the sequence of values taken by f by successively replacing `RootOf(P,x)` by all the roots of P. Whenever possible, these values are expressed with the help of radicals, otherwise MAPLE uses real numbers of type `float`.

Ex.15

```
> restart; alias(a=RootOf(x^2-2));
```
$$I \, , \, a$$
```
> f:=a^3-7;
```
$$f := a^3 - 7$$
```
> s:=allvalues(f);
```
$$2\sqrt{2} - 7, \ -2\sqrt{2} - 7$$
```
> s[2];
```
To extract the second element
$$-2\sqrt{2} - 7$$

In the previous example, selection operator [ ] was used to extract a specific value of the sequence returned by `allvalues`, which isn't reliable since the order of the elements of the sequence may vary from one session to another. It is better to use the function `select` as in the next example, in which the root which is smaller than -7 is extracted.

Ex.16

```
> select(x->evalf(x+7)<0,[s]);
```
Mind the square brackets
$$\left[-2\sqrt{2} - 7 \right]$$

In the next example, in which the function `allvalues` returns a sequence of elements of type `float`, the function `select` is used to extract the values whose imaginary part is negative.

Ex.17

```
> alias(b=RootOf(x^5+2*x+1));
```
$$I \, , \, a, \, b$$

```
> g:=b^2+3;
```
$$g := b^2 + 3$$

```
> s:=allvalues(g);
```
$$
\begin{array}{l}
2.718759347 + 1.234872424\,I, \\
2.718759347 - 1.234872424\,I, \\
3.236574294, \\
3.162953506 - 1.615154465\,I, \\
3.162953506 + 1.615154465\,I
\end{array}
$$

```
> select(x->Im(x)<0,[s]);
```
$$[2.718759347 - 1.234872424\,I, \, 3.162953506 - 1.615154465\,I]$$

When an expression `f` contains `RootOf`'s of different polynomials, the evaluation of `allvalues(f)` returns the sequence of values taken by `f` by combining all possible values of the `RootOf`'s.

Ex.18

```
> restart; a:=RootOf(x^2-2); b:=RootOf(x^2+2);
```
$$a := RootOf(\_Z^2 - 2)$$
$$b := RootOf(\_Z^2 + 2)$$

```
> f:=a+b;
```
$$f := RootOf(\_Z^2 - 2) + RootOf(\_Z^2 + 2)$$

```
> allvalues(f);
```
One obtains a sequence of 2×2 possible values

$$\sqrt{2} + I\,\sqrt{2}, \; \sqrt{2} - I\,\sqrt{2}, \; -\sqrt{2} + I\,\sqrt{2}, \; -\sqrt{2} - I\,\sqrt{2}$$

13.1.5 Conversion of `RootOf` Into Radicals

If `f` is an expression containing one or several `RootOf`, the evaluation of `convert(f,radical)` returns the expression `f` in which

- `RootOf(a*x^n+b,x)` is replaced by `(-b/a)^(1/n)`,
- `RootOf(a*x^2+b*x+c,x)` is replaced by `(-b+sqrt(b^2-4*a*c))/(2*a)`.

Ex.19

```
> restart; a:=RootOf(x^3-2);
```
$$a := RootOf(\_Z^3 - 2)$$
```
> convert(a^2+1,radical);
```
$$2^{2/3} + 1$$
```
> b:=5*a^4+1: convert(b,radical);
```
$$1 + 10\,2^{1/3}$$
```
> simplify(b);
```
$$1 + 10\,RootOf(\_Z^3 - 2)$$

One sees in the previous example that MAPLE automatically simplifies an expression written with radicals, which isn't the case for an expression written with `RootOf`'s.

The inverse transformation, `convert(f,RootOf)`, returns an expression of `f` in which the radicals of type `a^(1/q)` are replaced by `RootOf(x^q-a,x)`.

Ex.20

```
> convert(sqrt(2),RootOf);
```
$$RootOf(\_Z^2 - 2)$$

In the second part of this chapter, this last transformation will prove to be very important in order to transform polynomials with algebraic coefficients and express all their irrational terms using `RootOf`.

Ex.21

```
> f:=x^2-(sqrt(2)+sqrt(3))*x+sqrt(2)*sqrt(3);
```
$$f := x^2 - (\sqrt{2} + \sqrt{3})\,x + \sqrt{2}\,\sqrt{3}$$
```
> g:=convert(f,RootOf);
```
$$g := x^2 - \left(RootOf\left(\_Z^2 - 2\right) + RootOf\left(\_Z^2 - 3\right)\right)x$$
$$+ RootOf\left(\_Z^2 - 2\right)RootOf\left(\_Z^2 - 3\right)$$

13.2 Computation Over an Algebraic Extension

13.2.1 Factorization Over a Given Extension

The factorization of a polynomial can be carried out over an algebraic extension of the field generated by the polynomial's coefficients by using a second parameter when calling the function `factor`.

Let f be a polynomial. If K is a set of algebraic numbers, i.e.

- either a set of elements of type `radical`,
- or a set of `RootOf`'s,

then `factor(f,K)` returns f written as a product of irreducible polynomials over the field generated by the coefficients of f and the elements of K; the coefficients of the polynomials in such a decomposition are expressed as linear combinations of powers of elements of K with rational coefficients

For example, in the case of the polynomial $x^8 - 1$

- `factor(x^8-1)` returns the decomposition over $\mathbb{Q}$, which contains a polynomial of degree 4.
- `factor(x^8-1,sqrt(2))` returns a decomposition into a product of polynomials whose coefficients may contain $\sqrt{2}$. The maximum degree of these polynomials is 2.
- `factor(x^8-1,{sqrt(2),I})` returns a decomposition into a product of polynomials whose coefficients may contain $\sqrt{2}$ and i. All these polynomials are of degree 1.

Ex.22

```
> f:=x^8-1;
```
$$f := x^8 - 1$$
```
> factor(f);
```
$$(x - 1)(x + 1)(x^2 + 1)(x^4 + 1)$$
```
> factor(f,sqrt(2));
```
$$\left(x^2 + 1\right)\left(x^2 + \sqrt{2}\,x + 1\right)\left(x^2 - \sqrt{2}\,x + 1\right)(x + 1)(x - 1)$$
```
> factor(f,{sqrt(2),I});
```
$$\tfrac{1}{16}(x - I)(x + I)(2x + \sqrt{2} - I\sqrt{2})(2x - \sqrt{2} + I\sqrt{2})$$
$$(2x - \sqrt{2} - I\sqrt{2})(2x + \sqrt{2} + I\sqrt{2})(x - 1)(x + 1)$$

Example in which K is described with the help of `RootOf`'s:

Ex.23

```
> restart; alias(a=RootOf(x^2-5));
```
$$I, a$$
```
> f:=x^5-1;
```
$$f := x^5 - 1$$
```
> factor(f,a);
```
$$\frac{1}{4}(2x^2 + x - ax + 2)(2x^2 + x + ax + 2)(x - 1)$$

Note: To find the radicals which give such a factorization, the user may draw inspiration from classical factorization methods. One may also use the function `solve` which, for most classical examples, can be used to express the roots and to deduce the radicals one is looking for from them.

In describing the algebraic extension and the coefficients of a polynomial using `RootOf`, it is necessary to use only `RootOf`'s of irreducible polynomials, otherwise MAPLE returns an error message.

Ex.24

```
> f:=(x+1)^5-x^5-1; a:=RootOf(x^3-1);
```
$$f := (x + 1)^5 - x^5 - 1$$
$$a := RootOf(\_Z^3 - 1)$$
```
> factor(f,a);
```
Error, (in evala) reducible RootOf detected ...

13.2.2 Incompatibility Between Radicals and `RootOf`

When one uses `factor` with a second parameter K, the elements of K as well as the coefficients of the polynomial have to be either all written with radicals or all written with `RootOf`'s. The two notations cannot be mixed.

When K is described with the help of `RootOf`, the coefficients of f may not contain radicals, otherwise MAPLE returns an error message.

Ex.25

```
> restart; alias(a=RootOf(x^2-2));
  f:=x^2-2*sqrt(3)*x+1;
```

$$I , a$$

$$f := x^2 - 2\sqrt{3}\, x + 1$$

```
> factor(f,a);
  Error, (in factor) expecting a polynomial over
  an algebraic number field
```

This error message, which may at first sight seem rather strange since the user has indeed described an algebraic extension, is caused by the incompatibility between RootOf and radicals.

When such a conflict between RootOf and radicals is encountered, one usually expresses both the coefficients of the polynomial and the elements of the parameter K with RootOf: one may use convert(...,RootOf) to do this.

Ex.26

```
> alias(a=RootOf(x^2-3),b=RootOf(x^2-2));
```

$$I , a , b$$

```
> f:=convert(f,RootOf);
```

$$f := x^2 - 2a\, x + 1$$

```
> factor(f,b);
```

$$(x - a - b)(x - a + b)$$

Warning! This incompatibility between RootOf and sqrt appears in a more subtle way in the next example.

Ex.27

```
> f:=x^8-1; factor(f,{I,RootOf(Z^2-2)});
```

$$f := x^8 - 1$$

Error, (in factor) 2nd argument is not a valid algebraic extension

Indeed, I is the alias of sqrt(-1) in MAPLE. This definition of I allows a automatic simplification in the computations, which wouldn't be the case with RootOf(_Z^2+1), for which simplify would be required. On the other hand, such a definition makes the simultaneous use of I and RootOf(_Z^2-2) incompatible. One must therefore write: factor(f,{I,sqrt(2)}) in the previous example.

13.2.3 Irreducibility, Roots Over a Given Extension

Like the function `factor`, the functions `irreduc` and `roots` may be used with a second optional parameter K which describes an algebraic extension using radicals or `RootOf`.

If `f` is a polynomial with algebraic coefficients, `irreduc(f,K)` returns `true` if `f` is irreducible over the field generated by the coefficients of `f` and the elements of K.

Ex.28

```
> f:=x^4+x^3+x^2+x+1; irreduc(f);
```

$$f := x^4 + x^3 + x^2 + x + 1$$

$$true$$

```
> irreduc(f,sqrt(5)); factor(f,sqrt(5));
```

$$false$$

$$\frac{1}{4}\left(2x^2 + x + \sqrt{5}x + 2\right)\left(2x^2 + x - \sqrt{5}x + 2\right)$$

If `f` is a polynomial with algebraic coefficients, `roots(f,K)` returns the roots of `f` over the field generated by the elements of K and the coefficients of `f`.

Ex.29

```
> f:=7*x^8+21*x^7+56*x^6+98*x^5
    +126*x^4+112*x^3+63*x^2+21*x;
```

$$f := 7x^8 + 21x^7 + 56x^6 + 98x^5$$

$$+126x^4 + 112x^3 + 63x^2 + 21x$$

```
> alias(a=RootOf(x^2+x+1)): roots(f,a);
```

$$[[2a + 1, 1], [-1 - 2a, 1], [-1, 1], [0, 1], [-a - 1, 2], [a, 2]]$$

13.2.4 Factorization of a Polynomial Over Its Splitting Field

The function `split` factors a polynomial with algebraic coefficients over its splitting field.

If `f` is a polynomial in the variable `x`, `split(f,x)` returns the factorization of `f` into a product of first degree factors. This function must be loaded with the help of `readlib(split)` before its first use.

Ex.30

```
> restart; f:=x^4+4;
```
$$f := x^4 + 4$$

```
> readlib(split): g:=split(f,x);
```
$$g := (x + \%1)\,(x + 2 + \%1)\,(x - \%1)\,(x - 2 - \%1)$$
$$\%1 := RootOf(\_Z^2 + 2\_Z + 2)$$

The result reads more easily using the function `alias`.

Ex.31

```
> alias(a=%1);
```
$$I\,,\ a$$

```
> g;
```
$$(x + a)\,(x + 2 + a)\,(x - a)\,(x - 2 - a)$$

But the `RootOf`'s can also be converted into radicals.

Ex.32

```
> convert(g,radical);
```
$$(x + 1 + I)\,(x + 1 - I)\,(x - 1 + I)\,(x - 1 - I)$$

13.2.5 Divisibility of Polynomials with Algebraic Coefficients

The function `divide` (starting with a lower case d) shouldn't be used for polynomials with algebraic coefficients. One must use the inert form `Divide` (starting with an upper case D). This inert function returns an unevaluated form whose evaluation can be forced with the function `evala`. However, all irrational algebraic coefficients of the polynomials must then be defined with `RootOf`'s.

If f and g are polynomials with algebraic coefficients written using `RootOf`,

- the evaluation of `evala(Divide(f,g))` returns the value `true` if f is divisible by g and `false` otherwise.

- when `evala(Divide(f,g,'q'))` gives the value `true`, the variable q contains the quotient of the division of f by g after the evaluation.

Ex.33

```
> f:=x^2+x+3-RootOf(x^2+3);
  g:=x-RootOf(x^2+3);
```

$$f := x^2 + x + 3 - RootOf(\_Z^2 + 3)$$

$$g := x - RootOf(\_Z^2 + 3)$$

```
> evala(Divide(f,g,'q')); q;
```

$$true$$

$$x + 1 + RootOf(\_Z^2 + 3)$$

Warning! Do not use the function `divide` (lower case d) on polynomials with algebraic coefficients. Up to release 4, MAPLE doesn't give an error message but returns an answer that may be false, as for the polynomials of the previous example.

Ex.34

```
> divide(f,g);
```

$$false$$

Warning! If `evala(Divide( ))` is called for polynomials whose coefficients contain `sqrt`'s, the result may be false, as in the next example.

Ex.35

```
> f:=x*x-2; g:=x-sqrt(2);
```

$$f := x^2 - 2$$

$$g := x - \sqrt{2}$$

```
> evala(Divide(f,g,'q'));
```

$$false$$

```
> evala(convert(Divide(f,g,'q'),RootOf));
```

$$true$$

13.2.6 G.c.d. of Polynomials with Algebraic Coefficients

While the function `gcd` may only be used with polynomials with rational coefficients, the inert form, `Gcd`, can be used to compute the g.c.d. of polynomials with algebraic coefficients. As for `Divide`, irrational algebraic coefficients of polynomials must be defined with the function `RootOf`.

If `f` and `g` are polynomials whose algebraic coefficients are defined by `RootOf`'s, then `evala(Gcd(f,g))` returns the g.c.d. of the polynomials `f` and `g`.

Ex.36

```
> alias(a=RootOf(x^2-2));
  f:=x^4-2; g:=x^4-2*a*x^2+2;
```

$$I , a$$

$$f := x^4 - 2$$

$$g := x^4 - 2\,a\,x^2 + 2$$

```
> evala(Gcd(f,g));
```

$$x^2 - a$$

Like `Divide`, the function `Gcd` may give incorrect results if some coefficients of f and of g are expressed with radicals rather than `RootOf`'s.

Ex.37

```
> f:=x^4-2;
```

$$f := x^4 - 2$$

```
> g:=x^4-2*sqrt(2)*x^2+2;
```

$$g := x^4 - 2\sqrt{2}\,x^2 + 2$$

```
> evala(Gcd(f,g));
```
Inexact result

$$1$$

To carry out the extended Euclidean algorithm on polynomials with algebraic coefficients, `Gcdex` must be used. Its syntax is identical to that of `gcdex`, in that the irrational coefficients of polynomials must be expressed with `RootOf`. The evaluation of `evala(Gcdex(f,g,x,'u','v'))` returns the g.c.d. of the polynomials f and g and assigns to the variables u and v a pair of polynomials such that $u\,f + v\,g = gcd(f, g)$.

Ex.38

```
> alias(a=RootOf(x^2-2)):
  f:=x*x-2; g:=x*x-2*a*x+2;
```

$$f := x^2 - 2$$

$$g := x^2 - 2a\,x + 2$$

```
> evala(Gcdex(f,g,x,'u','v'));u;v;
```

$$-a + x$$

$$\frac{1}{4}\,a$$

$$-\frac{1}{4}\,a$$

13.3 Polynomials with Coefficients in $\mathbb{Z}/p\mathbb{Z}$

The functions studied up to this point only concern polynomials whose co-efficients are rational or algebraic. MAPLE has also functions for computing with polynomials whose coefficients belong to $\mathbb{Z}/p\mathbb{Z}$, where p is a prime natural number. These functions play a fundamental role in computer algebra since they are used in most algorithms related to polynomials with rational coefficients (g.c.d, factorization, etc ...).

In the following sections, p will denote a prime natural number.

13.3.1 Basic Polynomial Computations in $\mathbb{Z}/p\mathbb{Z}$

Remember that $\mathbb{Z}/p\mathbb{Z}$ can be represented either as elements of the set $\{0, 1, \ldots, p - 1\}$, or as integers in the interval $\left[-E\left(\frac{p-1}{2}\right), E\left(\frac{p}{2}\right)\right]$. MAPLE uses the first representation by default for its computations modulo p, but it can be forced to use the second by assigning the value `mods` to the variable `mod` (p. 53).

We assume the first representation to be used in what follows. Any polynomial in one or several indeterminates whose coefficients belong to $\mathbb{Z}/p\mathbb{Z}$ can then be represented as a unique polynomial with coefficients in $\{0, 1, \ldots, p-1\}$. The image of a polynomial in this representation is obtained using the operator `mod`.

Ex.39
```
> P:=x^2+7*x+1: P mod 5;
```
$$x^2 + 2x + 1$$

To compute the sum or the product of polynomials whose coefficients belong to $\mathbb{Z}/p\mathbb{Z}$, one first performes the computation on associated polynomials with coefficients in $\mathbb{Z}$ and then uses `mod` to obtain the representative of the result in $\mathbb{Z}/p\mathbb{Z}$.

Ex.40
```
> P:=x^2+7*x+1;
```
$$P := x^2 + 7x + 1$$
```
> Q:=x^2+4;
```
$$Q := x^2 + 4$$
```
> (P+Q) mod 5;
```
$$2x^2 + 2x$$
```
> expand(P*Q) mod 5;
```
$$x^4 + 2x^3 + 3x + 4$$

13.3.2 Divisibility of Polynomials in $\mathbb{Z}/p\mathbb{Z}$

Given two polynomials f and g whose coefficients belong to $\mathbb{Z}/p\mathbb{Z}$, the study of the divisibility of f by g cannot be reduced to the study of the divisibility of their representatives with coefficients in $\mathbb{Z}$, as we shall see in the next example with f=x^2+3*x+1, g=x+4 and p=5.

Therefore, one cannot use divide(f,g) mod p, since MAPLE starts by evaluating divide(f,g) which returns true or false depending on whether or not f divides g in $\mathbb{Z}[x]$, and this truth value alone does not always suffice to determine divisibility.

To study the divisibility of polynomials with coefficients in $\mathbb{Z}/p\mathbb{Z}$, the inert form Divide must be used, which is then evaluated within the context of the operator mod.

If f and g are polynomials in one or several variables with coefficients in $\mathbb{Z}/p\mathbb{Z}$,

- Divide(f,g) mod p returns the value true if f is divisible by g, and false otherwise.
- When Divide(f,g,'q') mod p evaluates to true, the variable q contains the quotient of the division of f by g in $\mathbb{Z}/p\mathbb{Z}$ after the evaluation.

Ex.41

```
> f:=x^2+3*x+1;
```
$$f := x^2 + 3x + 1$$

```
> g:=x+4;
```
$$g := x + 4$$

```
> Divide(f,g,'q') mod 5;
```
$$true$$

```
> q;
```
$$x + 4$$

```
> divide(f,g) mod 5;
```
$$false$$

13.3.3 Computation of the G.c.d. of Polynomials in $\mathbb{Z}/p\mathbb{Z}$

As for divisibility, the g.c.d. of polynomials whose coefficients belong to $\mathbb{Z}/p\mathbb{Z}$ is not determined by the g.c.d. of their representatives. One thus must use the inert function Gcd.

If f and g are two polynomials in one or several variables with coefficients in $\mathbb{Z}/p\mathbb{Z}$, Gcd(f,g) mod p returns the g.c.d. of f and g. One may use two optional parameters to the function Gcd which, after evaluation, contain the quotient modulo p of f by $gcd(f,g)$ and the quotient modulo p of g by $gcd(f,g)$, respectively.

Ex.42

```
> f:=x*x+6*x+6;
```
$$f := x^2 + 6\,x + 6$$
```
> g:=x*x+2*x+3;
```
$$g := x^2 + 2\,x + 3$$
```
> Gcd(f,g,f1,g1) mod 11;
```
$$x + 9$$
```
> f1; g1;
```
$$x + 8$$
$$x + 4$$

13.3.4 Euclidean Division, Extended Euclid's Algorithm

The inert forms Quo and Rem compute the quotient and remainder of the Euclidean division modulo p. If f and g are two polynomials in one or several variables with coefficients in $\mathbb{Z}/p\mathbb{Z}$

- Quo(f,g,x) mod p   returns the quotient of the Euclidean division of the polynomial f by the polynomial g.
- Rem(f,g,x) mod p   returns the remainder of the Euclidean division of the polynomial f by the polynomial g.

As for the functions quo and rem, the x is essential even for polynomials in one indeterminate.

A fourth optional parameter which is unassigned (or is between apostrophes) can be used in the function Quo or in the function Rem. It will respectively contain the remainder and the quotient of the Euclidean division after the evaluation.

Ex.43

```
> f:=x^4+4*x^3+7;
```
$$f := x^4 + 4x^3 + 7$$

```
> g:=2*x^2-2*x+1;
```
$$g := 2x^2 - 2x + 1$$

```
> Rem(f,g,x) mod 11;
```
$$2x + 2$$

```
> Quo(f,g,x,'r') mod 11;
```
$$6x^2 + 8x + 5$$

```
> r;
```
$$2x + 2$$

If **f** and **g** are two polynomials in one or several variables with coefficients in $\mathbb{Z}/p\mathbb{Z}$, Gcdex(f,g,'u','v') mod p determines polynomials u and v with coefficients in $\mathbb{Z}/p\mathbb{Z}$ such that the equation $uf + vg = gcd(f, g)$ is satisfied.

Ex.44

```
> f:=x^2-x+1;
```
$$f := x^2 - x + 1$$

```
> g:=2*x*x-x+1;
```
$$g := 2x^2 - x + 1$$

```
> Gcdex(f,g,x,'u','v') mod 13;
```
$$1$$

```
> u; v;
```
$$2x + 1$$
$$12x$$

13.3.5 Factorization of the Polynomials in $\mathbb{Z}/p\mathbb{Z}$

The inert function **Factor**, used together with **mod**, factors polynomial modulo a prime number **p**.

With the positive representation (by default), one has

Ex.45

```
> f:=x^4+x^2+1;
```
$$f := x^4 + x^2 + 1$$

```
> Factor(f) mod 13;
```
$$(x + 10)(x + 4)(x + 3)(x + 9)$$

In symmetrical representation, one obtains

Ex.46

```
> 'mod':=mods;          Do not forget the backward apostrophes
```
$$mod := mods$$
```
> Factor(f) mod 13;
```
$$(x - 3)\,(x + 4)\,(x + 3)\,(x - 4)$$

Warning! Don't forget to capitalize `Factor`, otherwise one obtains an image modulo p of the decomposition into products of irreducible factors over $\mathbb{Z}$ of the representatives of f and g instead of the expected decomposition.

Ex.47

```
> 'mod':=modp;     To switch back to the positive representation
```
$$mod := modp$$
```
> factor(f) mod 13;                    Here with a lower case f !
```
$$\left(x^2 + x + 1\right)\left(x^2 + 12\,x + 1\right)$$

The inert function `Irreduc` used with `mod` tests the irreducibility of a polynomial modulo a prime number **p**.

Ex.48

```
> f:=x^5+2;
```
$$f := x^5 + 2$$
```
> Irreduc(f) mod 11;
```
$$true$$
```
> Irreduc(f) mod 19;
```
$$false$$
```
> mods(Factor(f),19);                    To obtain a symmetrical
                                  representation without modifying
                                           the content of mod
```
$$\left(x^2 + x - 3\right)\left(x^2 + 3\,x - 3\right)(x - 4)$$

Warning! The inert functions `Divide`, `Factor` and `Irreduc` are not systematically protected against use with integers that aren't prime. They do, however, return error messages in some cases.

Ex.49

```
> f:=4*x+4; g:=2*x+2;
```
$$f := 4x + 4$$
$$g := 2x + 2$$
```
> Divide(f,g) mod 6;
```
Error, (in mod/Rem) the modular inverse does not exist

14. Rational Functions

Rational functions have a specific type `ratpoly`. However, as with polynomials, introducing such objects doesn't require an explicit type declaration. Rational functions are simply entered by the user with the help of the basic operators +, -, *, ^ and / . Like the type `polynom`, the type `ratpoly` isn't a basic type returned by `whattype`, but it can be tested for with the help of the function `type`.

Ex. 1

```
> f:=(4*x^3+1/2)/(2*x^2-15*x-8);
```
$$f := \frac{4\,x^3 + \frac{1}{2}}{2\,x^2 - 15\,x - 8}$$

```
> whattype(f); type(f,ratpoly);
```
$$*$$
$$true$$

14.1 Writing of the Rational Functions

14.1.1 Irreducible Form

If `f` is a rational function in one or several variables with rational coefficients, `normal(f)` returns an irreducible representative of the rational function `f`, i.e. a representative $k\,\frac{p}{q}$ in which k is a rational number and p and q are relatively prime polynomials with integer coefficients.

For the rational function from the previous example, one has

Ex. 2

```
> normal(f);
```
$$\frac{1}{2} \frac{4\,x^2 - 2\,x + 1}{x - 8}$$

Example of a rational function in several variables

Ex. 3

```
> g:=(x^4+x^2*y^2+y^4)/(x^3-y^3);
```
$$g := \frac{x^4 + x^2\,y^2 + y^4}{x^3 - y^3}$$

```
> normal(g);
```
$$\frac{x^2 - x\,y + y^2}{x - y}$$

In fact, the function `normal`, as we saw p. 27, puts any "rational expression" with rational coefficients in normal form, although it doesn't always put a rational function whose coefficients are not rational in irreducible form.

Ex. 4

```
> h:=(x^2-cos(a)^2)/(x-cos(a));
```
$$h := \frac{x^2 - \cos(a)^2}{x - \cos(a)}$$

```
> normal(h);
```
$$\cos(a) + x$$

```
> h:=(x-sqrt(2))/(x^2-2);
```
$$h := \frac{x - \sqrt{2}}{x^2 - 2}$$

```
> normal(h);
```
Here, normal has no effect

$$\frac{x - \sqrt{2}}{x^2 - 2}$$

14.1.2 Numerator and Denominator

If `f` is a rational function, `numer(f)` and `denom(f)` return, respectively, the numerator and the denominator of `f`.

Ex. 5

```
> f:=x+(x+1)/(2*x^2+x+1);
```
$$f := x + \frac{x + 1}{2\,x^2 + x + 1}$$

```
> numer(f);
```
$$2\,x^3 + x^2 + 2\,x + 1$$

```
> denom(f);
```
$$2\,x^2 + x + 1$$

14.2 Factorization of the Rational Functions

The function `factor` factors the numerators and denominators of rational functions. Its syntax is similar to what is used for polynomials.

14.2.1 Rational Functions with Rational Coefficients

If `f` is a rational function in one or several variables with rational coefficients, the evaluation of `factor(f)` returns an irreducible representative of the rational function `f` whose numerator and denominator are written as products of irreducible polynomials over the field of rational numbers.

Example with a rational function in one variable

Ex. 6

```
> f:=(x^3+1)/((x+1)^7-x^7-1);
```

$$f := \frac{x^3 + 1}{(x+1)^7 - x^7 - 1}$$

```
> normal(f);
```
normal normalizes but doesn't factorize

$$\frac{1}{7} \frac{x^2 - x + 1}{(x^4 + 2x^3 + 3x^2 + 2x + 1)x}$$

```
> factor(f);
```
factor gives the means to factorize

$$\frac{1}{7} \frac{x^2 - x + 1}{(x^2 + x + 1)^2 x}$$

Example with a rational function in several variables

Ex. 7

```
> f:=(3*x^5-7*x^4*y+3*x^3*y^2-3*x^2*y^3+4*y^5)/(x^3-y^3);
```

$$f := \frac{3x^5 - 7x^4 y + 3x^3 y^2 - 3x^2 y^3 + 4y^5}{x^3 - y^3}$$

```
> factor(f);
```

$$\frac{(3x + 2y)(x - 2y)(x^2 + y^2)}{x^2 + xy + y^2}$$

```
> normal(f);
```
normal normalizes but doesn't factorize

$$\frac{3x^4 - 4x^3 y - x^2 y^2 - 4xy^3 - 4y^4}{x^2 + xy + y^2}$$

14.2.2 Rational Functions with Any Coefficients

If f is a rational function, in one or several variables, whose coefficients are irrational, `factor(f)` returns an irreducible representation of f whose numerator and denominator are written as products of irreducible polynomials over the field generated by the coefficients of f.

Ex. 8

```
> f:=(x^2-2)*(x+2*sqrt(2))/(x^2-8);
```

$$f := \frac{(x^2 - 2)(x + 2\sqrt{2})}{x^2 - 8}$$

```
> factor(f);
```

$$\frac{(x - \sqrt{2})(x + \sqrt{2})}{x - 2\sqrt{2}}$$

```
> normal(f);
```

Here, normal has no effect

$$\frac{(x^2 - 2)(x + 2\sqrt{2})}{x^2 - 8}$$

14.2.3 Factorization Over an Algebraic Extension

As with polynomials, the factorization of a rational function can be carried out over an algebraic extension of the field generated by the function's coefficients by giving a second parameter K, which is a set of algebraic numbers, to the function `factor`,

If f is a rational function, the evaluation of `factor(f,K)` returns a representation of the rational function f whose numerator and denominator are written as products of irreducible polynomials over the field generated by the coefficients of f and the elements of K. As with polynomials (p. 227), the elements of K as well as the coefficients of f have to be either all written with radicals or all written with `RootOf`'s.

Example with radicals

Ex. 9

```
> f:=1/(x^4-x^2+1);
```

$$f := \frac{1}{x^4 - x^2 + 1}$$

```
> f:=factor(f,sqrt(3));
```

$$f := \frac{1}{(x^2 + \sqrt{3}x + 1)(x^2 - \sqrt{3}x + 1)}$$

Example with `RootOf`'s

Ex.10

```
> alias(a=RootOf(x^2-5)):
  f:=(x^2-5)/(x^5-1);
```

$$f := \frac{x^2 - 5}{x^5 - 1}$$

```
> factor(f,a);
```

$$4 \frac{(x+a)(x-a)}{(2x^2 + x - ax + 2)(2x^2 + x + ax + 2)(x-1)}$$

14.3 Partial Fraction Decomposition

The function `convert` together with the option `parfrac` decomposes a rational function into partial fraction form.

14.3.1 Decomposition of a Rational Function Over $\mathbb{Q}(x)$

If `f` is a rational function with rational coefficients in the free variable x, the evaluation of `convert(f,parfrac,x)` returns the decomposition of `f` into partial fraction form over $\mathbb{Q}(x)$. The x is required, even when the rational function `f` doesn't depend on another free variable.

Ex.11

```
> f:=(x^3+1)/(x*(x^4+4));
```

$$f := \frac{x^3 + 1}{x(x^4 + 4)}$$

```
> convert(f,parfrac,x);
```

$$\frac{1}{4}\frac{1}{x} + \frac{1}{8}\frac{1+x}{x^2 - 2x + 2} - \frac{1}{8}\frac{1+3x}{x^2 + 2x + 2}$$

```
> convert(f,parfrac);
  Error, (in convert/parfrac) convert/parfrac
  uses a 2nd argument, x, which is missing
> f:=1/(x^8-1);
```

$$f := \frac{1}{x^8 - 1}$$

```
> convert(f,parfrac,x);
```

$$\frac{1}{8}\frac{1}{x-1} - \frac{1}{8}\frac{1}{x+1} - \frac{1}{4}\frac{1}{x^2+1} - \frac{1}{2}\frac{1}{x^4+1}$$

14.3.2 Decomposition Over $\mathbb{R}(x)$ or Over $\mathbb{C}(x)$

Rational Function with Rational Coefficients

If f is a rational function with rational coefficients such that only polynomials with rational coefficients appear in the factorization of its denominator in $\mathbb{R}(x)$, the evaluation of `convert(f,parfrac,x)` returns the partial fraction decomposition of f over $\mathbb{R}(x)$.

Ex.12

```
> f:=1/(x^4+4);
```
$$f := \frac{1}{(x^4 + 4)}$$

```
> convert(f,parfrac,x);
```
$$+\frac{1}{8}\frac{-x+2}{x^2-2x+2} + \frac{1}{8}\frac{x+2}{x^2+2x+2}$$

On the other hand, if some algebraic coefficients appear in the factorization over $\mathbb{R}(x)$ or if one wishes a decomposition over $\mathbb{C}(x)$, then one must accomplish this in two steps: first use the function `factor` with a second parameter to obtain the factorization of the denominator, then call `convert`.

Ex.13

```
> f:=(x^2+1)/(x^4-4);
```
$$f := \frac{x^2+1}{x^4-4}$$

```
> g:=factor(f,sqrt(2));            factorization of f over ℝ(x)
```
$$g := \frac{x^2+1}{(x^2+2)(x-\sqrt{2})(x+\sqrt{2})}$$

```
> convert(g,parfrac,x);            Decomposition of f over ℝ(x)
```
$$\frac{1}{4}\frac{1}{x^2+2} + \frac{3}{16}\frac{\sqrt{2}}{x-\sqrt{2}} - \frac{3}{16}\frac{\sqrt{2}}{x+\sqrt{2}}$$

```
> h:=factor(f,{sqrt(2),I});        Factorization of f over ℂ(x)
```
$$h := \frac{(x+I)(x-I)}{(x-\sqrt{2})(x+\sqrt{2})(x+I\sqrt{2})(x-I\sqrt{2})}$$

```
> convert(h,parfrac,x);            Decomposition of f over ℂ(x)
```
$$\frac{3}{16}\frac{\sqrt{2}}{x-\sqrt{2}} - \frac{3}{16}\frac{\sqrt{2}}{x+\sqrt{2}} + \frac{1}{16}\frac{I\sqrt{2}}{x+I\sqrt{2}} - \frac{1}{16}\frac{I\sqrt{2}}{x-I\sqrt{2}}$$

Rational Function with Any Coefficients

For any rational function `f`, the evaluation of `convert(f,parfrac,x)` starts by carrying out `factor(denom(f))`, which returns a factorization of the denominator over the field generated by its coefficients.

- When this factorization only contains polynomials that are irreducible over $\mathbb{R}(x)$ (resp. over $\mathbb{C}(x)$), the result returned by this single call to `convert` provides the expected decomposition.
- Otherwise, the user has to use `factor` with a second parameter in order to factor the denominator into irreducible polynomials.

Example of decomposition that doesn't require a prior call to `factor`

Ex.14

```
> f:=1/(x^2-(sqrt(2)+sqrt(3))*x+sqrt(6));
```

$$f := \frac{1}{x^2 - \left(\sqrt{2} + \sqrt{3}\right)x + \sqrt{6}}$$

```
> convert(f,parfrac,x);
```

$$-\frac{\sqrt{3} + \sqrt{2}}{x - \sqrt{2}} + \frac{\sqrt{3} + \sqrt{2}}{x - \sqrt{3}}$$

Example of decomposition for which the user has to apply `factor`

Ex.15

```
> f:=(x^2-2)*(x+2)/(x^2-8);
```

$$f := \frac{\left(x^2 - 2\right)(x + 2)}{\left(x^2 - 8\right)}$$

```
> convert(f,parfrac,x);              Decomposition of f over ℚ(x)
```

$$x + 2 + \frac{6x + 12}{x^2 - 8}$$

```
> g:=factor(f,sqrt(2));
```

$$g := \frac{\left(x - \sqrt{2}\right)\left(x + \sqrt{2}\right)(x + 2)}{\left(x + 2\sqrt{2}\right)\left(x - 2\sqrt{2}\right)}$$

```
> convert(g,parfrac,x);              Decomposition of f over ℝ(x)
```

$$x + 2 - \frac{3}{2}\frac{\sqrt{2} - 2}{x + 2\sqrt{2}} - \frac{3}{2}\frac{\sqrt{2} + 2}{-x + 2\sqrt{2}}$$

Note: Since one only needs the factorization of the denominator in the previous example, computation time can be saved by replacing `factor(f,sqrt(2))` with `subs(denom(f)=factor(denom(f),sqrt(2)),f)`.

Example of decomposition using the function `split`

Ex.16

```
> f:=(x^4+1)/(x^8+x^4+1);
```

$$f := \frac{x^4 + 1}{x^8 + x^4 + 1}$$

```
> readlib(split):
  d:=split(denom(f),x):            to suppress useless echo
  d:=convert(d,radical);
```

$$d := (x - \%1)\left(x - \frac{1}{2} - \frac{1}{2}I\sqrt{3}\right)\left(x + \sqrt{\%1}\,(-\%1)\right)$$

$$(x + \%1)\left(x - \sqrt{\%1}\right)\left(x - \sqrt{\%1}\,(-\%1)\right)$$

$$\left(x + \sqrt{\%1}\right)\left(x + \frac{1}{2} - \frac{1}{2}I\sqrt{3}\right)$$

$$\%1 := \frac{1}{2} + \frac{1}{2}I\sqrt{3}$$

```
> convert(numer(f)/d,parfrac,x);
```

$$\frac{1}{12}\frac{3I - \sqrt{3}}{2x - \sqrt{3} + I} + \frac{1}{12}\frac{\sqrt{3} + 3I}{2x + \sqrt{3} + I} - \frac{1}{12}\frac{-3 + I\sqrt{3}}{2x + 1 - I\sqrt{3}}$$

$$-\frac{1}{12}\frac{\sqrt{3} + 3I}{2x - \sqrt{3} - I} - \frac{1}{12}\frac{3I - \sqrt{3}}{2x + \sqrt{3} - I} - \frac{1}{12}\frac{-3 + I\sqrt{3}}{2x - 1 + I\sqrt{3}}$$

$$+\frac{1}{12}\frac{3 + I\sqrt{3}}{2x + 1 + I\sqrt{3}} - \frac{1}{12}\frac{3 + I\sqrt{3}}{2x - 1 - I\sqrt{3}}$$

Looking at the previous decomposition, we see that the decomposition of the rational function f over $\mathbb{R}(x)$ could have been obtained by typing

Ex.17

```
> d:=factor(denom(f),sqrt(3));
```

$$d := \left(x^2 - x + 1\right)\left(x^2 + x + 1\right)\left(x^2 + \sqrt{3}x + 1\right)\left(x^2 - \sqrt{3}x + 1\right)$$

```
> convert(numer(f)/d,parfrac,x);
```

$$-\frac{1}{4}\frac{-1 + x}{x^2 - x + 1} + \frac{1}{4}\frac{1 + x}{x^2 + x + 1}$$

$$+\frac{1}{12}\frac{3 + \sqrt{3}x}{x^2 + \sqrt{3}x + 1} - \frac{1}{12}\frac{-3 + \sqrt{3}x}{x^2 - \sqrt{3}x + 1}$$

14.3.3 Decomposition of a Rational Function with Parameters

The function `convert` can also decompose a rational function in the variable x whose coefficients depend on parameters in partial fractions.

Ex.18

```
> f:=1/(x^4-4*x^2*a^2+2*x^2+1);
```

$$f := \frac{1}{x^4 - 4x^2 a^2 + 2x^2 + 1}$$

```
> convert(f,parfrac,x);
```

$$\frac{1}{4} \frac{2a + x}{a(x^2 + 2a\, x + 1)} - \frac{1}{4} \frac{-2a + x}{a(x^2 - 2a\, x + 1)}$$

In fact, in the previous example the function `convert` returns the decomposition of f while considering the coefficients of x as elements of $\mathbb{Q}(a)$, where a is symbolically different from 0, from 1 and from -1. Since a usually denotes a numerical parameter, one shouldn't forget to handle these special cases.

Ex.19

```
> convert(subs(a=0,f),parfrac,x);        Study of the case a=0
```

$$\frac{1}{(x^2 + 1)^2}$$

```
> convert(subs(a=1,f),parfrac,x);        Study of the case a=1
```

$$\frac{1}{4} \frac{1}{(x-1)^2} - \frac{1}{4} \frac{1}{(x-1)} + \frac{1}{4} \frac{1}{(x+1)^2} + \frac{1}{4} \frac{1}{(x+1)}$$

Another classical example of decomposition

Ex.20

```
> f:=1/(x^4-2*x^2*cos(a)+1);
```

$$f := \frac{1}{x^4 - 2x^2 \cos(a) + 1}$$

```
> f:=subs(cos(a)=2*cos(a/2)^2-1,f);
```

$$f := \frac{1}{x^4 - 2x^2 \left(2 \cos\left(\frac{1}{2}a\right)^2 - 1\right) + 1}$$

```
> convert(f,parfrac,x);
```

$$\frac{1}{4} \frac{2 \cos\left(\frac{1}{2}a\right) + x}{\cos\left(\frac{1}{2}a\right)\left(x^2 + 2 \cos\left(\frac{1}{2}a\right) x + 1\right)}$$

$$-\frac{1}{4} \frac{2 \cos\left(\frac{1}{2}a\right) - x}{\cos\left(\frac{1}{2}a\right)\left(-x^2 + 2 \cos\left(\frac{1}{2}a\right) x - 1\right)}$$

Study of the special case $a = 0$

Ex.21

```
> convert(subs(a=0,f),parfrac,x);                doesn't provide
                                                 the decomposition
                                            since cos(0) isn't evaluated
```

$$\frac{1}{4} \frac{2\cos(0) + x}{\cos(0)\,(x^2 + 2\cos(0)\,x + 1)}$$

$$-\frac{1}{4} \frac{2\cos(0) - x}{\cos(0)\,(-x^2 + 2\cos(0)\,x - 1)}$$

```
> convert(eval(subs(a=0,f)),parfrac,x);          after subs one
                                                 has to force the
                                                 evaluation with eval
```

$$\frac{1}{4}\frac{1}{(x-1)^2} - \frac{1}{4}\frac{1}{x-1} + \frac{1}{4}\frac{1}{(x+1)^2} + \frac{1}{4}\frac{1}{x+1}$$

14.4 Continued Fraction Series Expansions

The function convert together with the option confrac computes the continued fraction series expansion of any expression.

- If f is a rational function, then convert(f,confrac,x) returns the continued fraction series expansion of f with respect to the variable x. As for a rational number, this is just another way to write f.

- If f is not a rational expression in x, then convert(f,confrac,x,n) returns the continued fraction series expansion of f with respect to the variable x at order n. It is, in fact, the continued fraction series expansion of series(f,x,n). The parameter n is optional, and MAPLE chooses the default value n=Order (p. 127).

Example of the expansion of a rational function

Ex.22

```
> f:=(1+x+x^2)/(2-x+x^2+x^3);
```

$$f := \frac{1 + x + x^2}{2 - x + x^2 + x^3}$$

```
> convert(f,confrac,x);
```

$$\cfrac{1}{x - 2 - \cfrac{1}{x + 2 + 3\cfrac{1}{x - 1}}}$$

Another example: continued fraction series expansion of `cos(x)`, and a graphical study of the quality of the approximation.

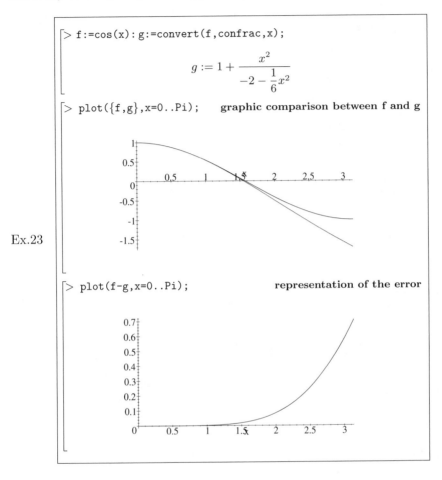

Ex.23

15. Construction of Vectors and of Matrices

15.1 The `linalg` Library

Most functions[1] for linear algebra operations don't belong to MAPLE's kernel but to the `linalg` library. There are several ways to proceed when one wishes to use them.

First Solution

If many functions from the library are needed, the whole library should be loaded with the `with(linalg)` command. MAPLE will indicate that it use new definitions of the identifiers `trace` and `norm`. It then displays a list of all functions that have been loaded into memory.

Ex. 1

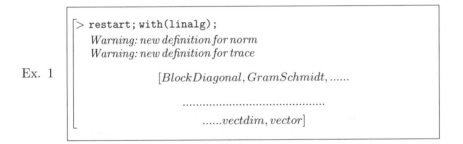

The user may replace the semicolon by a colon if he doesn't want this list to be displayed.

---

[1] except `vector`, `matrix` and `evalm`.

Second Solution

If one only needs a few functions and doesn't want to clutter up memory, they can loaded individually with

Ex. 2

```
> restart; with(linalg,det,vectdim,trace);
        Warning: new definition for trace

                        [det, vectdim, trace]
```

Third Solution

Use the full name of the function, including the name of the library, using square brackets. For the function vectdim, which will be studied in the next section, one may write

Ex. 3

```
> restart; v:=vector([1,2,3]): linalg[vectdim](v);

                        3
```

Warning! The function isn't loaded into memory in this case, and one will have to call it again with its full name, including the name of the library, for any future use.

We assume in the rest of this chapter that the linalg library has been loaded.

15.2 Vectors

MAPLE has a type vector, which is a specific array type: an array with one index, which starts with 1. It isn't a basic type returned by whattype, but it can, nevertheless, be tested with the help of the function type.

15.2.1 Definition of the Vectors

The function vector can be used to define vectors. vector supports two different syntaxes.

First Syntax

A vector can be defined by simply giving the list (between square brackets) of its components.

Ex. 4

```
> v:=vector([5,7,3]);
```
$$v := [5, 7, 3]$$

```
> vector(5,7,3);        If one forgets the square brackets...Error
```
Error, (in vector) invalid arguments

```
> v:=vector({5,7,3});            { } defines a set and not a list
```
Error, (in vector) invalid arguments

Second Syntax

A vector can be defined by giving its dimension and an rule specifying each component as function of its index. It can be either an anonymous function (p. 406) defined in the call to **vector**, or an application defined previously.

Ex. 5

```
> v:=vector(5,x->x*x);
```
$$v := [1, 4, 9, 16, 25]$$

```
> f:=x->x^2; v:=vector(5,f);
```
$$f := x \rightarrow x^2$$
$$v := [1, 4, 9, 16, 25]$$

Warning! It is essential to use a function and not an expression when defining a vector by giving its components as function of their indices.

Ex. 6

```
> x:='x': w:=vector(3,2*x+1);
```
$$w := [2\,x(1) + 1,\ 2\,x(2) + 1,\ 2\,x(3) + 1]$$

Warning! The dimension n must contain an integer numerical value when **vector(n,f)** is evaluated, otherwise an error results.

Ex. 7

```
> n:='n': v:=vector(n,t->t^2);
```
Error, (in vector) invalid argument

Note: A variable v can be assigned a vector for which not all components are defined. In the echo returned by MAPLE, every component of index i which isn't initialized is represented by v_i.

Ex. 8

```
> v:=vector(4,[3,1,2]);
```
$$v := [3, 1, 2, v_4]$$
```
> v:=vector(4);
```
                                    Particular case of an empty list
$$v := array\,(1..4, [\,])$$

15.2.2 Dimension and Components of a Vector

The function `vectdim` returns the number of components of its argument which is assumed to be a vector.

Ex. 9

```
> v:=vector([1,2,3]);
```
$$v := [1, 2, 3]$$
```
> vectdim(v);
```
                                    one assumes that with(linalg)
                                    has been executed !

$$3$$

Like most functions which are applied to vectors, the function `vectdim` allows lists to represent vectors.

Ex.10

```
> v:=[1,2,3];
```
$$v := [1, 2, 3]$$
```
> vectdim(v);
```
$$3$$

To obtain the value of a component of a vector, the vector is subscripted by the component's index between square brackets, as with any object of type `array`.

Ex.11

```
> v:=vector([3,2,4,5,1]); v[3];
```
$$v := [3, 2, 4, 5, 1]$$
$$4$$
```
> v[6];
```
                                    In case of overflowing ...Error
Error, 1st index, 6, larger than upper array bound 5

Likewise, to assign a value to the i-th component of the vector v, just make the assignment v[i]:=...

Ex.12

```
[> v[3]:=2.5;
```
$$v_3 := 2.5$$
```
[> eval(v);
```
                                    **eval gives the means to obtain
                                    the components of v (p. 258)**

$$[3, 2, 2.5, 5, 1]$$

15.3 Matrices

To handle matrices, MAPLE has the type matrix, which is a specific array type: an array with two indices both starting at 1. It isn't a basic type returned by whattype, but it can, nevertheless, be tested with the help of the function type.

15.3.1 Definition of Matrices

The function matrix defines matrices. It allows three different syntaxes.

First Syntax

A matrix can be defined by giving the list of its rows, each of these rows being itself a list of elements: thus, nested square brackets must be used.

If each object among L1,L2,...,Ln is a list of p elements, then the evaluation of matrix([L1,L2,...,Ln]) returns the matrix with n rows and p columns, whose i-th row is Li.

Ex.13

```
[> M:=matrix([[1,2,3],[4,5,6]]);
```
$$M := \begin{bmatrix} 1 & 2 & 3 \\ 4 & 5 & 6 \end{bmatrix}$$

Warning! The function `matrix` sees at least two arguments of type `list` if one forgets the outer square brackets: it returns an error message in this case.

Ex.14

```
> M:=matrix([1,2,3],[4,5,6] );
   Error, (in matrix)1st and 2nd arguments (dimensions)
   must be non negative integers
```

Second Syntax

A matrix can also be defined by first giving its dimensions, and then the list (between square brackets) of its elements; this list will be used to fill in the matrix row by row. For a matrix with `n` rows and `p` columns, the syntax is: `matrix(n,p,List_El)` where `List_El` is a list of `np` elements.

If the list isn't long enough to fill in the whole matrix, the last elements are left unspecified and appear as indexed coefficients. If the list is too long, MAPLE doesn't truncate, but instead returns an error message.

Ex.15

```
> M:=matrix(2,3,[1,2,3,4,5,6]);
```
$$M := \left[\begin{array}{ccc} 1 & 2 & 3 \\ 4 & 5 & 6 \end{array} \right]$$
```
> M:=matrix(2,3,[1,2,3,4]);
```
$$M := \left[\begin{array}{ccc} 1 & 2 & 3 \\ 4 & M_{2,2} & M_{2,3} \end{array} \right]$$
```
> M:=matrix(2,3,[1,2,3,4,5,6,7,8]);
   Error, (in matrix) 1st index, 3, larger than upper array bound 2
```

Third Syntax

A matrix can also be defined by giving its dimensions (specific values and not free variables) and a function in two variables that defines each coefficient as a function of its indices. This function may be previously defined, or an anonymous function (p. 406) defined in the call to `matrix`.

Ex.16

```
> f:=(i,j)->(i+j-1): matrix(3,3,f);
```
$$\left[\begin{array}{ccc} 1 & 2 & 3 \\ 2 & 3 & 4 \\ 3 & 4 & 5 \end{array} \right]$$
```
> M:= matrix(3,3,(x,y)->x+y-1):
```
Use of an anonymous function

Warning! A function and not an expression must be used when one defines a matrix by giving the elements as a function of their position.

Ex.17

$$\left[\begin{matrix} > \texttt{x:='x':y:='y':M:=matrix(3,3,x+y);} \\ \\ \left[\begin{matrix} x(1,1)+y(1,1) & x(1,2)+y(1,2) & x(1,3)+y(1,3) \\ x(2,1)+y(2,1) & x(2,2)+y(2,2) & x(2,3)+y(2,3) \\ x(3,1)+y(3,1) & x(3,2)+y(3,2) & x(3,3)+y(3,3) \end{matrix} \right] \end{matrix} \right.$$

Warning! The dimensions n and p have to contain integer numerical values when `matrix(n,p,f)` is evaluated, otherwise MAPLE returns an error message.

Ex.18

```
> n:='n':matrix(n,3,[1,2,3,4,5,6,7,8]);
```
Error, (in matrix)1st and 2nd arguments (dimensions) must be non negative integers

15.3.2 Dimensions and Coefficients of a Matrix

The functions `rowdim` and `coldim` give the number of rows and the number of columns of a matrix. If A is a matrix, the evaluation of `rowdim(A)` (resp. `coldim(A)`) returns the number of rows (resp. of columns) of the matrix A.

Ex.19

```
> A:=matrix([[1,2,3],[2,3,4],[3,4,5],[4,5,6]]);
```

$$A := \left[\begin{matrix} 1 & 2 & 3 \\ 2 & 3 & 4 \\ 3 & 4 & 5 \\ 4 & 5 & 6 \end{matrix} \right]$$

```
> rowdim(A);coldim(A);
```
$$4$$
$$3$$

Warning! The previous functions expect a matrix as argument and don't accept a vector, because MAPLE distinguishes between a vector and a column matrix.

Ex.20

```
> v:=vector(5,i->i);rowdim(v);
```

$$v := [1,2,3,4,5]$$

Error, (in rowdim) expecting a matrix

To obtain the value of an element of a matrix, one indicates its index between square brackets, the first value being the index of the row.

Ex.21

```
> M:=matrix(2,3,[1,2,3,4,5,6]):M[2,3];
```
$$6$$
```
> M[2,4];
   Error, 2nd index, 4, larger than upper array bound 3
```

Likewise, M[i,j]:=... assigns a value to the coefficient with index (i,j) of the matrix M.

Ex.22

```
> M[1,1]:=0: eval(M);                    eval (see p. 260
```

$$\begin{bmatrix} 0 & 2 & 3 \\ 4 & 5 & 6 \end{bmatrix}$$

15.4 Problems of Evaluation

15.4.1 Evaluation of Vectors

Contrary to what goes on with the variables of almost all types encountered so far, MAPLE doesn't carry out a full evaluation of an object of type vector (the same is true for all arrays).

It doesn't suffice to invoke the name of a vector to display its contents on the screen, since it only leads to an evaluation up to the last vector name encountered. To obtain a list of elements, one must use eval, which returns a full evaluation.

Ex.23

```
> v:=vector(5,t->t^2); w:=v;
```
$$v := [1, 4, 9, 16, 25]$$

$$w := v$$
```
> v,w;                                    v is the last name encountered
```
$$v \ , \ w$$
```
> eval(v); eval(w);
```
$$[1, 4, 9, 16, 25]$$
$$[1, 4, 9, 16, 25]$$

Of course, MAPLE handles vectors whose components are expressions depending on free variables. But if one assigns a value to one of these variables, `eval` doesn't suffice to obtain the new value of the vector. Instead `map(eval,...)` must be used, which applies `eval` to every component of the vector. Although the function `map` will be studied in detail in Chapter 22, the following examples indicate its use.

Ex.24

```
> x:='x'; v:=vector(4,t->t*x^(t-1));
```

$$x := x$$

$$v := \left[1, 2\,x, 3\,x^2, 4\,x^3\right]$$

```
> x:=2; eval(v); map(eval,v);
```

$$x := 2$$

$$\left[1, 2\,x, 3\,x^2, 4\,x^3\right]$$

$$[1, 4, 12, 32]$$

Another example with an assignment of a literal expression.

Ex.25

```
> x:=y+1; eval(v); map(eval,v);
```

$$x := y + 1$$

$$\left[1, 2\,x, 3\,x^2, 4\,x^3\right]$$

$$\left[1, 2\,y + 2, 3\,(y+1)^2, 4\,(y+1)^3\right]$$

When a vector v depends on a variable x, and this variable contains an expression depending on another variable, y for example, a second level use of `map` or a composition of functions may be required to simplify some results. With the notations of the previous example, one has

Ex.26

```
> map(expand ,map(eval ,v));
```

$$\left[1, 2\,y + 2, 3\,y^2 + 6\,y + 3, 4\,y^3 + 12\,y^2 + 12\,y + 4\right]$$

```
> map(expand@eval,v);                          other possibility
```

$$\left[1, 2\,y + 2, 3\,y^2 + 6\,y + 3, 4\,y^3 + 12\,y^2 + 12\,y + 4\right]$$

15.4.2 Evaluation of the Matrices

As with variables of type `vector`, MAPLE carries out an evaluation up to the last name encountered for matrices. It doesn't suffice to invoke the name of a matrix to obtain its contents; one must use `eval`.

Ex.27

```
> x:='x': M:=matrix(3,3,(i,j)->x^(i-1)*y^(j-1)): N:=M;
```
$$N := M$$
```
> N; eval(N);
```
$$M$$
$$\begin{bmatrix} 1 & y & y^2 \\ x & x\,y & x\,y^2 \\ x^2 & x^2\,y & x^2\,y^2 \end{bmatrix}$$

As with vectors, the function `eval` doesn't suffice to obtain the full evaluation of matrices whose components are expressions. Again, `map` must be used to apply `eval` to every coefficient of the matrix.

Ex.28

```
> M:=matrix(3,3,(i,j)->x^(i-1)*y^(j-1)):
  x:=1: eval(M); map(eval,M);
```
$$\begin{bmatrix} 1 & y & y^2 \\ x & xy & xy^2 \\ x^2 & x^2y & x^2y^2 \end{bmatrix}$$
$$\begin{bmatrix} 1 & y & y^2 \\ 1 & y & y^2 \\ 1 & y & y^2 \end{bmatrix}$$

As with vectors, when the variable x appearing in the matrix points contain an expression depending on another variable, two levels of `map` may be needed to obtain evaluations.

To expand the elements of the preceding matrix when y is set to z+1, write

Ex.29

```
> x:='x': y:=z+1:
  map(expand,map(eval,M));
```
$$\begin{bmatrix} 1 & z+1 & z^2+2z+1 \\ x & xz+x & xz^2+2xz+x \\ x^2 & x^2z+x^2 & x^2z^2+2x^2z+x^2 \end{bmatrix}$$

15.4.3 Example of Use of Matrices of Variable Size

MAPLE only allows matrices and vectors whose dimensions are integer numerical values. It is therefore impossible to work with a matrix or a vector with dimensions that depend on a "parameter", i.e. on an unassigned variable.

If one wishes to study the determinant of

$$
\begin{bmatrix}
1 & 1 & \cdots & \cdots & 1 \\
1 & \xi & \xi^2 & \cdots & \xi^{n-1} \\
1 & \xi^2 & \xi^4 & \cdots & \xi^{2(n-1)} \\
\vdots & \vdots & \vdots & & \vdots \\
1 & \xi^{n-2} & \xi^{2(n-2)} & \cdots & \xi^{(n-2)(n-1)} \\
1 & \xi^{n-1} & \xi^{2(n-1)} & \cdots & \xi^{(n-1)(n-1)}
\end{bmatrix}
$$

with $\xi = e^{2i\pi/n}$, it is impossible to define the corresponding matrix without having assigned an integer value to **n**.

Ex.30

```
> n:='n': M:=matrix(n,n,(i,j)->
  exp(2*I*Pi/n)^((i-1)*(j-1)));
  Error, (in matrix) 1st and 2nd arguments (dimensions)
  must be non egative integers
```

On the other hand, it is possible to first assign an integer value to **n**, and then to define M as a function of **n** and compute its determinant.

Ex.31

```
> n:=3:
  M:=matrix(n,n,(i,j)->exp(2*I*Pi/n)^((i-1)*(j-1))):
> det(M);
```
$$-3I\sqrt{3}$$

To compute the value of this determinant for **n=5**, it then suffices to modify the assignment of the first line and to re-execute the three commands.

It is, however, even better to write

Ex.32

```
> n:='n':
  M:='matrix(n,n,(i,j)->exp(2*I*Pi/n)^((i-1)*(j-1)))';
```
$$
M := matrix\left(n, n, (i,j) \rightarrow \left(e^{\left(2\frac{I\pi}{n}\right)}\right)^{(i-1)(j-1)}\right)
$$

The apostrophes postpone the evaluation of the function `matrix`, so that M points towards an expression depending on **n**. This way the computation of the determinant for different values of **n** can be written

Ex.33

```
> n:=3: det(eval(M));
```
$$-3I\sqrt{3}$$

```
> n:=5: evalc(det(eval(M)));
```
$$-25\sqrt{5}$$

```
> det(M);                    det refuses the computation because M
                                              is of type string
```
Error, (in det) expecting a matrix

One might also think about defining M as a function of **n** in order to carry out the computation of the determinant more quickly. One might then be tempted to write

Ex.34

```
> M:=n->matrix(n,n,(i,j)->exp(2*I*Pi/n)^((i-1)*(j-1)));
```
$$M := n \rightarrow matrix\left(n, n, (i,j) \rightarrow \left(e^{\left(2\frac{I\pi}{n}\right)}\right)^{(i-1)(j-1)}\right)$$

```
> simplify(det(M(3)));
```
$$1 - 2\,(-1)^{2/5} - 2\,(-1)^{1/5} + (-1)^{3/5}$$

The 5 appearing in the result seems surprising. It is a consequence of the way MAPLE manages the variables appearing in nested procedures or functions: the function `(i,j)->exp(2*I*Pi/n)^((i-1)*(j-1))` being nested in the function M, the **n** appearing in it is considered by MAPLE as the global variable **n**, thus 5, and not as the parameter **n** of the function M. The reader may refer to Section 24.2.2 for a more detailed explanation of this phenomenon.

The function **unapply** must be used to obtain a correct expression of the function M in this case.

Ex.35

```
> M:=n->matrix(n,n,unapply(exp(2*I*Pi/n)^((i-1)*(j-1)),
  i,j));
```
$$M := n \rightarrow matrix\left(n, n, unapply\left(\left(e^{\left(2\frac{I\pi}{n}\right)}\right)^{(i-1)(j-1)}, i, j\right)\right)$$

```
> n:='n': det(M(3)); evalc(det(M(5)));
```
$$-3I\sqrt{3}$$
$$-25\sqrt{5}$$

15.5 Special Matrices

15.5.1 Diagonal Matrix and Identity Matrix

The function `diag` creates diagonal matrices. If `Expr_seq` is a sequence of scalar numbers, then `diag(Expr_seq)` returns the diagonal matrix whose diagonal elements are the elements of `Expr_seq`.

Ex.36

```
> restart: with(linalg): diag(1,2,3);
```

$$\begin{bmatrix} 1 & 0 & 0 \\ 0 & 2 & 0 \\ 0 & 0 & 3 \end{bmatrix}$$

A diagonal matrix cannot be defined simply by a function defining the diagonal elements in terms of their indices. One may, however, use the function `seq` (p. 350).

Ex.37

```
> diag(seq(i*i,i=1..3));
```

$$\begin{bmatrix} 1 & 0 & 0 \\ 0 & 4 & 0 \\ 0 & 0 & 9 \end{bmatrix}$$

```
> id:=diag(seq(1,i=1..3));
```
Obtaining the identity matrix
One may also write diag(1$3)

$$id := \begin{bmatrix} 1 & 0 & 0 \\ 0 & 1 & 0 \\ 0 & 0 & 1 \end{bmatrix}$$

15.5.2 Tri-Diagonal or Multi-Diagonal Matrix

The function `band` can be used to create banded matrices, for which all the elements along a given diagonal are equal. If `a`, `b` and `c` are three scalar numbers, and if `n` is an integer, then `band([a,b,c],n)` returns the tridiagonal square matrix of order `n`

$$\begin{bmatrix} b & c & 0 & \cdots & 0 \\ a & b & c & \ddots & \vdots \\ 0 & a & \ddots & \ddots & 0 \\ \vdots & \ddots & \ddots & \ddots & c \\ 0 & \cdots & 0 & a & b \end{bmatrix}$$

Ex.38

```
> band([1,2,-1],4);
```

$$
\begin{bmatrix}
2 & -1 & 0 & 0 \\
1 & 2 & -1 & 0 \\
0 & 1 & 2 & -1 \\
0 & 0 & 1 & 2
\end{bmatrix}
$$

More generally, the function **band** creates a $(2p+1)$-diagonal matrix where all the elements on the same diagonal are equal. As before, a list of elements to use is given as well as the size of the matrix. The list is used to fill in the diagonals of the matrix from bottom to top, using the middle element for the principal diagonal.

15.5.3 Vandermonde Matrix

To obtain a Vandermonde matrix, use the function **vandermonde** and give it the list (between square brackets) of elements to be used.

Ex.39

```
> vandermonde([x,y,z,t]);
```

$$
\begin{bmatrix}
1 & x & x^2 & x^3 \\
1 & y & y^2 & y^3 \\
1 & z & z^2 & z^3 \\
1 & t & t^2 & t^3
\end{bmatrix}
$$

As the next example shows, one may use the function **seq** to construct a Vandermonde matrix with many rows, or to test an hypothesis about Vandermonde matrices of different sizes.

Ex.40

```
> n:=4: M:=vandermonde([seq(x[i],i=1..n)]);
```

$$
\begin{bmatrix}
1 & x_1 & x_1^2 & x_1^3 \\
1 & x_2 & x_2^2 & x_2^3 \\
1 & x_3 & x_3^2 & x_3^3 \\
1 & x_2 & x_4^2 & x_4^3
\end{bmatrix}
$$

The previous example uses the array x whose elements are written x_1, x_2, x_3, x_4. One thus must write x[i]:=... to modify the contents of x[i].

15.5.4 Hilbert Matrix

If n is a natural number, then `hilbert(n)` returns the Hilbert matrix of order n, i.e. the matrix of order n whose entries are given by $1/(i + j - 1)$.

Ex.41

```
> hilbert(3);
```

$$\begin{bmatrix} 1 & \dfrac{1}{2} & \dfrac{1}{3} \\[2mm] \dfrac{1}{2} & \dfrac{1}{3} & \dfrac{1}{4} \\[2mm] \dfrac{1}{3} & \dfrac{1}{4} & \dfrac{1}{5} \end{bmatrix}$$

15.5.5 Sylvester Matrix and Bézout Matrix

If P and Q are two polynomials in the variable x, then `sylvester(P,Q,x)` (resp. `bezout(P,Q,x)`) returns the Sylvester matrix (resp. the Bézout matrix) of P and Q.

```
> P:=a3*x^3+a2*x^2+a1*x+a0; Q:=b2*x^2+b1*x+b0;
```

$$P := a3\,x^3 + a2\,x^2 + a1\,x + a0$$

$$Q := b2\,x^2 + b1\,x + b0$$

```
> sylvester(P,Q,x);
```

$$\begin{bmatrix} a3 & a2 & a1 & a0 & 0 \\ 0 & a3 & a2 & a1 & a0 \\ b2 & b1 & b0 & 0 & 0 \\ 0 & b2 & b1 & b0 & 0 \\ 0 & 0 & b2 & b1 & b0 \end{bmatrix}$$

Ex.42

```
> bezout(P,Q,x);
```

$$\begin{bmatrix} a3\,b0 - b2\,a1 & b0\,a2 - a1\,b1 - b2\,a0 & -a0\,b1 \\ a3\,b1 - b2\,a2 & a3\,b0 - b2\,a1 & -b2\,a0 \\ b2 & b1 & b0 \end{bmatrix}$$

```
> bezout(P,(x+1)^2,x);
```

$$\begin{bmatrix} a3 - a1 & a2 - 2a1 - a0 & -2a0 \\ 2a3 - a2 & a3 - a1 & -a0 \\ 1 & 2 & 1 \end{bmatrix}$$

15.5.6 Matrix of a System of Equations

The function `genmatrix` produces a matrix of a system of linear equations. If `Eq` is a set or a list of equations and `var` is a set or a list of variables, then `genmatrix(Eq,var)` returns the matrix of the system of equations whose unknowns are the elements of `var`. It is strongly recommended to use lists, i.e. square brackets, since it keeps the initial order of the equations for the rows and the initial order of the variables for the columns.

Ex.43

```
> Eq:=[2*x+3*y-2*z=3,x+y+z-1,5*x+4*y+2*z];

        Eq := [2 x + 3 y − 2 z = 3, x + y + z − 1, 5 x + 4 y + 2 z]

> genmatrix(Eq,[x,y,z]);
```

$$\begin{bmatrix} 2 & 3 & -2 \\ 1 & 1 & 1 \\ 5 & 4 & 2 \end{bmatrix}$$

Used with `flag` as a third parameter, `genmatrix` returns the full matrix of the system with the "right-hand sides" in the last column.

Ex.44

```
> genmatrix(Eq,{x,y,z},flag);
```

$$\begin{bmatrix} 2 & 3 & -2 & 3 \\ 1 & 1 & 1 & 1 \\ 5 & 4 & 2 & 0 \end{bmatrix}$$

15.6 Random Vectors and Matrices

15.6.1 Random Vectors

If `n` is a natural number,

- `randvector(n)` returns a vector with `n` components which are integer random numbers contained between −99 and 99.
- `randvector(n,entries=rand(a..b))` returns a vector with `n` components which are integer random numbers contained between `a` and `b`.

Note: The user may be suprised to get the same "random" values as the ones given below. In fact, it is not a question of randomness, the function `rand` being a procedure that only marks out equidistant numbers from a basis. Use `readlib(randomize)()` to modify the value of this basis, and thus the values which are returned.

Ex.45

```
> randvector(5); randvector(5,entries=rand(-10..150));
```

$$[-85, -55, -37, -35, 97]$$

$$[139, 79, 63, 13, 50]$$

To obtain a vector whose components are decimals, multiply by an appropriate decimal step by using `scalarmul`.

Ex.46

```
> scalarmul(randvector(5,
   entries=rand(-1000..1000)),0.001);
```

$$[.600, -.100, .908, .151, -.515]$$

15.6.2 Random Matrices

MAPLE's function `randmatrix` constructs random matrices.

If n and m are two natural numbers,

- `randmatrix(n,m)` returns an $n \times m$ matrix whose coefficients are integer random numbers between -99 and 99.
- `randvector(n,entries=rand(a..b))` returns a $n \times m$ matrix whose coefficients are integer random numbers between a and b.

Ex.47

```
> randmatrix(3,3);
```

$$\begin{bmatrix} 92 & 43 & -62 \\ 77 & 66 & 54 \\ -5 & 99 & -61 \end{bmatrix}$$

```
> randmatrix(2,3,entries=rand(-500..500));
```

$$\begin{bmatrix} -134 & 201 & 316 \\ -360 & 93 & -151 \end{bmatrix}$$

To obtain a matrix whose components are decimals, multiply by an appropriate decimal number by using `scalarmul`.

Ex.48

```
> scalarmul(randmatrix(3,3,
   entries=rand(-1000..1000)),0.001);
```

$$\begin{bmatrix} -.899 & -.532 & -.761 \\ -.698 & .893 & .046 \\ -.914 & .503 & -.352 \end{bmatrix}$$

15.7 Functions to Extract Matrices

15.7.1 Submatrices

The function `submatrix` extracts a submatrix from a given matrix.

Given a matrix `A` and four natural numbers `i1,i2,j1,j2`, the evaluation of `submatrix(A,i1.. i2,j1..j2)` returns the matrix extracted from `A` by only keeping the rows `i1` to `i2` and the columns `j1` to `j2`.

Instead of using intervals as in the previous syntax, one may also describe the rows and the columns one wishes to keep as a list, which can be used to rearrange rows and columns.

Note: The two syntaxes may be used simultaneously, one for the rows and the other one for the columns.

Ex.49

```
> A:=vandermonde([x,y,z]);
  B:=submatrix(A,2..3,[3,1]);
```

$$A := \begin{bmatrix} 1 & x & x^2 \\ 1 & y & y^2 \\ 1 & z & z^2 \end{bmatrix}$$

$$B := \begin{bmatrix} y^2 & 1 \\ z^2 & 1 \end{bmatrix}$$

To extract a matrix with one row or one column, use intervals or lists of a single element.

Ex.50

```
> submatrix(A,2,[3,1]);
  Error, (in submatrix) wrong number (or type) of args
> submatrix(A,2..2,[3,1]);          or: submatrix(A,[2],[3,1]);
```

$$\begin{bmatrix} y^2 & 1 \end{bmatrix}$$

The functions `delrows` and `delcols` can also be used to extract a submatrix. Given a matrix `A` and two integers `i1` and `i2`, `delrows(A,i1..i2)` returns the matrix extracted from `A` by deleting rows `i1` to `i2`. The evaluation of `delcols(A,i1..i2)` does the same for columns. Lists may not be used in this case.

```
> delcols(A,1..1); delrows(A,2..3);
```

$$\begin{bmatrix} x & x^2 \\ y & y^2 \\ z & z^2 \end{bmatrix}$$

$$\begin{bmatrix} 1 & x & x^2 \end{bmatrix}$$

Ex.51

The matrices of one row or one column returned by the previous functions are always of type matrix and not of type vector, which explains the error message one obtains in the following example if one requests the dimension of the "row vector" that is returned. To obtain a result of type vector, use the functions row, col or subvector described in the next section.

```
> A:=vandermonde([x,y,z]);
```

$$A := \begin{bmatrix} 1 & x & x^2 \\ 1 & y & y^2 \\ 1 & z & z^2 \end{bmatrix}$$

```
> B:=submatrix(A,[3],1..3);
```

$$B := \begin{bmatrix} 1 & z & z^2 \end{bmatrix}$$

```
> vectdim(B);
```

Error, (in vectdim) expecting a vector

Ex.52

15.7.2 Column Vector and Row Vector

Given a matrix A and two natural numbers n and m

- col(A,n) returns the n-th column vector of the matrix A.
- col(A,n..m) returns the sequence of column vectors of A whose indices range from n to m.

The function row does the same with the row vectors.

```
> col(A,2); row(A,2..3);
```

$$[x, y, z]$$

$$\begin{bmatrix} 1, y, y^2 \end{bmatrix}, \begin{bmatrix} 1, z, z^2 \end{bmatrix}$$

Ex.53

Parts of column vectors or of row vectors can also be extracted from matrices with the help of the function `subvector`.

Given a matrix `A` and three natural numbers `i1`, `i2` and `j`, the evaluation of `subvector(A,i1..i2,j)` returns the vector whose components are the coefficients with indices `i1` to `i2` of the `j`-th column vector of matrix `A`. In the previous syntax, the coefficients one wishes to keep may also be described in the form of a list, which can be used to rearrange them.

Ex.54

```
> A:=vandermonde([x,y,z]);
```

$$A := \begin{bmatrix} 1 & x & x^2 \\ 1 & y & y^2 \\ 1 & z & z^2 \end{bmatrix}$$

```
> subvector(A,1..2,3);
```

$$\left[x^2, y^2 \right]$$

```
> subvector(A,[3,1],2);
```

$$[z, x]$$

There is a similar syntax to extract row "subvectors".

Ex.55

```
> subvector(A,1,[2,1]);
```

$$[x, 1]$$

The functions `col`, `row` and `subvector` all return objects of type `vector`.

15.8 Constructors of Matrices

15.8.1 Block-Diagonal Matrices

The function `diag` constructs block-diagonal matrices. Given the square matrices `A1`, `A2`, ..., `Ap`, `diag(A1,A2,...,Ap)` returns

$$\begin{bmatrix} A_1 & 0 & \cdots & 0 \\ 0 & A_2 & \ddots & \vdots \\ \vdots & \ddots & \ddots & 0 \\ 0 & \cdots & 0 & A_p \end{bmatrix}.$$

15.8.4 Copying a Matrix Into Another

The function copyinto copies one matrix into another. If A and B are two matrices and i and j are two natural numbers, copyinto(A,B,i,j) copies A into B from the position (i,j) and returns the matrix obtained in this way. This function modifies the contents of B. No error message is returned in case of overflow.

Ex.61

```
> A:=(n,p)->matrix(n,p,(i,j)->i+j-1);
  B:=vandermonde([x,y,z]);
```

$$A := (n, p) \rightarrow matrix(n, p, (i, j) \rightarrow i + j - 1)$$

$$B := \begin{bmatrix} 1 & x & x^2 \\ 1 & y & y^2 \\ 1 & z & z^2 \end{bmatrix}$$

```
> copyinto(A(2,2),B,2,1); eval(B);
```

$$\begin{bmatrix} 1 & x & x^2 \\ 1 & 2 & y^2 \\ 2 & 3 & z^2 \end{bmatrix} \quad \begin{bmatrix} 1 & x & x^2 \\ 1 & 2 & y^2 \\ 2 & 3 & z^2 \end{bmatrix}$$

While the function copyinto copies one matrix into another, the function copy creates a new matrix. If A is a matrix with n rows and p columns, the assignment B:=copy(A) creates a new matrix B and copies the contents of A into it. It is essential to use copy to create an independent copy of a given matrix, which C:=eval(A) doesn't do, as one can see in the following example.

Ex.62

```
> A:=vandermonde([x,y,z]);
```

$$A := \begin{bmatrix} 1 & x & x^2 \\ 1 & y & y^2 \\ 1 & z & z^2 \end{bmatrix}$$

```
> B:=copy(A); C:=eval(A);
```

$$B := \begin{bmatrix} 1 & x & x^2 \\ 1 & y & y^2 \\ 1 & z & z^2 \end{bmatrix}$$

$$C := \begin{bmatrix} 1 & x & x^2 \\ 1 & y & y^2 \\ 1 & z & z^2 \end{bmatrix}$$

Ex.63

```
[> A[1,1]:=0:
[> eval(A); eval(B); eval(C);
```

$$\begin{bmatrix} 0 & x & x^2 \\ 1 & y & y^2 \\ 1 & z & z^2 \end{bmatrix}$$

$$\begin{bmatrix} 1 & x & x^2 \\ 1 & y & y^2 \\ 1 & z & z^2 \end{bmatrix}$$

$$\begin{bmatrix} 0 & x & x^2 \\ 1 & y & y^2 \\ 1 & z & z^2 \end{bmatrix}$$

Note: The assignment $C:=evalm(A)$ also creates an independent copy of A. The function evalm will be studied in the next chapter.

16. Vector Analysis and Matrix Calculus

In this chapter, we assume that the `linalg` library has been loaded with the command `with(linalg)`.

16.1 Operations upon Vectors and Matrices

16.1.1 Linear Combinations of Vectors

In MAPLE, there are two ways to compute linear combinations of vectors

- either use the functions `scalarmul` and `matadd` from the `linalg` library.
- or write the linear combination in the usual way with + and *.

Using `scalarmul` and `add`

Given two vectors, u and v, and two scalar numbers, x and y,

- `scalarmul(u,x)` returns the vector $x\,u$.
- `matadd(u,v)` returns the vector $u + v$.
- `matadd(u,v,x,y)` returns the vector $x\,u + y\,v$.

Ex. 1

```
> with(linalg): u:=vector(3,1); v:=vector(3,t->t);
```
$$u := [1, 1, 1] \qquad v := [1, 2, 3]$$
```
> scalarmul(v,x);
```
$$[x, 2\,x, 3\,x]$$
```
> matadd(u,v);
```
$$[2, 3, 4]$$
```
> matadd(u,v,x,y);
```
$$[x + y, x + 2\,y, x + 3\,y]$$

Warning! The scalars must follow the vectors in both functions!

Using the Operators + and *

A linear combination of the vectors u and v can also be written in the usual way, i.e. as x*u+y*v. However, the object constructed in this way is not fully evaluated, but left as an expression of type + (likewise, x*u remains of type *). The function evalm must be used to fully evaluate the vector expression and obtain its components.

Ex. 2

```
> u:=vector([1,1,1]); v:=vector([1,2,3]);
```
$$u := [1, 1, 1]$$
$$v := [1, 2, 3]$$

```
> w:=2*u+3*v;
```
$$w := 2\,u + 3\,v$$

```
> eval(w);
```
eval doesn't work

$$2\,u + 3\,v$$

```
> evalm(w);
```
$$[5, 8, 11]$$

Warning! MAPLE carries out some simplifications automatically in every expression, and it may therefore happen that a linear combination expressed with the help of + and * evaluates to something that is no longer a vector. For example, a linear combination like u-u is automatically simplified to 0 (the number 0), which may lead to an error if a function like vectdim is called. It is thus better, especially when programming, to use the function matadd.

Ex. 3

```
> v:=evalm(u-u);
```
$$v := 0$$

```
> vectdim(v);
```
Error, (in vectdim) expecting a vector

```
> matadd(u,-u);
```
$$[0, 0, 0]$$

```
> vectdim(");
```
the function matadd returns always a vector:

$$3$$

16.1.2 Linear Combination of Matrices

Linear combinations of matrices are written, as with vectors, either with the help of scalarmul and matadd, or with the help of the operators + and * and evalm.

Examples using matadd or scalarmul:

Ex. 4

```
> A:=matrix(3,3,(i,j)->i+j-1); B:=matrix(3,3,1);
```

$$A := \begin{bmatrix} 1 & 2 & 3 \\ 2 & 3 & 4 \\ 3 & 4 & 5 \end{bmatrix}$$

$$B := \begin{bmatrix} 1 & 1 & 1 \\ 1 & 1 & 1 \\ 1 & 1 & 1 \end{bmatrix}$$

```
> matadd(A,B);
```

$$\begin{bmatrix} 2 & 3 & 4 \\ 3 & 4 & 5 \\ 4 & 5 & 6 \end{bmatrix}$$

```
> matadd(A,B,x,y); scalarmul(A,2);
```

$$\begin{bmatrix} x+y & 2x+y & 3x+y \\ 2x+y & 3x+y & 4x+y \\ 3x+y & 4x+y & 5x+y \end{bmatrix}$$

$$\begin{bmatrix} 2 & 4 & 6 \\ 4 & 6 & 8 \\ 6 & 8 & 10 \end{bmatrix}$$

Example using * and +, followed by the function evalm

Ex. 5

```
> C:=x*A+y*B; evalm(C);
```

$$C := x\,A + y\,B$$

$$\begin{bmatrix} x+y & 2x+y & 3x+y \\ 2x+y & 3x+y & 4x+y \\ 3x+y & 4x+y & 5x+y \end{bmatrix}$$

As with vectors, the result might not remain a matrix when using + or *, which may lead to problems if a function like rowdim or coldim is then used.

16.1.3 Transposition of Matrices and of Vectors

To transpose a matrix, the function `transpose` is called with the matrix to be transposed as its only argument.

Ex. 6

```
[> A:=vandermonde([x,y,z]);
```

$$A := \begin{bmatrix} 1 & x & x^2 \\ 1 & y & y^2 \\ 1 & z & z^2 \end{bmatrix}$$

```
[> transpose(A);
```

$$\begin{bmatrix} 1 & 1 & 1 \\ x & y & z \\ x^2 & y^2 & z^2 \end{bmatrix}$$

The function `transpose` may also take a vector v as argument, in which case it returns a result which is displayed in the form `transpose(v)`: MAPLE handles row vectors in this way, the type `vector` corresponding to column vectors.

Ex. 7

```
[> transpose(vector([1,2,3]));
```

$$transpose([1,2,3])$$

The function `evalm` should be used when one wishes to apply `transpose` to a variable.

Ex. 8

```
[> u:=vector([1,2,3]):
   v:=transpose(evalm(u));w:=transpose(u);
```

$$v := transpose([1,2,3])$$

$$w := transpose(u)$$

```
[> u:=vector([1,2]): eval(v);map(eval,w);
```

$$transpose([1,2,3])$$

$$transpose([1,2])$$

The function `htranspose` gives the transpose of the conjugate of a matrix. This function can also be applied to vectors. The function `htranspose` presents the same evaluation problems as the function `transpose`.

16.1.4 Product of a Matrix by a Vector

The function `multiply` computes the product of a matrix by a vector. Given a matrix `A` and a vector `u` of compatible dimensions, `mutiply(A,u)` returns the product of the matrix `A` by the vector `u`.

Ex. 9

```
> A:=matrix(3,2,(i,j)->i+j-1);u:=vector([1,1]);
```

$$A := \begin{bmatrix} 1 & 2 \\ 2 & 3 \\ 3 & 4 \end{bmatrix}$$

$$u := [1,1]$$

```
> multiply(A,u);
```

$$[3,5,7]$$

The function `multiply` can also multiply a row vector by a matrix. A row vector is written with the function `transpose` (or `htranspose`). The result of the multiplication is a row vector, and thus is written with the function `transpose`.

Ex.10

```
> v:=vector([1,-1,1]):multiply(transpose(v),A);
```

$$transpose\,([2,3])$$

16.1.5 Product of Matrices

The Function `multiply`

If `A` and `B` are two matrices of compatible dimensions, `mutiply(A,B)` returns the product $A\,B$. Likewise, `multiply(A`$_1$`,A`$_2$`,...,A`$_p$`)` returns the product $A_1\,A_2\ldots A_p$.

Ex.11

```
> A:=matrix(3,3,(i,j)->i+j-1);B:=matrix(3,2,1);
```

$$A := \begin{bmatrix} 1 & 2 & 3 \\ 2 & 3 & 4 \\ 3 & 4 & 5 \end{bmatrix}$$

$$B := \begin{bmatrix} 1 & 1 \\ 1 & 1 \\ 1 & 1 \end{bmatrix}$$

```
> multiply(A,B);
```

$$\begin{bmatrix} 6 & 6 \\ 9 & 9 \\ 12 & 12 \end{bmatrix}$$

The Multiplication Operator &*

The operator * should not be used to multiply matrices, although one might be tempted to do so. MAPLE forbids it, in most cases, for a product of two matrices.

Ex.12

```
> A:=matrix(3,3,(i,j)->i+j-1); B:=matrix(3,3,1);
```

$$A := \begin{bmatrix} 1 & 2 & 3 \\ 2 & 3 & 4 \\ 3 & 4 & 5 \end{bmatrix} \qquad B := \begin{bmatrix} 1 & 1 & 1 \\ 1 & 1 & 1 \\ 1 & 1 & 1 \end{bmatrix}$$

```
> evalm(A*B);
```
Error, (in evalm/evaluate) use the & operator*
for matrix multiplication

MAPLE doesn't return any error message for a product of three matrices written this way, but it returns a wrong result, as we verify in the next example

Ex.13

```
> evalm(A*B*A); multiply(A,B,A);
```

$$\begin{bmatrix} 60 & 60 & 60 \\ 87 & 87 & 87 \\ 114 & 114 & 114 \end{bmatrix}$$

$$\begin{bmatrix} 36 & 54 & 72 \\ 54 & 81 & 108 \\ 72 & 108 & 144 \end{bmatrix}$$

The reader can verify that the first result MAPLE returns is the product A^2B. When MAPLE encounters expressions like A*B*A or P^(-1)*A*P, it considers them as rational expressions and starts by applying the simplifications which are automatically carried out for such expressions. For example:

- if one first evaluates A*B*C and then tries to compute B*A*C, MAPLE recognizes that an expression which is equivalent to the second, in the sense of polynomial multiplication, already belongs to its table of expressions, and therefore replaces B*A*C by A*B*C before starting any matrix computation.

- A*B*A is automatically transformed into A^2*B, or B*A^2 depending on the context.

- An expression like P^(-1)*A*P is automatically simplified into A.

Therefore, one shouldn't be surprised by the next result, which is obtained without any matrix computation using only polynomial simplification.

Ex.14

```
> A*B-B*A;
```
$$0$$

To sum up, MAPLE handles any multiplication denoted by ∗ as a commutative multiplication, which may lead to nonsensical results!

If one wishes to use a multiplicative notation that is closer to our own than the function `multiply`, the operator `&*` should be used instead of the operator ∗ to represent this noncommutative multiplication and prevent MAPLE from starting to carry out polynomial simplifications. The function `evalm` is then required to obtain a full evaluation.

Ex.15

```
> A:=matrix(3,3,(i,j)->i+j-1);B:=matrix(3,3,1);
```
$$A := \begin{bmatrix} 1 & 2 & 3 \\ 2 & 3 & 4 \\ 3 & 4 & 5 \end{bmatrix} \quad B := \begin{bmatrix} 1 & 1 & 1 \\ 1 & 1 & 1 \\ 1 & 1 & 1 \end{bmatrix}$$

```
> A&*B-B&*A;
```
$$(A\& * B) - (B\& * A)$$

```
> evalm(A&*B-B&*A);
```
$$\begin{bmatrix} 0 & -3 & -6 \\ 3 & 0 & -3 \\ 6 & 3 & 0 \end{bmatrix}$$

16.1.6 Inverse of a Matrix

If A is an invertible matrix, `inverse(A)` returns the inverse matrix of A. One may also use `evalm(1/A)` or `evalm(A^(-1))`.

Ex.16

```
> A:=matrix([[a,b],[-b,a]]);
```
$$A := \begin{bmatrix} a & b \\ -b & a \end{bmatrix}$$

```
> B:=inverse(A);
```
One may also use
evalm(1/A) and evalm(A^(-1))

$$B := \begin{bmatrix} \dfrac{a}{a^2 + b^2} & -\dfrac{b}{a^2 + b^2} \\ \dfrac{b}{a^2 + b^2} & \dfrac{a}{a^2 + b^2} \end{bmatrix}$$

16.1.7 Powers of Square Matrices

To compute a power of a matrix, one may use the operator ^ or, better, the operator &^, possibly followed by an evalm in order to obtain a full evaluation.

Ex.17

```
> A:=matrix([[a,b],[-b,a]]);
```

$$A := \left[\begin{array}{cc} a & b \\ -b & a \end{array} \right]$$

```
> B:=A&^2; evalm(B);
```

$$B := A \,\&^{\wedge}\, 2$$

$$\left[\begin{array}{cc} a^2 - b^2 & 2\,ab \\ -2\,ab & a^2 - b^2 \end{array} \right]$$

When the matrix is invertible, one may compute negative powers.

Ex.18

```
> evalm(A&^(-2));
```

$$\left[\begin{array}{cc} \dfrac{a^2 - b^2}{(a^2 + b^2)^2} & -\,2\,\dfrac{ab}{(a^2 + b^2)^2} \\[2ex] 2\,\dfrac{ab}{(a^2 + b^2)^2} & \dfrac{a^2 - b^2}{(a^2 + b^2)^2} \end{array} \right]$$

Warning! As with the operator *, the use of the operator ^ (instead of &^) may lead to an improper automatic simplification. For example, when the exponent is equal to zero, then the scalar number 1 and not the identity matrix is returned. One should remember this when using the functions coldim and rowdim, especially when programming.

Incorrect method

Ex.19

```
> B:=A^n;
```

$$B := A^n$$

```
> n:=0: B;
```

$$1$$

```
> rowdim(B);
   Error, (in rowdim) expecting a matrix
```

Correct method

```
> n:='n': B:=A&^n;
                              B := A &^ n

> n:=0: evalm(B);
                              ⎡ 1  0 ⎤
                              ⎣ 0  1 ⎦

> rowdim(B);
                                 2
```

Ex.20

16.2 Basis of a Vector Subspace

16.2.1 Subspace Defined by Generators

The function **basis** produces a basis for a vector space defined by a family of generators.

- If **Lst** is a list of vectors, **basis(Lst)** returns a sublist of **Lst** which is a basis of the vector space generated by these vectors.
- If **Ens** is a set of vectors, **basis(Ens)** returns a subset of **Ens** which is a basis of the vector space generated by these vectors.

It is better to apply the function **basis** to a list in order so that the basis is returned in a list whose order corresponds to the order of the input.

```
> a:= vector([1,2,0,1]): b:=vector([2,1,3,1]):
  c:= vector([1,-1,1,2]): d:=vector([2,4,2,0]):

> Base:=basis([a,b,c,d]);
                          Base := [a, b, c]

> Base:=basis({a,b,c,d});   the answer depends on the session
                          Base := {b, a, d}
```

Ex.21

To obtain the dimension of the corresponding vector space, use the function **nops** (p. 339) which returns the number of elements of the basis.

```
> nops(Base);
                                 3
```

Ex.22

16.2.2 Kernel of a Matrix

The functions `kernel` or `nullspace` produce a basis for the kernel of a matrix. If A is a matrix, `kernel(A)` returns a basis of the kernel of A as a set.

Ex.23

```
> M:=matrix(2,4,[1,2,3,4,2,3,4,5]);
```
$$M := \begin{bmatrix} 1 & 2 & 3 & 4 \\ 2 & 3 & 4 & 5 \end{bmatrix}$$

```
> kernel(M);                          one may also use nullspace(M)
```
$$\{ [1, -2, 1, 0] , [2, -3, 0, 1] \}$$

The function `kernel` can also be used with a second parameter, which is either unassigned or between apostrophes. If A is a matrix and k is a variable, `kernel(A,'k')` returns a basis for the kernel of A and assigns the dimension of this subspace to k.

Ex.24

```
> kernel(M,'k');
```
$$\{ [1, -2, 1, 0] , [2, -3, 0, 1] \}$$

```
> k;
```
$$2$$

16.2.3 Subspace Generated by the Lines of a Matrix

- If A is a matrix and r is a free variable, `colspace(A,r)` returns a basis of the vector space generated by the column vectors of A as a set, and assigns the dimension of this subspace to r.
- If A is a matrix and r is a free variable, `rowspace(A,r)` returns a basis of the vector space generated by the row vectors of A as a set, and assigns the dimension of this subspace to r.

The second argument is optional in both cases.

Ex.25

```
> colspace(M,r);
```
$$\{[0, 1] , [1, 0]\}$$

```
> r;
```
$$2$$

```
> rowspace(M);
```
$$\{[1, 0, -1, -2] , [0, 1, 2, 3]\}$$

The function `rowspan` also returns a basis of the vector subspace generated by the row vectors of a matrix. It is better to use it when the matrix has entries that are expressions. The function `rowspace` puts the matrix in triangular form using Gaussian elimination, while the function `rowspan` uses a fraction-free method.

The function `colspan` operates similarly on the columns of the matrix.

Ex.26

```
> A:=matrix(2,2,[(x-1)^2,(x^2-1),(x-1),(x+1)]);
```

$$A := \begin{bmatrix} (x-1)^2 & x^2-1 \\ x-1 & x+1 \end{bmatrix}$$

```
> rowspace(A);
```

$$\left\{ \left[1, \frac{x+1}{x-1}\right] \right\}$$

```
> rowspan(A);
```

$$\{ [x-1, x+1] \}$$

```
> colspan(A);
```

$$\left\{ \left[x^2-1, x+1\right] \right\}$$

16.2.4 Subspace Defined by Equations

To construct a basis for a vector subspace defined by a set of equations, one first extracts the matrix of the system of equations using the function `genmatrix`, and then uses `kernel`, which gives a basis for the kernel of the matrix.

Ex.27

```
> Eq:=[x+2*y+3*z+4*t=0,2*x+3*y+4*z+5*t=0];
```

$$Eq := [x + 2y + 3z + 4t = 0, \ 2x + 3y + 4z + 5t = 0]$$

```
> M:=genmatrix(Eq,[x,y,z,t]);
```

$$M := \begin{bmatrix} 1 & 2 & 3 & 4 \\ 2 & 3 & 4 & 5 \end{bmatrix}$$

```
> kernel(M);                    one may also use nullspace(M)
```

$$\{[1, -2, 1, 0], [2, -3, 0, 1]\}$$

16.2.5 Intersection and Sum of Vector Subspaces

Given vector subspaces E1,E2,...,Ep, each defined by a list or a set of generators,

- intbasis(E1,E2,...,Ep) returns a basis of the intersection of these subspaces.
- sumbasis(E1,E2,...,Ep), returns a basis of the sum of these subspaces.

Ex.28

```
> E1:=[vector([1,2,0]),vector([2,1,3])];
  E2:=[vector([1,2,1]),vector([-1,1,1]),
       vector([-2,-1,0])];
```
$$E1 := [[1,2,0], [2,1,3]]$$
$$E2 := [[1,2,1], [-1,1,1], [-2,-1,0]]$$
```
> intbasis(E1,E2);
```
$$\{[-5,-7,-3]\}$$
```
> sumbasis(E1,E2);
```
$$[[1,2,0,], [2,1,3], [1,2,1]]$$

Note: A family of vector subspaces can be described by lists or sets of generators. MAPLE always returns a set of linearly independent generators (between braces) for an intersection of vector subspaces. For a sum, MAPLE returns a list (between square brackets) when all the subspaces are described by lists and a set otherwise.

16.2.6 Rank of a Matrix

The function **rank** returns the rank of a matrix, regardless of whether it is square. If A is a matrix whose entries are rational expressions with rational coefficients, the evaluation of rank(A) returns the rank of A.

Ex.29

```
> A:=matrix(3,4,(i,j)->i+j-1);
```
$$A := \begin{bmatrix} 1 & 2 & 3 & 4 \\ 2 & 3 & 4 & 5 \\ 3 & 4 & 5 & 6 \end{bmatrix}$$
```
> rank(A);
```
$$2$$

Warning! The function `rank` cannot be used with a matrix that has an entry containing an irrational value like `sqrt(2)` or `Pi`.

Ex.30

```
> rank(diag(1,sqrt(2)));
   Error, (in linalg[gausselim]) unable to find a provably
   non-zero pivot
```

16.2.7 Evaluation Problem

Problems can arise using functions like `rank`, `colspace`, and `kernel` with matrices whose entries are expressions in bound variables. The following example may be surprising.

Ex.31

```
> A:=vandermonde([x,y,z]);
```

$$A := \begin{bmatrix} 1 & x & x^2 \\ 1 & y & y^2 \\ 1 & z & z^2 \end{bmatrix}$$

```
> x:=1: y:=1:
> rank(A);
                          3
> det(A);
                          0
```

This is a consequence of the programming of the function `rank`, which uses a superficial evaluation of a matrix whose coefficients are expressions: the function `rank` calls the procedure `linalg[ffgausselim]` with A, which sends the initial expression of A to `ffgausselim`, and not a full evaluation of the matrix. Hence, the function `rank` returns the rank of A without taking into account the values assigned to x and y.

As we saw on page 260, the function `eval` doesn't produce the full evaluation of a matrix whose coefficients depend on variables that point towards other values. It doesn't suffice to apply the function `rank` to `eval(A)` to obtain the expected result in the previous example, one must write `rank(map(eval,A))`.

Ex.32

```
> rank(eval(A));
                          3
> rank(map(eval,A));
                          2
```

16.2.8 An Exercise About the Commuting Matrices

A classical problem is to look for the matrices B which commute with a given matrix A. To solve this problem, one may first compute C=A*B-B*A where B is an unknown matrix.

Ex.33

```
> restart; with(linalg):
  A:=matrix(3,3,[1,1,1,0,2,1,0,0,3]);
```

$$A := \begin{bmatrix} 1 & 1 & 1 \\ 0 & 2 & 1 \\ 0 & 0 & 3 \end{bmatrix}$$

```
> B:=matrix(3,3);
```

$$B := array(1..3, 1..3, [])$$

```
> C:=evalm(A&*B-B&*A):
```

The initial problem is equivalent to solving the equation C=0. Since MAPLE cannot solve such an equation directly, we need to recover each element of C in order to obtain the set of equations corresponding to C equal to zero.

First Possibility

Since every 3×3 matrix is defined by the list L of its 9 elements, looking for B is equivalent to looking for this list. The function **seq** can be used to pass B to L, and then to recover the coefficients of C which provide the left-hand sides of the system whose unknowns are the elements of L.

Ex.34

```
> Lst_Inc:=[seq(seq(B[i,j],j=1..3),i=1..3)];
```

$$Lst\_Inc := [B_{1,1}, B_{1,2}, B_{1,3}, B_{2,1}, B_{2,2}, B_{2,3}, B_{3,1}, B_{3,2}, B_{3,3}]$$

```
> Ens_Eq:={seq(seq(C[i,j],j=1..3),i=1..3)}:
```

Solving this system of equations is equivalent to looking for the kernel of the corresponding 9×9 matrix, which can be constructed with **genmatrix**.

Ex.35

```
> N:=kernel(genmatrix(Ens_Eq,Lst_Inc));
```

$$N := \{ [1, 0, 0, 0, 0, 1, 0, 0, 0, 1] ,$$
$$[-1, 1, 0, 0, 0, 0, 0, 0, 0] , [-1, 0, 1, 0, -1, 1, 0, 0, 0] \}$$

The function `matrix` can be applied to every element of `N` to recover the corresponding matrices. The function `map` can be used instead of writing three assignments. One then easily obtains the general form of all the matrices that commute with `A`.

Ex.36

```
> M:=map(m->matrix(3,3,m),N);
```

$$M := \left\{ \begin{bmatrix} -1 & 1 & 0 \\ 0 & 0 & 0 \\ 0 & 0 & 0 \end{bmatrix}, \begin{bmatrix} 1 & 0 & 0 \\ 0 & 1 & 0 \\ 0 & 0 & 1 \end{bmatrix}, \begin{bmatrix} -1 & 0 & 1 \\ 0 & -1 & 1 \\ 0 & 0 & 0 \end{bmatrix} \right\}$$

```
> evalm(a*M[1]+b*M[2]+c*M[3]);
```

$$\begin{bmatrix} a-b-c & b & c \\ 0 & a-c & c \\ 0 & 0 & a \end{bmatrix}$$

Second Possibility

Use the function `solve`, which can be used to choose the coefficients of `B` to be used in parametrizing the result. To achieve this, one must give the set of unknowns with respect to which one wishes to solve as second argument to `solve`. This second argument of `solve` can be constructed by subtracting the set of unknowns from the set of parameters, using the function `minus`.

If one wishes to express the general solution as a function of the diagonal elements of `B`, one may write:

Ex.37

```
> Ens_Inc:=convert(Lst_Inc,set);        To transform
```
                                   the list into a set (p. 356)

$$Ens\_Inc := \{ B_{1,1}, B_{1,2}, B_{1,3}, B_{2,1}, B_{2,2}, B_{2,3}, B_{3,1}, B_{3,2}, B_{3,3} \}$$

```
> Sol := solve(Ens_Eq,
  Ens_Inc minus{B[1,1],B[2,2],B[3,3]});
```

$$Sol := \{ B_{1,3} = B_{3,3} - B_{2,2} ,\ B_{1,2} = B_{2,2} - B_{1,1},\ B_{3,1} = 0,$$
$$B_{2,3} = B_{3,3} - B_{2,2} ,\ B_{2,1} = 0 ,\ B_{3,2} = 0 \}$$

```
> subs(Sol,evalm(B));        to realize the previous conditions
```

$$\begin{bmatrix} B_{1,1} & B_{2,2} - B_{1,1} & B_{3,3} - B_{2,2} \\ 0 & B_{2,2} & B_{3,3} - B_{2,2} \\ 0 & 0 & B_{3,3} \end{bmatrix}$$

17. Systems of Linear Equations

In this chapter, we always assume that the `linalg` library has been loaded with the command `with(linalg)`.

17.1 Solution of a Linear System

17.1.1 Linear System Given in Matrix Form

Given a matrix **A** with **n** rows and **p** columns,

- if B is a vector with **n** components, `linsolve(A,B)` returns the general solution of the system $AX = B$, written as a vector with **p** components.
- if B is a matrix with **n** rows and **q** columns, `linsolve(A,B)` returns the general solution of the system $AX = B$, written as a matrix with **p** rows and **q** columns.

System with a Single Solution

Example of the solution of a system in which the unknown is a vector

Ex. 1

```
> A:=evalm(matrix(3,3,1)+1);
```

$$\begin{bmatrix} 2 & 1 & 1 \\ 1 & 2 & 1 \\ 1 & 1 & 2 \end{bmatrix}$$

```
> B:=vector([a,b,c]);
  v:=linsolve(A,B);
```

$$B := [a, b, c]$$

$$v := \left[\frac{3}{4}a - \frac{1}{4}b - \frac{1}{4}c, -\frac{1}{4}a + \frac{3}{4}b - \frac{1}{4}c, -\frac{1}{4}a - \frac{1}{4}b + \frac{3}{4}c \right]$$

When the matrix A is invertible (and thus square), as in the previous example, v:=linsolve(A,B) can be replaced by v:=evalm(A^(-1)&*B). However, the function linsolve can also solve a system whose matrix isn't square, as in the following example.

Ex. 2

> A:=matrix(3,2,[2,1,1,2,1,1]); B:=vector([3,3,2]);

$$A := \begin{bmatrix} 2 & 1 \\ 1 & 2 \\ 1 & 1 \end{bmatrix}$$

$$B := [3, 3, 2]$$

> linsolve(A,B);

$$[1, 1]$$

> X:=evalm(A^(-1)&*B);
Error, (in linalg[inverse]) expecting a square matrix

Example of the solution of a system in which the unknown is a matrix

Ex. 3

> A:=matrix(3,2,[2,1,1,2,1,1]);
B:=matrix(3,3,[5,4,-3,4,5,-3,3,3,-2]);

$$A := \begin{bmatrix} 2 & 1 \\ 1 & 2 \\ 1 & 1 \end{bmatrix} \qquad B := \begin{bmatrix} 5 & 4 & -3 \\ 4 & 5 & -3 \\ 3 & 3 & -2 \end{bmatrix}$$

> linsolve(A,B);

$$\begin{bmatrix} 2 & 1 & -1 \\ 1 & 2 & -1 \end{bmatrix}$$

System Without Solution

When the system has no solution, the function linsolve returns an empty sequence, which has no echo on the screen.

Ex. 4

> A:=matrix(3,2,[2,1,1,2,1,1]); B:=vector([1,1,1]);

$$A := \begin{bmatrix} 2 & 1 \\ 1 & 2 \\ 1 & 1 \end{bmatrix} \qquad B := [1, 1, 1]$$

> v:=linsolve(A,B);

Without assignment, there would be no echo

$$v :=$$

System with More Than One Solution

When a system has more than one solution, `linsolve` returns the expression of the general solution using additional variables that begin with the *underscore* character.

Example with a vector on the right-hand side

Ex. 5

```
> A:=matrix(3,3,1)-3;
```

$$A := \begin{bmatrix} 1 & 1 & 1 \\ 1 & 1 & 1 \\ 1 & 1 & 1 \end{bmatrix} - 3$$

```
> evalm(A);
```

One can check that MAPLE treats M-3 as M-3 I if M is a matrix

$$\begin{bmatrix} -2 & 1 & 1 \\ 1 & -2 & 1 \\ 1 & 1 & -2 \end{bmatrix}$$

```
> B:=vector([0,3,-3]);
```

$$B := [0, 3, -3]$$

```
> v:=linsolve(A,B);
```

$$v := [\_t_1 - 1, \_t_1 - 2, \_t_1]$$

Example with a matrix on the right-hand side

Ex. 6

```
> B1:=vector([3,-3,0]);
```

$$B1 := [3, -3, 0]$$

```
> C:=concat(B,B1);
```

$$C := \begin{bmatrix} 0 & 3 \\ 3 & -3 \\ -3 & 0 \end{bmatrix}$$

```
> v:=linsolve(A,C);
```

$$v := \begin{bmatrix} -1 + \_t_{1_1} & -1 + \_t_{2_1} \\ -2 + \_t_{1_1} & 1 + \_t_{2_1} \\ \_t_{1_1} & \_t_{2_1} \end{bmatrix}$$

System of the Form $XA = B$

In MAPLE, there is no special function to solve a linear system of the form $XA = B$. This can be overcome by using **transpose** twice, as in the following example.

Ex. 7

```
> A:=matrix(2,3,[2,1,1,1,2,1]);
```
$$A := \begin{bmatrix} 2 & 1 & 1 \\ 1 & 2 & 1 \end{bmatrix}$$

```
> B:=matrix(3,3,[4,5,3,5,4,3,1,-4,-1]);
```
$$B := \begin{bmatrix} 4 & 5 & 3 \\ 5 & 4 & 3 \\ 1 & -4 & -1 \end{bmatrix}$$

```
> linsolve(transpose(A),transpose(B));
```
$$\begin{bmatrix} 1 & 2 & 2 \\ 2 & 1 & -3 \end{bmatrix}$$

```
> transpose(");
```
$$\begin{bmatrix} 1 & 2 \\ 2 & 1 \\ 2 & -3 \end{bmatrix}$$

Note: The previous result can be obtained directly by typing

Ex. 8

```
> transpose(linsolve(transpose(A),transpose(B)));
```

17.1.2 Linear System Specified by Equations

In this section, we will solve systems specified by equations.

Using solve

If **solve** is used to solve a system of linear equations, the result is returned as a sequence, which requires the use of the functions **subs** and **vector** to convert to a vector.

```
> Eq:={2*x+3*y-2*z-3,x+y+z-1,5*x+4*y+2*z};
```
$$Eq := \{2\,x + 3\,y - 2\,x - 3,\, x + y + z - 1,\, 5\,x + 4\,y + 2\,z\}$$

```
> S:=solve(Eq,{x,y,z});
```
$$S := \left\{ y = \frac{23}{7},\, x = \frac{-20}{7},\, z = \frac{4}{7} \right\}$$

Ex. 9

```
> v:=vector(subs(S,[x,y,z]));
```
$$v := \left[\frac{-20}{7},\, \frac{23}{7},\, \frac{4}{7} \right]$$

Using linsolve

For a linear system which is specified by equations, one may use the function linsolve after constructing the matrix of the system and of the "right-hand sides" using the functions genmatrix and submatrix.

Ex.10

```
> S:=genmatrix(Eq,[x,y,z],flag);
```
$$S := \begin{bmatrix} 2 & 3 & -2 & 3 \\ 1 & 1 & 1 & 1 \\ 5 & 4 & 2 & 0 \end{bmatrix}$$

```
> A:=submatrix(S,1..3,1..3);
  B:=col(S,4);
```
$$A := \begin{bmatrix} 2 & 3 & -2 \\ 1 & 1 & 1 \\ 5 & 4 & 2 \end{bmatrix}$$
$$B := [3,\, 1,\, 0]$$

```
> linsolve(A, B);
```
$$\left[\frac{-20}{7},\, \frac{23}{7},\, \frac{4}{7} \right]$$

The order of the variables must not be changed if one uses this method: these variables must therefore be given as a list. On the other hand, the set of equations defined can be used directly, which may change the order of the rows of matrix A, but won't change the result.

17.2 The Pivot's Method

17.2.1 Operations on the Rows and the Columns of a Matrix

Although MAPLE can solve linear systems by itself, it is sometimes necessary to carry out transformations on the rows or the columns of a matrix.

Given a matrix A, two integers i and j and a scalar x, the following table summarizes the syntax of the various functions for manipulating rows and columns.

Command	The returned matrix is obtained by ...
swapcol (A,i,j)	swapping columns i and j of A
swaprow (A,i,j)	swapping rows i and j of A
mulcol (A,j,x)	multiplying the ith column of A by x
mulrow (A,i,x)	multiplying the ith row of A by x
addcol (A,i,j,x)	replacing the jth column Cj by Cj+x*Ci
addrow (A,i,j,x)	replacing the jth row Lj by Lj+x*Li

Note: None of these functions modifies the original matrix. With addcol and addrow, be careful of the strange order of the parameters: addcol(A,i, j,x) adds the product of x by the ith column to the jth column.

Ex.11

```
> A:=matrix(4,3,(i,j)->i+j-1);
```
$$A := \begin{bmatrix} 1 & 2 & 3 \\ 2 & 3 & 4 \\ 3 & 4 & 5 \\ 4 & 5 & 6 \end{bmatrix}$$

```
> B:=swapcol(A,2,3); C:=swaprow(A,1,4);
```
$$B := \begin{bmatrix} 1 & 3 & 2 \\ 2 & 4 & 3 \\ 3 & 5 & 4 \\ 4 & 6 & 5 \end{bmatrix} \quad C := \begin{bmatrix} 4 & 5 & 6 \\ 2 & 3 & 4 \\ 3 & 4 & 5 \\ 1 & 2 & 3 \end{bmatrix}$$

```
> mulrow(A,2,w);
```
$$\begin{bmatrix} 1 & 2 & 3 \\ 2w & 3w & 4w \\ 3 & 4 & 5 \\ 4 & 5 & 6 \end{bmatrix}$$

17.2.2 The Function `pivot`

The function `pivot` eliminates entries in a column by forming linear combinations of rows.

Given a matrix A and a pair of indices `(i,j)` for which the entry `A[i,j]` (the pivot) is non-zero, the command `pivot(A,i,j)` returns a matrix that has the same size and rank as A whose coefficients below the pivot are all zero. This matrix is obtained by subtracting from each row below the ith row a multiple of the ith row.

Ex.12

```
> A:=matrix(4,3,(i,j)->i+j-1);
```

$$A := \begin{bmatrix} 1 & 2 & 3 \\ 2 & 3 & 4 \\ 3 & 4 & 5 \\ 4 & 5 & 6 \end{bmatrix}$$

```
> A1:=pivot(A,1,1);
  A2:=pivot(A1,2,2);
```

$$A1 := \begin{bmatrix} 1 & 2 & 3 \\ 0 & -1 & -2 \\ 0 & -2 & -4 \\ 0 & -3 & -6 \end{bmatrix}$$

$$A2 := \begin{bmatrix} 1 & 0 & -1 \\ 0 & -1 & -2 \\ 0 & 0 & 0 \\ 0 & 0 & 0 \end{bmatrix}$$

By using an interval as a fourth parameter, the effect of the function `pivot` can be restricted to the rows whose index lies between the bounds of this interval.

Ex.13

```
> pivot(A,1,1,2..3);
```

$$\begin{bmatrix} 1 & 2 & 3 \\ 0 & -1 & -2 \\ 0 & -2 & -4 \\ 4 & 5 & 6 \end{bmatrix}$$

17.2.3 Gaussian Elimination: The Function `gausselim`

The function `gausselim` performs Gaussian elimination. If `A` is a matrix whose entries are numbers or rational expressions, `gausselim(A)` returns an "upper triangular" matrix that has the same rank as `A`.

When the coefficients of the matrix are rational functions whose coefficients are of type `complex(rational)` (p. 348), the computations are exact, although MAPLE sometimes permutates the rows in such a way that it can divide by an element of minimal length, in order to keep the denominators as simple as possible.

Example with a matrix which has rational entries

Ex.14

```
> A:=matrix(4,3,(i,j)->i+j-1); gausselim(A);
```

$$A := \begin{bmatrix} 1 & 2 & 3 \\ 2 & 3 & 4 \\ 3 & 4 & 5 \\ 4 & 5 & 6 \end{bmatrix}$$

$$\begin{bmatrix} 1 & 2 & 3 \\ 0 & -1 & -2 \\ 0 & 0 & 0 \\ 0 & 0 & 0 \end{bmatrix}$$

Example with a matrix with polynomial entries

Ex.15

```
> A:=matrix(3,3,(i,j)->(x+i+j-1)^2); gausselim(A);
```

$$A := \begin{bmatrix} (x+1)^2 & (x+2)^2 & (x+3)^2 \\ (x+2)^2 & (x+3)^2 & (x+4)^2 \\ (x+3)^2 & (x+4)^2 & (x+5)^2 \end{bmatrix}$$

$$\begin{bmatrix} (x+1)^2 & (x+2)^2 & (x+3)^2 \\ 0 & -\dfrac{2x^2+8x+7}{(x+1)^2} & -4\dfrac{x^2+5x+5}{(x+1)^2} \\ 0 & 0 & 8\dfrac{1}{2x^2+8x+7} \end{bmatrix}$$

If the matrix has numerical entries among which one is of type `float`, then
all computations are carried out using floating point arithmetic. In this case,
MAPLE uses the classical method of the partial pivot by choosing an element
of maximal absolute value.

Ex.16

```
[> A:=matrix(3,3,(i,j)->i+j-1):
[> A[1,1]:=1.: evalm(A);                          notice the decimal point
```

$$\begin{bmatrix} 1. & 2 & 3 \\ 2 & 3 & 4 \\ 3 & 4 & 5 \\ 4 & 5 & 6 \end{bmatrix}$$

```
[> gausselim(A);
```

$$\begin{bmatrix} 3. & 4. & 5. \\ 0 & .666666667 & 1.333333333 \\ 0 & 0 & .4\,10^{-9} \end{bmatrix}$$

The matrix cannot contain a variable if it contains a element of type `float`.
MAPLE returns an error message in this case.

Ex.17

```
[> A:=matrix(3,3,(i,j)->i+j-1): A[1,1]:=1.: A[2,2]:=x:
   evalm(A);
```

$$\begin{bmatrix} 1. & 2 & 3 \\ 2 & x & 4 \\ 3 & 4 & 5 \end{bmatrix}$$

```
[> gausselim(A);
   Error, (in gausselim) matrix entries must all evaluate to
   complex floats
```

The function `gausselim` also requires that none of its entries contain a real
value which isn't of type `numeric`, like `sqrt(2)`. Trying to carry out the
Gaussian elimination with the following matrix A produces an error message.

Ex.18

```
[> A:=matrix(3,3,(i,j)->i+j-1): A[1,1]:=sqrt(2):
[> gausselim(A);
   Error, (in gausselim) unable to find a provably non zero pivot
```

In such cases, one may force MAPLE to carry out the computation with real
numbers either by writing one of the integers with a decimal point or by
applying the function `gausselim` to `map(evalf,A)` or to `evalf(eval(A))`.

17.2.4 Gaussian Elimination Without Denominator: `ffgausselim`

The function `ffgausselim` performs Gaussian elimination as well, but only on matrices whose entries are polynomials with coefficients of type `complex` (`rational`), i.e. written `a+i*b` where `a` and `b` are rational numbers. The elimination doesn't introduce denominators, so all computations are carried out in a ring of polynomials with coefficients of type `complex(rational)`.

Like the function `gausselim`, the function `ffgausselim` may permutate rows in order to use an entry of minimal length as "pivot". Unlike the function `gausselim`, the absolute value of the determinant of the matrix isn't preserved.

The following example shows the different results obtained with the functions `gausselim` and `ffgausselim`.

Ex.19

```
> A:=matrix(3,3,(i,j)->(6-i-j)^2);
```

$$A := \begin{bmatrix} 16 & 9 & 4 \\ 9 & 4 & 1 \\ 4 & 1 & 0 \end{bmatrix}$$

```
> gausselim(A); ffgausselim(A);
```

$$\begin{bmatrix} 9 & 4 & 1 \\ 0 & -\dfrac{7}{9} & -\dfrac{4}{9} \\ 0 & 0 & \dfrac{8}{7} \end{bmatrix}, \begin{bmatrix} 9 & 4 & 1 \\ 0 & -7 & -4 \\ 0 & 0 & -8 \end{bmatrix}$$

It can be seen in the previous example that MAPLE begins by swapping the first row with the second, whose entry is of minimal length (not value) among the elements of the first column.

Another example with a matrix with polynomial coefficients

Ex.20

```
> A:=matrix(3,3,(i,j)->(x+i+j-1)^2);
```

$$A := \begin{bmatrix} (x+1)^2 & (x+2)^2 & (x+3)^2 \\ (x+2)^2 & (x+3)^2 & (x+4)^2 \\ (x+3)^2 & (x+4)^2 & (x+5)^2 \end{bmatrix}$$

```
> ffgausselim(A);
```

$$\begin{bmatrix} x^2+2x+1 & x^2+4x+4 & x^2+6x+9 \\ 0 & -2x^2-8x-7 & -4x^2-20x-20 \\ 0 & 0 & -8 \end{bmatrix}$$

17.2.5 Optional Parameters of `gausselim` and `ffgausselim`

Each of the two previous functions, `gausselim` and `ffgausselim`, allows optional parameters allowing one to recover the rank and the determinant of the matrix, or to specify the index of a row at which the elimination is to be stopped.

Given a matrix `A`,

- if `i` contains an integer numerical value, then `gausselim(A,i)` or of `ffgausselim(A,i)` carries out a partial Gaussian elimination stopping at the row with index `i`.
- if `r` is a free variable, then `gausselim(A,r)` or `ffgausselim(A,r)` carries out a total Gaussian elimination and `r` contains the rank of `A` after this evaluation.
- if `r` and `d` are free variables and if `A` is a square matrix, then the evaluation of `gausselim(A,r,d)` or `ffgausselim(A,r,d)` carries out a total Gaussian elimination and `r` and `d` contain the rank and the determinant respectively of `A` after the evaluation.

Example of partial elimination

Ex.21

```
> A:=matrix(4,4,(i,j)->(i+j)^2);
```

$$A := \begin{bmatrix} 4 & 9 & 16 & 25 \\ 9 & 16 & 25 & 36 \\ 16 & 25 & 36 & 49 \\ 25 & 36 & 49 & 64 \end{bmatrix}$$

```
> gausselim(A,2);
```

$$\begin{bmatrix} 4 & 9 & 16 & 25 \\ 0 & -11 & -28 & -51 \\ 0 & 0 & -\dfrac{2}{11} & -\dfrac{6}{11} \\ 0 & 0 & \dfrac{6}{11} & \dfrac{18}{11} \end{bmatrix}$$

Example with the computation of the rank and the determinant:

Ex.22

```
> A:=matrix(3,3,(i,j)->(6-i-j)^2):
> gausselim(A,'r','d'): r; d;
```

$$3$$

$$-8$$

An equality is used to test if the pivot is equal to zero: this can give incorrect results for the rank and the determinant when the computations are carried out with values of type `float`.

Ex.23

```
[> A:=matrix(3,3,(i,j)->(i+j-1)): A[1,1]:=1.:
[> evalm(A);
```
$$A := \begin{bmatrix} 1. & 2 & 3 \\ 2 & 3 & 4 \\ 3 & 4 & 5 \end{bmatrix}$$
```
[> gausselim(A,'r','d'):
[> r; d;
```
MAPLE doesn't take the rounding errors into account to determine the rank

$$3$$

$$8.000000004 \ 10^{-9}$$

17.2.6 Gauss–Jordan Elimination

Gauss–Jordan elimination is a Gaussian elimination method which normalizes each pivot to one, and eliminates entries above as well as below the pivot. After this elimination, the "diagonal" elements are all 1 or 0;

One use of this function is the computation of matrix inverses, as described below.

The matrix A is augmented with the identity matrix:

Ex.24

```
[> A:=matrix(3,3,(i,j)->(i+j-1)^2);
```
$$A := \begin{bmatrix} 1 & 4 & 9 \\ 4 & 9 & 16 \\ 9 & 16 & 25 \end{bmatrix}$$
```
[> B:=concat(A,diag(1,1,1));
```
$$B := \begin{bmatrix} 1 & 4 & 9 & 1 & 0 & 0 \\ 4 & 9 & 16 & 0 & 1 & 0 \\ 9 & 16 & 25 & 0 & 0 & 1 \end{bmatrix}$$

And the resulting matrix is put in Gauss–Jordan form.

Ex.25

```
> B1:=gaussjord(B);
```

$$B1 := \begin{bmatrix} 1 & 0 & 0 & \dfrac{31}{8} & -\dfrac{11}{2} & \dfrac{17}{8} \\[2ex] 0 & 1 & 0 & -\dfrac{11}{2} & 7 & -\dfrac{5}{2} \\[2ex] 0 & 0 & 1 & \dfrac{17}{8} & -\dfrac{5}{2} & \dfrac{7}{8} \end{bmatrix}$$

Then the right block is extracted to obtain the inverse of A.

Ex.26

```
> C:=submatrix(B1,1..3,4..6);
```

$$C := \begin{bmatrix} \dfrac{31}{8} & -\dfrac{11}{2} & \dfrac{17}{8} \\[2ex] -\dfrac{11}{2} & 7 & -\dfrac{5}{2} \\[2ex] \dfrac{17}{8} & -\dfrac{5}{2} & \dfrac{7}{8} \end{bmatrix}$$

```
> multiply(A,C);                              let's verify
```

$$\begin{bmatrix} 1 & 0 & 0 \\ 0 & 1 & 0 \\ 0 & 0 & 1 \end{bmatrix}$$

18. Normalization of Matrices

In this chapter, we assume that the `linalg` library has been loaded with the command `with(linalg)`.

18.1 Determinant, Characteristic Polynomial

18.1.1 Determinant of a Matrix

The function `det` computes the determinant of a matrix. If `A` is a square matrix, `det(A)` returns the determinant of `A`.

Example with a matrix with integer elements

Ex. 1

```
> with(linalg): A:=matrix(5,5,(i,j)->irem(i+j-2,5)+1);
```

$$A := \begin{bmatrix} 1 & 2 & 3 & 4 & 5 \\ 2 & 3 & 4 & 5 & 1 \\ 3 & 4 & 5 & 1 & 2 \\ 4 & 5 & 1 & 2 & 3 \\ 5 & 1 & 2 & 3 & 4 \end{bmatrix}$$

```
> det(A);
```
$$1875$$

Example of the famous Vandermonde determinant

Ex. 2

```
> A:=vandermonde([x,y,z,t]):
  factor(det(A));
```

$$(t-y)(y-x)(t-x)(z-y)(t-z)(z-x)$$

18.1.2 Characteristic Matrix and Characteristic Polynomial

Characteristic Matrix of a Matrix

If A is a square matrix of order n, charmat(A,x) returns the matrix $x\, I_n - A$, where I_n is the identity matrix of order n. The variable x must be specified.

Ex. 3

```
> A:=matrix(3,3,(i,j)->i^j): B:=charmat(A,x);
```

$$B := \begin{bmatrix} x-1 & -1 & -1 \\ -2 & x-4 & -8 \\ -3 & -9 & x-27 \end{bmatrix}$$

```
> C:=charmat(A);
```
If one forgets the x ... Error

Error, (in charmat) invalid arguments

Characteristic Polynomial of a Matrix

If A is a square matrix of order n, charpoly(A,x) returns the determinant of the matrix $xI_n - A$, where I_n is the identity matrix of order n. One thus obtains the characteristic polynomial of A up to the multiplicative factor $(-1)^n$. The variable x must be specified in this case as well.

Ex. 4

```
> A:=matrix(3,3,(i,j)->i^j);
```

$$A := \begin{bmatrix} 1 & 1 & 1 \\ 2 & 4 & 8 \\ 3 & 9 & 27 \end{bmatrix}$$

```
> p:=charpoly(A);
```
Error, (in charpoly) wrong number of parameters

```
> p:=charpoly(A,x);
```

$$p := x^3 - 32x^2 + 62x - 12$$

```
> subs(x=A,p);
```
Let's verify
Cayley-Hamilton's theorem

$$A^3 - 32\, A^2 + 62\, A - 12$$

```
> evalm(");
```

$$\begin{bmatrix} 0 & 0 & 0 \\ 0 & 0 & 0 \\ 0 & 0 & 0 \end{bmatrix}$$

The polynomial obtained may not be normalized if all the coefficients of the matrix A are not rational numbers.

Ex. 5

```
> A:=evalm(matrix(3,3,1)+a);
```
$$A := \begin{bmatrix} 1+a & 1 & 1 \\ 1 & 1+a & 1 \\ 1 & 1 & 1+a \end{bmatrix}$$

```
> p:=charpoly(A,x);
```
$$p := x^3 - 3x^2 - 3x^2a + 6xa + 3xa^2 - 3a^2 - a^3$$

```
> collect(p,x);
```
$$x^3 + (-3 - 3a)x^2 + (3a^2 + 6a)x - 3a^2 - a^3$$

```
> factor(p);
```
$$-(a - x + 3)(-x + a)^2$$

18.1.3 Minimal Polynomial of a Matrix

If A is a square matrix of order n, the evaluation of minpoly(A,x) returns the minimal polynomial of matrix A.

Ex. 6

```
> A:=matrix(3,3,[4,4,6,-6,-7,-12,3,4,7]);
```
$$A := \begin{bmatrix} 4 & 4 & 6 \\ -6 & -7 & -12 \\ 3 & 4 & 7 \end{bmatrix}$$

```
> q:=minpoly(A,x);
```
$$q := 2 - 3x + x^2$$

```
> p:=charpoly(A,x);
```
$$p := x^3 + 5x - 4x^2 - 2$$

```
> divide(p,q);
```
One can check that the minimal polynomial divides the characteristic polynomial

$$true$$

18.2 Eigenvalues and Eigenvectors of a Matrix

18.2.1 Eigenvalues

The function eigenvals returns the eigenvalues of a matrix. If A is a square matrix, the evaluation of eigenvals(A) returns the sequence of eigenvalues of A, written explicitly or implicitly.

If the order of the matrix A is less than or equal to 3, then eigenvals(A) returns the sequence of eigenvalues of A expressed in radicals.

Ex. 7

```
> A := matrix(3,3,[1,1,1,1,1,1,1,2,3]);
```

$$A := \begin{bmatrix} 1 & 1 & 1 \\ 1 & 1 & 1 \\ 1 & 2 & 3 \end{bmatrix}$$

```
> eigenvals(A);
```

$$0, \frac{5}{2} + \frac{1}{2}\sqrt{13}, \frac{5}{2} - \frac{1}{2}\sqrt{13}$$

If the matrix A is of order 4, then eigenvals(A) will return either a result using radicals or an implicit form using the function RootOf, according to the value of the global variable _EnvExplicit (p. 103).

Ex. 8

```
> A:=matrix(4,4,[0,0,0,a,0,0,0,b,0,0,0,c,a,b,c,d]);
```

$$A := \begin{bmatrix} 0 & 0 & 0 & a \\ 0 & 0 & 0 & b \\ 0 & 0 & 0 & c \\ a & b & c & d \end{bmatrix}$$

```
> eigenvals(A);
```

$$0, 0, \frac{d}{2} - \frac{1}{2}\sqrt{d^2 + 4c^2 + 4b^2 + 4a^2}, \frac{d}{2} + \frac{1}{2}\sqrt{d^2 + 4c^2 + 4b^2 + 4a^2}$$

If the order of the matrix A is greater than 5, it is in general impossible to express the eigenvalues with radicals; eigenvals(A) returns a result written either with the help of trigonometric functions or with the function RootOf.

Example of a result using RootOf's

Ex. 9

```
> A:=matrix(5,5,(i,j)->gcd(i,j)): eigenvals(A);
```

$$RootOf(-16 + 88\_Z + 134 - Z^2 + 72\_Z^3 - 15\_Z^4 + \_Z^5)$$

Example of a result using trigonometric functions

```
> A:=band([0,0,1],7): A[7,1]:=1: eval(A);
```

$$\begin{bmatrix} 0 & 1 & 0 & 0 & 0 & 0 & 0 \\ 0 & 0 & 1 & 0 & 0 & 0 & 0 \\ 0 & 0 & 0 & 1 & 0 & 0 & 0 \\ 0 & 0 & 0 & 0 & 1 & 0 & 0 \\ 0 & 0 & 0 & 0 & 0 & 1 & 0 \\ 0 & 0 & 0 & 0 & 0 & 0 & 1 \\ 1 & 0 & 0 & 0 & 0 & 0 & 0 \end{bmatrix}$$

Ex.10

```
> eigenvals(A);
```

$$1,\ \cos\left(\frac{2\pi}{7}\right) + I\sin\left(\frac{2\pi}{7}\right),\ -\cos\left(\frac{3\pi}{7}\right) + I\sin\left(\frac{3\pi}{7}\right),$$
$$-\cos\left(\frac{\pi}{7}\right) + I\sin\left(\frac{\pi}{7}\right),\ -\cos\left(\frac{\pi}{7}\right) - I\sin\left(\frac{\pi}{7}\right),$$
$$-\cos\left(\frac{3\pi}{7}\right) - I\sin\left(\frac{3\pi}{7}\right),\ \cos\left(\frac{2\pi}{7}\right) - I\sin\left(\frac{2\pi}{7}\right)$$

```
> charpoly(A,x);
```
To verify

$$1 - x^7$$

If **A** is a matrix whose elements are rational functions with algebraic elements, eigenvals(A,implicit) forces MAPLE to return a result written with the help of RootOf's (of irreducible polynomials).

With the matrix **A** of the previous example, one obtains

Ex.11

```
> eigenvals(A,implicit);
```

$$1, RootOf(\_Z^6 + \_Z^5 + \_Z^4 + \_Z^3 + \_Z^2 + \_Z + 1)$$

Irrational numbers appearing in the matrix must be written with RootOf when one uses the option implicit, otherwise MAPLE returns an error message. The function convert can be used to transform radicals into RootOf's, but the rule used to evaluate matrices requires that convert be applied to eval(A), not A.

Ex.12

```
> A:=matrix(3,3,[sqrt(2),-1,1,2,1,-1,-2,1,-1]);
```

$$A := \begin{bmatrix} \sqrt{2} & -1 & 1 \\ 2 & 1 & -1 \\ -2 & 1 & -1 \end{bmatrix}$$

```
> eigenvals(A,implicit);
```
Error, (in eigenvals) radicals in input matrix
must be converted to RootOf's

18.2.2 Eigenvectors, Diagonalization

If A is a square matrix, eigenvects(A) returns a sequence of lists $[\lambda, \alpha, B_\lambda]$, where λ is an eigenvalue of A, α is its order of multiplicity and B_λ is a basis (in the form of a set) of the subspace associated with the eigenvalue λ.

First Example

Ex.13

```
> A:=matrix(3,3,(i,j)->a^(i+j-2));
```

$$A := \begin{bmatrix} 1 & a & a^2 \\ a & a^2 & a^3 \\ a^2 & a^3 & a^4 \end{bmatrix}$$

```
> s:=eigenvects(A);
```

$$s \; : \; = \left[0, 2, \left\{\left[-a^2, 0, 1\right], [-a, 1, 0]\right\}\right],$$
$$\left[1 + a^2 + a^4, 1, \left\{\left[\frac{1}{a}, 1, a\right]\right\}\right]$$

The previous matrix can thus be diagonalized and a transformation matrix can be constructed with the help of the functions op and union.

Ex.14

```
> Ens_Vect:=op(3,s[1]) union op(3,s[2]);
```

$$Ens\_vect := \left\{\left[-a^2, 0, 1\right], [-a, 1, 0], \left[\frac{1}{a}, 1, a\right]\right\}$$

```
> P:=concat(op("));          op transforms the set into a sequence
```

$$P := \begin{bmatrix} -a & -a^2 & \frac{1}{a} \\ 1 & 0 & 1 \\ 0 & 1 & a \end{bmatrix}$$

```
> map(normal,evalm(P^(-1)&*A&*P));
```

$$\begin{bmatrix} 0 & 0 & 0 \\ 0 & 0 & 0 \\ 0 & 0 & 1 + a^2 + a^4 \end{bmatrix}$$

Second Example

Ex.15

```
> A:=matrix(4,4,(i,j)->irem(i+j-2,4));
```

$$A := \begin{bmatrix} 0 & 1 & 2 & 3 \\ 1 & 2 & 3 & 0 \\ 2 & 3 & 0 & 1 \\ 3 & 0 & 1 & 2 \end{bmatrix}$$

```
> s:=eigenvects(A);
```

$$s \quad := \quad [[6, 1, \{[1, 1, 1, 1]\}], [-2, 1, \{[1, -1, 1, -1]\}],$$
$$[2\sqrt{2}, 1, \{[-1, \sqrt{2}+1, 1, -1-\sqrt{2}]\}],$$
$$[-2\sqrt{2}, 1, \{[-1, 1-\sqrt{2}, 1, \sqrt{2}-1]\}],]$$

```
> P:=concat(op('union'(seq(op(3,x),x=s))));
```

Ex.16

$$P := \begin{bmatrix} 1 & 1 & -1 & -1 \\ 1 & -1 & \sqrt{2}+1 & 1-\sqrt{2} \\ 1 & 1 & 1 & 1 \\ 1 & -1 & -1-\sqrt{2} & \sqrt{2}-1 \end{bmatrix}$$

```
> map(normal,evalm(P^(-1)&*A&*P));
```
To verify

$$P := \begin{bmatrix} 6 & 0 & 0 & 0 \\ 0 & -2 & 0 & 0 \\ 0 & 0 & 2\sqrt{2} & 0 \\ 0 & 0 & 0 & -2\sqrt{2} \end{bmatrix}$$

Note: The expression `seq(op(3,x),x=s)` is an abbreviated form of `seq(op(3,s[i]),i=1..nops([s]))`, it returns a sequence of sets whose union can be obtained with the help of the function `union` (p. 357).

Third Example

```
> A:=matrix(5,5,(i,j)->gcd(i,j)): s:=eigenvects(A);
```

$$s := [[\%1, 1, \{[-\frac{397}{8}\%1 + \frac{237}{8}\%1^2 - \frac{103}{16}\%1^3 + \frac{7}{16}\%1^4 + \frac{91}{4},$$
$$\frac{67}{4}\%1 - 9\%1^2 + \frac{15}{8}\%1^3 - \frac{1}{8}\%1^4 - 10,$$

Ex.17

$$\frac{109}{8}\%1 - \frac{41}{4}\%1^2 + \frac{41}{16}\%1^3 - \frac{3}{16}\%1^4 - 5, 1,$$
$$-\frac{7}{4} + \frac{7}{2}\%1 - \frac{11}{8}\%1^2 + \frac{1}{8}\%1^3]\}]]$$

$$\%1 = RootOf(-16 + 88\_Z + 34 - Z^2 + 72\_Z^3 - 15\_Z^4 + \_Z^5)$$

The function `allvalues` gives approximate values of the algebraic expressions.

Ex.18

```
> Digits:=5; s1:=allvalues([s]);
```

$$[.29364, 1, \{[10.572, -5.8109, -1.8195, 1, -.83766]\}],$$
$$[.78114, 1, \{[-.843, -1.5604, .54029, 1, .2046]\}],$$
$$[2.3743, 1, \{[-.320, .1586, -2.0916, 1, .4819]\}],$$
$$[3.7812, 1, \{[.070, .482, .181, 1, -1.4160]\}],$$
$$[7.7698, 1, \{[.550, .74, .73, 1, 1.0680]\}]$$

```
> P:=concat(op('union'(seq(op(3,x),x=s))));
```

$$P := \begin{bmatrix} 10.572 & -.843 & -.320 & .070 & .550 \\ -5.8109 & -1.5604 & .1586 & .482 & .74 \\ -1.8195 & .54029 & -2.0916 & .181 & .73 \\ 1 & 1 & 1 & 1 & 1 \\ -.83766 & 2046 & 4819 & -1.4160 & 1.0680 \end{bmatrix}$$

```
> evalm(P^(-1)&*A&*P);
```
To verify.

18.2.3 Testing if a Matrix Can Be Diagonalized

There is no MAPLE function that tests whether a matrix can be diagonalized, but one need only compute the number of eigenvectors returned by the function `eigenvals` and compare it with the order of the matrix, as in the following example.

Ex.19

```
> A:=matrix(3,3,1);
```

$$A := \begin{bmatrix} 1 & 1 & 1 \\ 1 & 1 & 1 \\ 1 & 1 & 1 \end{bmatrix}$$

```
> s:=eigenvects(A);
```

$$s := [0, 2, \{[-1, 0, 1], [-1, 1, 0]\}], [3, 1, \{[1, 1, 1]\}]$$

```
> Ens_Vect:= 'union'(seq(op(3,x),x=s));
```

$$Ens\_Vect := \{[-1, 0, 1], [-1, 1, 0], [1, 1, 1]\}$$

```
> nops(Ens_Vect);
```
$$3$$

18.2.4 Matrices That Have an Element of Type `float`

Given a matrix A whose entries are all numerical values, at least one among them being of type `float` or of type `complex(float)` (p. 348),

- `eigenvals(A)` returns the sequence of approximate values of the (real and complex) eigenvalues of A.
- `eigenvects(A)` returns a result which is similar to the one described on page 310 but using approximate values.

The number of significant digits of these results is specified by the variable `Digits`.

Ex.20

```
> A:=matrix(3,3,[0,-1,3.0,2,1,1,-2,1,-1]);
```

$$A := \begin{bmatrix} 0 & -1 & 3.0 \\ 2 & 1 & 1 \\ -2 & 1 & -1 \end{bmatrix}$$

```
> eigenvals(A);
```

$$-.735139262 + 2.760668258\,I,$$
$$-.735139262 - 2.760668258\,I,\ 1.70278519$$

```
> Digits:=3; eigenvects(A);
```

$$[-.74 + 2.75\,I, 1, \{[-.723 - 1.02\,I, -.514 + .503\,I, .948 - .241\,I]\}],$$
$$[-.74 - 2.75\,I, 1, \{[-.723 + 1.02\,I, -.514 - .503\,I, .948 + .241\,I]\}],$$
$$[1.48, 1, \{[.030, .669, .242]\}]$$

The matrix may not contain a variable if it contains any coefficient of type `float`, otherwise MAPLE returns an error message.

Ex.21

```
> A:=matrix(3,3,[u,-1,3.0,2,1,1,-2,1,-1]);
```

$$A := \begin{bmatrix} u & -1 & 3.0 \\ 2 & 1 & 1 \\ -2 & 1 & -1 \end{bmatrix}$$

```
> eigenvals(A);
```
Error, (in linalg/evalf) matrix entries must all evaluate to float

```
> eigenvects(A);
```
Error, (in linalg/evalf) matrix entries must all evaluate to float

18.2.5 The Inert Function Eigenvals

When one only needs numerical approximations of the eigenvalues, the results can be obtained more quickly using the inert form `Eigenvals`. If A is a matrix with real or complex coefficients, `evalf(Eigenvals(A))` returns a list of approximations of the complex eigenvalues of A in the form of a vector. However, such a method can only be applied to a matrix whose coefficients are all numerical values.

Warning ! Since the function `evalf` uses a `remember` table and since a matrix isn't fully evaluated, one must write `evalf(Eigenvals(eval(A)))` if one wishes to carry out this computation for several values of A.

Ex.22

```
> A:=matrix(3,3,[0,-1,3,2,1,1,-2,1,-1]);
```

$$A := \begin{bmatrix} 0 & -1 & 3 \\ 2 & 1 & 1 \\ -2 & 1 & -1 \end{bmatrix}$$

```
> evalf(Eigenvals(eval(A)));
```

$$[-.735 + 2.76\,I,\ -.735 + 2.76\,I,\ 1.47]$$

If A is a matrix with real entries and real eigenvalues which can be diagonalized, and if P is a free variable, `evalf(Eigenvals(A,P))` returns the sequence of approximate values of the eigenvalues of A and assigns to P a transformation matrix which diagonalizes A.

Ex.23

```
> A:=matrix(3,3,[1,1,1,1,2,1,1,1,3]);
```

$$A := \begin{bmatrix} 1 & 1 & 1 \\ 1 & 2 & 1 \\ 1 & 1 & 3 \end{bmatrix}$$

```
> Digits:=3: P:='P': evalf(Eigenvals(eval(A),P));
```

$$[.328,\ 1.50,\ 4.24]$$

```
> eval(P);                    To display the transformation matrix
```

$$\begin{bmatrix} .891 & -.228 & .398 \\ -.427 & -.745 & .535 \\ -.173 & .638 & .747 \end{bmatrix}$$

18.2.6 Normalization to the Jordan Form

Jordan Block Matrix

The function JordanBlock constructs a Jordan block matrix. If n is a natural number and x is an expression, JordanBlock(x,n) returns the square matrix of order n with copies of x on the principal diagonal, 1's on the diagonal just above it and 0's everywhere else.

Ex.24

```
> x:='x'; J:=JordanBlock(x,5);
```

$$J := \begin{bmatrix} x & 1 & 0 & 0 & 0 \\ 0 & x & 1 & 0 & 0 \\ 0 & 0 & x & 1 & 0 \\ 0 & 0 & 0 & x & 1 \\ 0 & 0 & 0 & 0 & x \end{bmatrix}$$

Normalization to the Jordan Form

If A is a square matrix, jordan(A) returns Jordan form of A, i.e. a block-diagonal matrix $\mathtt{diag}(J_1, J_2, ..., J_r)$, where the matrices J_k are Jordan block matrices, two J_k's being allowed to have the same diagonal elements.

Ex.25

```
> A:=matrix(3,3,[2,-3,-1,1,-2,-1,-2,6,3]);
```

$$A := \begin{bmatrix} 2 & -3 & -1 \\ 1 & -2 & -1 \\ -2 & 6 & 3 \end{bmatrix}$$

```
> jordan(A);
```

$$\begin{bmatrix} 1 & 1 & 0 \\ 0 & 1 & 0 \\ 0 & 0 & 1 \end{bmatrix}$$

A second optional parameter can be used in the function jordan. If A is a square matrix and P is a free variable, the evaluation of jordan(A,P) returns a matrix J, the Jordan form of A, and assigns to P an invertible matrix such that $J = P^{-1}AP$. When J is diagonal, P is a transformation matrix from the canonical basis to a basis of eigenvectors of A.

Ex.26

```
> A:=matrix(4,4,[5,10,-19,4,1,7,-8,3,1,4,-5,2,0,-1,1,1]);
```

$$A := \begin{bmatrix} 5 & 10 & -19 & 4 \\ 1 & 7 & -8 & 3 \\ 1 & 4 & -5 & 2 \\ 0 & -1 & 1 & 1 \end{bmatrix}$$

```
> P:='P'; jordan(A,P);
```

$$\begin{bmatrix} 2 & 1 & 0 & 0 \\ 0 & 2 & 0 & 0 \\ 0 & 0 & 2 & 1 \\ 0 & 0 & 0 & 2 \end{bmatrix}$$

```
> eval(P);
```

$$\begin{bmatrix} 8 & 9 & 5 & 8 \\ 1 & 0 & 0 & 0 \\ 2 & 1 & 1 & 1 \\ 1 & 0 & 1 & 0 \end{bmatrix}$$

The function **jordan** can be applied to matrices whose elements are algebraic expressions. The computation time, however, may become very long with such matrices.

Ex.27

```
> x:=sqrt(2): A:=matrix(3,3,[-1,0,1,x+1,x,-1,-x-2,-x+2,3]);
```

$$A := \begin{bmatrix} -1 & 0 & 1 \\ \sqrt{2}+1 & \sqrt{2} & -1 \\ \sqrt{2}-2 & -\sqrt{2}+2 & 3 \end{bmatrix}$$

```
> J:=jordan(A);
```

$$J := \begin{bmatrix} \sqrt{2} & 0 & 0 \\ 0 & 1 & 1 \\ 0 & 0 & 1 \end{bmatrix}$$

The function **jordan** accepts matrices with coefficients of type **float**, but it may return error messages that aren't very explicit or strange results when the eigenvalues are not distinct.

With the matrix in Example 17, one obtains

Ex.28

```
[> Digits=5; A:=matrix(5,5,(i,j)->gcd(i,j)):
[> jordan(map(evalf,A));
```

$$
\begin{bmatrix}
.29364 & 0 & 0 & 0 & 0 \\
0 & 0.78114 & 0 & 0 & 0 \\
0 & 0 & 2.3743 & 0 & 0 \\
0 & 0 & 0 & 3.78112 & 0 \\
0 & 0 & 0 & 0 & 7.7698
\end{bmatrix}
$$

An error message is produced for the matrix in Example 26.

Ex.29

```
[> A:=matrix(4,4,[5.,10,-19,4,1,7,-8,3,1,4,-5,2,0,-1,1,1]);
[> jordan(A);
    Error, (in linalg[inverse]) singular matrix
```

And a nonsensical result is returned for the matrix in Example 25.

Ex.30

```
[> A:=matrix(3,3,[2,-3,-1,1,-2,-1,-2,6,3]):
```

$$
A := \begin{bmatrix}
2 & -3 & -1 \\
1 & -2 & -1 \\
-2 & 6 & 3
\end{bmatrix}
$$

```
[> jordan(map(evalf,A));
```

$$
\begin{bmatrix}
1 & 0 & 0 \\
0 & 1 & 0 \\
0 & 0 & J_{3,3}
\end{bmatrix}
$$

19. Orthogonality

19.1 Euclidean and Hermitean Vector Spaces

In this chapter, we use functions from the `linalg` library, which is assumed to have been loaded at the beginning of the session using the command `with(linalg)`.

19.1.1 Scalar Product, Hermitean Scalar Product

The function `dotprod` computes the scalar product of two real vectors or the Hermitean scalar product of two complex vectors.

- If u and v are two vectors with real numerical components that have the same dimension, the evaluation of `dotprod(u,v)` returns the (real) scalar product of u and v.
- If u and v are two vectors with complex numerical components that have the same dimension, the evaluation of `dotprod(u,v)` returns the hermitean scalar product of u and v.

Ex. 1

```
> u:=vector([1,2,3]); v:=vector([1,1,1]);
```
$$u \quad : \quad = [1, 2, 3]$$
$$v \quad : \quad = [1, 1, 1]$$
```
> dotprod(u,v);
```
$$6$$
```
> u:=vector([1,I,-1]); v:=vector([-I,1,1]);
```
$$u \quad : \quad = [1, I, -1]$$
$$v \quad : \quad = [-I, 1, 1]$$
```
> dotprod(u,v);
```
$$2I - 1$$

When the components of u and v contain free variables, these variables are assumed to be real numbers. If the complex number I appears in u or v, then dotprod(u,v) returns the hermitean product of u and v; otherwise dotprod(u,v) returns the (real) scalar product of the vectors u and v.

Ex. 2

```
> u:=vector([1,x]): v:=vector([1,y]): w:=vector([1,I*y]):
  dotprod(u,v);
```
$$1 + x\,y$$
```
> dotprod(u,w);
```
$$1 - I\,x\,y$$

When Hermitean products of vectors with variable components must be computed, each "complex" variable that is introduced has to be explicitly written in the form x+I*y.

Ex. 3

```
> restart: with(linalg):
  Warning, new definition for norm
  Warning, new definition for trace
> z1:=x1+I*y1: z2:=x2+I*y2:
  u:=vector([1,1]); v:=vector([z1,z2]);
```
$$u := [\,1,1\,]$$
$$v := [\,x1 + I\,y1\,, x2 + I\,y2\,]$$
```
> dotprod(u,v);
```
$$x1 - I\,y1 + x2 - I\,y2$$

It can be seen in the following example that the evaluation must be forced with map(eval,) if one explicitly writes the complex variables in the form x+I*y **after having used the function** vector.

Ex. 4

```
> uu:=vector([1,1]); vv:=vector([zz1,zz2]);
```
$$uu := [\,1,1\,]$$
$$vv := [\,zz1,\,zz2\,]$$
```
> zz1:=x1+I*y1: zz2:=x2+I*y2: dotprod(uu, vv); eval(");
```
$$zz1 + zz2$$
$$x1 + I\,y1 + x2 + I\,y2$$
```
> dotprod(u,map(eval,v));
```
$$x1 - I\,y1 + x2 - I\,y2$$

19.1.2 Norm

The function `norm(...,2)` computes the Euclidean or Hermitean norm of a vector. If the complex number `I` appears in `u`, then `norm(u,2)` returns the Hermitean norm of `u`, otherwise `norm(u,2)` returns the Euclidean norm of `u`.

Ex. 5

```
> u:=vector([1,1]): norm(u,2);
```
$$\sqrt{2}$$
```
> v:=vector([1+2*I,1+3*I]): norm(v,2);
```
$$\sqrt{15}$$

19.1.3 Cross Product

The function `crossprod` computes the cross product of two vectors in $\mathbb{R}^3$. Given two vectors with three components `u=(x1,x2,x3)` and `v=(y1,y2,y3)`, the evaluation of `crossprod(u,v)` returns the vector whose components are $(x2\,y3 - x3\,y2,\ x3\,y1 - x1\,y3,\ x1\,y2 - x2\,y1)$.

Ex. 6

```
> u:=vector([1,1,2]); v:=vector([1,2,1]);
```
$$u := [1, 1, 2]$$
$$v := [1, 2, 1]$$
```
> crossprod(u,v);
```
$$[-3, 1, 1]$$

19.1.4 Gram–Schmidt Orthogonalization

If `A` is a list of linearly independent vectors with real or complex numerical coefficients, `GramSchmidt(A)` returns a list of pairwise orthogonal vectors obtained by the Gram–Schmidt orthogonalization process. MAPLE uses the real scalar product if the given vectors have real coefficients, otherwise it uses the Hermitean scalar product.

The function `GramSchmidt` can be used with an optional second argument `normalized`, in which case it returns a list of vectors whose norm is 1.

Ex. 7

```
> u:=vector([1,1]); v:=vector([2,1]); GramSchmidt([u,v]);
```
$$u := [1, 1]$$
$$v := [2, 1]$$
$$\left[[1, 1], \left[\frac{1}{2}, \frac{-1}{2}\right]\right]$$

```
> GramSchmidt([u,v],'normalized');
```
$$\left[\left[\frac{1}{2}\sqrt{2}, \frac{1}{2}\sqrt{2}\right], \left[\frac{1}{2}\sqrt{2}, -\frac{1}{2}\sqrt{2}\right]\right]$$

```
> u:=vector([1+I,1]): v:=vector([1,1-I]):
  GramSchmidt([u,v]);
```
$$\left[[1 + I, 1], \left[\frac{-1}{3}, \frac{1}{3} - \frac{1}{3}I\right]\right]$$

When the list `A` isn't made up of linearly independent vectors, the evaluation of `GramSchmidt(A)` returns a shorter list, which contains pairwise orthogonal nonzero vectors.

Ex. 8

```
> u:=vector([1,1,1]): v:=vector([1,0,1]):
  w:=vector([2,1,2]): GramSchmidt([u,v,w]);
```
$$\left[[1, 1, 1], \left[\frac{1}{3}, \frac{-2}{3}, \frac{1}{3}\right]\right]$$

```
> det(concat(u,v,w));
```
to verify the dependence of the vectors

$$0$$

Warning! The function `GramSchmidt` accepts only vectors whose coefficients are real or complex numerical values, and returns an error message when one of the components contains a free variable.

Ex. 9

```
> a:='a': u:=vector([1,1]): v:=vector([a,1]):
```
$$u := [1, 1]$$
$$v := [a, 1]$$

```
> GramSchmidt([u,v]);
```
Error, (in GramSchmidt) not implemented for non numerical cases

19.1.5 Positive Definite and Positive Semidefinite Real Symmetric Matrices

Let us remind ourselves that a real symmetric matrix A is positive definite (resp. positive semidefinite) if for every nonzero column matrix X, ${}^t X A X > 0$ (resp. ${}^t X A X \geq 0$). Negative definite and negative semidefinite symmetric matrices are defined in a similar way. The function `definite` can be used to test whether a real symmetric matrix `A` is positive semidefinite, positive definite, etc.

If `A` is a square matrix,

- `definite(A,'positive_def')` returns a boolean expression `Expr`.
  * If `A` has numerical coefficients, `Expr` equals `true` (resp. `false`) if `A` is (resp. isn't) positive definite,
  * otherwise `Expr` is a boolean expression which is true if and only if `A` is positive definite.
- `definite(A,'positive_semidef')` returns a boolean expression `Expr`.
  * If `A` has numerical coefficients, `Expr` equals `true` (resp. `false`) if `A` is (resp. isn't) positive semidefinite,
  * otherwise `Expr=true` is equivalent to A being positive semidefinite.
- `definite(A,'negative_def')` and `definite(A,'negative_semidef')` do the same for negative definite matrices and negative semidefinite matrices.

Examples of matrices with numerical coefficients

Ex.10
```
> A:=matrix(2,2,[2,1,1,3]);
  B:=matrix(3,3,[4,1,1,1,4,1,1,1,4]);
```
$$A := \begin{bmatrix} 2 & 1 \\ 1 & 3 \end{bmatrix} \quad B := \begin{bmatrix} 4 & 1 & 1 \\ 1 & 4 & 1 \\ 1 & 1 & 4 \end{bmatrix}$$
```
> definite(A,'positive_def');
```
$$true$$
```
> definite(B,'positive_semidef');
```
$$true$$

Examples of matrices whose coefficients are variables

Ex.11
```
> A:=matrix(2,2,[a,b,b,c]);
```
$$A := \begin{bmatrix} a & b \\ b & c \end{bmatrix}$$
```
> definite(A,'positive_def');
```
necessary and sufficient condition for A to be positive definite
$$-a < 0 \; and \; -ac + b^2 < 0$$

Another example: condition for a matrix to be negative semidefinite

Ex.12

```
> B:=matrix(3,3,[a,2,-5,2,-2,4,-5,4,-9]);
```

$$B := \begin{bmatrix} a & 2 & -5 \\ 2 & -2 & 4 \\ -5 & 4 & -9 \end{bmatrix}$$

```
> definite(B,'negative_semidef');
```

$$a \leq 0 \text{ and } a + 2 \leq 0 \text{ and } a + 3 \leq 0$$

Warning! The function `definite` returns an error message when the matrix isn't square. On the other hand, it returns the value *false* when the matrix isn't symmetric.

Ex.13

```
> A:=matrix(2,3,1); definite(A,'positive_def');
```

$$A := \begin{bmatrix} 1 & 1 & 1 \\ 1 & 1 & 1 \end{bmatrix}$$

Error, (in definite) expecting a square matrix

```
> A:=matrix(2,2,[1,1,-1,1]); definite(A,'positive_def');
```

$$A := \begin{bmatrix} 1 & 1 \\ -1 & 1 \end{bmatrix}$$

$$false$$

19.1.6 Hermitian Transpose of a Matrix

The function `htranspose` returns the Hermitian transpose of a given matrix. If A is matrix, not necessarily square, the evaluation of `htranspose(A)` returns the conjugate of the transpose of A.

Ex.14

```
> A:=matrix(3,2,[1,1-I,2*I,1+2*I,3,1-5*I]); htranspose(A);
```

$$A := \begin{bmatrix} 1 & 1 - I \\ 2 - I & 1 + 2I \\ 3 & 1 - 5I \end{bmatrix}$$

$$\begin{bmatrix} 1 & 2 + I & 3 \\ 1 + I & 1 - 2I & 1 + 5I \end{bmatrix}$$

19.1.7 Orthogonal Matrix

The function `orthog` tests whether a real square matrix is orthogonal. This function returns the value `true` when it can determine that the matrix is orthogonal, `false` when it can determine that it isn't orthogonal, and *FAIL* when it cannot decide. The function `orthog` returns *FAIL* in the latter case because it uses the function `testeq` (on-line help with `?testeq`) to compare the different scalar products with 0 or with 1.

Ex.15

```
> A:=matrix(2,2,[sqrt(2)/2,sqrt(2)/2,-sqrt(2)/2,
  sqrt(2)/2]);
```
$$A := \begin{bmatrix} \dfrac{1}{2}\sqrt{2} & \dfrac{1}{2}\sqrt{2} \\ -\dfrac{1}{2}\sqrt{2} & \dfrac{1}{2}\sqrt{2} \end{bmatrix}$$

```
> orthog(A);
```
$$true$$

19.1.8 Normalization of Real Symmetric Matrices

As an example, let us show how the previous functions can be used to obtain an orthonormal basis of eigenvectors of a given real symmetric matrix A, and find an orthogonal matrix P such that ^tPAP is a diagonal matrix.

We first call the function `eigenvects`, which returns a sequence from which the eigenvectors of the matrix A can be extracted using `op`. The evaluation of `GramSchmidt` next returns the expected orthonormal basis.

Ex.16

```
> A:=matrix(3,3,[2,-2,-2,-2,2,-2,-2,-2,2]);
```
$$A := \begin{bmatrix} 2 & -2 & -2 \\ -2 & 2 & -2 \\ -2 & -2 & 2 \end{bmatrix}$$

```
> T:=eigenvects(A);
```
$$T := [4, 2, \{[-1, 0, 1], [-1, 1, 0]\}], [-2, 1, \{[1, 1, 1]\}]$$

```
> B:=[seq(op(x[3]),x=T)];          op to remove the braces
```
$$B := [[-1, 0, 1], [-1, 1, 0], [1, 1, 1]]$$

```
> U:=GramSchmidt(B,normalized);
```
$$\left[\left[-\frac{1}{2}\sqrt{2}, \frac{1}{2}\sqrt{2}, 0\right], \left[-\frac{1}{6}\sqrt{3}\sqrt{2}, -\frac{1}{6}\sqrt{3}\sqrt{2}, \frac{1}{3}\sqrt{3}\sqrt{2}\right],\right.$$
$$\left.\left[\frac{1}{3}\sqrt{3}, \frac{1}{3}\sqrt{3}, \frac{1}{3}\sqrt{3}\right]\right]$$

The matrix P whose columns are the previous vectors, can then be constructed. We can then verify that it solves the problem.

Ex.17

```
> P:=transpose(matrix(U));                              to construct
                                            the transformation matrix
```

$$P := \begin{bmatrix} -\dfrac{1}{2}\sqrt{2} & -\dfrac{1}{6}\sqrt{3}\sqrt{2} & \dfrac{1}{3}\sqrt{3} \\[2mm] 0 & \dfrac{1}{3}\sqrt{3}\sqrt{2} & \dfrac{1}{3}\sqrt{3} \\[2mm] \dfrac{1}{2}\sqrt{2} & -\dfrac{1}{6}\sqrt{3}\sqrt{2} & \dfrac{1}{3}\sqrt{3} \end{bmatrix}$$

```
> orthog(P);              to check that U is an orthonormal basis
```

$$true$$

```
> evalm(transpose(P) &* A &* P);              to verify that U is
                                             a basis of eigenvectors
```

$$\begin{bmatrix} 4 & 0 & 0 \\ 0 & 4 & 0 \\ 0 & 0 & -2 \end{bmatrix}$$

19.2 Orthogonal Polynomials

The functions presented in this section, which can be used to obtain the classical orthogonal polynomials, belong to the `orthopoly` library, which must be loaded using `with(orthopoly)`.

Ex.18

```
> restart: with(orthopoly);
```

$$[\, G,\ H,\ L,\ P,\ T,\ U \,]$$

We assume this library has been loaded for the remainder of this chapter.

19.2.1 Chebyshev Polynomials of the First Kind

The Chebyshev polynomials of the first kind are the polynomials defined by

$$T_0(X) = 1, \quad T_1(X) = X$$

$$\forall n \geq 2, \quad T_n(X) = 2\,X\,T_{n-1}(X) - T_{n-2}(X)$$

The evaluation of `T(n,x)` returns the value of T_n at `x`.

If m and n are two different natural numbers, T_n and T_m are orthogonal for the scalar product defined by $\langle P, Q \rangle = \int_{-1}^{1} \frac{P(t) \cdot Q(t)}{\sqrt{1-t^2}} \, dt$.

Ex.19

```
> T(5,cos(x));
```
$$16 \cos(x)^5 - 20 \cos(x)^3 + 5 \cos(x)$$
```
> combine(",trig);
```
$$\cos(5\,x)$$

19.2.2 Chebyshev Polynomials of the Second Kind

The Chebyshev polynomials of the second kind are the polynomials defined by

$$U_0(X) = 1 , \quad U_1(X) = 2\,X$$

$$\forall n \geq 2, \quad H_n(X) = 2\,X\,H_{n-1}(X) - 2\,(n-1)\,H_{n-2}(X)$$

The evaluation of U(n,x) returns the value of U_n at x.

If m and n are two different natural numbers, U_n and U_m are orthogonal for the scalar product defined by $\langle P, Q \rangle = \int_{-1}^{1} P(t)\,Q(t)\,\sqrt{1-t^2}\,dt$.

Ex.20

```
> U(5,sin(x))*cos(x);
```
$$\left(32\sin(x)^5 - 32\sin(x)^3 + 6\sin(x)\right)\,\cos(x)$$
```
> combine(",trig);
```
$$\sin(6x)$$

19.2.3 Hermite Polynomials

The Hermite polynomials are the polynomials defined by

$$H_0(X) = 1 , \quad H_1(X) = 2\,X$$

$$\forall\, n \geq 2,\ H_n(X) = 2\,X\,H_{n-1}(X) - 2\,(n-1)\,H_{n-2}(X)$$

The evaluation of H(n,x) returns the value of H_n at x.

If m and n are two different natural numbers, H_n and H_m are orthogonal for the scalar product defined by $\langle P, Q \rangle = \int_{-\infty}^{+\infty} P(t) \, Q(t) \, e^{-t^2} \, dt$.

Let us verify the formula $e^{t^2} \frac{d^n}{dt^n} \left(e^{-t^2} \right) = (-1)^n \, H_n(t)$ for $n = 4$ and $n = 5$

Ex.21

```
> n:=4: H(n,t);
```
$$16\,t^4 - 48\,t^2 + 12$$

```
> expand(exp(t^2)*diff(exp(-t^2),t$n));
```
$$16\,t^4 - 48\,t^2 + 12$$

```
> n:=5; H(n,t);
```
$$32\,t^5 - 160\,t^3 + 120\,t$$

```
> expand(exp(t^2)*diff(exp(-t^2),t$n));
```
$$-120\,t + 160\,t^3 - 32\,t^5$$

19.2.4 Laguerre Polynomials

The generalized Laguerre polynomials with parameter a are defined by

$$L_0(a, X) = 1 \,, \quad L_1(a, x) = -X + 1 + a$$

$$\forall n \geq 2, \ L_n(a, X) = \tfrac{2n+a-1-X}{n} \, L_{n-1}(a, X) - \tfrac{n+a-1}{n} \, L_{n-2}(a, X)$$

$L(n,a,x)$ returns the value at x of the nth generalized Laguerre polynomial with parameter a, and $L(n,x)$ returns $L(n,0,x)$, the ordinary Laguerre polynomial of degree n.

If m and n are two different natural numbers and a is a real number greater than -1, the polynomials $L_n(a, X)$ and $L_m(a, X)$ are orthogonal for the scalar product defined by $\langle P, Q \rangle = \int_0^\infty P(t) \, Q(t) \, e^{-t} t^a \, dt$.

Ex.22

```
> L(2,-1/2,x);
```
$$\frac{3}{8} - \frac{3}{2}x + \frac{1}{2}x^2$$

```
> L(2,x);
```
Ordinary Laguerre polynomial of degree 2

$$1 - 2\,x + \frac{1}{2}x^2$$

19.2.5 Legendre and Jacobi Polynomials

The Jacobi polynomials with parameters a and b are defined by

$$P_0(a, b, X) = 1 \qquad P_1(a, b, X) = \frac{a-b}{2} + \frac{a+b+2}{2} X$$

$$\forall\, n \geq 2, \quad P_n(a, b, X) = A_n\, P_{n-1}(a, b, X) + B_n\, P_{n-2}(a, b, X)$$

with

$$A_n = \frac{(2n+a+b-1-X)\,(a^2+b^2+(2n+a+b-2)\,(2n+a+b)\,X)}{2\,n\,(n+a+b)\,(2n+a+b-2)}$$

$$B_n = -\frac{2\,(n+a-1)\,(n+b-1)\,(2n+a+b)}{2\,n\,(n+a+b)\,(2n+a+b-2)}$$

The evaluation of `P(n,a,b,x)` returns the value at `x` of the nth Jacobi polynomial with parameters `a` and `b`, and `P(n,x)` returns `P(n,0,0,x)`, the Legendre polynomial of degree `n`.

If m and n are two different natural numbers, $P_n(a, b, X)$ and $P_m(a, b, X)$ are orthogonal for the scalar product $\langle P, Q \rangle = \int_{-1}^{+1} P(t)\, Q(t)\, (1-t)^a\, (1+t)^b\, dt$.

Examples of Legendre and Jacobi polynomials:

Ex.23

```
> P(3,x);P(2,1,1/2,x);
```

$$\frac{5}{2}x^3 - \frac{3}{2}x$$

$$-\frac{21}{32} + \frac{9}{16}x + \frac{99}{32}x^2$$

19.2.6 Gegenbauer Polynomials

The Gegenbauer polynomials with parameter a are defined by :

- if a does not equal zero,

$$G_0(a, X) = 1\,, \quad G_1(a, X) = 2\,a\,X$$

$$\forall\, n \geq 2,\; G_n(a, X) = \frac{2n+2a-2}{n} X\, G_{n-1}(a, X) - \frac{n+2a-2}{n} G_{n-2}(a, X).$$

- if a is equal to zero,

$$G_0(0, X) = 1$$

$$\forall\, n \geq 1,\; G_n(0, X) = \frac{2}{n} T_n(X)$$

$T_n(X)$ being the nth Chebyshev polynomial of the first kind.

The evaluation of G(n,a,x) returns the value at x of the nth Gegenbauer polynomial with parameter a.

If m and n are two different natural numbers, $G_n(a, X)$ and $G_m(a, X)$ are orthogonal for the scalar product defined by
$$\langle P, Q \rangle = \int_{-1}^{+1} P(t)\, Q(t)\, (1 - t^2)^{a-1/2}\, dt.$$

Ex.24

```
> G(3,4,x);
```
$$160\, x^3 - 40\, x$$

20. Vector Analysis

The functions that are described in this chapter belong to the `linalg` library. We always assume that the `linalg` library has been been loaded using the command `with(linalg)` for the remainder of this chapter.

In general, these functions use vector or matrix expressions as data or return them as result. A vector expression provided as data can be either a list or an object of type `vector`. Any non-scalar results which are returned are always of type `vector` or `matrix`.

20.1 Jacobian Matrix, Divergence

20.1.1 Jacobian Matrix

The function `jacobian` produces the Jacobian matrix of a vector expression. Given a vector expression `p=[p1,p2, ..,pn]` and a vector expression `x=[x1,x2,..,xm]` whose components are free variables, the evaluation of `jacobian(p,x)` returns the Jacobian matrix of `[p1,p2,..,pn]` with respect to `[x1,x2,..,xm]`, i.e. the matrix with n rows and m columns $\left(\dfrac{\partial p_i}{\partial x_j} \right)_{\substack{1 \le i \le n \\ 1 \le j \le m}}$.

Ex. 1

```
> restart: with(linalg): p:=[r*cos(t),r*sin(t)]; v:=[r,t];
```
$$p := [r\,\cos(t), r\,\sin(t)]$$
$$v := [r, t]$$

```
> A:=jacobian(p,v); simplify(det(A));
```
$$A := \left[\begin{array}{cc} \cos(t) & -r\,\sin(t) \\ \sin(t) & r\,\cos(t) \end{array} \right]$$

```
> simplify(det(A));
```
$$r$$

Warning! The evaluation of `jacobian(p,x)` returns the following error message if one of the variables of the vector expression `[x1,x2,..,xm]` isn't free.

Ex. 2

```
> r:=sqrt(x*x+y*y);
```

$$r := \sqrt{x^2 + y^2}$$

```
> jacobian([r*cos(t),r*sin(t)],[r,t]);
    Error, (in jacobian) wrong number (or type) of parameters in
    funct diff
```

20.1.2 Divergence of a Vector Field

The function `diverge` produces the divergence of a vector field. Given a vector expression `p=[p1,p2,..,pn]` and a vector expression `x =[x1,x2,..,xn]` whose components are free variables, the evaluation of `diverge(p,x)` returns the divergence of `[p1,p2,..,pn]` with respect to `[x1,x2,..,xn]`, i.e. the expression $\sum_{i=1}^{n} \dfrac{\partial p_i}{\partial x_i}$.

Ex. 3

```
> p:=[arctan(y/x),1/(x^2+y^2)];
```

$$p := \left[\arctan(\frac{y}{x}) \ , \ \frac{1}{x^2 + y^2} \right]$$

```
> normal(diverge(p,[x,y]));
```
                                    normal to simplify the result

$$-\frac{y\,(x^2 + y^2 + 2)}{(x^2 + y^2)^2}$$

In three dimensions, the function `diverge` may be used with the option `coords=cylindrical` (resp. `coords=spherical`) as third argument. The computation of the divergence is then carried out in cylindrical (resp. spherical) coordinates, the elements of `p` containing the components of the vector function in the moving frame that corresponds to the coordinates used.

Ex. 4

```
> unassign('r','u','v');
```
                                    To unassign r, u and v

```
> diverge([1/(r^2),0,0],[r,u,v],coords=spherical);
```
            Computation of the divergence of a field at 1/r^2

$$0$$

20.2 Gradient, Laplacian, Curl

20.2.1 Gradient

The function `grad` determines the gradient of an expression. Given a scalar expression `p` and the vector `x=[x1,x2,..,xn]` whose components are free variables, the evaluation of `grad(p,x)` returns the gradient of `p` with respect to `[x1,x2,..,xn]`, i.e. the vector $\left(\dfrac{\partial p}{\partial x_1}, \dfrac{\partial p}{\partial x_2}, ..., \dfrac{\partial p}{\partial x_n} \right)$.

Ex. 5

```
> g:=arctan(y/x); G:=grad(g,[x,y]);
```

$$g := \arctan(\frac{y}{x})$$

$$G := \left[-\frac{y}{x^2 \left(1 + \frac{y^2}{x^2} \right)} , \frac{1}{x \left(1 + \frac{y^2}{x^2} \right)} \right]$$

```
> map(normal,G);
```
                                        **To apply normal
                                        to every component of G**

$$\left[-\frac{y}{x^2 + y^2} , \frac{x}{x^2 + y^2} \right]$$

In three dimensions, the function `grad` may be used with the option `coords=cylindrical` (resp. `coords=spherical`) as a third argument: the function `f` must then be expressed in cylindrical (resp. spherical) coordinates, the computation of the gradient is carried out in cylindrical (resp. spherical) coordinates and the result which is returned is expressed in the moving frame corresponding to the coordinates used.

Ex. 6

```
> grad(1/r,[r,u,v],coords=spherical);
```

$$\left[-\frac{1}{r^2} , 0 , 0 \right]$$

20.2.2 Laplacian

The function `laplacian` gives the means to compute a Laplacian. If `f` is an expression in the free variables $x_1, x_2, ..., x_n$, then the evaluation of

`laplacian(f,[x1,x2,.., xn])` returns $\displaystyle\sum_{i=1}^{n} \frac{\partial^2 f}{\partial x_i^2}$.

Example of the computation of a Laplacian

Ex. 7

```
> p:=ln(1+cos(x)/cosh(y));
```

$$p := \ln\left(1 + \frac{\cos(x)}{\cosh(y)}\right)$$

```
> simplify(laplacian(p,[x,y]));
```

$$-\frac{1}{\cosh(y)^2}$$

In three dimensions, the function laplacian may be used with the option coords=cylindrical (resp. coords=spherical) as a third argument; the function f must then be expressed in cylindrical (resp. spherical) coordinates, the computation of the Laplacian is carried out in cylindrical (resp. spherical) coordinates and the result which is returned is expressed as a function of the corresponding coordinates.

As an example, let us show how the function laplacian, together with the option coords=spherical, can be used to find the harmonic functions in the three variables (x, y, z) that only depend on $\sqrt{x^2 + y^2 + z^2}$.

Ex. 8

```
> f:='f': p:=f(r):
> laplacian(p,[r,theta,phi],coords=spherical);
```

$$\frac{2r\sin(\theta)\left(\frac{\partial}{\partial r}f(r)\right) + r^2\sin(\theta)\left(\frac{\partial^2}{\partial r^2}f(r)\right)}{r^2\sin(\theta)}$$

```
> Eq:=normal(");
```

$$Eq := \frac{2\left(\frac{\partial}{\partial r}f(r)\right) + r\left(\frac{\partial^2}{\partial r^2}f(r)\right)}{r}$$

```
> S:=dsolve(Eq,f(r));
```

$$S := f(r) = \_C1 + \frac{\_C2}{r}$$

```
> subs(S,r=sqrt(x^2+y^2+z^2),f(r));
```

$$\_C1 + \frac{\_C2}{\sqrt{x^2 + y^2 + z^2}}$$

20.2.3 Hessian Matrix

The function `hessian` constructs the Hessian matrix of an expression. Given a scalar expression `p` and a vector expression `x=[x1,x2,..,xn]` whose components are free variables, the evaluation of `hessian(p,x)` returns the Hessian matrix of `p` with respect to `[x1,x2,..,xn]`, i.e. the square matrix

$$\left(\frac{\partial^2 p}{\partial x_i \, \partial x_j} \right)_{\substack{1 \le i \le n \\ 1 \le j \le n}}.$$

Ex. 9

```
> p:=x^2+y^2+z^2-2*x*y*z;
```

$$p := x^2 + y^2 + z^2 - 2\,x\,y\,z$$

```
> A:=hessian(p,[x,y,z]);
```

$$A := \begin{bmatrix} 2 & -2\,z & -2\,y \\ -2\,z & 2 & -2\,x \\ -2\,y & -2\,x & 2 \end{bmatrix}$$

One may use the Hessian matrix to determine if an expression `p` has an extremum at a point where its gradient is equal to zero. For example, with the previous expression `p`: one first looks for the points where the gradient is equal to zero; next, for each of them, one determines the sign of the eigenvalues of the associated Hessian matrix.

Ex.10

```
> v:=grad(p,[x,y,z]);
```

$$v := [\, 2\,x - 2\,y\,z \,,\ 2\,y - 2\,x\,z \,,\ 2\,z - 2\,x\,y \,]$$

```
> S:=solve({v[1],v[2],v[3]},{x,y,z});
```

$$S := \{x = 0,\ z = 0,\ y = 0\} \,,\ \{x = 1,\ y = 1,\ z = 1\},$$
$$\{y = 1,\ x = -1,\ z = -1\} \,,\ \{x = -1,\ y = -1,\ z = 1\},$$
$$\{\, x = 1,\ z = -1,\ y = -1\}$$

```
> A1:=subs(S[1],eval(A)): eigenvals(A1);
```

$$2\,,\ 2\,,\ 2$$

```
> A2:=subs(S[2],eval(A)): eigenvals(A2);
```

$$-2\,,\ 4\,,\ 4$$

The previous computations prove that `p` has a minimum at the origin but that this expression has no extremum at $(1, 1, 1)$.

20.2.4 Curl of a Vector Field of $\mathbb{R}^3$

The function `curl` computes the curl of a vector field. Given a vector expression p=[p1, p2,p3] and a vector expression x=[x1, x2,x3] whose components are free variables, the evaluation of `curl(p,x)` returns the curl of p with respect to the variables of x, i.e. the vector with components

$$\left(\frac{\partial p_3}{\partial x_2} - \frac{\partial p_2}{\partial x_3} , \ \frac{\partial p_1}{\partial x_3} - \frac{\partial p_3}{\partial x_1} , \ \frac{\partial p_2}{\partial x_1} - \frac{\partial p_1}{\partial x_2} \right) .$$

Ex.11

```
> p:=[(x^2-y^2)*x,y*(x*x-z^2),z*(y^2-x^2)];
```
$$p := \left[(x^2 - y^2)x , \ y(x^2 - z^2) , \ z(y^2 - x^2) \right]$$
```
> curl(p,[x,y,z]);
```
$$[4yz , \ 2xz , \ 4xy]$$

The function `curl` can be used with the option `coords=cylindrical` (resp. `coords=spherical`) as a third argument: the field p must then be expressed in cylindrical (resp. spherical) coordinates, the computation of the curl is carried out in cylindrical (resp. spherical) coordinates and the result which is returned is expressed in the corresponding frame.

20.3 Scalar Potential, Vector Potential

20.3.1 Scalar Potential of a Vector Field

The function `potential` tests whether a vector field derives from a scalar potential, and determines a potential from which it derives if it does. If p is a vector expression and x is the vector x=[x1,x2,...,xn] whose components are free variables, the evaluation of `potential(p,x,'V')` returns `true` if the field p derives from a scalar potential and `false` otherwise. When `potential(p,x,'V')` returns `true`, the variable V is assigned the expression of a scalar potential from which the field p derives.

Ex.12

```
> p:=[2*x+y+z,x+2*y+z,x+y+2*z];
```
$$p := [2x + y + z , \ x + 2y + z , \ x + y + 2z]$$
```
> potential(p,[x,y,z],'V'); V;
```
$$true$$
$$x y + x^2 + y^2 + x z + z^2 + y z$$

20.3.2 Vector Potential of a Vector Field

The function `vectpotent` tests whether a vector field of $\mathbb{R}^3$ derives from a vector potential, and determines a vector potential from which it derives if it does. If `p=[p1,p2,p3]` is a vector expression and `x` is the vector `[x1,x2,x3]` whose components are free variables, the evaluation of `vectpotent(p,x,'V')` returns `true` if the field `p` derives from a vector potential and `false` otherwise. When `vectpotent(p,x,'V')` returns `true`, the variable `V` is assigned the expression of a vector potential from which the field `p` derives.

Ex.13

> `p:=[y*z,-x*z,x^2+x*y];`

$$p := \left[y\, z, -x\, z, x^2 + x\, y \right]$$

> `vecpotent(p,[x,y,z],'V'); eval(V);`

$$true$$

$$\left[-\frac{1}{2} z^2 x - \frac{1}{2} x\, y^2 - x^2 y \quad -\frac{1}{2} z^2 y, \; 0 \right]$$

21. The MAPLE Objects

21.1 Basic Expressions

21.1.1 The Types $+$, $*$ and $\char`\^$

MAPLE classifies the basic expressions, involving only rational constants, names of variables and the operators +, -, *, / and ^, according to three types: the type +, the type * and the type ^.

- Expressions like x+y and x+y+z are of type +, as are x-y+z, which MAPLE stores as x+(-1)*y+z, and (x*y)+(z*t), which is the sum of the two terms x*y and z*t. For MAPLE, the operator + isn't a binary operator that is generalized by recurrence but an n-ary operator whose operands all play a symmetric role.
- Expressions like x*y and x*y*z are of type *, as are x*y/z, which MAPLE stores as x*y*z^(-1), and (x+y)*(z+t) which, written like this, is the product of the two terms (x+y) and (z+t). Like the operator +, the operator * is an n-ary operator.
- Expressions like x^y, 1/x, (x+y)^(-3) as well as x^(1/2) or (x-y+z)^(1/3) are of type ^. For MAPLE, the operator ^ is a binary operator and MAPLE doesn't accept x^y^z, one must thus specify x^(y^z) or (x^y)^z.

21.1.2 The Functions whattype, op and nops

- The function whattype determines the type of a basic expression and more generally the basic type of a MAPLE object. If Obj is a MAPLE object, whattype(Obj) returns the basic type of Obj. A list of the MAPLE basic types can be obtained by typing: ?datatype
- The function op can be used to break up an expression into subexpressions. Given an expression Expr, any element belonging to the sequence returned by op(Expr) is called an operand of Expr or a first level subexpression of Expr.
- The function nops returns the number of these subexpressions.

Ex. 1

```
> Expr_1:=2*x*y-3*x^2+4*x/y^2;
```

$$Expr\_1 := 2\,x\,y - 3\,x^2 + 4\,\frac{x}{y^2}$$

```
> whattype(Expr_1); op(Expr_1); nops(Expr_1);
```

$$+$$

$$2\,x\,y \ , \ -3\,x^2 \ , \ 4\,\frac{x}{y^2}$$

$$3$$

```
> Expr_2:=(x+2*y^2)*(z+4)/(x+2);
```

$$Expr\_2 := \frac{(x + 2\,y^2)\,(z + 4)}{x + 2}$$

```
> whattype(Expr_2); op(Expr_2);
```

$$*$$

$$x + 2\,y^2 \ , \ z + 4 \ , \ \frac{1}{x + 2}$$

```
> Expr_3:=(x^2+2*y*z)^2;
```

$$Expr\_3 := (x^2 + 2\,y\,z)^2$$

```
> whattype(Expr_3); op(Expr_3);
```

$$\wedge$$

$$x^2 + 2\,y\,z \ , \ 2$$

The function op can also be used with two arguments. If n contains a positive integer value, the evaluation of op(n,Expr) returns the nth operand of the expression Expr.

Ex. 2

```
> Expr_11:=op(1,Expr_1);
```

$$Expr\_11 := 2\,x\,y$$

```
> Expr_12:=op(2,Expr_1);
```

$$Expr\_12 := -3\,x^2$$

```
> Expr_13:=op(3,Expr_1);
```

$$Expr\_13 := 4\,\frac{x}{y^2}$$

Warning! One should only call op(n,Expr) with a positive integer value of n which is less than or equal to nops(Expr), otherwise MAPLE returns an error message.

Ex. 3

```
> op(5,Expr_1);
  Error, improper op or subscript selector
```

If Expr is of type +, * or ^, the evaluation of op(0,Expr) returns the type of Expr; it is a synonym of whattype(Expr) in this case and although op(0,Expr) is defined, it doesn't appear within the sequence op(Expr) and it isn't counted within the result of nops(Expr).

Ex. 4

```
> op(0,Expr_1);
```
$$+$$

21.1.3 The Type function

In addition to +, *, /, and ^, writing mathematical expressions requires the use of terms like ln(2) or sin(x+1), which MAPLE keeps in their literal forms. If the evaluation of Expr returns a form like f(Expr1), then Expr is of type function and this object has Expr1 as its sole operand, returned at once by op(Expr) and op(1,Expr). On the other hand, the name f is returned by op(0,Expr).

Ex. 5

```
> x:='x':                           to free x in order to ensure
                              a non evaluated form after the evaluation
> y:=sin(x+1): whattype(y);
```
$$function$$
```
> op(y);
```
$$x+1$$
```
> op(0,y), op(1,y);
```
$$sin \quad , \quad x+1$$

Warning! It isn't f which is of type function, but the expression f(x). The identifier f is free or points towards an object of type procedure (Chapter 24).

Ex. 6

```
> whattype(sin(2));
```
$$function$$
```
> whattype(eval(sin));             one has to force the evaluation
                                    of an object of type procedure
```
$$procedure$$

21.1.4 Structure of Basic Mathematical Expressions

Basic mathematical expressions are constructed with the help of the four operations +, *, /, ^ and expressions of type function, like ln(2) or sin(x+1).

Such expressions are of type +, *, ^ or function. It is the "outermost" operator, i.e. the one that is carried out "last" that gives its type to an expression.

- $\frac{\sin(x)+\sqrt{2}}{y}$ is of type *, it is the product of $\sin(x) + \sqrt{2}$ and of $1/y$.
- The first subexpression $\sin(x) + \sqrt{2}$ is itself of type +, it is made up of $\sin(x)$ which is of type function and of $\sqrt{2}$ which is of type ^.
- $\sin(\frac{x+\sqrt{2}}{y})$ is of type function, its only first level subexpression is $\frac{x+\sqrt{2}}{y}$ which is of type * and has two operands ...

Ex. 7

```
> restart; Expr_4:=(sin(x)+sqrt(2))/y;
```
$$Expr\_4 := \frac{\sin(x) + \sqrt{2}}{y}$$

```
> whattype(Expr_4);
```
$$*$$

```
> op(Expr_4);
```
$$\sin(x) + \sqrt{2} \ , \ \frac{1}{y}$$

```
> op(1,Expr_4); op(2,"); whattype(");
```
$$\sin(x) + \sqrt{2}$$
$$\sqrt{2}$$
$$\wedge$$

```
> Expr_5:=sin((x+sqrt(2))/y);
```
$$Expr\_5 := \sin\left(\frac{x + \sqrt{2}}{y}\right)$$

```
> whattype(Expr_5),op(0,Expr_5),op(1,Expr_5);
```
$$function \ , \quad \sin \ , \quad \frac{x + \sqrt{2}}{y}$$

Repeated use of the function op allows one to reach subexpressions of any level of a MAPLE expression, as the following example shows.

Ex. 8

> `Expr_1:=2*x*y-3*x^2+4*x/y^2;`

$$Expr\_1 := 2\,x\,y - 3\,x^2 + 4\,\frac{x}{y^2}$$

> `Expr_13:=op(3,Expr_1);`

$$Expr\_13 := 4\,\frac{x}{y^2}$$

> `op(Expr_13);`

$$4\,,\,x\,,\,\frac{1}{y^2}$$

> `Expr_133:=op(3,Expr_13);`

$$Expr\_133 := \frac{1}{y^2}$$

> `whattype(");`

$$\wedge$$

> `op(Expr_133);`

$$y\,,-2$$

This little game can be continued ad infinitum and the curious user may use the function op to explore the maze of his favourite expressions. This function op, used with one or two arguments, can be used to rapidly become acquainted with the structure of MAPLE objects.

21.2 Real and Complex Numerical Values

With real values, MAPLE distinguishes

- values it calls `numeric`: integers, fractions, decimal values.
- values that it keeps in literal form, like `sqrt(2)` and `ln(2)`, or that it represents by a specific name, like `Pi`, `gamma`,...

With complex values, a similar distinction exists for the real and the complex parts.

21.2.1 The Values of Type numeric

The Type integer

A positive or negative integer is an object of type integer. It is exactly represented in memory and always displayed in base 10 on the screen. It is a basic object that cannot be broken up with the help of op.

Ex. 9

```
> x:=2^(2^15)+1:                    the reader may replace : by ;
                                           to see the value of x

> whattype(x);
                                integer

> length(x);        number of digits of the decimal writing of x
                                  9865
```

The Types fraction and rational

A rational number that isn't an integer is represented by two integers, its numerator and its denominator: the denominator being strictly positive and relatively prime to the numerator. Such an object is of type fraction.

Ex.10

```
> x:=3/4-5;
                                x := \frac{-17}{4}

> whattype(x);
                                fraction
```

An object of type fraction is composed of two operands. The user can retrieve each of these operands with the help of the function op or with the specific functions numer and denom.

Ex.11

```
> op(1,x); op(2,x);
                                  -17
                                   4
> numer(x); denom(x);
                                  -17
                                   4
```

The type `rational` is the union of the types `integer` and `fraction`. It isn't a basic type returned by `whattype`, like the types `integer` and `fraction`, but it can, nevertheless, be tested with the function `type`. The list of types recognized by the function `type` can be obtained by typing: `? type`.

Ex.12

```
> whattype(3), whattype(17/4);
```
$$integer \ , \ fraction$$
```
> type(3,fraction), type(3,rational);
```
$$false \ , \ true$$
```
> type(17/4,rational);
```
$$true$$

The Type `float`

A number that explicitly contains a decimal point is represented in memory by two integers: the mantissa and the exponent. It is an object of type `float`. The mantissa and the exponent can be retrieved with the function `op`. If `x` contains a value of type `float`, then `op(1,x)` returns the mantissa of `x` and `op(2,x)` returns its exponent.

Ex.13

```
> x:=123.456;
```
$$x := 123.456$$
```
> op(x);
```
$$123456 \ , \ -3$$
```
> op(1,x);
```
$$123456$$

The Type `numeric`

The type `numeric` is the union of the three types `integer, fraction` and `float`. It isn't a basic type returned by the function `whattype`, but it can, nevertheless, be tested with the function `type`. MAPLE uses often `type(...,numeric)` within its procedures in order to determine whether an argument contains an integer, fractional or decimal value.

Ex.14

```
> type(1.414,numeric),type(2^(1/2),numeric);
```
$$true \ , \ false$$

21.2.2 The Values of Type `realcons`

While a classical programming language like PASCAL replaces $\sqrt{2}$ or $\log(3)$ by an approximate numerical value, MAPLE keeps an exact symbolic representation of such numbers.

A quantity like `sqrt(2)` is stored in the form `2^(1/2)`. It is an expression of type `^`.

Ex.15

```
> x:=sqrt(2); whattype(x); op(x);
```

$$x := \sqrt{2}$$

$$\wedge$$

$$2 \; , \; \frac{1}{2}$$

A quantity like `ln(2)` is left as an unevaluated expression of type `function`.

Ex.16

```
> x:=ln(2); whattype(x); op(x);
```

$$x := \ln(2)$$

$$function$$

$$2$$

```
> op(0,x);
```

$$\ln$$

A quantity like `Pi` is an identifier that represents a constant and for such an object the type returned by `whattype` is `string`. Such an object cannot be broken up with the help of the function `op`.

The other identifiers of numerical constants MAPLE knows are `gamma`, `infinity`, `Catalan` and `I`. These identifiers are protected and the user cannot assign values to them (except by using `unprotect`). For more information about these identifiers of constants, type `? constants` or `? gamma, ? Pi`, etc.

Ex.17

```
> x:=gamma; whattype(x);                        Euler's constant
```

$$x := \gamma$$

$$string$$

```
> op(x);
```

$$\gamma$$

As can verified by the function `type`, MAPLE doesn't regard the previous values to be of type `numeric`.

Ex.18

```
> type(ln(2),numeric);
                    false
> x:=Pi+1; whattype(x); type(x,numeric);
                  x := π + 1

                       +

                    false
```

There exists a type in MAPLE that corresponds to what one usually calls a real number, it is the type `realcons`. It isn't a basic type returned by the function `whattype` but it can nevertheless be tested with the help of `type`. If the evaluation of `type(Expr,realcons)` returns the value `true`, an approximate value of `Expr` can be computed by the function `evalf`.

Ex.19

```
> x:=Pi+1+sqrt(2); whattype(x);
  type(x,realcons); type(x,numeric);
              x := π + 1 + √2

                       +

                     true
                    false
> y:=evalf(x); whattype(y); type(y,numeric);

                y := 5.555806216

                    float
                     true
```

Warning! Quantities in an inequality test must be of type `numeric`. Objects of type `realcons` that are not of type `numeric` must be converted using `evalf`. The constant `Pi`, for example, cannot be used within a test like `x<Pi`. This test should be written `x<evalf(Pi)`.

Ex.20

```
> if 1<Pi then 'true' else 'false' fi;
  Error, cannot evaluate boolean
> if 1<evalf(Pi) then 'true' else 'false' fi;
                     true
```

21.2.3 The Complex Values

MAPLE has no specific basic type for complex values. If Expr contains a complex value, then whattype(Expr) can be +, *, ^ or function according to the outermost operator appearing in Expr. The operands returned by op(Expr) are therefore the ones that correspond to the type returned by whattype(Expr).

Ex.21

```
> x:=1+I; whattype(x); op(x);
```
$$x := 1 + I$$
$$+$$
$$1 \ , \ I$$

```
> y:=(1+sqrt(2)*I)^2; whattype(y); op(y);
```
$$y := (1 + I\sqrt{2})^2$$
$$\wedge$$
$$1 + I\sqrt{2} \ , \ 2$$

```
> z:= ln(-2); whattype(z); op(z); op(0,z);
```
$$z := \ln(-2)$$
$$function$$
$$-2$$
$$\ln$$

As for real numbers, MAPLE provides a type for expressions representing a complex value: the type complex. This type isn't returned by whattype, but can nevertheless be tested with the function type. When the evaluation of type(Expr, complex) returns true, an approximate value of Expr can be computed with the help of the function evalf.

Ex.22

```
> z:= ln(-2): type(z,complex); evalf(z);
```
$$true$$
$$0.6931471806 + 3.141592654 \ I$$

```
> evalc(z);
```
$$\ln(2) + I\pi$$

As can be seen in previous example, one shouldn't confuse evalf(z), which writes z in the form a+I*b where a and b are approximate values of the real and imaginary parts of z, with evalc(z) which writes z in the form a+I*b where a and b are the exact values of the real and imaginary parts of z.

The type `complex` has derived types corresponding to the type of the real and imaginary parts of an expression. For example

- `type(Expr,complex(integer))` returns `true` if `Expr` is written in the form a+I*b, where a and b are both of type `integer`.
- `type(Expr,complex(numeric))` returns `true` if `Expr` is written in the form a+I*b, where a and b are both of type `numeric`.

More generally, `type(Expr,complex(Expr_Type))` returns `true` if `Expr` is written in the form a+I*b, where a and b are both of type `Expr_Type`. To test whether `Expr` is a quantity of type `complex(Expr_Type)`, it is thus better to transform it before the evaluation of `type(Expr,complex(Expr_Type))`.

Ex.23

> `z:=(1+I*(sqrt(2)+1))^3*(1-I*(sqrt(2)-1))^3;`

$$z := \left(1 + I\left(\sqrt{2} + 1\right)\right)^3 \left(1 - I\left(\sqrt{2} - 1\right)\right)^3$$

> `z1:=expand(z);`

$$z1 := -16 + 16\,I$$

> `type(z,complex(integer));`

$$false$$

> `type(z1,complex(integer));`

$$true$$

21.3 Expression Sequences

A sequence or expression sequence appears in the form of a finite family of objects separated with commas. The comma is the operator used to construct sequences. A sequence can be constructed

- either by writing elements separated by commas,
- or by joining two sequences with a comma.

Ex.24

> `s1:=Lun,Mar,Mer; s2:=1,2,3;`

$$s1 := Lun, Mar, Mer$$

$$s2 := 1, 2, 3$$

> `s:=s1,s2;`

$$s := Lun , Mar , Mer , 1 , 2 , 3$$

The type `exprseq` is a basic type returned by `whattype` that cannot be tested with the help of the function `type`.

Ex.25

```
> whattype(s);
                           exprseq
> type(s,exprseq);
  Error, wrong number (or type) of parameters in function type
```

21.3.1 The Function seq

The function seq constructs a sequence whose elements are defined as a function of their rank. Given an expression f(i) depending on the variable i, and a and b, two values of type numeric such that a<=b, the evaluation of seq(f(i),i=a..b) returns the sequence f(a),f(a+1),...,f(a+n), where n is the integer part of b-a. If a and b are two integers, which is typically the case, the sequence returned is f(a),f(a+1),...,f(b-1),f(b).

Ex.26

```
> seq(cos(i*Pi/6),i=0..6);
```

$$1\,,\,\frac{1}{2}\sqrt{3}\,,\,\frac{1}{2}\,,\,0\,,\,-\,\frac{1}{2}\,,\,-\frac{1}{2}\sqrt{3}\,,\,-1$$

```
> whattype(");
                           exprseq
> f:='f'; s:=seq(f(i),i=1.55..5);
```

$$s := f(1.55)\,,\,f(2.55)\,,\,f(3.55)\,,\,f(4.55)$$

Note: The function seq is in fact an abbreviation of a for loop (Chapter 23). The previous single expression seq(f(i),i=1.55..5) is equivalent to

Ex.27

```
> s:=NULL:                    NULL denotes the empty sequence
  for i from 1.55 to 5 do s:=s,f(i); od:
```

But seq is more efficient because it avoids constructing intermediate sequences, which would slow down execution speed and using unnecessarily the memory.

Warning! Since seq(f(i),i=a..b) is an abbreviation of a for loop, the variable i need not be free. On the other hand, the variable i recovers the value it contained when seq was called after the execution of seq(f(i),i=a..b). Despite the syntactic similarity, i has to be a free variable in sum(f(i),i=a..b), since sum begins with a full evaluation of all its arguments (p. 175).

21.3.2 The Operator $

The operator $ also constructs sequences but with a syntax which reads less easily than seq. The only practical use of the operator $ is the construction of a sequence of n elements all equal to an object x, using the syntax x$n. It is mainly used with diff in order to specify an order of derivation.

Ex.28

```
> restart; x$6;
```
$$x, x, x, x, x, x$$

```
> diff(arctan(x),x$3);          for a third derivative
```
$$8\frac{x^2}{(1+x^2)^3} - 2\frac{1}{(1+x^2)^2}$$

```
> normal(");
```
$$2\frac{3x^2 - 1}{(1+x^2)^3}$$

21.3.3 Sequence of Results

Some MAPLE functions, providing a variable number of results, return a sequence. This is, for example, true of solve:

Ex.29

```
> P:=x^3-6*x^2+11*x-6;
```
$$P := x^3 - 6x^2 + 11x - 6$$

```
> solve(P);
```
$$1, 2, 3$$

When such a function seems not to return anything, it in fact returns an empty sequence corresponding to MAPLE's NULL identifier.

Ex.30

```
> P:=x^2+1; S:=fsolve(P);          gives the real roots of P
```
$$P := x^2 + 1$$
$$S :=$$

```
> whattype(S);
```
$$exprseq$$

```
> evalb(S=NULL);     evalb to force the evaluation of the boolean
```
$$true$$

21.3.4 Sequence of Components of an Expression

If `Expr` is any expression, `op(Expr)` returns the sequence of first level components of `Expr`. Likewise, if `a` and `b` are two integers, `op(a..b,Expr)` returns the sequence made up of the first level components of `Expr` whose rank lies between `a` and `b`.

Ex.31

```
> P:=x^3-6*x^2+11*x-6;
```
$$P := x^3 - 6x^2 + 11x - 6$$
```
> op(P);
```
$$x^3 \,,\, -6x^2 \,,\, 11x \,,\, -6$$
```
> op(2..3,P);
```
$$-6x^2 \,,\, 11x$$
```
> z:=ln(2);
```
$$z := \ln(2)$$
```
> op(0..1,z);
```
$$\ln \,,\, 2$$

21.3.5 Sequence of Parameters of a Procedure

Sequences are also used in a symbolic way to represent the sequence of parameters to a procedure (Chapter 24).

Internally, a MAPLE procedure operates upon a sequence of arguments, allowing procedures which, from the point of view of the user, manipulate a variable number of parameters. The ith argument passed to a procedure is simply the ith element of the sequence which is passed to the procedure. The number of arguments which are passed is the number of elements in this sequence. We shall see in Chapter 24, p. 424, how the ith argument or the number of arguments passed to a procedure can be recovered using the functions `args` and `nargs`.

This explains why, if `Expr` is a sequence, one cannot extract the ith element from it with the help of `op(i,Expr)`, as for the objects encountered previously: when evaluating `op(i,Expr)`, the function `op` encounters the sequence `i,Expr` which in general contains more than two elements (it has $n + 1$ elements if `Expr` is a sequence of n elements) and the verification test by which the function `op` begins thus gives an error. For the same reason, it is impossible to compute the number of elements of `Expr` with `nops(Expr)`, or to test the type `exprseq` with `type(Expr,exprseq)`.

Ex.32

```
> P:=x^3-3*x^2+x+1;
```
$$P := x^3 - 3x^2 + x + 1$$
```
> S:= solve(P);
```
$$S := \ 1 \ , \ \sqrt{2}+1 \ , \ 1-\sqrt{2}$$
```
> op(2,S);
```
Error, wrong number (or type) of parameters in function op

One may use the selection operator [] to extract an element from a sequence: if Expr is an expression sequence and if i is a natural number at most equal to the number of elements of Expr, the evaluation of Expr[i] returns the ith element of Expr.

Ex.33

```
> S2:=S[2];
```
$$S2 := \sqrt{2}+1$$

Like op, the selection operator can be used with a range of integers a..b. If Expr is a sequence, Expr[a..b] returns the sequence of elements of Expr whose rank lies between a and b.

Ex.34

```
> S[1..2];
```
$$1 \ , \ \sqrt{2}+1$$

21.4 Ranges

One constructs an object of type **range** by joining two expressions with the help of the .. operator. Such objects are mainly used to write an integral, to create expression sequences with **seq**, to define sums or products of a large number of quantities with **sum** or **product**, etc.

Ex.35

```
> Rng:=a..b;
```
$$Rng := a..b$$

The range `a..b` is of type `..` and it is made up of two operands `a` and `b`.

Ex.36

```
> whattype(Rng);
```
$$..$$
```
> op(Rng);
```
$$a\,,\,b$$
```
> op(1,Rng);
```
$$a$$

One can test if an expression is of type range with the function **type**. One may use **range**, which is a synonym of `..`, as a second argument. If one really wishes to use `..`, one must, as for `+` and `*`, put this symbol between backward apostrophes, in order to avoid an inappropriate evaluation leading to a syntax error.

Ex.37

```
> type(Rng,range);
```
$$true$$
```
> type(Rng,'..');
```
$$true$$
```
> type(Rng,.. );
  syntax error, '..' unexpected
```

The function **seq** used with a range, as second argument, whose bounds evaluate to values of type **numeric** quickly and effectively constructs an expression sequence. When one of the bounds of the range contains a value which is of type **realcons** without being of type **numeric**, **evalf** must be used.

Ex.38

```
> f:='f': seq(f(i),i=1.55..5);
```
$$f(1.55)\,,\;f(2.55)\,,\;f(3.55)\,,\;f(4.55)$$
```
> Rng:=1..Pi;
```
$$Rng := 1..\pi$$
```
> seq(i,i=Rng);
  Error, unable to execute seq
```
```
> seq(i,i=evalf(Rng));
```
$$1.\,,\;2.\,,\;3.$$

21.5 Sets and Lists

21.5.1 The Operators { } and [ ]

Syntactically, we construct

- a set by adding a pair of braces { } around a sequence.
- a list by adding a pair of square brackets [ ] around a sequence.

If `Expr` is an expression sequence,

- {Expr} is the set made up of the elements appearing in `Expr`. As usual in a set, MAPLE never duplicates elements, and it sorts elements in an order it choses. This order can vary from one session to another, but remains constant within a session.
- [Expr] is the list containing the elements of `Expr` in the order in which they appear in the sequence `Expr`. A list may contain the same element several times.

Ex.39

```
> s:=b,a,c;
                        s := b , a , c
> Ens:={s}; Liste:=[s];
                     Ens := { c , a , b }
                     Liste := [ b , a , c ]
> s:=seq(i*i,i=-3..3): Ens:={s}; Liste:=[s];
                     Ens := { 0 , 1 , 4 , 9 }
                 Liste := [ 9 , 4 , 1 , 0 , 1 , 4 , 9 ]
```

If `Ens_Lst` is a set or a list,

- op(Ens_Lst) returns the sequence of its elements.
- nops(Ens_Lst) returns the number of its elements.
- op(i,Ens_Lst) returns its ith element.

Ex.40

```
> nops(Ens); op(Ens);
                        4
                   0 , 1 , 4 , 9
> nops(Liste); op(Liste);
                        7
                9 , 4 , 1 , 0 , 1 , 4 , 9
> op(3,Liste);
                        1
```

Warning! An object of type set or list is considered as a unique object by a procedure while a sequence is considered as an aggregate of several objects if it contains more than one element. If Expr is an expression sequence, the evaluation of nops(Expr) returns an error message, since the function nops expects a single argument. On the other hand, the evaluation of nops([Expr]) returns the number of elements of the list [Expr] and thus of Expr.

Ex.41

```
> Sol:=solve(x^3-3*x^2+x+1);
```
$$Sol := 1,\ \sqrt{2}+1,\ 1-\sqrt{2}$$
```
> nops(Sol);
   Error, wrong number (or type) of parameters in function nops
> nops([Sol]);
```
$$3$$

The function member tests whether an element belongs to a set or to a list. When X is a set or a list which is completely described,

- the evaluation of member(x,X) returns *true* if x is an element of X.
- if member(x,X,'rg') returns the value true, then rg contains the rank of the first occurrence of x within X after the evaluation.

Ex.42

```
> Liste:=[1,3,5,7,9,7,5]:member(7,Liste,'rg');
```
$$true$$
```
> rg;
```
$$4$$
```
> restart:member(7,L);                    Case where L is free
   Error, wrong number (or type) of parameters in function member;
```

One may use the function convert together with the option list (resp. the option set) to transform sets into lists (resp. lists into sets).

- If Lst is a list, convert(Lst,set) returns the set of elements of Lst. Duplicates are deleted and MAPLE sorts the elements of the set without taking into account the order of the elements of the list.
- If Ens is a set, convert(Ens,list) returns a list containing the elements of Ens and MAPLE keeps the elements of the list in the order in which they appear in Ens.

Ex.43

```
> convert([1,3,4,2,4,6],set);
```
$$\{1,\ 2,\ 3,\ 4,\ 6\}$$

21.5.2 Operations Upon the Sets

The operators `intersect`, `union` and `minus` perform operations on sets. If E1 and E2 are sets

E1 union E2   returns the union $E1 \cup E2$.

E1 intersect E2 returns the intersection $E1 \cap E2$.

E1 minus E2   returns the set difference $E1 \setminus E2$.

Ex.44

```
> Ens_1:={1,2,3,4,5}; Ens_2:={3,5,7,9};
```
$$Ens\_1 := \{\,1\,,\,2\,,\,3\,,\,4\,,\,5\,\}$$
$$Ens\_2 := \{\,3\,,\,5\,,\,7\,,\,9\,\}$$
```
> Ens_1 intersect Ens_2;
```
$$\{\,3\,,\,5\,\}$$
```
> Ens_1 union Ens_2;
```
$$\{\,1\,,\,2\,,\,3\,,\,4\,,\,5\,,\,7\,,\,9\,\}$$
```
> Ens_1 minus Ens_2;
```
$$\{\,1\,,\,2\,,\,4\,\}$$

One may use the *functions* intersect, union and minus to write an intersection or a union of more than two sets more compactly. The names of these functions must appear between backward apostrophes in order to avoid confusing these functions with the operators bearing the same names.

Ex.45

```
> Ens:='union'(Ens_1,Ens_2,Ens_3);
```
$$Ens := Ens\_3 \ union \ \{\,1\,,\,2\,,\,3\,,\,4\,,\,5\,,\,7\,,\,9\,\}$$
```
> Ens_3:={a,1,2}; Ens;
```
$$Ens\_3 := \{\,a\,,\,1\,,\,2\,\}$$
$$\{a\,,\,1\,,\,2\,,\,3\,,\,4\,,\,5\,,\,7\,,\,9\,\}$$

As can be seen in the previous example, MAPLE can symbolically express the union of sets that haven't been completely described. The same can be done for intersections or set differences.

21.5.3 Operations on Lists

Value of an Element

As for vectors and arrays, elements of a list can be retrieved or modified using the index operator `[ ]`. Given a list L and a positive integer i which is less than or equal to `nops(L)`

- one obtains the ith element of L by `L[i]`.
- one modifies the ith element of L by an assignment like `L[i]:=`...

Ex.46

```
> L:=[1,3,5,7,9]: L[3];
                              5
> L[3]:=11;
                          L_3 := 11
> L;
                     [1, 3, 11, 7, 9]
> L[6]:=11;                               If one exceeds nops(L)
  Error, out of bound assignment to a list
```

Concatenation

Given p lists L1, L2, ..., Lp, the evaluation of `[op(L1),op(L2),...,op(Lp)]` returns the list obtained by concatenating these p lists

Ex.47

```
> L1:=[1,3,5,7,9]; L2:= [7,9,11,13];
                   L1 := [1, 3, 5, 7, 9]
                   L2 := [7, 9, 11, 13]
> L3:= [op(L1),op (L2)];
            L3 := [1, 3, 5, 7, 9, 7, 9, 11, 13]
```

One can construct `L4:=[L1,L2]` with the lists L1 and L2 of the previous example. But note that L4 isn't equal to the list L3 obtained by concatenating L1 and L2. The list L4 only contains two elements, which are lists, while L3 contains 9 elements, which are numbers.

Ex.48

```
> L4:=[L1,L2];
            L4 := [[1, 3, 5, 7, 9], [7, 9, 11, 13]]
> op(L4); op(L3);
            [1, 3, 5, 7, 9], [7, 9, 11, 13]
            1, 3, 5, 7, 9, 7, 9, 11, 13
```

21.5.4 Extraction

Given a list L and two integers a, b such that 0<=a<=b<=nops(L), the evaluation of op(a..b,L) returns the sequence of elements of L whose rank lies between a and b; the corresponding sublist is thus: [op(a..b,L)].

Ex.49

```
> [op(2..4,L1)];
                    [ 3 , 5 , 7 ]
```

Given a list (resp. a set) X and a function (or a procedure) f in one variable that returns a boolean result,

- the evaluation of select(f,X) returns the list (resp. the set) of elements x of X verifying f(x)=true.
- the evaluation of remove(f,X) returns the list (resp. the set) of elements x of X verifying f(x)=false.

Example with a MAPLE function

Ex.50

```
> L:=[seq(i,i=100..150)]:
  select(isprime,L);
            [101, 103, 107, 109, 113, 127, 131, 137, 139, 149]
```

Example with a function defined by the user

Ex.51

```
> Digits:=3:
  s:=fsolve(x^5+x+1,x,complex):        To extract the roots
  select(x->Re(x)>=0,[s]);        whose real part is positive
            [.877 − .745 I , .877 + .745 I]
```

Given a list (resp. a set) X, a MAPLE expression a and a function (or procedure) f in two variables that returns a boolean result,

- the evaluation of select(f,X,a) returns the list (resp. the set) of elements x of X verifying f(x,a)=true.
- the evaluation of remove(f,L,a) returns the list (resp. the set) of elements x of X verifying f(x,a)=false.

For example, the list of rational roots of a polynomial can be constructed by writing

Ex.52

```
> P:=6*x^6-17*x^5+10*x^4+x^3+5*x^2+x-6;
```
$$q := 6\,x^6 - 17\,x^5 + 10\,x^4 + x^3 + 5\,x^2 + x - 6$$
```
> s:=solve(q):
  select(type,[s],rational); select(type,[s],fraction);
```
$$[1, -2/3, 3/2]$$
$$[-2/3, 3/2]$$

Note: The function `select` can also be used with a set or with any MAPLE expression as second argument: it then returns an expression of the same type consisting only of those operands that agree with the criterion.

Ex.53

```
> p:=factor(x^8+x^4+1,sqrt(3));
```
$$(x^2 + x + 1)\,(x^2 - x + 1)\,(x^2 + \sqrt{3}\,x + 1)\,(x^2 - \sqrt{3}\,x + 1)$$
```
> select(has,p,sqrt(3));
```
                                          **to get the product
                                  of the trinomials containing** $\sqrt{3}$
$$(x^2 + \sqrt{3}\,x + 1)\,(x^2 - \sqrt{3}\,x + 1)$$

21.5.5 Back to the Function `seq`

Given a list or a set `X`,

- If `f` is a function (or a procedure) in one variable, then `seq(f(x),x=X)` is synonymous with `seq(f(X[i]),i=1..nops(X))`.
- If `p` is an expression in the free variable `x`, then `seq(p,x=X)` is synonymous with `seq(subs(x=X[i],p),i=1..nops(X))`.

For example, the sequence of expressions $t\,e^x + x^2$ when t takes the values $-1, 1, 2, 5, 7$ can be obtained by writing

Ex.54

```
> p:=t*exp(x)+x^2;
```
$$p := t\,e^x + x^2$$
```
> seq(p,t=[-1,1,2,5,7]);
```
$$-e^x + x^2, e^x + x^2, 2\,e^x + x^2, 5\,e^x + x^2, 7\,e^x + x^2$$

21.6 Unevaluated Integrals

MAPLE has no specific type unevaluated integrals. Such an expression may have been returned

- either because MAPLE cannot express it with the help of the functions in its library,
- or because the user has called the inert function `Int`.

MAPLE then stores it as an object of type `function`.

As for any object of type `function`, the name of the function is the operand of rank 0: this name is `int` for an integral MAPLE hasn't succeeded in expressing in terms of basic functions, and `Int` for an integral written with the inert form `Int`.

Applied to such an expression, the function `op` returns a sequence of two operands. The first is the expression to be integrated and the second is

- the name of the integration variable for a primitive.
- an equation of type `nom_var=Interv_intgr` for an integral.

Ex.55

```
> Intg_1:=int(sin(x)/(1+exp(x)),x=0..1);
```

$$Intg_1 := \int_0^1 \frac{\sin(x)}{1+e^x} dx$$

```
> whattype(Intg_1);
```

$$function$$

```
> op(Intg_1);
```

$$\frac{\sin(x)}{1+e^x} \ , \ x = 0..1$$

```
> op(0,Intg_1);
```

$$int$$

21.7 Polynomials

MAPLE has no specific basic type for polynomials. If the variable P points towards a polynomial, `whattype(P)` may return `+`, `*`, `^` according to the outermost operator appearing in P. The operands returned by `op(P)` are those corresponding to the type returned by `whattype(P)`.

Ex.56

```
> x:='x': y:='y': P:=3*x^4+5*x^3+2*x+1;
  whattype(P); op(P);
```

$$P := 3\,x^4 + 5\,x^3 + 2\,x + 1$$

$$+$$

$$3\,x^4,\ 5\,x^3,\ 2\,x\,,1$$

```
> Q:=(x+y*sqrt(2))^2*(x-y*sqrt(2))^2;
  whattype(Q); op(Q);
```

$$Q := (x + y\sqrt{2})^2(x - y\sqrt{2})^2$$

$$*$$

$$(x + y\sqrt{2})^2\,,\ (x - y\sqrt{2})^2$$

However MAPLE provides the type `polynom`, which tests whether an expression represents a polynomial: it isn't a basic type returned by `whattype` but it can nevertheless by tested with `type`.

Ex.57

```
> type(P,polynom); type(Q,polynom);
```

$$true$$

$$true$$

```
> R:=3*sin(x)^2+2*sin(x); type(R,polynom);
```

$$R := 3\sin(x)^2 + 2\sin(x)$$

$$false$$

Like the type `complex`, the type `polynom` has derived types which can be used to determine what kind of coefficients a polynomial has. In general, `type(P,polynom(Expr_Type))` returns `true` if P is a polynomial and if all the coefficients appearing in P are of type `Expr_Type`.

For example,

- `type(P,polynom(integer))` returns `true` if P is a polynomial and if all coefficients of P are of type integer.
- `type(P,polynom(realcons))` returns true if P is a polynomial and if all coefficients of P are of type `realcons`.

This test doesn't carry out any transformations of the polynomial P, and it may happen that the evaluation of `type(P,polynom(Expr_Type))` returns `false` even though P could be written with coefficients of type `Expr_Type`.

With the previous polynomials, one can write

Ex.58

```
> type(P,polynom(integer));
                       true
> type(Q,polynom(realcons)); type(Q,polynom(integer));
                       true
                       false
> Q1:=expand(Q); type(Q1,polynom(integer));
            Q1 := x^4 - 4 x^2 y^2 + 4 y^4
                       true
```

Other types derived from the type `polynom` can be used to test whether a quantity is a polynomial expression in some variables whose coefficients belong to a given domain. For example

- `type(P,polynom(integer,x))` returns `true` if P is written as a polynomial in the variable x with coefficients of type `integer`.
- `type(P,polynom(realcons,[x,y]))` returns `true` if P is written as a polynomial in the variables x and y whose coefficients are of type `realcons`.
- `type(P,polynom(rational,sin(x)))` returns `true` if P is written as a polynomial expression in `sin(x)` whose coefficients are of type `rational`.

As before, these tests don't carry out any preliminary reductions.

Ex.59

```
> type(P,polynom(integer,x));
                       true
> type(Q1,polynom(integer,x));
                       false
> type(Q1,polynom(integer,[x,y]))
                       ;true
> type(R,polynom(integer,sin(x)));
                       true
> P:=(x-sqrt(y))*(x+sqrt(y));
            P := (x - \sqrt{y}) (x + \sqrt{y})
> type(P,polynom(integer,x));
                       false
```

21.8 Truncated Series Expansions

21.8.1 Taylor Series Expansions

MAPLE has a specific type for Taylor series expansion: the type `series`. It is a basic type returned by `whattype`.

Ex.60

> `S:=series(sin(x),x=Pi/2); whattype(S);`

$$S := 1 - \tfrac{1}{2}\left(x - \tfrac{1}{2}\pi\right)^2 + \tfrac{1}{24}\left(x - \tfrac{1}{2}\pi\right)^4 + O\left(\left(x - \tfrac{1}{2}\pi\right)^6\right)$$

series

If S contains a Taylor series expansion of order n whose polynomial part has p non zero terms, then in general $2p + 2$ first level subexpressions are returned by the function `op` for S. The first $2p$ expressions are grouped together two by two: a coefficient and the corresponding exponent in the series expansion. The two last contain O(1) and n+1. The increment x-a doesn't appear in the sequence returned by the function `op` but it can be obtained as the subexpression of index 0.

Ex.61

> `r:=nops(S): op(1..r-2,S);`

$$1 , 0 , \frac{-1}{2} , 2 , \frac{1}{24} , 4$$

> `op(r-1..r,S);`

$$O(1) , 6$$

> `op(0,S);`

$$x - \frac{1}{2}\pi$$

Note: The representation used to store a Taylor series expansion is commonly called a sparse representation: only the coefficients and the powers of the nonzero terms are written.

One may use the function `convert`, together with the option `polynom`, to retrieve the polynomial part of a Taylor series expansion.

Ex.62

> `convert(S,polynom);`

$$S := 1 - \frac{1}{2}\left(x - \frac{1}{2}\pi\right)^2 + \frac{1}{24}\left(x - \frac{1}{2}\pi\right)^4$$

One exception to the Taylor series expansion structure described previously arises in the series expansion of a polynomial to an order greater than its degree: there is no supplementary term in this case, and S has only $2\,p$ first level subexpressions.

Ex.63

```
> S:=series(x^2+x+1,x=1,4);
```
$$S := 3 + 3\,(x - 1) + (x - 1)^2$$
```
> whattype(S);                    S is nevertheless of type series
```
$$series$$
```
> op(S);                but it doesn't contain a supplementary term
```
$$3\,,\,0\,,\,3\,,\,1\,,\,1\,,\,2$$

21.8.2 Other Series Expansions

Generalized truncated series expansions, Puiseux series, as well as asymptotic series expansions and the series expansions at infinity are not stored as objects of type series but simply as objects of type +, where each operand is a "monomial" of the series expansion, the last containing the supplementary term which is an object of type function.

Ex.64

```
> S:=series(x^2/(x^2+1),x=infinity);
```
$$S := 1 - \frac{1}{x^2} + \frac{1}{x^4} + O\left(\frac{1}{x^6}\right)$$
```
> whattype(S); op(S);
```
$$+$$
$$1\,,\,\frac{1}{x^2}\,,\,\frac{1}{x^4}\,,\,O\left(\frac{1}{x^6}\right)$$
```
> whattype(op(4,S)); op(0..1,op(4,S));
```
$$function$$
$$O\,,\,\frac{1}{x^6}$$

Although the regular part of such a series expansion isn't a polynomial, it can still be extracted with the help of convert(,polynom).

Ex.65

```
> S:=subs(O(1)=0,S);
```
$$S := 1 - \frac{1}{x^2} + \frac{1}{x^4}$$

21.9 Boolean Relations

21.9.1 The Type relation

Given two expressions a and b, the relations a=b, a<>b, a<b and a<=b are
MAPLE objects whose types are respectively '=', '<>', '<' and '<='. The
union of these four types make up the type relation. The type relation
isn't a basic type returned by the function whattype, but it can nevertheless
be tested with the help of the function type.

Ex.66

```
> Eq:=x=y+1;
```
$$Eq := x = y + 1$$
```
> whattype(Eq);
```
$$=$$
```
> Ineq:=2*x+1>0;
```
$$Ineq := 0 < 2x + 1$$
```
> whattype(Ineq);
```
$$<$$

As can be seen in the previous example, an inequality is automatically put
in the form a<b for a strict inequality and a<=b for a loose inequality.

To test each of the previous types with the function type, the symbol corresponding to the type must appear between backward apostrophes, in order
to prevent the syntactic analyzer from returning an error message.

Ex.67

```
> type(Ineq,'<');
```
true
```
> type(Ineq,'=');
```
false
```
> type(Ineq,relation);
```
true
```
> type(Ineq,<);
```
syntax error) unexpected

Each object of type relation has two first level subexpressions; the two
members of the relation. They can be extracted either with the function op
or with the functions rhs (right hand side) and lhs (left hand side).

```
> op(Ineq); op(0,Ineq);
```
$$0 \,,\, 2x + 1$$
$$<$$

Ex.68

```
> rhs(Ineq);
```
One may also use op(2,Ineq)
$$2x + 1$$

```
> lhs(Ineq);
```
One may also use op(1,Ineq)
$$0$$

21.9.2 The Type boolean

Objects of type **relation** encountered in the previous section belong to a more general type: the type **boolean**. The type **boolean** contains the type **relation**, the type **logical** which groups together the types 'and', 'or' and 'not', as well as the constants **true** and **false**.

The types 'and', 'or' and 'not' are basic types returned by the function whattype while the type **boolean** can only be tested with the function type.

Ex.69

```
> restart; test:=x<y and(y>0 or y<z);
```
$$test := x - y < 0 \; and \; (-y < 0 \; or \; y - z < 0)$$

```
> whattype(test);
```
$$and$$

Note: An inequality contained within a boolean expression is always put in the canonical form of comparison to 0.

The subexpressions of a boolean expression can be extracted with the help of the function op.

Ex.70

```
> op(test);
```
$$x - y < 0 \quad,\quad -y < 0 \; or \; y - z < 0$$

```
> op(2,test);
```
$$-y < 0 \; or \; y - z < 0$$

21.10 Tables and Arrays

The objects of type `table` and `array` allow families of values to be stored and retrieved by index.

21.10.1 Tables

An object of type `table` can store data indexed by any quantity. It can be used without any explicit prior declaration. If `ind` and `val` are basic MAPLE expressions, the assignment `A[ind]:=val` creates the table `A`, if it doesn't yet exist, and assigns the value `val` to its element of index `ind`.

Ex.71

```
> restart; Rg_Jour[Lu]:=1; Rg_Jour[Ma]:=2; Rg_Jour[Je]:=4;
```
$$Rg\_Jour_{Lu} := 1$$
$$Rg\_Jour_{Ma} := 2$$
$$Rg\_Jour_{Je} := 4$$

The previous assignments can be carried out as a single operation with the help of the function `table`, by the assignment `Rg_Jour:=table([Lu=1,Ma=2, Je=4])`.

Unlike basic MAPLE objects, a table is not fully evaluated every time it is used. One must thus explictly request the evaluation of a table using `eval` in order to display its contents.

Ex.72

```
> Rg_Jour;
```
$$Rg\_Jour$$
```
> eval(Rg_Jour);
```
                                One may also use print(Rg_Jour)

$$table \quad ([\\ Ma = 2\\ Lu = 1\\ Je = 4\\ ])$$

An object can be removed from a table with the functions `unassign` or `evaln` (described on page 371).

Ex.73

```
> unassign('Rg_Jour[Lu]'); eval(Rg_Jour);
```
$$table \quad ([\\ Ma = 2\\ Je = 4\\ ])$$

The type `table` is often used by MAPLE in order to store the results of procedures that use the option `remember` (p. 407).

The rule of evaluation for objects of type `table` states that

- the assignment `B:=A` only causes B to point towards A: every subsequent change to the value of an element of A therefore modifies the corresponding element of B.
- the assignment `B:=eval(A)` causes B to point towards the table of values towards which A is pointing, without creating a new table of values. Contrary to what happens for the other MAPLE objects, every subsequent change to the value of an element of A thus also modifies the corresponding element of B.

One should use the function `copy` in order to create a table B which is independent of A. If A is a table, the evaluation of `B:=copy(A)` creates a new table B and copies out the content of A into it.

Ex.74

```
> R:=Rg_Jour: S:=eval(Rg_Jour): T:=copy(Rg_Jour):
  Rg_Jour[Lu]:=8: eval(S); eval(T);
```

$$table \quad ([$$
$$Me = 3$$
$$Ma = 2$$
$$Lu = 8$$
$$Je = 4$$
$$])$$

$$table \quad ([$$
$$Me = 3$$
$$Ma = 2$$
$$Lu = 1$$
$$Je = 4$$
$$])$$

As for functions and procedures, the evaluation of an object of type `table` is an evaluation up to the last name encountered. In the previous example, R points towards the table `Rg_Jour` which points towards its contents: the last table name encountered within the evaluation of R is thus `Rg_Jour`. On the other hand, neither S nor T point towards another table since S points towards the contents of the table `Rg_Jour` and T points towards its own content: the last table names encountered within the evaluations of S and of T are thus respectively S and T.

Ex.75

```
> R; S; T;
```

$$Rg\_Jour$$
$$S$$
$$T$$

21.10.2 Tables, Indexed Variables

For MAPLE, the type `array` is a specialization of the type `table` whose indices are integers belonging to intervals specified by the user. An object of type `array` must be explicitly declared using the function `array`.

One-Dimensional Tables

If m and n are integers such that m<n, the assignment `A:=array(m..n)` creates a one-dimensional table whose index may vary from m up to n.

Moreover, if L is the list of equations `[i1=expr1,...,ik=exprk]` where i1, ..., ik are integer values belonging to the range m..n, then the assignment `A:=array(m..n,L)` creates the table A and carries out the assignments `A[i1] :=expr1`, ..., `A[ik]:=exprk` .

The advantage of a table whose dimension is specified is that MAPLE gives an error message for any attempt to access an element whose index doesn't belong to the range m..n.

Ex.76

> Nom_Jour:=array(0..3,[0=Dimanche,1=Lundi,2=Mardi]);

$$Nom\_Jour; = array(0..3, [$$
$$(0) = Dimanche$$
$$(1) = Lundi$$
$$(2) = Mardi$$
$$])$$

Ex.77

> Nom_Jour[4]:=Mercredi;

Error, 1st index, 4, larger than upper array bound 3

When the lower bound of a table is equal to 1, it is displayed as a vector, between two square brackets like a list. It is displayed as a table in the other cases. As for objects of type `table`, the tables are not fully evaluated and it is essential to use the function `copy` in order to create a new copy which is independent of an existing table.

Ex.78

> Nom_Jour:=array(1..4,[1=Lundi,2=Mardi,4=Jeudi]);

$$Nom\_Jour := [\, Lundi, \; Mardi, \; Nom\_Jour_3, \; Jeudi\,]$$

> Nom_Jour;

$$Nom\_Jour$$

> eval(Nom_Jour);

$$Nom\_Jour := [\, Lundi \quad Mardi \quad ?_3 \quad Jeudi\,]$$

Warning! The function `array` has to be followed by parentheses like all MAPLE functions. The use of square brackets doesn't produce any error message, but doesn't specify the dimension of a table.

Ex.79

```
> A:=array[1..5];
```
$$A := array_{1..5}$$

```
> A[6]:=1;
```
          doesn't return any error message since the dimension of the array hasn't been specified

$$A_6 := 1$$

```
> eval(A)
```
          In fact, A is a table

$$table \quad ([\atop 6 = 1 \atop])$$

One cannot use the assignment `A[i]='A[i]'` to free the element of index `i` in a table `A`, where `i` points towards a numerical value, because the `i` in the right hand side isn't evaluated. On should either use `unassign('A[i]')` or use `A[i]=evaln(A[i])`. Since the function `evaln` restricts the evaluation up to the level where it finds a name, it evaluates the `i` and stops the evaluation at the name `A[i]`.

Two-Dimensional Tables

If m, n, p, and q contain integer values such that m<n and p<q, the assignment `A:=array(m..n,p..q)` creates a two-dimensional table whose indices may vary from m up to n and from p up to q respectively.

If L is the list `[(i1,j1)=expr1,...,(ik,jk)=exprk]` with (i1,j1), ..., (ik,jk) elements of [m,n]×[p,q], then the assignment `A:=array(m..n, p..q,L)` creates the table A and carries out the assignments `A[i1,j1]:= expr1, ...,A[ik,jk]:=exprk`.

All remarks concerning one-dimensional tables remain true for two-dimensional tables.

22. Working More Cleverly with the Subexpressions

22.1 The Substitution Functions

22.1.1 The Function subs

The function subs replaces elements of a MAPLE expression by the given objects. This substitution is syntactic, not algebraic: the function subs only modifies subexpressions of the initial expression, i.e. terms which can be obtained using the function op.

Unique Substitution

Given two expressions Expr and S_Expr and an object a, the evaluation of subs(S_Expr=a,Expr) returns the expression obtained from Expr by substituting the object a for each subexpression of Expr which is equal to S_Expr.

Warning! The use of the function subs doesn't affect the contents of the variable Expr. To modify this content, use an assignment like: Expr:=subs (S_Expr=a,Expr).

The most basic use of subs is to compute the value of an expression depending on a variable x while keeping x free.

Ex. 1

```
> P:=x^2+x+1; subs(x=2,P);
```
$$x^2 + x + 1$$
$$7$$
```
> x; P;
```
$$x$$
$$x^2 + x + 1$$

Contrary to what the previous example may suggest, the function **subs** doesn't carry out any evaluation of the returned result; automatic arithmetic simplifications are the only ones that are carried out. The following example shows that the use of the function **eval** is most often required in order to force the evaluation and obtain a given simplification of the result returned by **subs**.

Ex. 2

```
> P:=sin(x*Pi);
```
$$P := \sin(x\pi)$$

```
> subs(x=2,P);
```
$$\sin(2\pi)$$

```
> eval(subs(x=2,P));
```
$$0$$

The Limits of the Function subs

One should be aware of the fact that the function **subs** can only replace subexpressions of a given expression: a subexpression is an entity that can be obtained by calling the function **op** one or several times.

In the next example, the function **subs** doesn't produce any substitution, since x+y isn't a subexpression of x+y+z:

Ex. 3

```
> subs(x+y=t,x+y+z);
```
$$x + y + z$$

```
> op(x+y+z);
```
op returns the list of all the operands
$$x , y , z$$

In the next example, only two replacements of a+b by t take place, even if each of the three terms a+b are written in parentheses. Indeed, the quantity a+b appears one time as a level 2 subexpression and one time as a level 3 subexpression in the expression stored by MAPLE, as shown by the latter use of the function **op**.

Ex. 4

```
> restart; Expr:=(a+b)^2*c+(a+b)+(a+b)*d;
```
$$Expr := (a+b)^2 c + a + b + (a+b) d$$

```
> subs(a+b=t,Expr);
```
$$t^2 c + a + b + t d$$

```
> op(Expr);
```
$$(a+b)^2 c \,,\, a \,,\, b \,,\, (a+b)\, d$$

Ex. 5

```
> op((1,op(1,op(1,Expr))));        level 3 subexpression
```
$$a+b$$

```
> op(1,op(4,Expr));                level 2 subexpression
```
$$a+b$$

If one wishes to get the simplification of the expression of the previous example by imposing the condition a+b=t, use

- the function subs in the form subs(a=b-t,Expr),
- or the function simplify with a second argument that specifies the simplification relation, in the form simplify(Expr,[a+b=t]),
- or the function algsubs, in the form algsubs(a+b=t,Expr), which carries out an "algebraic substitution" similar to that of simplify.

Ex. 6

```
> simplify(Expr,[a+b=t]);
```
$$(1+d)\, t + c\, t^2$$

Simultaneous Multiple Substitutions

Given expressions Expr, S_Expr$_1$, ..., S_Expr$_n$ and objects a$_1$, ..., a$_n$, the evaluation of subs({S_Expr$_1$=a$_1$,..., S_Expr$_n$ = a$_n$,Expr}) or of subs([S_Expr$_1$=a$_1$, ...,S_Expr$_n$=a$_n$,Expr]) returns the expression obtained by replacing in Expr, S_Expr$_1$ by a$_1$, S_Expr$_2$ by a$_2$, ... and S_Expr$_n$ by a$_n$.

Ex. 7

```
> restart; Expr:=x*y^2+1;
```
$$Expr := x\, y^2 + 1$$

```
> subs({x=a,y=b},Expr);
```
$$a\, b^2 + 1$$

```
> subs({x=y,y=x},Expr);         Easy way to exchange x and y
```
$$y\, x^2 + 1$$

Using the function subs with a set or a list as first argument is a convenient way to exploit some results MAPLE returns as sets or as lists of equations: examples of this arise when solving systems of equations with solve (p. 105) and when solving differential systems with dsolve (p. 148).

Successive Multiple Substitutions

Given expressions Expr, S_Expr$_1$, ..., S_Expr$_n$ and objects a$_1$, ..., a$_n$, the evaluation of subs(S_Expr$_1$=a$_1$, ...,S_Expr$_n$=a$_n$, ,Expr) returns the expression obtained by replacing S_Expr$_1$ by a$_1$ in Expr, then by replacing S_Expr$_2$ by a$_2$ in that expression, and so on, until finally replacing S_Expr$_n$ by a$_n$. This command, which carries out a stream of substitutions, is equivalent to

$$\texttt{subs(S\_Expr}_n\texttt{=a}_n\texttt{, ...subs(S\_Expr}_1\texttt{=a}_1\texttt{,Expr)...)}.$$

Example for which the syntaxes with and without braces are equivalent.

Ex. 8

```
> restart: Expr:=x*y^2+1;
```
$$Expr := x\,y^2 + 1$$
```
subs({x=a,y=b},Expr);                Simultaneous substitutions
```
$$a\,b^2 + 1$$
```
> subs(x=a,y=b,Expr);                 Successive substitutions
```
$$a\,b^2 + 1$$

Example for which the syntaxes with and without braces are not equivalent.

Ex. 9

```
> subs({x=y,y=x},Expr);              Simultaneous substitutions
```
$$y\,x^2 + 1$$
```
> subs(x=y,y=x,Expr);                Successive substitutions
```
$$x^3 + 1$$

Other examples of successive substitutions

Ex.10

```
> subs(y=t,x=y,Expr);
```
equivalent to subs(x=y,subs(y=t,Expr))
$$y\,t^2 + 1$$
```
> subs(x=y,y=t,Expr)
```
equivalent to subs(y=t,subs(x=y,Expr))
$$t^3 + 1$$

Particular Cases of Vectors and Matrices

If one wishes to use the function subs to modify all occurrences of a subexpression appearing in a vector, a matrix or more generally an array A, the rules of evaluation for objects of type array forces us to use eval(A) as a final argument to the function subs.

Ex.11

```
> A:=linalg[vandermonde]([x,y,z]);
```

$$A := \begin{bmatrix} 1 & x & x^2 \\ 1 & y & y^2 \\ 1 & z & z^2 \end{bmatrix}$$

```
> C:=eval(subs(x=y,A));
```
                                                No substitution !

$$C := \begin{bmatrix} 1 & x & x^2 \\ 1 & y & y^2 \\ 1 & z & z^2 \end{bmatrix}$$

```
> B:=subs(x=y,eval(A));
```

$$B := \begin{bmatrix} 1 & y & y^2 \\ 1 & y & y^2 \\ 1 & z & z^2 \end{bmatrix}$$

22.1.2 The Function subsop

The function **subsop** is used to modify a first level subexpression of a given expression by locating it through its rank. Given an expression **Expr**, an object **a** and an integer **n** lying between 1 and **nops(Expr)**, the evaluation of **subsop(n=a,Expr)** returns the expression obtained from **Expr** by replacing the nth first level subexpression of **Expr** by **a**.

The function **subsop** can be used to modify an element of given rank in a list.

Ex.12

```
> L:=[seq(i^2,i=-3..3)];L:= subsop(5=123,L);
```

$$L := [\,9\,,\,4\,,\,1\,,\,0\,,\,1\,,\,4\,,\,9\,]$$
$$L := [\,9\,,\,4\,,\,1\,,\,0\,,\,123\,,\,4\,,\,9\,]$$

If **u** is a Puiseux expansion, the function **subsop** can also be used to extract its regular part, by replacing the supplementary term of the expansion by zero. This supplementary term is the last operand of the expression **u**, i.e. the operand with rank **nops(u)**.

Ex.13

```
> p:=arcsin(x)/sqrt(x): u:=series(p,x);
```

$$u := \sqrt{x} + \frac{1}{6}x^{5/2} + \frac{3}{40}x^{9/2} + O\left(x^{11/2}\right)$$

```
> op(u);
```

$$\sqrt{x}\,,\,\frac{1}{6}x^{5/2}\,,\,\frac{3}{40}x^{9/2}\,,\,O\left(x^{11/2}\right)$$

```
> subsop(nops(u)=0,u);
```

$$\sqrt{x} + \frac{1}{6}x^{5/2} + \frac{3}{40}x^{9/2}$$

22.2 The Function map

The function `map` can be used to apply a function or a procedure to every first level subexpression of a given expression.

22.2.1 Using map with a Function Which Has a Single Argument

If `Expr` is an expression and `f` is a function (or a procedure) in a single variable, the evaluation of `map(f,Expr)` returns the expression obtained from `Expr` by replacing the ith first level subexpression of `Expr` by `f(op(i,Expr))` for every `i` from 1 to `nops(Expr)`.

The first example one usually gives to illustrate the behaviour of `map` is squaring the elements of a list:

Ex.14

```
> L:=[seq(i,i=1..5)];
```
$$L := [\,1\,,\,2\,,\,3\,,\,4\,,\,5\,]$$

```
> f:=x->x*x;
```
$$f := x \rightarrow x^2$$

```
> map(f,L);
```
$$[\,1\,,\,4\,,\,9\,,\,16\,,\,25\,]$$

```
> f(L);
```
Result which is syntactically correct, but useless
$$[\,1\,,\,2\,,\,3\,,\,4\,,\,5\,]^2$$

The previous example can also be treated by introducing the squaring function as an anonymous function in the call to the function `map`.

Ex.15

```
> map(x->x^2,L);
```
$$[\,1\,,\,4\,,\,9\,,\,16\,,\,25\,]$$

The function `map` can also be used with a MAPLE function, as in the next example with the function `sqrt`.

Ex.16

```
> map(sqrt,L);
```
$$[1,\ \sqrt{2},\ \sqrt{3}\,,2\,,\sqrt{5}]$$

The previous examples are useful in understanding what's happening, but aren't very interesting as such. However, there are cases for which it is almost impossible to avoid the use of `map`.

If for example one tries to obtain a simple expression of the factorization of $\sin(x)^3 - \cos(x)^3$, map must be used to simplify the second factor returned by factor, since the effect of the function simplify, used directly, is to reconstitute the expression one has just factored.

Ex.17

```
> f:=factor(sin(x)^3-cos(x)^3);
```
$$f := -(-\sin(x) + \cos(x))(\cos(x)^2 + \cos(x)\sin(x) + \sin(x)^2)$$

```
> op(f);
```
to see the first level subexpressions
upon which simplify will work

$$\sin(x) - \cos(x) \ , \ \cos(x)^2 + \cos(x)\sin(x) + \sin(x)^2$$

```
> map(simplify,f);
```
$$-(-\sin(x) + \cos(x))(\cos(x)\sin(x) + 1)$$

```
> simplify(f);
```
while simplify redevelops everything

$$-\cos(x)^3 - \sin(x)\cos(x)^2 + \sin(x)$$

Note: To explain the "simplified" form returned after the last use of simplify, keep in mind that MAPLE simplifies the trigonometric expressions by replacing $\sin(x)^2$ by $1 - \cos(x)^2$.

Likewise, for a polynomial P given as a product, the function map must be used to reduce each term of the product while keeping the factorized form.

Ex.18

```
> P:=((x+1)^3-2*(x-3)^2)*((x+1)^3-(x+1)^2);
```
$$P := \left((x+1)^3 - 2(x-3)^2\right)\left((x+1)^3 - (x+1)^2\right)$$

```
> map(expand,P);
```
develops each subexpression

$$(x^3 + x^2 + 15x - 17)(x^3 + 2x^2 + x)$$

```
> expand(P,x);
```
develops everything

$$x^6 + 3x^5 + 18x^4 + 14x^3 - 19x^2 - 17x$$

```
> factor(P);
```
gives a more advanced factorization

$$x(x-1)(x^2 + 2x + 17)(x+1)^2$$

One may sometimes be surprised at the result when using map: this is the case in the following example where we wish to expand the numerator and the denominator of a fraction. As the use of the function expand doesn't suffice, since expand is only applied to the numerator, one might try map(expand,...). But this is useless since, as one can see by using op, the expression has 4 first level subexpressions and not 2 as the writing of the fraction would suggest.

Ex.19

```
> R:=(x-1)*(x-2)/((x-3)*(x-4));
```
$$R := \frac{(x-1)(x-2)}{(x-3)(x-4)}$$

```
> expand(R);
```
$$\frac{x^2}{(x-3)(x-4)} - 3\frac{x}{(x-3)(x-4)} + 2\frac{1}{(x-3)(x-4)}$$

```
> map(expand,R);
```
$$\frac{(x-1)(x-2)}{(x-3)(x-4)}$$

```
> op(R);
```
$$x-1,\ x-2,\ \frac{1}{x-3},\ \frac{1}{x-4}$$

To get the expected result in the previous example, one should apply `expand` to the numerator and to the denominator separately and reconstruct the fraction afterwards.

Ex.20

```
> expand(numer(R))/expand(denom(R));
```
$$\frac{x^2 - 3x + 2}{x^2 - 7x + 12}$$

22.2.2 Using `map` with a Function of Several Arguments

Given $n+1$ expressions `Expr`, $Expr_1$, ..., $Expr_n$ and a function `f` that may use $n+1$ arguments, `map(f,Expr,Expr₁,...,Exprₙ)` returns the expression obtained from `Expr` by replacing, for i from 1 to `nops(Expr)`, the ith subexpression of `Expr` by `f(op(i,Expr),Expr₁,...,Exprₙ)`.

If, for example, one wishes to integrate a vector function written as a list, one may write

Ex.21

```
> L:=[sin(x),cos(x),tan(x),cot(x)]:map(int,L,x);
```
$$[-\cos(x)\ ,\ \sin(x)\ ,\ -\ln(\cos(x))\ ,\ \ln(\sin(x))]$$

Another example arises when trying to group together the terms with like powers in each of the two factors of a polynomial written in factored form. The function `collect` doesn't suffice, since it starts by calling `expand`, which breaks the factorization. On the other hand, `map` can be used to apply `collect` to every term of the product and indeed provides the expected result.

```
> i:='i': P:=sum(z^i,i=0..4);
```
$$P := 1 + z + z^2 + z^3 + z^4$$

```
> Q:=factor(P,sqrt(5));
```
p. 227
$$Q := \frac{1}{4}\left(2z^2 + z - \sqrt{5}z + 2\right)\left(2z^2 + z + \sqrt{5}z + 2\right)$$

Ex.22

```
> map(collect,Q,z);
```
$$\frac{1}{4}\left(2z^2 + (1-\sqrt{5})z + 2\right)\left(2z^2 + (1+\sqrt{5})z + 2\right)$$

```
> collect(Q,z);
```
$$z^4 + z^3 + \left(2 + \frac{1}{4}\left(1-\sqrt{5}\right)\left(1+\sqrt{5}\right)\right)z^2 + z + 1$$

22.2.3 Using map Upon a Sequence

The syntax needed to use **map** with a function that requires several parameters explains why **map** cannot be used in order to carry out an operation upon the elements of a sequence.

If, for example, one wishes to use the function **Re** to construct a list of real parts of the roots of an algebraic equation, one may be tempted to write

Ex.23

```
> P:=x^3+2*x^2+2*x+1: s:=solve(P);
```
$$s := -1,\ -\frac{1}{2} + \frac{1}{2}I\sqrt{3},\ -\frac{1}{2} - \frac{1}{2}I\sqrt{3}$$

```
> map(Re,s);
```
Error, wrong number (or type) of parameters in function Re

This way, the first element of the sequence **s** is considered as the expression upon which the function **Re** should be applied and the next elements are considered as supplementary arguments to **Re**. This explains the error message, since the function **Re** accepts only one argument.

To solve the previous problem, use **map** with the list **[s]**. The function **op** can be used if a sequence is really needed.

Ex.24

```
> op(map(Re,[s]));
```
$$-1,\ -\frac{1}{2},\ -\frac{1}{2}$$

Likewise, if one wishes to construct the list of images under $x \mapsto \frac{1}{x+2}$ of the roots of the same algebraic equation, one may be tempted to write

Ex.25

```
> map(x->1/(x+2),s);
                                    1
```

In this case, one doesn't get an error message but an unexpected result. This can be explained by carefully observing what happened: the anonymous function x->1/(x+2) expects one value and receives three of them; it takes the first value, computes its image and returns the result while ignoring the two others. There is no error message since an anonymous function doesn't verify the number of arguments it receives.

As previously, one may write

Ex.26

```
> map(x->1/(x+2), [s]);
```
$$\left[1, \frac{1}{\frac{3}{2} + \frac{1}{2}I\sqrt{3}}, \frac{1}{\frac{3}{2} - \frac{1}{2}I\sqrt{3}} \right]$$
```
> op(");
```
$$1, \frac{1}{\frac{3}{2} + \frac{1}{2}I\sqrt{3}}, \frac{1}{\frac{3}{2} - \frac{1}{2}I\sqrt{3}}$$

22.2.4 Avoiding the Use of `map`

If one tries to apply the functions `diff` and `int` directly to a list L, the former returns the expected result while the latter returns an error message.

Ex.27

```
> L:=[sin(x),cos(x),tan(x),cot(x)]: diff(L,x);
```
$$\left[\cos(x), -\sin(x), 1 + \tan(x)^2, -1 - \cot(x)^2 \right]$$
```
> int(L,x);
  Error, (in int) wrong number (or type) of arguments
```

This difference can be explained: some functions (or procedures) like, for example, the function `diff` call `map` directly when they test whether one of their arguments is a list, while others, like `int`, return an error because they find that the types of the arguments don't correspond. There is no general rule for determining whether a function automatically calls `map`, and this rarely appears in the documentation. It is best therefore to experiment.

As an example, let us construct a function `inT` which, like `diff`, works with both functions or lists of functions. After referring to Ch. 24 to find out how to correctly write a procedure, one might write

Ex.28

```
> inT:=
  proc(f,u)
  if type(f,list) then map(inT,f,u) else int(f,u) fi;
  end;
```
$$inT := proc(f,u)$$
$$if\ type(f,list)\ then\ map(inT,f,u)\ else\ int(f,u)\ fi\ end$$

```
> L:=[sin(x), cos(x), tan(x), cot(x)]: inT(L,x);
```
$$[-\cos(x),\ \sin(x),\ -\ln(\cos(x)),\ \ln(\sin(x))]$$

Note: One could have used `map(int,f,u)` instead of `map(inT,f,u)` within the definition of the function `inT`. However, the use of `map(inT,f,u)` results in a function that can be applied to nested lists of any level.

The function `inT` can also be used to compute definite integrals.

Ex.29

```
> inT(L,x=0..Pi/4);
```
$$\left[-\frac{1}{2}\sqrt{2}+1,\ \frac{1}{2}\sqrt{2},\ -\frac{1}{2}\ln(2),\ \infty\right]$$

23. Programming: Loops and Branches

Although MAPLE is an interactive language, it is programmable. Despite the language's simplicity, one can quickly and effectively code most problems encountered in Mathematics, in Physics or in Chemistry and even more generally in symbolic computation. This chapter is devoted to the study of loops and branches, while functions and procedures will be studied in Chapter 24.

23.1 Loops

Iterated actions that are controlled by counters can be programmed using for-loops. Counters can be

- either numerical values
- or generic operands of MAPLE expressions.

23.1.1 for Loop with a Numerical Counter

The syntax using a numerical counter is

    for i from i1 to i2 by h do <sequence_of_instructions> od;

in which

- i is the name of a MAPLE variable.
- i1, i2 and h are expressions containing numerical values (not necessarily integral) when the execution of the loop begins. The value of h may be either positive or negative, the latter used for loop counters that decrease.

The three expressions i1, i2 and h are evaluated only once, when the loop begins. Therefore, it is pointless to change their contents inside the loop.

The keywords do and od delimit the sequence of commands to be repeated, they are mandatory even if there is only one command to be repeated.

When h is positive, i is initialized to i1, then its value is compared with i2. If i is less than or equal to i2, <sequence_of_instructions> is executed, i is then increased by h, and the process repeats, starting at the test comparing i and i2. As soon as i is strictly greater than i2, the program proceeds to the instruction following the loop. When i1 is strictly greater than i2, <sequence_of_instructions> isn't executed.

Everything is the same when h is negative, except that one tests whether i is greater than or equal to i2.

In order to display the cubes of the three first even numbers, one may write:

Ex. 1

```
> for i from 0 to 5 by 2 do print(i^3); od;

                    0
                    8
                   64
```

In writing a loop, one may omit from i1 (i1 has then the default value 1) or by h (h has then the default value 1).

To compute the cubes of the three first integers, one may write:

Ex. 2

```
> for i to 3 do print(i^3); od;

                    1
                    8
                   27
```

The next example demonstrates that upon completion of the loop, the counter variable contains the value last assigned it in the loop. In particular, the counter variable is not free.

Ex. 3

```
> i;                    value of i assigned by the previous loop

                    4
> for i from 1.5 to 3 do i^3; od:
> i;                        here, the last value assigned to i is 3.5

                   3.5
```

Note: A command for ... do ... od carries out work, but isn't itself a MAPLE expression; therefore it cannot be assigned to an identifier.

Warning! If the evaluation of i1, of i2 or of h doesn't provide a value of type numeric when entering the loop, MAPLE returns a message stating that it cannot execute the loop. Remember that some values, like sqrt(5), or Pi, considered as numerical by the user, are in fact not of type **numeric** for MAPLE. The function evalf must then be used.

Ex. 4

```
> n:='n': for i from 1 to n do print(i^3); od;
    Error, unable to execute for statement
> for i from 1 to sqrt(5) do i od;                sqrt(5) is not
                                                  of type numeric
    Error, unable to execute for statement
> for i from 1 to evalf(sqrt(5)) do i od;

                            1
                            2
```

23.1.2 for Loop Upon Operands

In MAPLE, the "counter" of a **for** loop can describe the set of operands of a given expression, which is most often a list or a set but can also be any MAPLE expression. The syntax is then

for x in expr do <sequence_of_instructions> od

where x is an identifier and expr is a MAPLE expression.

When this command is executed, the variable i successively receives each operand, i.e. each first level subexpression (Chapter 21) of expr, and <sequence_of_instructions> is executed for each of the values of i.

For example, the sum of the elements of a list L can be computed by writing

Ex. 5

```
> L:=[1,4,7,3,4,5,12,3,5,9]:
  s:=0: for x in L do s:=s+x od:
  s;
                            53
```

which can be written with a numerical counter as:

Ex. 6

```
> s:=0: for i from 1 to nops(L) do s:=s+op(i,L) od:
  s;
                            53
```

23.1.3 How to Write a Loop That Spans Several Lines

With more intricate loops than the easy ones described above, it is better to write loops on several lines using a good indentation, which facilitates reading, correcting, and modifying the code.

- These lines have to belong to the same execution group (Chapter 26), i.e. they have to be collected together by a large square bracket located on the left side when the option **Show Group Range** of the **View** menu is selected. The default shows **Group Ranges**.
- When the cursor is in a command area, i.e. when the key $\boxed{\Sigma}$ is depressed, one may introduce a new line within the same execution group by using $\boxed{\text{SHIFT}}$ $\boxed{\text{ENTER}}$.

A loop computing the Chebyshev polynomials of degree 1 up to 4 can be written in the following way

Ex. 7

```
▷ restart:                         use SHIFT ENTER
  for i from 1 to 4                use SHIFT ENTER
     do                            use SHIFT ENTER
        expand(cos(i*x));          use SHIFT ENTER
        subs(cos(x)=t,");
     od;
```

$$\cos(x)$$

$$t$$

$$2\cos(x)^2 - 1$$

$$2t^2 - 1$$

$$4\cos(x)^3 - 3\cos(x)$$

$$4t^3 - 3t$$

$$8\cos(x)^4 - 8\cos(x)^2 + 1$$

$$8t^4 - 8t^2 + 1$$

Note: Within an execution group, new lines can be inserted with the $\boxed{\text{SHIFT}}$ $\boxed{\text{ENTER}}$ key and deleted with the $\boxed{\text{DEL}}$ and $\boxed{\leftarrow}$ keys. All the commands in the group are executed if the $\boxed{\text{ENTER}}$ key is pressed while the cursor stands within the execution group.

The delimiters do ... od cannot be omitted, even when the loop is reduced to a single instruction.

- Forgetting the first delimiter, (the do) results in the error message *Syntax error,....*
- Forgetting the second delimiter, (the od) results in a warning message, which shows great improvement over release 3, in which MAPLE didn't reply at all. One may then continue to write the loop in the area where one had started.

Ex. 8

```
> for i from 0 to 3 print(i^3);          Forgetting the initial do
  Syntax error, missing operator or ';'

> for i from 0 to 3 do print(i^3);       Forgetting the final od
>
  Warning, incomplete statement or missing semicolon
```

23.1.4 Echo of the Instructions of a Loop

If you feel that too many results are being displayed in the previous example and only want to see results which are polynomial in t, you might think about replacing the *semicolon* ending the line containing expand with a *colon*. However, this doesn't effect the echo displayed on the screen.

In fact,

- if the od ending the loop is followed by a *semicolon*, all intermediary results are displayed on the screen.
- if the od ending the loop is followed by a *colon*, there is no echo to the screen.

To print only the polynomial results, put a colon at the end of the loop, and an explicit print statement (using the function print) for the results of the substitution.

Ex. 9

```
> for i from 1 to 4
  do
     expand(cos(i*x));
     print(subs(cos(x)=t,"));        print to force the display
  od:                          the : avoids the undesirable displays
```

$$t$$
$$2t^2 - 1$$
$$4t^3 - 3t$$
$$8t^4 - 8t^2 + 1$$

23.1.5 Nested Loops and Echo on the Screen: `printlevel`

The printed results the next example, which contains two nested loops, may be puzzling for a beginner:

Ex.10

```
> for i to 3
    do
        x:=2*i;
        for j from 2 to 3 do x^j od;
    od;
                        x := 2
                        x := 4
                        x := 6
```

While the echo of the assignments `x:=2*i` is displayed on the screen, there is no trace of the powers `x^j`. This could lead to useless investigations within a more complicated program, because the user may believe that these lines are not executed. They are in fact executed, but not displayed on the screen because of their nesting level.

Nesting Level

During a session, MAPLE assigns a *level* to every instruction it encounters. This *level* is computed in the following way:

- Instructions at the conversational level are at level 0.
- The level is increased by 1 when entering a loop.
- The level is decreased by 1 when leaving a loop.

The only instructions for which MAPLE gives an echo on the screen are those whose level is less than or equal to the value of `printlevel`, which is an environment variable.

- The assignment `printlevel:=n` tells MAPLE to echo all instructions whose level is less than or equal to n and appearing in *an instruction of level 0 followed by a semicolon.*
- One may execute `printlevel:=1` or `restart` to go back to the initial situation.
- In all cases, no instruction appearing in *an instruction of level 0 followed by a colon* can have an echo on the screen.

By default, `printlevel` is 1 and the evaluations of `x^j` in the previous example, which are of level 2, thus have no echo on the screen. On the other hand, if `printlevel` is set to two, then all instructions encountered are echoed.

```
> printlevel:=2;
                            printlevel := 2
> for i to 3
    do
      x:=2*i;
      for j from 2 to 3 do x^j od;
    od;
                                x := 2
                                   4
                                   8
                                x := 4
                                   16
                                   64
                                a := 6
                                   36
                                  216
```

Ex.11

Modifying the value of the variable `printlevel` allows you to follow the
progress of instructions, either to fix a program that doesn't return the expected result, or to try to understand how MAPLE works. An assignment
like `printlevel:=1000` is very common in the latter case.

Note: The value of the variable `printlevel` has no effect on output produced
with the functions `print` and `printf`.

23.1.6 Avoiding `for` Loops

Although `for` loops are easy to use, it is sometimes better to call `seq` or even
`map`. The next example, wich involves constructing an expression sequence
containing the cubes of the three first integers, reveals the parallels between
`for` and `seq`.

With a `for` loop, one would write

```
> sq:=NULL; for i from 1 to 3 do sq:=sq,i^3; od;
                              sq :=
                              sq := 1
                              sq := 1, 8
                           sq := 1, 8, 27
```

Ex.12

While with **seq** one only has to write:

Ex.13

> restart: sq:=seq(i^3,i=1..3);
>
> $$sq := 1, 8, 27$$

Not only is the latter more compact and more rapidly executed that the former, it avoids cluttering memory with the intermediary sequences produced by the former.

Similarly, the sequence of the first 4 Chebyshev polynomials can be coumputed by writing:

Ex.14

> sq:=seq(subs(cos(x)=t,expand(cos(i*x))),i=0..3);
>
> $$sq := 1, t, 2t^2 - 1, 4t^3 - 3t$$

In order to compute the sum of the elements of a list of numbers, the function **convert** can be used with the option '+'. The list is then converted into a sum which is automatically simplified by MAPLE since it only contains integers. Compare the following with example 5 on p. 387 .

Ex.15

> L:=[1,4,7,3,4,5,12,3,5,9]:
>
> s:=convert(L,'+');   **Mind the backward apostrophes**
>
> $$s := 53$$

Note: The result can also be obtained with **add(x,x=L)**.

23.1.7 while **Loop**

The **while** loop is used to produce iteration controlled by boolean expressions. A statement of the form

> while bool_expr do <*sequence_of_instructions*> od

executes <*sequence_of_instructions*> as long as the boolean expression **bool _expr** evaluates to **true**.

The warnings of page 388 about **for** loops hold for **while** loops as well, i.e.

- that the pair do ... od is required even for a single instruction, and
- that large loops are better written spanning several lines of an execution group.

Statements concerning the echo on screen as depending on whether a colon or semicolon follows the final od, as well as remarks about nesting levels are all valid. As with a `for` loop, entering a `while` loop increases the level of the instructions encountered by one, and leaving the loop decreases this level by one.

A good example using a while loop is the computation of the g.c.d. of two integers or of two polynomials. The Euclidean algorithm is an almost universally known method for computing univariate polynomial g.c.d's. It computes a sequence of remainders of polynomial divisions, and the last non-zero element of this sequence is the g.c.d of the two input polynomials. Let us test this algorithm with the following example.

Ex.16

```
> P:=x^7+5*x^2+1:  Q:=x^5+3*x^2-3:
  while Q<>0
    do
      R:=rem(P,Q,x); P:=Q; Q:=R;
      print(P);
    od:
```

$$x^5 + 3\,x^2 - 3$$

$$8\,x^2 - 3\,x^4 + 1$$

$$\tfrac{8}{3}\,x^3 + 3\,x^2 + \tfrac{1}{3}\,x - 3$$

$$\tfrac{293}{64}\,x^2 - \tfrac{243}{64}\,x + \tfrac{307}{64}$$

$$\tfrac{159808}{85849}\,x - \tfrac{726336}{85849}$$

$$\tfrac{32766245377}{399040576}$$

Note: These results highlight a phenomenon that is well known users of computer algebra: the growth of intermediate expressions. Although the coefficients of the initial polynomials in our example are less than 5 in absolute value and the g.c.d. is 1, since the g.c.d. is typically normalized to be monic, the coefficients of the polynomials encountered in the sequence reach such a size that they are not easy to read. When the input polynomials are more complicated, storing these coefficients can start to tax memory.

As a consequence of this phenomenon of intermediate expression growth, which doesn't take place in numerical computations, where a number's representation has constant length, Euclid's algorithm has been superceded in many areas of computer algebra by new algorithms, which are more effective. Most of them work with the images of polynomials in $\mathbb{Z}/p\mathbb{Z}$, since coefficients then always lie between 0 and $p - 1$. The reader who wants to know more about this may refer to Geddes: Algorithms for Computer Algebra, Kluwer Academic Publishers.

23.2 Branches

23.2.1 The Conditional Branch: if ... then ... elif ... else

MAPLE has an extended conditional instruction that acts both as the *if* and the *case* of a language like PASCAL. Its syntax is:

```
if cond_1
        then <sequence_of_instructions_1>
elif cond_2
        then <sequence_of_instructions_2>
.../...
elif cond_n
        then <sequence_of_instructions_n>
else
        <sequence_of_instructions_else>
fi;
```

Each condition `cond_1`, ... `cond_n` is a boolean expression that can be fully evaluated when the `if` instruction is executed.

When one of the conditions is satisfied, the corresponding sequence of instructions is executed, and control is passed on to the instruction following the `fi`. When several conditions are satisfied, only the sequence of instructions corresponding to the first true condition is executed.

When none of the conditions `cond_1`, ... `cond_n` is fulfilled, the instructions in *<sequence_of_instructions_else>* are executed.

Each of the *<sequence_of_instructions_xx>* contains an arbitrary number of instructions separated by *semicolons* or *colons*. There is no delimiter for the end of a block of instructions, this role being played by the reserved word `elif`, `else` or `fi` that follows. Each of the `elif` or `else` blocks is optional.

Basic boolean expressions are written in MAPLE as they usually are in computer science, i.e. by using the operators =, <, >, <= (less than or equal), >= (greater than or equal), <> (not equal). These basic conditions can be composed using the operators: `and`, `or`, `not`.

As with loops, long conditional instructions should written on several lines, and formatted logically.

Ex.17

```
> x:=1;
  if x<2
        then print('x is smaller than two')
        else print('x is bigger than two')
  fi;
                    x is smaller than 2
```

Performing the test of the previous example with unassigned variable x produces an error message, since MAPLE cannot evaluate the boolean value x<2.

Ex.18

```
> x:='x';                          To be sure that x is free
  if x<2
      then print('x is smaller than two')
      else print('x is bigger than two')
  fi;
```
$$x := x$$
Error, cannot evaluate boolean

Warning ! This same error message is produced for conditions containing quantities like sqrt(5) or Pi, which are considered numerical values by the user but aren't of type numeric for MAPLE.

Ex.19

```
> if sqrt(5)<2
      then print('x is smaller than two')
      else print('x is bigger than two')
  fi;
```
Error, cannot evaluate boolean

As with loops, forgetting the terminal fi produces a warning message, even if there is only one instruction to be executed:

Ex.20

```
> if 2<5 then print('O.K.');
>
```
Warning, incomplete statement or missing semicolon

To test the primality of a few Mersenne numbers, one may write

Ex.21

```
> for i from 4 to 7
  do
      x:=2^i-1;
      if isprime(x)
        then print(x,'is prime')
        else print(x,'isn't prime')
      fi;
  od:
```
$$15,\ \textit{isn't prime}$$
$$31,\ \textit{is prime}$$
$$63,\ \textit{isn't prime}$$
$$127,\ \textit{is prime}$$

As with loops, entering a conditional structure increases the level of the instructions encountered by 1, while leaving such a structure decreases this level by 1. This should be taken into account when adjusting the variable `printlevel` to faithfully echo all instructions executed.

23.2.2 next and break

`next` and `break` are specific identifiers which, when evaluated within a `for` loop or a `while` loop, modify the loop's normal progress. MAPLE returns an error if one of these identifiers is encountered outside the context of a loop.

`next` leaves the execution of the current iteration of the innermost loop in which it appears, and passes control to the loop test for the execution of the next iteration. Using `next` is the best way to write an instruction which passes on to the next iteration while skipping the rest of the loop body.

`break` completely leaves the execution of the innermost loop in which it appears, and passes control to the instruction following the `od` that terminates that loop. After the execution of `break`, the values of all variables, in particular the counter of a `for` loop, are the same as at the moment `break` was executed.

In order to determine the rank of an element x within a list L, returning 0 if x doesn't belong to L, one may write

Ex.22

```
> L:=[a,b,c,d,e]; x:=d;
```
$$L := [a, b, c, d, e]$$

```
> j:=0;
  for i from 1 to nops(L)
  do if L[i]=x then j:=i; break; od;
```

```
> j;
```
$$4$$

Note: In the previous example, the instruction `j:=i` is within a conditional statement, which is itself within a loop: it therefore is of level 2, and has no echo on the screen since the default value of `printlevel` is equal to 1.

Dropping the requirement that 0 be returned when x doesn't belong to L, one may use a loop that combines `for` and `while` by writing

Ex.23

```
> L:=[a,b,c,d,e]; x:=b;
```

$$L := [a, b, c, d, e]$$

```
> for i from 1 to nops(L) while L[i]<>x then do od;
> i;
```

$$2$$

23.2.3 MAPLE's Three-State-Logic

MAPLE's logic encompasses three truth values: `true`, `false` and `FAIL`. The two first are well known and of common use. The third corresponds to an answer like: "I don't know" or: "the algorithm used cannot conclude" and is returned when MAPLE cannot answer yes or no.

A simple example of an answer of type FAIL involves the functions `assume` and `is`: the function `assume` is used to state hypotheses about variables within a session, and the function `is` is used to test properties of expressions containing these variables.

Ex.24

```
> restart ;assume(x>=0);
> is(x*(y-1)^2>=0);
```

$$FAIL$$

```
> assume(y,real); is(x*(y-1)^2>=0);
```

$$true$$

In this example, with the single hypothesis about x given by `assume(x>=0)`, MAPLE can't determine if $x(y-1)^2$ is positive, since y isn't necessarily real: thus it returns *FAIL*. But MAPLE can conclude that the expression is positive and returns *true*, once the hypothesis y real is added.

The use of a three-state-logic requires particular care when writing tests. Indeed, habits aquired with boolean logic are no longer valid, and in particular the order in which one writes the clauses of an instruction if ... then ... elif ... else is not immaterial.

Although FAIL isn't strictly speaking a MAPLE constant like true and false, it has the same behaviour. The relations between the "three truth values" and the operators and, or and not are summarized in the following tables

and	false	true	FAIL
false	false	false	false
true	false	true	FAIL
FAIL	false	FAIL	FAIL

or	false	true	FAIL
false	false	true	FAIL
true	true	true	true
FAIL	FAIL	true	FAIL

	false	true	FAIL
not	true	false	FAIL

24. Programming: Functions and Procedures

In PASCAL, a function returns a result while a procedure carries out an action: a modification of variables may be the outcome of such an action, but a procedure doesn't return a value, and is not directly usable within an expression. Such a distinction doesn't exist with MAPLE whose functions and procedures both return a result which is usable within an expression: the difference mainly lies in the complexity of the definition.

24.1 Functions

24.1.1 Definition of a Simple Function

From the beginning of this book, we have used mathematical functions which are easily written in MAPLE with the help of the operator $->$ (operator *arrow*). For a function of the p variables var_1, var_2, ..., var_p, the syntax is:

$$(\text{var\_1}, \text{var\_2}, \dots, \text{var\_p}) -> \text{Expr}$$

where Expr is an expression, written explicitly as a function of var_1, var_2, ..., var_p, which corresponds to the result returned by the function.

In general, this function is assigned to an identifier by an instruction like

$$\text{Id\_fonct} := (\text{var\_1}, \text{var\_2}, \dots, \text{var\_p}) -> \text{Expr}$$

For example, to assign to f_1 the function which is mathematically defined by $x \mapsto (x+1)^2$, one writes

Ex. 1

```
> f_1:=x->(x+1)^2;
```
$$f\_1 := x \rightarrow (x+1)^2$$

Writing a function of two or more variables requires the use of parentheses around its arguments. For example, the function f_2 that returns the sum of its two arguments can be defined by

Ex. 2

```
> f_2:=(x,y)->x+y;
```
$$f\_2 := (x, y) \rightarrow x + y$$

Forgetting the parentheses around the symbolic parameters of the previous function doesn't produce an error message, but the object that is defined is an expression sequence and not a function. Hence, in the following example, f points towards the expression sequence whose first element is x and whose second element is the application $y \mapsto x+y$: it isn't a function of two variables.

Ex. 3

```
> f:=x,y->x+y;
```
$$f := x, y \rightarrow x + y$$

24.1.2 Use of a Function

As with any MAPLE function, a user defined function's identifier may appear bound to arguments, i.e. followed by a list of objects in parentheses whose types corresponds the those of the functions arguments, or on its own.

Examples with the previous functions

Ex. 4

```
> f_1(2); 1+f_2(sin(x),1);
```
$$9$$
$$\sin(x) + 2$$

```
> plot (f_1,-5..5);
```

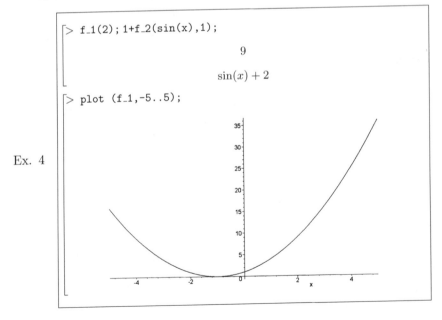

24.1.3 Function Using Tests

A function defined with the help of the operator *arrow* may use not only an expression but also a test: the result returned by the function is then the last quantity evaluated within the test instruction. The syntax of such a function is:

$$(\text{var\_1}, \text{var\_2}, \ldots, \text{var\_p}) \text{ -> } <\!Instruction\_test\!>$$

Ex. 5

```
> f_3:=x->if (x<=1) then -1 elif (x<1) then 0 else 1 fi;
  f_3 := proc(x) options operator,arrow;
    if x <= -1 then -1 elif x<1 then 0 else 1 fi end
```

The echo for such a function definition is no longer a faithful copy of the line entered by the user. In fact, MAPLE then considers the function as a procedure and adds a line `options` as well as the reserved words `proc` and `end` in order to delimit the body, which corresponds to the instruction written by the user. Procedures will be studied in detail in Section 24.2.

The function `f_3` defined previously may be used on a value of type `numeric`. On the other hand, it returns an error message if one tries to evaluate `f_3(x)` when x isn't of type `numeric`.

Ex. 6

```
> f_3(2);
                        1
> f_3(sqrt(2));                          sqrt(2) isn't of type numeric
  Error, (in f_3) cannot evaluate boolean
```

This error message, already encountered on page 395, can be explained by the fact that MAPLE cannot evaluate `x<=-1` when x doesn't represent a value of type `numeric`.

The same error message appears if one tries to represent `f_3` graphically by writing `plot(f_3(x),x=-3..3)`, since the evaluation of the arguments of `plot` causes `f_3(x)` to be evaluated while x is a free variable. One must write `plot(f_3,-3..3)` or `plot('f_3(x)',x=-3..3)` to obtain the expected graphical representation.

Ex. 7

```
> plot(f_3(x),x=-3..3);
  Error, (in f_3) cannot evaluate boolean
> plot(f_3,-3..3);                    returns the corresponding graph
```

A more intricate version of f_3 that begins by testing whether x is of type
numeric avoids the previous problems.

Ex. 8

```
> f_3:= x ->
  if type(x,numeric)
  then if (x <= -1)
      then -1
      elif (x<1) then 0
      else 1
      fi;
  else 'f_3(x)';             for a non evaluated form if x isn't
  fi;                                    a numerical value

  f_3:=proc(x)options operator,arrow;
  if type(x,numeric) then if x <= -1 then -1 elif x<1 then 0 else 1 fi
  else 'f_3(x)' fi
  end
```

As for loops (p. 388), all the previous lines have been written within a same
group, each one ending with SHIFT ENTER. The content of the group, i.e.
the definition of the function, is executed once the single key ENTER is
pressed. MAPLE then echoes a procedure in which the field *options* contains
operator,arrow, indicating a procedure defined with the help of the operator
arrow.

In the previous example, the presence of the test if type(x,numeric)...fi
allows the function f_3

- to carry out tests to compare with -1 and 1, and to return a number only
  if the evaluation of x returns a value of type numeric.
- to return the unevaluated form f_3(x) if the evaluation of x doesn't return
  a value of type numeric.

Warning! Mind the apostrophes appearing on the next to last line: they prevent
the evaluation of f_3(x), which would generate an infinite loop that would give the
message *Error, (in f_3), too many levels of recursion.* when calling f_3(x).

Ex. 9

```
> x:='x': f_3(x);              f_3(x)
```

With this version of `f_3` a plot can be produced with the syntax `plot(f_3(x), x=-3..3)`

Ex.10

```
[> plot(f_3(x),x=-3..3);
```

The previous version of `f_3` returns an unevaluated form for arguments that aren't of type `numeric`, in particular for values like `sqrt(3)`, `ln(2)` or `Pi`.

Ex.11

```
[> f_3(sqrt(2));
```
$$f\_3(\sqrt{2})$$

To define a new version of `f_3` that returns a numerical value even for values of type `realcons` like `sqrt(3)`, `ln(2)` or `Pi`, it suffices to recursively call `f_3` with `evalf(x)` when x is of type `realcons`.

Ex.12

```
[> f_3:=x->
   if type(x,numeric)
     then if x <= -1
             then -1
             elif x < 1 then 0
             else 1
          fi
     elif type(x,realcons) then f_3(evalf(x))
     else 'f_3'(x)
   fi;
```
$$f\_3 := proc(x)$$
$$options\ operator,arrow;$$
$$\quad if\ type(x,numeric)\ then$$
$$\quad\quad if\ x <= -1\ then\ -1\ elif\ x < 1\ then\ 0\ else\ 1\ fi$$
$$\quad elif\ type(x,realcons)\ then\ f\_3(evalf(x))$$
$$\quad else\ 'f\_3'(x)$$
$$\quad fi$$
$$end$$

One can then verify

Ex.13

```
[> f_3(sqrt(2)+sqrt(3));
```
$$1$$

24.1.4 Evaluation Problem for a Function

Evaluating a variable that contains a function produces a result that may be surprising: the function's identifier. Indeed, functions, like tables, are an exception to the full evaluation principle: evaluation stops at the last name encountered (*last name evaluation*) and a function identifier is returned without any detail about its content, i.e. about the instructions of the function.

In the case of the function f_2 defined above, one obtains

Ex.14
```
> f_2;
```
$$f\_2$$

But if another function g is defined by the assignment g:=f_2, and if the evaluation of g is requested, one still obtains f_2 which is the last name encountered before the body of the function.

Ex.15
```
> g:=f_2: g;
```
$$f\_2$$

In order to display the body of a function, one must explicitly request its full evaluation using the function eval.

Ex.16
```
> eval(f_2);
```
$$f_2 := (x, y) \rightarrow x + y$$

Last name evaluation is a distinctive feature that isn't limited to user defined functions: one must also use eval in order to see the source code of a MAPLE function, although interface(verboseproc=2) must be excuted first, as explained in the chapter devoted to MAPLE functions (Chapter 25).

24.1.5 Number of Arguments Passed on to a Function

In MAPLE, there is no automatic syntactic verification of the number of arguments passed to a function. It is only when executing an instruction in the body of the function requiring the use of such-and-such a parameter that a lack of arguments can be noticed. However, too many arguments will never be detected automatically.

MAPLE returns an error message if one tries to use the previous function f_2 with a single argument, but calling the function with three arguments doesn't pose any probmen to MAPLE, which simply uses the first two and ignores the third.

Ex.17

```
> f_2(1);
     Error, (in f_2) f_2 uses a 2nd argument, y, which is missing
> f_2(1,2,5);
                              3
```

One may program in a more secure way by testing for an incorrect number of arguments. The system variable **nargs** is equal to the number of arguments passed to a function. If the wrong number of arguments have been supplied, the **ERROR** instruction may be used to exit the function and display an error message.

Given a function f and p expressions expr_1, ..., expr_p, the evaluation, during the execution of f, of ERROR(expr_1,...,expr_p) stops the execution of f and displays the message *Error, (in f)*, followed by the evaluation of the sequence expr_1, ..., expr_p (except if the function f has been called within a traperror).

For the previous function f_2, for example, we may write

Ex.18

```
> f_2:=(x,y)->
  if nargs<>2
    then
        ERROR('expects 2 arguments and obtains',nargs)
    else x+y
  fi:
```

Warning! The message is a string that has to be delimited by backward apostrophes.

If this new function f_2 is called with three arguments, one obtains

Ex.19

```
> f_2(1,2,5);
     Error, (in f_2) expects 2 arguments and obtains , 3
```

The strange comma between *obtains* and *3* can be suppressed by using the concatenation operator, which is the *point*, and by writing: ERROR('expects 2 arguments and obtains'.nargs). One then gets:

Ex.20

```
> f_2(1,2,5);
     Error, (in f_2) expects 2 arguments and obtains 3
```

24.1.6 Other Ways to Write a Function

Function unapply

When one has an expression Expr depending on the free variable x (a solution of a differential equation for example) and needs the associated function, one should not write fnct:=x->Expr, as the following example clearly shows.

Ex.21

```
> S:=dsolve(diff(y(x),x)-y(x),y(x));Expr:=rhs(S);
```

$$S := y(x) = e^x \_C1$$

$$Expr := e^x \_C1$$

```
> fnct:=x->Expr;                                  Not to be used !
```

$$fnct := x \rightarrow Expr$$

```
> fnct(2);
```

$$e^x \_C1$$

The result of a function defined with the operator -> (i.e. the expression to the right of the ->) is syntactically verified, but not evaluated. In the previous example, MAPLE doesn't identify the x in the symbolic expression to the right of the -> as being same x as appears in the parameter list. Thus, fnct is assigned a constant function, and returns Expr for any value of the variable.

The function unapply should be used (p. 40) to obtain the function associated with a known expression.

Ex.22

```
> fnct:=unapply(Expr,x);
```

$$Fnct := x \rightarrow e^x \_C1$$

```
> fnct(2);
```

$$e^2 \_C1$$

Anonymous Functions

Anonymous functions are functions that aren't assigned to any identifier. They are often used with the function map (p. 378), or to define matrices or vectors (Chapter 15, p. 253). For example with map, one may square the elements of a list by writing

Ex.23

```
> L:=[1,5,4,3,2]: map(x->x^2,L);
```

$$[1, \; 25, \; 16, \; 9, \; 4]$$

24.1.7 Particular Values: remember Table

For some functions, like for example f defined by

$$\forall x \neq 0 \quad f(x) = \frac{\sin(x)}{x} \quad \text{and} \quad f(0) = 1$$

there are particular values of the variable for which the definition has a different analytic form. Such a function can, of course, be written with conditionals.

Ex.24

```
> f:=x->if x=0 then 1 else sin(x)/x fi;
  f :=
  proc(x) options operator,arrow;
     if x ≐ 0 then 1 else sin(x)/x fi
  end
```

While this is syntactically correct, it doesn't use one of MAPLE's most effective tools: the remember table, which is a table in which particular values are stored.

This remember table is consulted any time a function is called, and if the function's argument belongs to the set of indices in the table (see below), the corresponding value is directly returned without executing a line of the function.

In order to associate the value 1 with the argument 0 for this function, just type $f(0) := 1$.

Ex.25

```
> f:=x->sin(x)/x; f(0):=1;
```
$$f := x \rightarrow \frac{\sin(x)}{x}$$
$$f(0) := 1$$

One may define as many particular values as one wishes (within the limits of the memory size). For the previous function one may also define

Ex.26

```
> f(infinity):=0;
```
$$f(\infty) := 0$$

The remember table of a function is the fourth operand of the object function which is of type procedure (p. 419). It is a table in which the *indices* are the values of the arguments and the *entries* are the corresponding values.

The `remember` table of `f` can be displayed on the screen by typing

Ex.27

> op(4,eval(f));   **Make sure to use eval!**
> table([
>   0 = 1
>   ∞ = 0
>   ])

Warning! When one defines particular values of functions, all particular assignments should occur after the general definition of the function, since the general definition resets the function's *remember* table.

The following sequence of instructions produces an error message when `f(0)` is evaluated, since the general definition deletes the particular value `f(0):=1`.

Ex.28

```
> f(0):=1; f:=x->sin(x)/x;
```

$$f(0) := 1$$

$$f := x \to \frac{\sin(x)}{x}$$

```
> f(0);
```
Error, (in f) division by zero

remember **Table and Recursion**

The factorial function is one of the basic MAPLE functions and it is therefore pointless to program it. It is, however, a good example of the use of the `remember` table to program recursively without testing for a base case.

A classical definition would be

Ex.29

```
> fact:= n->if n=0 then 1 else n*fact(n-1) fi;
```
fact :=
proc(n) options operator,arrow;
if n = 0 then 1 else n*fact(n-1) fi end

Using the `remember` table, one has

Ex.30

```
> fact:=n->n*fact(n-1); fact(0):=1;
```

$$fact := n \to nfact(n-1)$$

$$fact(0) := 1$$

Neither of the previous `fact` functions is protected and, using them with a negative argument leads to the message *Error, (in fact) too many levels of recursion*. The next version corrects this problem.

Ex.31

```
> fact_0 :=n->n*fact_0(n-1):
  fact_0(0):=1:
  fact:=n->if type(n,integer) and (n>=0)
             then fact_0(n) else 'fact'(n); fi:
```

The first function `fact_0`, which carries out the actual computation of the factorial of a positive numerical value, is defined without any verification. The function `fact` tests whether the value which is passed on is integral and nonnegative. Using two levels of functions allows us to write a correct definition, while avoiding testing at each computation step.

When it is called with an argument n which isn't a natural number, the latter function doesn't lead to an error, but instead returns the unevaluated value `fact(n)`.

Ex.32

```
> fact(5);
```
$$120$$
```
> fact(n);
```
$$fact(n)$$
```
> fact(1.5);
```
$$fact(1.5)$$

24.2 Procedures

24.2.1 Definition of a Procedure

A MAPLE procedure performs an action (displaying on the screen, for example) but in general, like a function, it also returns a value which is usable within an expression.

The result returned by a procedure is the last quantity evaluated before it passes control to the calling process.

Since a procedure may consist of several instructions, its definition must be delimited by two reserved words: `proc` and `end`.

The syntax for defining procedure is as follows:

```
proc(var_1,.... ,var_p)
    local lvar_1,....,lvar_q;
    global gvar_1,.... gvar_r;
    options<Seq_options>;
    <Instruct_1>;
    .../...
    <Instruct_n>;
end
```

- var_1, ... , var_p are the symbolic parameters of the procedure. They are formal parameters that are of use to describe the procedure, but are replaced by variables or by expressions when the procedure is called.
- local is a reserved word, and lvar_1, ..., lvar_q are local variables used within the procedure. This line is optional. Local variables will be studied in detail in Section 24.2.2.
- global is a reserved word, and gvar_1, ... gvar_r are global variables used within the procedure. This line is optional. Global variables will be studied in detail in Section 24.2.2.
- options is a reserved word, and <Seq_options> is the sequence of options relating to this procedure. This line is optional and is mainly of use in the case of the option remember (cf. p. 417).
- <Instruct_1>, .../...<Instruct_n> are the instructions the procedure has to execute.

In general, a procedure is assigned to an identifier by an instruction like

```
Id_proc:=proc(var_1,... ,var_p) ... end
```

but there exist cases where, as for functions, one may use an anonymous procedure, i.e. a procedure which isn't associated with any identifier.

As for a function (p. 402), the lines defining a procedure must be written in the same execution group.

If the **end** terminating the procedure is followed by a *semicolon*, MAPLE returns an echo on the screen that displays the body of the procedure in a special format. But, whether there is a *semicolon* following the final **end** or not, syntactic errors are displayed, as well as some warnings (*Warning....*).

If one forgets the final **end**, MAPLE indicates it with the message *Warning, incomplete statement or missing semicolon*

By way of example, the factorial function can be written as a procedure

Ex.33

```
> fact := proc(n) if n=0 then 1 else n*fact(n-1); fi; end;
  fact := proc(n) if n = 0 then 1 else n*fact(n-1) fi end
```

or, as for functions, by using the **remember** table.

Ex.34

```
> fact:=proc(n) n*fact(n-1); end; fact(0):=1;
  fact := proc(n) n*fact(n-1) end
```

$$fact(0) := 1$$

This procedure doesn't carry out any test to verify the type of the argument it receives, it only carries out a computation and returns, for any positive integer value of **n**, the last evaluated quantity which is indeed the value of **n!**.

Ex.35

```
> fact(5);
                        120
> fact(-1);                    stack overflow for a negative integer
  Error, (in fact) too many levels of recursion
> x:='x': fact(x);                    or for a non numerical value
  Error, (in fact) too many levels of recursion
```

24.2.2 Local Variables and Global Variables

The definition of a procedure involves three types of variables: symbolic parameters (the identifiers following **proc**), local variables (the identifiers following **local**), global variables (the identifiers following **global**).

- A local variable is a temporary variable for working within the procedure, which disappears when the procedure is exited. "Localizing" a variable lets you use it without worrying about the risk of conflicts with a variable of the same name in another part of the program.
- A global variable is a variable whose content can be used or modified at the conversational level as well as within any procedure. When a procedure modifies the value of a global variable, the modified value is retained when the procedure passes control back to the calling process.

Warning ! The system variable `Digits` is an environment variable which is available to a procedure, but only as a local copy. Thus, a modification of its value within a procedure has no effect outside the procedure.

In order to properly understand the difference between a local variable and a global variable, let us consider the two following versions of the factorial function.

The first version, `fact_1`, uses one symbolic parameter n and two local variables y and i. It doesn't use any global variable. The second, `fact_2`, uses one gobal variable i and one local variable y.

Ex.36

```
> fact_1 :=
  proc(n)
    local i,y;
    y:=1;
    for i to n do y:=i*y; od
  end:
> fact_2 :=
  proc(n)
    local y; global i;
    y:=1;
    for i to n do y:=i*y; od
  end:
```

Let us compare their use in the following context.

Ex.37

```
> i:='i': fact_1(5); i;
                    120

                     i
> fact_2(5); i;
                    120

                     6
```

The first procedure doesn't modify the value of the variable i at the conversational level, while with the second procedure, one finds the value 6 in i after the procedure has returned.

Automatic Localization of Some Variables

If the procedure `fact` is written without using either `local` or `global`, MAPLE (from release 3) automatically detects that y and i ought to be local variables and after having warned the user (*Warning...*) it adds `local y,i` to the procedure, as one can see from the echo it returns.

```
> fact :=
  proc(n)
    y:=1;
    for i to n do y:=i*y; od
  end;
  Warning, 'y' is implicitly declared local
  Warning, 'i' is implicitly declared local
  fact := proc(n) local y,i; y := 1; for i to n do y := i*y od end
```

Ex.38

Thus MAPLE takes the liberty of assuming that any variable is local if it is not explicitly declared global, and it either appears on the left side of an assignment, or is the counter of a **for** loop. When this liberty is taken, it is indicated with a warning: such a warning often corresponds to a forgotten **local** declaration. Even if the procedure works properly, it is of course safer for the user to modify its definition to make it agree with the logic of his programming.

However, there are cases where a variable appears in a procedure on the left side of an assignment although it is not local. We shall see such an example in the next section, in Example 46, page 416. In this case, one must explicitly declare the variable as being global.

Evaluation Level of the Different Variables

Let us indicate one final difference between global variables and local variables: while global variables are, in general, fully evaluated, as at the conversational level, local variables are only evaluated at the first level. When a full evaluation of a local variable is required, one must force it with the function **eval**.

The following procedures may, for example, be compared:

Ex.39

```
> ess_1:=proc() local x; global y;
  y:=x; x:=1; print(y); end:
> ess_2:=proc() local x,y;
  y:=x; x:=1; print(y); end:
> ess_1();ess_2();
                              1
                              x
```

In each of these procedures, the variable y points towards x which points towards 1. In the first, y is a global variable and its evaluation in the **print** is carried out fully, as at the conversational level. In the second, y is a local variable and its evaluation within the **print** is only carried out at the first level, which only returns x.

Global Variables and Nested Procedures

Unlike most structured languages, like Pascal, if a procedure `proc2` is defined within a procedure `proc1`, a local variable or an argument of `proc1` can only be passed to `proc2` as a parameter or with the function `unapply`.

Since a function defined with the operator `->` is a procedure, one often comes up against this communication problem when defining such a function within a procedure.

To determine, for example, the affine function that coincides with a function `f` at given points `a` and `b`, one may write

Ex.40

```
> restart;
  P:=x->u*x+v:
  s:=solve({P(a)=f(a),P(b)=f(b)},{u,v});
  subs(s,eval(P);
```

$$\left\{ u = \frac{-f(b) + f(a)}{a - b}, v = -\frac{b\,f(a) - f(b)\,a}{a - b} \right\}$$

$$x \rightarrow -\frac{(f(a) - f(b))\,x}{b - a} + \frac{-a\,f(b) + f(a)\,b}{b - a}$$

Trying to write a procedure with one variable

Ex.41

```
> restart;
  Interpol1:=proc(f) local P,s,u,v
    P:=x->u*x+v:
    s:=solve({P(a)=f(a),P(b)=f(b)},{u,v});
    subs(s,eval(P));
  end;
```

$Interpol1 := \text{proc } (f)$
$\text{local } P,s,u,v; P := x \rightarrow u^*x + v;$
$s := solve(\{P(b) = f(b), P(a) = f(a)\},\{u, v\});$
$subs(s,eval(P))$
end

```
> Interpol1(sin);
```

$$x \rightarrow u * x + v$$

doesn't provide the expected result. The variables `u` and `v` involved in the system of equations `{P(a)=f(a),P(b)=f(b)}` are global variables of the procedure `P`, so they don't correspond to the local variables `u` and `v` appearing in the list of unknowns `{u,v}` of the function `solve`. Therefore, the result returned by `solve` is empty, which explains the result returned by the procedure `Interpol1`.

One way to solve this problem is not to localize the variables u and v at the beginning of the procedure Interpol1, which in this case is the same as defining them as global variables. But this isn't very satisfactory, since the procedure ends with an error when u or v isn't free.

A second way is to use the function unapply, which allows us to keep the outline of the first program.

Ex.42

```
> restart;
  Interpol2:=proc(f) local P,s,u,v,x
    P:=unapply(u*x+v,x):                          (*)
    s:=solve({P(a)=f(a),P(b)=f(b)},{u,v});
    subs(s,eval(P));
  end;
```

$$Interpol2 := proc\ (f)\ local\ P,s,u,v,x;$$
$$P := unapply(u*x+v,x);$$
$$s := solve(\{P(b) = f(b),\ P(a) = f(a)\},\{u,v\});$$
$$subs(s,eval(P))$$
$$end$$

```
> Interpol2(sin);
```

$$x \rightarrow -\frac{(f(a) - f(b))\,x}{b - a} + \frac{-a\,f(b) + f(a)\,b}{b - a}$$

This way, the definition of P begins at (*) with an evaluation of the arguments of unapply and in particular of u*x+v, for which u and v are indeed the local variables of the procedure Interpol2.

One final way is to write the polynomial as an expression of x, but then subs must be used in order to compute its values.

Ex.43

```
> restart;
  Interpol3:=proc(f) local P,s,u,v,x
    P := u*x+v;
    s := solve({subs(x=a,P)=f(a),subs(x=b,P)=f(b)},{u,v});
    subs(s,P);
  end;
```

$$Interpol3 := proc\ (f)\ local\ P,s,u,v,x;$$
$$P := u*x+v;$$
$$s := solve(\{subs(x=a,P)=f(a),subs(x=b,P)=f(b)\},\{u,\ v\});$$
$$subs(s,P)$$
$$end$$

```
> Interpol3(sin);
```

$$\frac{(f(a) - f(b))\,x}{b - a} + \frac{-a\,f(b) + f(a)\,b}{b - a}$$

Although less intuitive, this last version, which uses expressions instead of functions, should be kept in mind. The procedure Interpol3 returns an expression instead of a function. However, the user may use `unapply` before the final `end` if he prefers a function.

24.2.3 Recursive Procedures

As for functions, recursive procedures can be written in MAPLE, which provide natural translations of many recursive definitions.

If one considers the Chebyshev polynomial of degree n, for example, i.e. the polynomial T_n verifying $\cos(nt) = T_n(\cos(t))$, a basic trigonometric formula gives

$$T_n(x) + T_{n-2}(x) = 2\,x\,T_{n-1}(x) \quad \text{with } T_0(x) = 1 \text{ and } T_1(x) = x.$$

One can then write the following recursive procedure, which returns the Chebyshev polynomial of degree n for a given positive integer n.

Ex.44

```
> Tcheb_1:=proc(n)
    if n=0 then 1
    elif n=1 then x
    else expand(2*x*Tcheb_1(n-1)-Tcheb_1(n-2));
    fi;
  end:
```

Using the next line, anyone can compute the time this procedure takes to compute the Chebyshev polynomial of degree 20 on his own machine.

Ex.45

```
> Debut:=time():Tcheb_1(20):time()-Debut;
                        6.55
```

The function `time` counts the number of seconds during which the processor has worked for MAPLE since the beginning of the current session. By storing this time within `Debut` before calling the procedure, the evaluation of `time()-Debut` measures the computation time used by this procedure. On a DX4/100 it takes approximately takes 6 seconds to carry out this computation, which is quite long, and can be explained by adding a counter (global variable) that totals the number of times the procedure is called:

Ex.46

```
> Tcheb_1 :=
  proc(n) global cmpt;
    cmpt:=cmpt+1;
    if n=0 then 1
    elif n=1 then x
    else expand(2*x*Tcheb_1(n-1)-Tcheb_1(n-2));
    fi;
  end :
```

If one then executes:

Ex.47

```
> cmpt:=0: Tcheb_1(20): cmpt;

                    21891
```

one understands why 6 seconds have been used.

Warning ! In the previous example,

- the variable `cmpt` must be declared **global**: otherwise, MAPLE declares it **local** automatically, since it appears on the left side of an assignment, which won't count much.
- one absolutely should not forget to initialize `cmpt` before calling `Tcheb_1`, otherwise the assignment `cmpt:=cmpt+1` causes an infinite recursive call, which in turn causes a stack overflow (p. 20).

24.2.4 `remember` Table Versus Recursion

Like functions, procedures have a `remember` table in which specific values can be directly stored. This table can be used to store either special values or values which are hard to compute. MAPLE often uses the `remember` tables in order to store a few exact values of some kernel functions, like `sin`, `cos`, `ln`, `exp`, ... This kind of use has already been encountered (p. 411) in writing the factorial procedure.

But a function or procedure can also be programmed to automatically store all the values it computes within its `remember` table. This is of utmost relevance either for a recursive procedure, in order to avoid useless recursive calls, or for a procedure which is often used, when the computations are relatively long and few results need to be stored.

If one redefines the procedure computing the Chebyshev polynomial of degree n, adding `remember` on the line `option`.

Ex.48

```
> Tcheb_2 :=
  proc(n) global cmpt;
    option remember;
    cmpt:=cmpt+1;
    if n=0 then 1
    elif n=1 then x
    else expand(2*x*Tcheb_2(n-1)-Tcheb_2(n-2));
    fi;
  end :
```

And if one then executes

Ex.49

```
> cmpt:=0: Debut:=time(): Tcheb_2(20) :
    time()-Debut, cmpt;

                        0.55 , 21
```

One sees that the computation time has significantly decreased (less than one second on a DX4/100), and that the number of times the procedure is called is only 21! Thanks to the option **remember**, the procedure has kept all the polynomials which are computed within its table, which prevents many recursive calls. As for functions, one may view this table by requesting

Ex.50

```
> op(4,eval(Tcheb_2));
```
$$table([$$
$$3 = 4x^3 - 3x$$
$$.../...$$
$$0 = 1$$
$$.../...$$
$$1 = x$$
$$.../...$$
$$2 = 2x^2 - 1$$
$$.../...$$
$$])$$

The previous table contains 21 elements, only the simplest values have been copied above.

However, a drawback of the **remember** table is that it can quickly overflow memory. If one tries to use the previous procedure for **n=40** with only 4 Megabytes of RAM, one gets the message *Error, (in Tcheb_2) STACK OVERFLOW*. This shows the limits of the method ... although one doesn't need this polynomial of degree 40 every day!

Finally, let us give one last procedure computing Chebyshev polynomials, which is as effective as the previous one although it doesn't use the **remember** table. More analysis is required to write it, since it doesn't use the facilities of MAPLE, but it can be used for huge values of n without risk of memory overflow.

Ex.51

```
> Tcheb_3 := proc(n) local i,u,v,w;
    u:=1; v:=x;
    for i from 2 to n do w:=expand(2*x*v-u); u:=v; v:=w; od;
  end;
```

24.2.5 Structure of an Object Function or Procedure

Functions or procedures, whether internal to MAPLE or defined by the user, share the same type in MAPLE: the type procedure. However, to verify this with the help of the function whattype one must first force the evaluation of the procedure or function with eval, since, by default, a procedure isn't fully evaluated.

Ex.52

```
> whattype(sin);
                              string
> whattype(eval(sin));
                                    procedure
> whattype(eval(Tcheb_3));
                                    procedure
```

Warning! The type function corresponds to a form f(...), whether f is a function, a procedure or a free variable.

The structure of the objects of type procedure can be studied using the examples of procedures encountered previously. Each object of this type contains 6 operands or, equivalently, 6 first level sub-objects.

- The operand of rank 1 contains the list of parameters of the function.
- the operand of rank 2 contains the sequence of local variables.
- the operand of rank 6 contains the sequence of global variables.

Ex.53

```
> nops(eval(sin));
                              6
> nops(eval(Tcheb_3));
                              6
> op(1,eval(Tcheb_3));              symbolic parameters
                              n
> op(2,eval(Tcheb_3));                 local variables
                         i, u, v, w
> op(6,eval(Tcheb_2));                 global variables
                         cmpt
```

The operands of rank 3 and 4 contain respectively the option line and the remember table of the procedure. When the procedure contains the option remember, the remember table is updated every time the procedure is used, otherwise it is only updated by a assignment carried out by the user.

Ex.54

```
[> op(3,eval(Tcheb_2));                          Options

                            remember

[> op(4,eval(Tcheb_2));                      remember table
   table([
   3 = 4x³ − 3x
   .../...
   0 = 1
   .../...
   ])
```

$3 = 4x^3 - 3x$

$0 = 1$

24.3 About Passing Parameters

24.3.1 Automatic Verification of the Types of Arguments

In MAPLE, the type of some arguments passed to a procedure can be automatically verified. Within the definition of the procedure, just put the symbol : : followed by the desired type behind the corresponding arguments. For the factorial function, for example,

Ex.55

```
[> fact :=
   proc(n::integer) local i,y;        :: to verify the type of n
      y:=1;
      for i to n do y:=i*y; od
   end;
```

If one then tries to use this function with a value like 1.5, one has

Ex.56

```
[> fact(1.5);
   Error, fact expects its 1st argument, n, to be of type integer,
   but received 1.5
```

24.3.2 Testing the Number and the Kind of Arguments Which Are Passed

As with functions, there is no automatic syntactic verification of the number of arguments which are passed to a procedure. However, the user can include such a verification using the system variable **nargs**, which returns the number of arguments that are actually passed to the procedure. With the function **type**, the user can also verify the type of arguments which haven't been declared of a given type within the header of the procedure.

In the example of the factorial function studied previously, this yields

Ex.57

```
> fact:=
  proc(n) local y,i;
    if nargs<> 1
    then
      ERROR('expects a single argument')
    else
      if type(n,numeric)
      then if not type(n,integer) or (n<0)
        then
          ERROR('expects a positive integer')
        else
          if n=0
          then 1
          else y:=1;
            for i from 1 to n do y:=y*i; od;
          fi;
        fi;
      else 'fact'(n);              to return a non evaluated form
      fi;
    fi;
  end :
```

With this procedure, if the number of arguments passed to the procedure is different from 1, the function **ERROR** (p. 405) causes the procedure to exit with the error message: *Error, (in fact) expects a single argument*. If the argument is of type **numeric**, the function tests if it is a positive integer and it leaves with an error if it isn't. The function returns an unevaluated form when **n** isn't of type **numeric** .

Ex.58

```
> fact(1,2);
  Error, (in fact) expects a single argument
> fact(-1);
  Error, (in fact) expects a positive integer
```

24.3.3 How to Test a Type

The function **type** tests whether the value of a variable or of an expression satisfies some criteria. It can be used to prevent a function from operating on incorrect types, or computing with values outside its domain. For example

- the evaluation of **type(expr,integer)** returns **true** if **expr** evaluates to an integer.
- the evaluation of **type(expr,rational)** returns **true** if **expr** evaluates to a rational number (fraction or integer).

- the evaluation of `type(expr,numeric)` returns `true` if `expr` is of type numeric (integer, rational or `float`). Mind that some values that are considered numerical by the user, like `sqrt(2)` or `Pi`, are not of type `numeric`, but of type `realcons`.
- the evaluation of `type(expr,polynom)` returns `true` if `expr` evaluates to a polynomial.

Examples using the function type with numerical expressions.

Ex.59

```
> x:=5/2; y:=sqrt(2);
```

$$x := 5/2 \quad , \quad y := \sqrt{2}$$

```
> type(x,numeric);
```
$$true$$

```
> type(y,numeric);
```
$$false$$

```
> type(x,integer);
```
$$false$$

```
> type(x,rational);
```
$$true$$

```
> type(y,realcons);
```
$$true$$

Examples using the function type with polynomials.

Ex.60

```
> x:='x': P:=sqrt(2)*x^2+x+1;
```

$$P := \sqrt{2}\, x^2 + x + 1$$

```
> type(P,polynom);
```
$$true$$

```
> y:='y': Q:=x*sin(y);
```

$$Q := x * \sin(y)$$

```
> type(Q,polynom);
```
$$false$$

The types above are simple. Structured types are built on top of these types. On top of the type `polynom`, for example, there are types for testing more precisely the type of the coefficients of a polynomial (p. 362). One may use `polynom(integer)` to test for polynomials with integer coefficients, `polynom(integer)` for polynomials with coefficients of type `numeric` and `polynom(algebraic)` for polynomials with algebraic coefficients.

With the previous polynomial P, for example:

Ex.61

```
> type(P,polynom(integer));

                                false

> type(P,polynom(algebraic));

                                true
```

The few examples given above are a small sample of the possibilities MAPLE offers regarding types. We won't give all the available types here, but the user may call the on-line help by typing ?type in order to get all the available types (there are about a hundred of them). For more information about each specific type, the user should type ?type/<nom_type>, for example: ?type/polynom:

Finally, the user may read the source code for the functions and procedures in MAPLE, since they give valuable examples of testing types in cases that are quite interesting. In order to do this, use eval(<nom_proc>) after executing (Chapter 25) interface(verboseproc=2).

24.3.4 Procedure Modifying the Value of Some Parameters

One of the most fundamental problems relating to the use of procedures is the way parameters are passed. When a procedure modifies a symbolic parameter appearing in its definition, what happens to the argument which is actually passed in the procedure called?

We shall study this problem with a simple procedure that returns the remainder of the division of two given integers, and uses a third argument to return the quotient of the division.

We start by limiting ourselves to a procedure that always requires three parameters. The first definition one might think of is:

Ex.62

```
> remainder :=
  proc(a,b,q)
    q := trunc(a/b);
    a-b*q;
  end;
    remainder := proc(a,b,q) q := trunc(a/b); a-b*q end
```

At first sight this seems to be correct, since the value of the quotient has been assigned to q, and the last computed value (the value returned by the procedure), is a-bq, i.e. the remainder of the division. If one calls this procedure with 13, 5 and q0, one obtains

Ex.63

```
> q0:='q0';
  remainder(13,5,q0);
                                    13 − 5 q0

> q0;
                                         2
```

it is best to free q0

which isn't the expected result and highlights an important rule.

The evaluation of the parameters which are actually passed to a procedure, whether they are expressions or simply identifiers of variables, is a full evaluation which is carried out at the moment the procedure is called, but these parameters are never re-evaluated during the execution of the procedure.

In the previous example, q is replaced by q0 at the moment of the call, which allows the first instruction to assign the value 2 to q0 as can be verified afterwards by requesting the evaluation of q0. But in the second instruction q still points towards the value which was assigned at the beginning of the procedure, i.e. q0, hence the result $13 - 5\,q0$ since there is no other evaluation of q.

A way to solve the previous problem is to force a full evaluation of a−b*q with the function `eval`. Hence, the second instruction carries out a full evaluation of a−b*q, which has the value 13-5*q0, i.e. $13 - 5 * 2 = 3$, and the result which is returned is indeed the remainder of the division.

Ex.64

```
> remainder :=
  proc(a,b,q)
    q := trunc(a/b);
    eval(a-b*q);
  end;
        remainder := proc(a,b,q) q := trunc(a/b); eval(a-b*q) end

> q0:='q0': remainder(13,5,q0);

                                    3

> q0;
                                    2
```

We shall study this example again in the next section in order to give a more flexible version of this procedure that allows the use of either 2 or 3 parameters.

24.3.5 Procedure with a Variable Number of Arguments

If one wishes to use the procedure `remainder` defined previously but only needs the remainder, one may wish to call it with only two parameters. In this case, MAPLE displays an error message at the moment of using `q` within the assignment `q:=trunc(a/b)`.

Ex.65

```
> remainder(13,5);
    Error, (in remainder) remainder uses a 3rd argument, q,
    which is missing
```

When writing a procedure that accepts a variable number of parameters, make sure that when executing, the procedure only uses the parameters that actually belong to the calling list.

There is no verification of the number of parameters which are passed when a procedure is called, but MAPLE exits with an error if the execution of the procedure requires the use of a parameter that doesn't belong to the calling list.

In order to rewrite our procedure remainder to manage a variable number of parameters, we use **nargs**, which contains the number of parameters actually passed to the procedure.

Ex.66

```
> remainder:=proc(a,b,q) local qq;
    if nargs<2
      then ERROR('at least 2 parameters are required');
    fi;
    qq:=trunc(a/b);
    if nargs>2 then q:=qq; fi;
    a-b*qq;
  end:

  remainder := proc(a,b,q) local qq;
    if nargs < 2 then ERROR('at least 2 parameters are required')
    fi;
    qq := trunc(a/b); if 2 < nargs then q := qq fi;
    a-b*qq
  end
```

We have used **nargs** in the previous procedure, on the one hand in order to verify that at least two parameters are passed on to the procedure (otherwise the procedure exits with an error using the function **ERROR**), and on the other hand in order to detect the preserve of a third parameter, `q`, and assign it a value `q` if a third parameter belongs to the calling list.

Using this procedure gives

Ex.67

```
> remainder(1);
  Error, (in remainder) at least two arguments are required
> remainder(13,5);
                                        3
> q:='q': remainder(13,5,q), q;
                                      3, 2
```

24.3.6 Procedure with an Unspecified Number of Arguments

In MAPLE, there are procedures that can use an unspecified number of arguments. One example of this is the procedure that determines the maximum of any family of elements. This isn't a procedure that can use either two or three arguments, but a procedure that can use an arbitrarily large number of arguments.

Such a procedure cannot be written with symbolic parameters which are completely identified, as in previous examples. It is written as a procedure without symbolic parameters, and the variable args is used to manage the parameters that are passed to the procedure. This variable contains the sequence of arguments with which the procedure has been called, and every argument can be accessed with the help of the selection operator [] : args[1] is the first element of the calling sequence, args[2] is the second one, etc.

As an exercise, let us write a procedure My_max (it is better not to use the same name as the MAPLE procedure) returning the maximum of any number of numerical values.

Ex.68

```
> My_max :=
  proc() local i,j,L;                   Procedure without parameters.
    L:=evalf([args]);                   evalf to handle the realcons values.
    j:=1;
    for i from 2 to nargs
      do if L[i]>L[j] then j:=i; fi; od;
    args[j];                            To define the value that is returned
  end:
> My_max(1,5+sqrt(2),3-sqrt(3));
                          5 + √2
```

Written like this, the procedure isn't at all protected against other uses than the one it has been written for, i.e. handling families of numbers only. It can be protected against improper use by using the type list(numeric), to test that all the entries are indeed numerical, and avoid exiting with the error message: *Error, (in My_max) cannot evaluate boolean.*

Ex.69

```
> My_max_2:=
  proc() local i,j,L;
    L:=evalf([args]);
    if not type(L,list(numeric))
      then RETURN('Mon_max(args)');                    (*)
    fi;
    j:=1;
    for i from 2 to nargs
      do if L[i]>L[j] then j:=i; fi; od;
    args[j];
  end:
> My_max(1,5+sqrt(2),3-sqrt(3));
```
$$5 + \sqrt{2}$$
```
> My_max_2(a,1,2);
```
$$Mon\_max\_2(a, 1, 2)$$

If one of the arguments passed to My_Max_2 isn't numerical, the function RETURN is used at (*) to directly exit from the procedure while returning an unevaluated form of type function.

24.4 Follow-up of the Execution of a Procedure

24.4.1 The Variable printlevel

Returning to the procedure **remainder** (defined in Example 66, p. 425), which returns the remainder of a Euclidean division and stores the quotient in an third argument, and executing it twice with the same arguments, we see that the second execution terminates with an error message.

Ex.70

```
> q:='q': remainder(13,5,q); q;
```
$$3$$
$$2$$
```
> remainder(13,5,q);
  Error, (in remainder) Illegal use of a formal parameter
```

In order to understand where this error is coming from, we can track the execution of the program by increasing the value of **printlevel** in order to echo each step of the program. Every instruction executed by MAPLE has a "level" which is defined as follows:

- instructions at the interactive level are at level 0,
- upon entering a loop or a test, the level is increased by 1,
- upon exiting a loop or a test, the level is decreased by 1,
- upon entering a procedure (or a function), the level is increased by 5,
- upon exiting a procedure (or a function), the level is decreased by 5.

Every instruction appearing within a level 0 instruction followed by a semi-colon and of level at most equal to `printlevel`, is echoed when executed. The value of `printlevel` is equal to 1 by default, which only echoes instructions whose level is less than or equal to 1. Hence, one needs at least `printlevel:=5` in order to echo the instructions executed within our program.

Ex.71

```
> printlevel:=5: remainder(13,5,q); printlevel:=1:
    {-> enter remainder, args = 13, 5, 2                    (1)
    qq:=2                                                   (2)
    <- ERROR in remainder (now at top level) =             (3)
            Illegal use of a formal parameter}
    Error, (in remainder) Illegal use of a formal parameter (4)
    executing statement: q := qq                           (4)
    locals defined as: qq = 2
    remainder called with arguments: 13, 5, 2
```

The echo on the screen tells us that the procedure is called ((1)) with arguments 13, 5 and 2. The assignment (2) takes place correctly, but the trouble begins at (3) and are caused by the assignment `q:=qq`, as MAPLE tells us at (4). And one indeed realizes that such an assignment is meaningless if q contains the value 2. The problem is thus caused by the previous computation, which had assigned a numerical value to q.

There are three ways to solve this problem:

- either one frees the variable q before calling `remainder`, with the assignment: `q:='q'`
- or one calls `remainder` with q between apostrophes `remainder(a,b,'q')`.
- or, as in the example that follows, one defines the procedure `remainder` with `q::evaln`, which restricts the evaluation of the argument at the last name.

Ex.72

```
> remainder:=proc(a,b,q::evaln) local qq;
      if nargs<2 then ERROR('You need at least 2 values')
  fi;
      qq:=trunc(a/b);
      if nargs>2 then q:=qq fi;
      a-b*qq
  end:
```

24.4.2 The Functions userinfo and infolevel

MAPLE provides other means by which users can follow an algorithm: the functions userinfo and infolevel.

The function userinfo allows you to embed information in a procedure definition which will be displayed at the user's request during the procedure's execution. The syntax is userinfo(level,name,expr_1,expr_2,..., expr_p) where

- level is an integer lying between 1 and 5.
- name is a name, in general the name of a procedure, although it can also be a set of names,
- expr_1, expr_2,..., expr_p are p expressions which are evaluated then displayed if infolevel[name] is greater than or equal to level.

To see the messages associated with a given name, a level is assigned to the name by modifying the associated value in the table infolevel, i.e. by typing: infolevel[name]:=n, where n is an integer lying between 1 and 5.

If the names of the procedures used within an algorithm one wishes to follow are unknown, one may type infolevel[all]:=n. During execution, the messages of userinfo instructions encountered whose level is at most n will then be displayed.

To see what factor does with a given polynomial, type:

Ex.73

```
> infolevel[all]:=2;
```

$$infolevel\_all := 2$$

```
> factor(x^^5+3*x^2+1);
```

factor/polynom: polynomial factorization: number of terms 3
convert/sqrfree/sqrfree: square-free factorization in x
factor/unifactor: entering
factor/fac1mod: entering
factor/fac1mod: found prime 2
factor/fac1mod: distinct degree factorization
modp1/DistDeg: polynomial has degree 5
factor/fac1mod: polynomial proven irreducible by degree analysis
factor/unifactor: exiting

$$x^5 + 3\,x^2 + 1$$

If you want more information and request a higher information level, you will be unpleasantly surprised not to get any message at all.

Ex.74
```
> infolevel[all]:=5: factor(x^5+3*x^2+1);
```
$$x^5 + 3\,x^2 + 1$$

It's not that MAPLE is tired of spitting out information, but rather a consequence of **remember** tables. As is verified below, the result of the factorization of the polynomial is in the **remember** table of the procedure **factor**, and MAPLE thus doesn't need any computation to return the result.

Ex.75
```
> op(4,eval(factor));
```
$$table\,([\\ x^5 + 3x^2 + 1 = x^5 + 3x^2 + 1 \\ ])$$

To get another trace of the functions used by **factor** for this polynomial, you can erase the **remember** table of the function **factor**, either with **restart**, or with the help of **readlib(forget)(factor)**.

You can see for yourself how the function **userinfo** is used within **factor/ polynom** by typing:

Ex.76
```
> interface(verboseproc=2); eval('factor/polynom');
```
$proc(x)$ *local* $v,a,k,l,lx,c;$
options '*Copyright 1993 by Waterloo Maple Software*';
if type(x,numeric) then RETURN(x) fi;
userinfo(1,factor, '*polynomial factorization:number of terms*',
nops(x));
$c := icontent(x);$
divide(x,c,'lx');
.... / .....
end

Note: Be sure not to forget the backward apostrophes around the name **factor/polynom**, otherwise MAPLE tries to evaluate the quotient of **factor** and **polynom**, which isn't at all what's expected.

24.5 Save and Reread a Procedure

Once a procedure or a function has been written and tested, there are two ways to use it later:

- The first is to save the procedure within a file, like all the sessions executed so far have been saved. To use it again, just open the file, reexecute it completely with the menu option **Format/Execute/Worksheet**, and go to the end of the file and write the instructions related to the problem you want to solve.
- The second way is to save an executable version of the procedure, which can later be loaded within a session, as has already been done with all the functions of the *Maple.lib* library.

To save one or several functions, one may write either

$$\text{save file\_name}$$
or
$$\text{save Ident\_1,Ident\_2,....,Ident\_n ,file\_name}$$

The first saves all variables that have a content, together with their content, within the file `file_name`. The second does the same, but only for the identifiers before `file_name`.

It isn't necessary to give the filename an extension. However, objects are saved in an internal format which is more rapidly reread, and hence reloaded, if the extension .*m* is used.

In order to reload values (variables, procedures or functions) saved in this way, just type:

$$\text{read file\_name}$$

The functions **save** and **read** work in the current directory by default. To specify a different directory, write the filename in full including the path, and thus \ characters. Don't forget to put this name between backward apostrophes, and to double each \.

In order to save the function **remainder** previously defined to the file `rem_file` in the current directory, type:

Ex.77
```
> save remainder,'rem_file';
```

In order to reload the previous function into memory, type

Ex.78
```
▷ read 'rem_file':
```

In order to save the previous function in the directory **MAPLEV4\lib** you must, as in the C language, double all \ characters, and thus should type

Ex.79
```
▷ save remainder,'\\MAPLEV4\\lib\\rem_file.m':
```

In order to reload the function into memory, type

Ex.80
```
▷ read '\\MAPLEV4\\lib\\rem_file.m':
```

25. The Mathematical Functions

25.1 Catalogue of Mathematical Functions

The ordinary mathematical functions are either internal functions or functions of the standard library. The internal functions, written in C, belong to the kernel and are automatically loaded when MAPLE is started. As for the functions of the standard library, some are automatically loaded when they are used for the first time, while other must be explicitly loaded with the command `readlib`.

You might notice that a function must be read in with `readlib` when MAPLE returns it in an unevaluated form. The function can be loaded before it is used, but `readlib` can also be used directly as part of the first call to that function.

Ex. 1

```
> ilog(3.14);
                    ilog (3.14)
> readlib(ilog): ilog(3.14);          loading before use

                         1
> restart;                             restart suppresses
                              the functions loaded by readlib
> ilog(3.14);
                    ilog (3.14)
> readlib(ilog)(3.14);                loading when using

                         1
```

In the following table of functions, a special note in the first column indicates those functions which must be loaded with `readlib`.

25.1.1 Arithmetical Functions

Syntax	Description
ceil(x)	Smallest integer bigger or equal to x
floor(x)	Biggest integer smaller or equal to x
round(x)	Integer the closest to x
trunc(x)	Integer part of x **trunc(-x)=-trunc(x)**
signum(x)	Sign of x, assumed real **signum(0)=1**
sqrt(x)	Square root of x **(x real, complex or polynomial)**
conjugate(x)	Conjugate of x **(x complex value or complex expression)**
csgn(x)	"Sign" of x, for x complex, defined by $+1$ if $Re(\mathbf{x})>0$ or $(Re(\mathbf{x})=0$ and $Im(\mathbf{x})\leq 0)$ -1 otherwise
csgn(1,x)	Derivative of csgn at x.

25.1.2 Counting Functions and Γ Function

Syntax	Description
factorial(n)	Factorial of n ; can also be written n!
binomial(n,p)	Number of de combinations of n elements taken p by p
GAMMA(a)	Γ function verifying $\Gamma(a) = \int_0^\infty e^{-t}t^{a-1}dt$ For $n \in \mathbb{N}^*$, $\Gamma(n) = (n-1)!$
GAMMA(a,x)	Incomplete Γ functions : $\Gamma(a,x) = \int_x^\infty e^{-t}t^{a-1}dt$
LnGAMMA(x) **readlib**	Logarithm of the Γ function

25.1.3 Exponentials, Logarithms and Hypergeometric Function

Syntax	Description
`exp(x)`	Exponential of x, $\quad \exp(x) = \sum_{n=0}^{\infty} \frac{x^n}{n!} = \lim_{n \to \infty} \left(1 + \frac{x}{n}\right)^n$
`ln(x)` or `log(x)`	Natural logarithm of x, $\qquad$ **(see definition p. 41)**
`log10(x)`	Logarithm with base 10 of x, `log10(x)=ln(x)/ln(10)`
`log[b](x)`	Logarithm with base b of x, `log[b](x)=ln(x)/ln(b)`
`ilog[b](x)` `readlib`	Integer logarithm with base b of x. For x real, `ilog[b](x)` is the integer r verifying $b^r \le \|x\| < b^{r+1}$
`ilog(x)` `readlib`	Integer natural logarithm, `ilog(x)=ilog[exp(1)](x)`
`ilog10(x)`	Integer logarithm with base 10, `ilog10(x)=ilog[10](x)`

`hypergeom`
`(n,d,z)`
`readlib`
	`hypergeom` is the generalized hypergeometric function The evaluation of
	`hypergeom([n`$_1$`,...,n`$_j$`],[d`$_1$`,,...,d`$_m$`])`
	returns $\displaystyle\sum_{k=0}^{\infty} \frac{\left(\prod_{i=1}^{j} \frac{\Gamma(n_i+k)}{\Gamma(n_i)}\right) z^k}{\left(\prod_{i=1}^{m} \frac{\Gamma(d_i+k)}{\Gamma(d_i)}\right) k!}$

25.1.4 Circular and Hyperbolic Trigonometric Functions

Syntax	Description and examples
`sin(x)` `cos(x)`	trigonometric sine and cosine
`tan(x)` `cot(x)`	trigonometric tangent and cotangent
`sec(x)` `csc(x)`	trigonometric secant and cosecant `sec(x)=1/(cos(x))` `csc(x)=1/(sin(x))`

Syntax	Description and examples
`sinh(x)` `cosh(x)`	hyperbolic sine and cosine
`tanh(x)` `coth(x)`	hyperbolic tangent and cotangent
`sech(x)` `csch(x)`	hyperbolic secant and cosecant `sech(x)=1/(cosh(x))` `csch(x)=1/(sinh(x))`

For the functions of the two previous tables, the classical formulas, which are well known for real x, are also valid for complex x.

$$\sin(x) = \frac{e^{ix} - e^{-ix}}{2i} \quad , \quad \cos(x) = \frac{e^{ix} + e^{-ix}}{2}$$

$$\sinh(x) = \frac{e^x - e^{-x}}{2} \quad , \quad \cosh(x) = \frac{e^x + e^{-x}}{2}$$

$$\tan x = \frac{\sin x}{\cos x} \, , \quad \cot x = \frac{\cos x}{\sin x} \, , \quad \tanh x = \frac{\sinh x}{\cosh x} \, , \quad \coth x = \frac{\cosh x}{\sinh x}$$

25.1.5 Inverse Trigonometric Functions

Syntax	Description
`arcsin(x)`	Inverse sine function For $x \in \mathbb{C}$, `arcsin(x)` $= -i \ln \left(ix + \sqrt{1 - x^2} \right)$ For $x \in [-1, 1]$ one recovers the ordinary arcsin function
`arccos(x)`	Inverse cosine function For $x \in \mathbb{C}$, `arccos(x)` $= \frac{\pi}{2} - \arcsin(x)$ For $x \in [-1, 1]$ one recovers the ordinary arccos function
`arctan(x)`	Inverse tangent function. For $x \in \mathbb{C} \setminus \{-i, i\}$, one has `arctan(x)` $= \frac{1}{2i} \ln \left(\frac{1+ix}{1-ix} \right)$ For x real one recovers the ordinary arctan function
`arctan(y,x)`	`arctan(y,x)` returns `argument(x+I*y)`
`arccot(x)`	Inverse cotangent Function. For $x \in \mathbb{C} \setminus \{-i, i\}$, one has `arccotan(x)` $= \frac{\pi}{2} - \arctan(x)$ For x real one recovers the arccotan function

Syntax	Description
arcsinh(x)	Inverse hyperbolic sine function For $x \in \mathbb{C}$ $\texttt{arcsinh(x)} = \ln\left(x + \sqrt{x^2 + 1}\right)$ For x real one recovers $\operatorname{arcsinh}(x) = \ln(x + \sqrt{x^2 + 1})$
arccosh(x)	Inverse hyperbolic cosine function For $x \in \mathbb{C}$ $\texttt{arccosh (x)} = i\, csgn(i(1 - x))\, \arccos(x)$ For x real one recovers $\operatorname{arccosh}(x) = \ln(x + \sqrt{x^2 - 1})$
arctanh(x)	Inverse hyperbolic tangent function For $x \in \mathbb{C} \setminus \{-1, 1\}$, $\texttt{arctanh(x)} = \frac{1}{2}\ln\left(\frac{1+x}{1-x}\right)$ One recovers $\forall x \in\,]-1, 1[$, $\operatorname{arctanh}(x) = \frac{1}{2}\ln\left(\frac{1+x}{1-x}\right)$
arccoth(x)	Inverse hyperbolic cotangent function For $x \in \mathbb{C} \setminus \{-1, 1\}$, $\texttt{arccoth(x)} = i\,\frac{\pi}{2} - \operatorname{arctanh}(x)$ For $x \in \mathbb{R} \setminus [-1, 1]$, $\operatorname{arccotanh}(x) = \frac{1}{2}\ln(|\frac{1+x}{1-x}|)$

25.1.6 Integral Exponential and Related Functions

Syntax	Description
Si(x)	Integral sine of x, with $\operatorname{Si}(x) = \int_0^x \frac{\sin(t)}{t}\,dt$
Ci(x)	Integral cosine of x defined by $\operatorname{Ci}(x) = -\int_x^\infty \frac{\cos(t)}{t}\,dt\ = \gamma + \ln(x) + \int_0^x \frac{\cos(t)-1}{t}\,dt$
Shi(x)	Integral hyperbolic sine of x, $\operatorname{Shi}(x) = \int_0^x \frac{sh(t)}{t}\,dt$
Chi(x)	Integral hyperbolic cosine of x $\operatorname{Chi}(x) = \gamma + \ln(x) + \int_0^x \frac{ch(t)-1}{t}\,dt$

Syntax	Description
Ei(x)	Integral exponential defined by $$\forall x \in \mathbb{R}_+^*, \ Ei(x) = \text{p.v.} \left(\int_{-\infty}^x \frac{\exp(t)}{t} dt \right)$$
Ei(n,x)	Indexed integral exponential defined by $$\forall n \in \mathbb{N}^* \ \forall x \ \text{Re}(x) > 0 \Rightarrow Ei(n,x) = \left(\int_1^\infty \frac{\exp(-xt)}{t^n} dt \right)$$ Remark: `diff(Ei(n,x),x)=-Ei(n-1,x)`
Li(x) readlib	Integral logarithm defined by $$\forall x > 1, \ Li(x) = \text{v.p.} \left(\int_0^x \frac{1}{Ln(t)} dt \right)$$

The notation p.v. denotes (Cauchy's principal value), i.e.

$$\text{p.v.} \left(\int_{-\infty}^x \frac{\exp(t)}{t} dt \right) = \lim_{\varepsilon \to 0^+} \left(\int_{-\infty}^{-\varepsilon} \frac{\exp(t)}{t} dt + \int_\varepsilon^x \frac{\exp(t)}{t} dt \right)$$

$$\text{p.v.} \left(\int_0^x \frac{1}{\ln t} dt \right) = \lim_{\varepsilon \to 0^+} \left(\int_0^{1-\varepsilon} \frac{1}{\ln t} dt + \int_{1+\varepsilon}^x \frac{1}{\ln t} dt \right)$$

25.1.7 Bessel Functions

For non-negative real numbers n, the Bessel functions of index n are solutions of the differential equation (Bessel equation of index n)

$$x^2 \frac{d^2 y}{dx^2} + x \frac{dy}{dx} + (x^2 - n^2) y = 0 \qquad (E_1)$$

The functions classically denoted J_n and Y_n are called the Bessel function of the first and of the second kind respectively; they form a basis of the vector space of solutions of the equation (E_1), and are defined by

$$J_n(x) = \sum_{r=0}^\infty (-1)^r \frac{1}{r! \Gamma(n+r+1)} \left(\frac{x}{2} \right)^{2r+n},$$

$$Y_n(x) = \frac{\cos n\pi \, J_n(x) - J_{-n}(x)}{\sin n\pi}$$

The formula defining Y_n must be considered as a limit when n is an integer.

The modified Bessel functions of index n are solutions of the differential equation (Modified Bessel equation of index n)

$$x^2 \frac{d^2y}{dx^2} + x \frac{dy}{dx} - (x^2 + n^2) y = 0 \tag{E_2}$$

The functions classically denoted I_n and K_n are called the modified Bessel function of the first and of the second kind respectively; they form a basis of the vector space of solutions of the equation (E_2), and are defined by

$$I_n(x) = (-1)^n J_n(ix), \quad K_n(x) = \frac{\pi}{2} \frac{I_{-n}(x) - J_n(x)}{\sin n\pi}$$

The formula defining K_n must be considered as a limit when n is an integer.

Syntax	Description
`BesselJ(n,x)`	Bessel function of the first kind $J_n(x)$
`BesselY(n,x)`	Bessel function of the second kind $Y_n(x)$
`BesselI(n,x)`	Modified Bessel function of the first kind $I_n(x)$
`BesselK(n,x)`	Modified Bessel function of the second kind $K_n(x)$

25.1.8 Elliptic Functions

The elliptic functions, which are used to express elliptic integrals, are in Jacobi's algebraic form in MAPLE.

Syntax	Description
EllipticF(x,k)	Incomplete elliptic integral of the first order denoted $F(k,x)$ and defined by: $F(k,x) = \int_0^x \frac{1}{\sqrt{(1-t^2)(1-k^2t^2)}} dt$
EllipticE(x,k)	Incomplete elliptic integral of the second order denoted $E(k,x)$ and defined by: $E(k,x) = \int_0^x \frac{\sqrt{1-k^2t^2}}{\sqrt{1-t^2}} dt$
EllipticPi (x,a,k)	Incomplete elliptic integral of the third order denoted $\pi(a,k,x)$ such that: $\pi(a,k,x) = \int_0^x \frac{1}{(1-at^2)\sqrt{(1-t^2)(1-k^2t^2)}} dt$
EllipticK(k)	Complete elliptic integral of the first order denoted $K(k)$ and defined by $K(k) = F(k,1)$
EllipticE(k)	Complete elliptic integral of the second order denoted $E_c(k)$ and defined by: $E_c(k) = E(k,1)$
EllipticPi (a,k)	Complete elliptic integral of the third order denoted $\pi_c(a,k)$ and defined by: $\pi_c(a,k) = \pi(a,k,1)$
EllipticCK(c)	Complete associated elliptic integral of the first order denoted $K_1(c)$ defined by $K_1(c) = K(\sqrt{1-c^2})$
EllipticCE(c)	Complete associated elliptic integral of the second order denoted $E_{c1}(c)$ defined by $E_{c1}(c) = E_c(\sqrt{1-c^2})$
EllipticCPi (a,c)	Complete associated elliptic integral of the third order denoted $\pi_{c1}(a,c)$; one has: $\pi_{c1}(a,c) = \pi_c(a,\sqrt{1-c^2})$

25.2 How Does a MAPLE Function Work?

25.2.1 Numerical Return Values

This section discusses MAPLE functions returning numerical values.

- Integer results are always returned fully evaluated.
- When the value to be returned is of type `float`, a numerical approximation of the result is displayed with a precision given by the variable `Digits`.
- For some exceptional values an "exact value", possibly using radicals, may be returned.
- In the other cases, unevaluated forms are returned, which is disappointing, but this keeps exact results for further computations.

Ex. 2

```
> sin(2.);
                        .9092974268
> floor(sqrt(2));
                              1
> sin(Pi/4);
                           1
                           - √2
                           2
> sin(2);
                           sin(2)
```

One may use `evalf` to force a decimal numerical evaluation of a result.

Ex. 3

```
> evalf(sin(2));
                        .9092974268
```

25.2.2 An Example: The Function `arcsin`

In order to understand how a MAPLE function works, let us examine the case of the function `arcsin`, which is part of the standard MAPLE library.

The function `arcsin` is automatically loaded when it is first called. In fact, the identifier `arcsin` contains `readlib('arcsin')` at the beginning of a MAPLE session, which can be verified by using `eval` with a single level.

Ex. 4

```
> restart: eval(arcsin,1);

                      readlib(arcsin);
```

Hence, the code of the function doesn't clutter up the memory as long as it isn't used, but with the first call, MAPLE evaluates `arcsin`, and thus executes `readlib('arcsin')`, which loads the function.

After the first use of `arcsin`, the same call to the function `eval` returns

Ex. 5

```
> restart; arcsin(1/3):

                      arcsin(1/3)

> eval(arcsin,1);

                      proc(x)...end
```

Only the header of the function has been displayed. In order to get more information, it is necessary to modify the value of the environmental variable `verboseproc`, using the function `interface`. By default, the value of `verboseproc` is 1, and `eval(f)` displays only one line if `f` is a MAPLE function (or procedure).

For more information, one must execute

Ex. 6

```
> interface(verboseproc=2);
```

The function `eval` is then more verbose, and tells more about MAPLE programming to curious users. Even if you don't understand everything at first, analysing a few points of the source code on the opposite page is enlightening in terms of the way a MAPLE function works.

You can see in the following example that this function starts (1) by testing the number of arguments passed to it, and that it may exit with an error message using the function `ERROR`.

Next (2), it tests whether the argument `x` is of type `complex(float)` and, if so, numerically evaluates the value with `evalf`.

Next (3), it tests whether `x` is pure imaginary and, if so, expresses the quantity as a function of `arcsinh`.

You may then notice a few simplifications which are possible if `x` is of type `function`

- If x begins with `cos` (4), it returns `Pi/2-arccos(x)` so that it can simplify the result afterwards.
- Likewise (5), if x is itself an object of type `function` whose argument (`op(1,x)`) is a numerical value and begins with `sin`, it simplifies the inverse functions.

Finally, pay particular attention to (6) which, if no interesting transformation has been found, returns the initial expression in an unevaluated form. Notice the apostrophes that prevent the evaluation of `arcsin(x)`, which would cause an infinite loop.

Ex. 7

```
> eval(arcsin,1);
    proc(x) local x1r,k;
    options 'Copyright 1992 by the University of Waterloo';
(1) if nargs <> 1 then ERROR('expecting 1 argument, got '.nargs)
(2) elif type(x,'complex(float)') then evalf('arcsin'(x))
(3) elif type(x,'*') and member(I,{op(x)}) then I*arcsinh(-I*x)
    elif type(x,'complex(numeric)') then
        if csgn(x) < 0 then -arcsin(-x) else 'arcsin'(x) fi
    elif type(x,'*') and type(op(1,x),'complex(numeric)')
                and csgn(op(1,x)) < 0 then -arcsin(-x)
    elif type(x,'+') and traperror(sign(x)) = -1
            then -arcsin(-x)
    elif type(x,'function') and nops(x) = 1
            then x1 := op(1,x);
(4)     if op(0,x) = cos then RETURN(1/2*Pi-arccos(x))
        elif op(0,x) = cosh and (type(x1,'numeric') or
                type(x1,'constant') and Im(x1) = 0)
            then RETURN(1/2*Pi-I*abs(x1))
(5)     elif op(0,x) = sin and (type(x1,'complex(numeric)') or
(5)             type(x1,'constant') and
(5)             type(evalf(x1,10),'complex(numeric)'))
(5)         then s := csgn(I*x1);
(5)         if type(s,'integer')
(5)             then k := s*ceil(s*Re(x1)/Pi-1/2);
(5)             if type(k,'integer')
(5)                 then RETURN((-1)^k*(x1-k*Pi))
            fi
        fi
    fi;
    arcsin(x) := 'arcsin'(x)
(6) else arcsin(x) := 'arcsin'(x)
    fi
    end
```

25.2.3 Case of the Functions `builtin`

For *builtin* functions, which are written in C for increased efficiency, it is impossible to list the source code, and the function `eval` only returns a function number no matter what value `verboseproc` has.

Ex. 8

```
> interface(verboseproc=2); eval(iquo);
    proc() options builtin; 96 end
```

25.2.4 `remember` Table

Finally, let us say a few words about an important point that always impresses newcomers. How can MAPLE return exact results like

Ex. 9

```
> arcsin(sqrt(3)/2);
```
$$\frac{1}{3}\pi$$

It is simply thanks to a table. The function `arcsin`, like most MAPLE functions, has a `remember` table in which about fifteen particular values are initially stored. This table can be displayed by requesting the evaluation of `op(4,eval(arcsin))`

Ex.10

```
> op(4,eval(arcsin));                    see Chapter 24 if necessary
```
$$table([$$
$$\tfrac{1}{4}\sqrt{5} + \tfrac{1}{4} = \tfrac{3}{10}\pi$$
$$\tfrac{1}{4}\sqrt{2}\sqrt{5 + \sqrt{5}} = \tfrac{2}{5}\pi$$
$$.../...$$
$$0 = 0$$
$$.../...$$
$$I = I\,\mathrm{arcsinh}\,(1)$$
$$\tfrac{1}{2}\sqrt{2 + \sqrt{2}} = \tfrac{3}{8}\pi$$
$$])$$

This table is a sequence of equations assigning to every index (argument on the left side of the = sign) a value (on the right side of the = sign). These equations are arranged in an order that may at first sight seem strange, but is a consequence of the method (hash-coding) MAPLE uses to search the elements of a table.

The values contained in this table are both those MAPLE puts in it when loading the function, and, however odd, values entered by the user.

Ex.11

```
> arcsin(2):=3: op(4,eval(arcsin));
```
$$table([$$
$$.../...$$
$$2 = 3$$
$$.../...$$
$$])$$

26. MAPLE Environment in Windows

26.1 The MAPLE Worksheet

Once MAPLE is started, the user is presented with a typical Windows window
that looks like

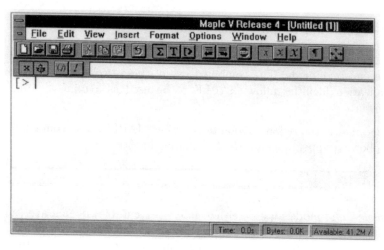

Within this window, you see from top to bottom

- the header bar, with *MAPLE V Release 4 - [Untitled(1)]*,

- the menu bar containing the options: **File Edit View Insert Format** ... ,

- the tool bar allowing direct access to some functions through icons.

- the context bar, which changes according to the current area: command
  area, text area or graphical area.

- the worksheet itself (*MAPLE Worksheet*) where the user works.

- the status line, at the bottom, where certain information is displayed.

The user can then compute with MAPLE, as explained in Chapter 2. MAPLE the results of computations within the worksheet, as well as the graphics plotted with `plot` and `plot3d` (by default).

The worksheet is far bigger than what appears on the screen, and the user can move within it with the help of the arrow keys or the scrollbar on the right side. The user should refer to a manual for more details about the standard use of the Windows environment.

However, beware of the fact that you may move through the worksheet in different directions, and modify some lines of data without executing them again: after working in a worksheet for some time, the lines of results are not necessarily the consequence of the lines of input in top-down order. When in doubt, it is better to reexecute all instructions in the worksheet, in order, with the option **Execute** from the **Edit** menu.

26.1.1 Text and Maple-input Modes

To enter data in a worksheet, the user may choose between *Maple-input* mode and text mode. The combined use of these two modes and the pre-visualization facilities allow MAPLE to be used as a mini-scientific word processor.

Maple-input is the default mode on starting MAPLE. The context bar has the following appearance in *Maple-input* mode

- *Maple-input* mode may be either active (executable) or inactive (non executable). One can switch from one mode to the other by clicking on the icon in the context bar representing a maple leaf: when the button is depressed, the mode is active and characters are displayed in red (by default), otherwise the mode is inactive and the display is in black.

- *Maple-input* mode can be formated or not. One switches from one mode to the other by clicking on the icon ⌊x⌋ in the context bar. When the button is up, the mode is formatted and mathematical formulas appear in their familiar form, otherwise (by default) they are displayed in bold *Courrier New*.
  To modify an expression written in formated mode, one must work on the unformatted field in the context bar.

One can switch from *Maple-input* mode to text mode with the icon ⌊T⌋ in the tool bar. Text mode appears on the screen in *Times New Roman* by default, and the style of each paragraph can be modified with the help of the command **Format/Styles**.

In text mode, the context bar looks like

and is mainly useful for modifying the style of the current paragraph. One can switch back from text mode to *Maple-input* mode with the icon $\boxed{\Sigma}$ in the tool bar.

26.1.2 Groups and Sections

Groups

For MAPLE, an execution group is an area of the worksheet whose lines are collected together by a large square bracket located to their left – if the option **Show Group Ranges** of the **View** menu is selected. Within an execution group, one may mix text mode and *Maple-input* mode whether formated or not, active or not.

- All active *Maple-input* expressions of a group are executed
  - either if one depresses $\boxed{\text{ENTER}}$ when the cursor is located within one of the active *Maple-input* areas of the group
  - or if one clicks on the icon $\boxed{!}$ in the context bar.

- Within an execution group, one introduces a newline.
  - by depressing $\boxed{\text{ENTER}}$ when located within a text area or an inactive *Maple-input* area
  - by depressing $\boxed{\text{SHIFT}}\boxed{\text{ENTER}}$ when located within an active *Maple-input* area.

Sections

The use of sections, even subsections, allows the user to stucture his worksheet.

A section is made up of a title (possibly empty) followed by execution groups or even of subsections.

- If closed, one only sees its title preceded by the box $\boxed{+}$.

- If expanded, its title is preceded by the box $\boxed{-}$ and, if the option **Show Section Ranges** of the **View** menu is selected, its elements are collected together by a large square bracket.

One may switch from one form to another by clicking on the box $\boxed{+}$ or $\boxed{-}$ located to the left of the section's title.

A new section can be introduced with the option **Section** of the **Insert** menu or with the icon ⊟→ in the tool bar.

Several execution groups can be collected together within a same section by selecting them with the mouse and using the icon ⊟→ in the tool bar.

26.1.3 The Menu Bar

The user can use options in the menu bar to print or save his work, modify its presentation or access the on-line help.

File   Edit   View   Insert   Format   Options   Window   Help

He can activate one of the options

- either by clicking upon it with the left button of the mouse,
- or by typing *Alt < Underlined_letter >*.

He then accesses submenus with specific options.

File	Operations to read from and write to the disk, and to print.
	End of session and return to the operating system.
Edit	Management of blocks, execution groups and regions, search, insertion of OLE objects.
View	Modification of the worksheet's presentation.
Insert	Insertion of a text area, of a command area, of a section, of a subsection, etc.
Format	Management of the text styles of the different areas of the worksheet.
Options	Management of the display and work options.
Window	Management of the windows.
Help	Access the on-line help.

When the user opens a menu, the corresponding options appear:

- if one of these options is tinted grey, it cannot be accessed at the moment.
- control sequences like *F3* or *Ctrl C* appear to the right of some of these options, indicating how function can be accessed directly.
- when a letter of one of these options is underlined, the user can access the corresponding function directly by typing this letter.

26.2 The File Menu

When one activates the **File** menu, the screen looks like this:

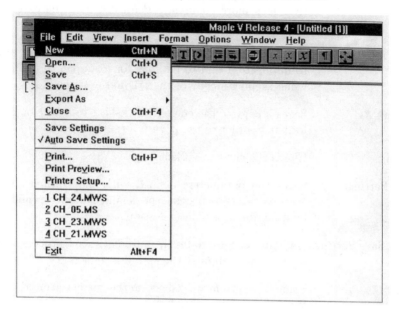

The options of the **File** menu can be used to load or to save a worksheet, to print the current sheet, or a part of it, and to leave MAPLE.

New

Opens a new blank worksheet, without resetting the variables.

Open

Opens, i.e. loads into memory, an existing worksheet. This function uses a typical Windows dialogue box, and presents only files whose extension is *.ms* (old *release* 3 extension) or *.mws* (new *release* 4 extension). In order to get other names in this list, modify the selection criterion *.ms appearing in the box Filename.

Warning! *Release* 4, by default, no longer resets the variables when the user loads a worksheet. It doesn't execute any command line of the worksheet being loaded, and the actual content of the variables appearing within the sheet has nothing to do with what the user sees on the screen. To be sure that the worksheet and memory match, it is therefore better, when in doubt, to reexecute all lines; this can be done with the command **Execute/Worksheet** of the **Edit** menu.

Save   Saves the current worksheet. Do from time to time to avoid losing work in case of a power outage (which doesn't happen frequently), or memory overflow or infinite loops (which is more common). *Release* 4 uses the extension *.mws* by default.

Save As   Saves the current worksheet with a new name in order to duplicate it and to be able, for example, to modify it while keeping a copy of the original worksheet.

Export As   Saves a copy of the current worksheet in a text or *Latex* format in order to use it with a text processor.

Close   Closes the current worksheet.

Save Settings   Saves the parameters defined with the **Options** menu. These parameters become the default parameters and will be used during any later session.

Auto Save Settings Validates or invalidates the automatic save process of the default parameters at the end of a session.

Print   Prints the current worksheet on the current printer, using Windows' printer manager.

Print Preview   Provides a preview on the screen of how the current worksheet will be printed, either to modify its presentation or to select the pages to be printed.

Printer Setup   Allows you to configure the printer.

<Files>   List of the last files which have been used, or quick access.

Exit   To properly exit MAPLE, which then prompts you to save the worksheets which have been modified since they were last saved.

26.3 The Edit Menu

When the **Edit** menu is active, the screen looks like

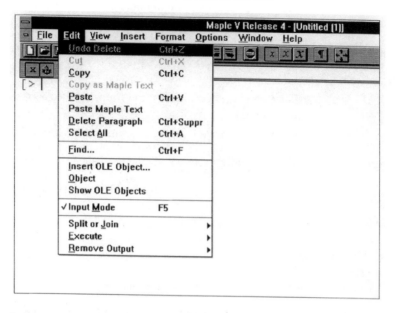

The first options of the **Edit** menu concern ordinary word processing operations: deleting, copying, moving a selected block, searching a string.

To select a block with the mouse, position the cursor at the beginning of the
block, press the left button of the mouse, move the cursor until the end of
the block with the button down, then release the button. The selected block
is highlighted.

Undo Delete   Undoes the last deletion.

Cut   Deletes the selected block and copies it into the clipboard.

Copy   Copies the selected block into the clipboard without
                     deleting it.

Paste   Insert the copy of the clipboard at the location of the
                     cursor.

Delete Paragraph Deletes the paragraph in which the cursor is located.

Select All   Selects the whole worksheet.

Find   Searches for a string within the current worksheet, which
                     is especially useful when consulting the on-line help.

One next finds

Insert OLE Object, **Object**, **Show OLE Objects**

which are functions for managing OLE links, which can be used to include several objects (graphics, sounds, etc.)

Input Mode   Switches from text mode to command mode.

Split or Join   Joins or splits execution groups or sections.

The join is carried out on the groups or the sections that are selected.

The split is carried out at the cursor's location.

Execute   Automatically executes all the worksheet or a part of it.

Remove Output   Removes all the results returned by MAPLE from the worksheet.

26.4 The View Menu

When the **View** menu is activated, the screen looks like

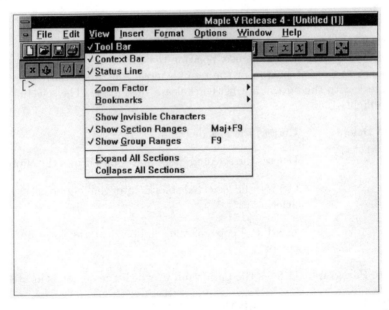

Tool Bar   When this option is selected, MAPLE displays a tool bar under the menu bar, which is made up of icons providing direct access to common functions. If one presses the left button of the mouse when its pointer is located on one of these icons, a message explaining how it works appears within the status line. Just move the cursor off the icon before letting up the button if you don't want to execute the function.

This message appears within a balloon when the pointer is over an icon, provided that **Balloon Help** has been selected in the **Help** menu.

Context Bar When this option is selected, MAPLE displays a context bar under the tool bar, which provides direct access to common functions.

Status Line When this option is selected, MAPLE displays a status line at the bottom of the screen that indicates how the processor and memory have been used since the beginning of the session, as well as the memory which is still available.

Zoom Factor To modify the magnification factor of the worksheet's image.

Bookmarks To insert or modify bookmarks and access them later on.

Show Invisible Characters

When this option is selected, MAPLE displays invisible characters like carriage returns, blanks, etc.

Show Section Ranges

When this option is selected, MAPLE displays a square bracket to the left of sections and subsections.

Show Group Ranges

When this option is selected, MAPLE displays a square bracket to the left of execution groups.

Expand All Sections

To expand all sections.

Collapse All Sections

To collapse all sections.

26.5 The Insert Menu

When the **Insert** menu is activated, the screen looks like

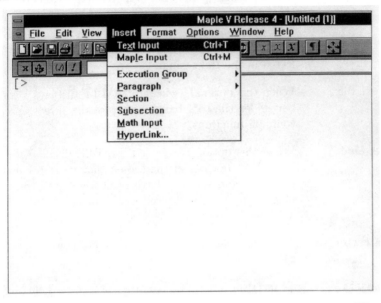

Text Input	Switching to text mode, equivalent to the icon $\boxed{T}$ of the tool bar.
Maple Input	Switching to *Maple-input* mode, equivalent to the icon $\boxed{\Sigma}$ of the tool bar.
Execution Group	Inserts an execution group *before* or *after* the one where the cursor is located.
Paragraph	Inserts a paragraph *before* or *after* the cursor location.
Section	Inserts a section whose level is the same as the current one after the section in which the cursor is located.
Subsection	Inserts a section of lower level inside the one in which the cursor is located.
Math Input	Inserts a field in *Maple-input* format.
HyperLink	Creates a hyper-text link that may point either towards a MAPLE worksheet or towards a keyword of the on-line help. In order to modify the properties of an existing link, click upon the right button of the mouse and choose the **Properties** heading of the contextual menu that is displayed.

26.6 The Format Menu

When the **Format** menu is activated, the screen looks like

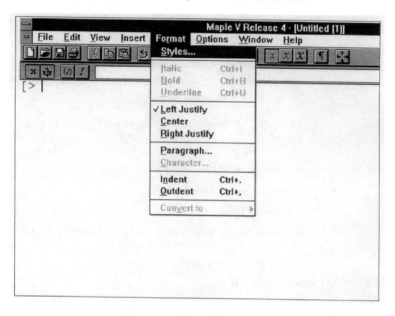

In MAPLE's *Release 4*, the user can define and modify styles he may afterwards apply to the different regions of his worksheet: *Title*, titles of the sections and subsections (*Heading*), *Maple-input*, results returned by MAPLE (*2D Output*), etc. The first options of the **Format** menu manage these styles.

Styles	Accesses the menu to create/modify the different styles.
Italic	Changes the text area in which the cursor is located to italic.
Bold	Changes the text area in which the cursor is located to bold.
Underline	Changes the text area in which the cursor is located to underline.
Left Justify	Left justifies the current paragraph.
Center	Centers the current paragraph.
Right Justify	Right justifies the current paragraph.
Paragraph	Modifies the style of the current paragraph. The most attractive option is **Start New Page**, which forces the

paragraph to start at the beginning of the page. Used together with **File/Print Preview**, this functionality provides a nice presentation when the worksheet is printed.

Character   Chooses the style of the text area within which the cursor is located.

Indent   Indents all sections contained within the current selection. Next, one may use **Edit/Split or Join/Join Section** in order to join these subsections.

Outdent   Outdents all sections contained within the current selection.

Convert to   For the selected text:

- creates a hyper-text link,
- transforms it into inactive formated *Maple-input*,
- transforms it into active and unformatted *Maple-input*.

26.7 The Options Menu

When the **Options** menu is activated, the screen looks like

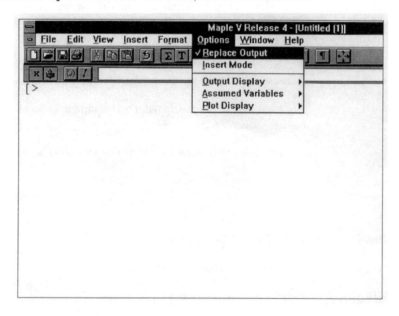

Replace Output   When this option is selected and the computation of an execution group is restarted, MAPLE erases the old results before writing the new ones. When this option isn't selected, the new results are displayed behind the old ones.

Insert Mode   When this option is selected and one evaluates the expressions in a group, MAPLE, after having computed and possibly written the results, inserts a new group and positions the cursor there. This mode should be used when one wishes to insert a sequence of computations in the middle of an existing worksheet.

When this option isn't selected and one executes a group, MAPLE, after having computed and possibly written the results, positions the cursor in the first executable area of the next group. It is the most commonly used mode, and it allows you to reexecute a whole part of a worksheet using the ENTER key.

Output Display   To choose the mode used for the outputs.

Assumed Variables To choose whether a variable submitted to a hypothesis with the help of assume is displayed on the screen without annotation (*No Annotation*), followed by a tilde (*Trailing Tildes*) or followed by the phrase *with assumption on ...* (*Phrase*).

Plot Display   To choose whether the graphics (obtained with plot and plot3d) are inserted within the worksheet or displayed within a new window.

26.8 The Window Menu

The first options are typical for Windows, and allow the relative positions of the various open windows to be modified.

The function **Close All** closes all MAPLE windows, while **Close All Help** closes all help sheets.

The rest of this menu contains the list of all the open MAPLE windows, which can be used to navigate from one sheet to another. One should, however, notice that *Alt Tab* allows switches programs, while *Ctrl Tab* navigates between the worksheets and MAPLE's help windows.

26.9 On-line Help

26.9.1 The Help Menu

The option **Help** from the menu bar provides access to MAPLE's on-line help. This help is made up of pages which are the electronic version of the *Library Reference Manuel* and are often more up-to-date than the version in paper format.

Contents	Provides access to the table of contents for the on-line help, organized by subject and consisting of a help page in which one can expand the sections and click on hypertext links.
	In particular, the first section, **What's New**, can be used to quickly locate the new features of *Release* 4.
Help on ...	Displays, if possible, a help page concerning the word located beneath the cursor. The same function can be obtained directly with the key F1.
Topic Search	Provides access the on-line help through a list of keywords.
Full Text Search	Gives a list of help pages containing a given word or phrase.
History	Provides the list of the last help pages consulted by the user, and allows him to access them directly.
Save to Database	Transforms the current sheet into a help page.
Remove Topic	Removes a help page.
Using Help	Provides help for the on-line help.
Balloon Help	Displays an explanatory message within a balloon when the pointer is over an icon or a menu option.
About Maple V	Displays the usual information about the origin of the software.

26.9.2 Accessing the On-line Help Directly

Remember that the on-line help can be accessed directly from a worksheet with the question mark. By entering for example

Ex. 1 $\triangleright$? convert

the help page for the function convert is displayed on the screen.

When there are special pages describing some specific applications of the function, as is the case for `convert`, one can access them by writing the second keyword behind the first, separated by a slash or a comma.

Ex. 2   `> ? convert/parfrac`   **For help about**
                                              the partial fraction decomposition

Note: When the keyword appears within the worksheet, the corresponding help page can be retrieved by positioning the cursor on the word and by typing F1.

When a specific help page has been accessed, one can scan it with the help of the scrollbar or the arrows, select text with the mouse to copy, which avoids typing errors when bringing examples back to the worksheet.

To exit a help page, either click upon its **Exit** button (the x to the immediate top right of the **Help** menu), or use the option **Close Help Topic** in the **File** menu of the window, or use the control sequence Ctrl F4. All help pages can also be closed with the option **Close All Help** of the **Window** menu.

One can also leave the help page open and move to another open help page or MAPLE worksheet with Ctrl Tab or by using the **Window** menu.

26.9.3 Structure of a Help Page

Every help page related to a MAPLE function follows the same model and contains 4 headings which are, in fact, sections that can be expanded or collapsed.

- **Function** which gives the name of the function, a brief description, the different possible syntaxes, as well as the kind of parameters the user must pass the function and what they do.

- **Description** which explains in more detail how the function works.

- **Examples** which provides a few examples to help better understand how the function works. These examples can be copied through the clipboard.

- **See Also** which lists related keywords written as hyper-text links which can be clicked on in order to access the corresponding sheet.

Index

Production: Druckhaus Beltz, Hemsbach